The Oxford Book of
Satirical Verse

The Oxford Book of Satirical Verse

Chosen by
Geoffrey Grigson

Oxford New York Toronto Melbourne
OXFORD UNIVERSITY PRESS
1980

Oxford University Press, Walton Street, Oxford OX2 6DP

OXFORD LONDON GLASGOW
NEW YORK TORONTO MELBOURNE WELLINGTON
KUALA LUMPUR SINGAPORE HONG KONG TOKYO
DELHI BOMBAY CALCUTTA MADRAS KARACHI
NAIROBI DAR ES SALAAM CAPE TOWN

© *Preface and compilation Geoffrey Grigson 1980*

British Library Cataloguing in Publication Data
The Oxford book of satirical verse.
1. Satire, English
2. English poetry
I. Grigson, Geoffrey
821'.07   PR1195.S3   79–41738
ISBN 0–19–214110–4

*Filmset by Northumberland Press Ltd,
Gateshead, Tyne and Wear
Printed in Great Britain by
Richard Clay (The Chaucer Press) Ltd,
Bungay, Suffolk*

PREFACE

Whatever satirical poets may have said about their moral or reforming or punitive intentions—and they have made some rather grand claims —we may be sure that writing their satires never caused them pain. They have enjoyed it; and we enjoy what they have written, without apology. T. S. Eliot, who did not quite bring himself to satire, wrote of a 'certain divine levity' which gives their 'sparkle' to the lines of Dryden and Pope; he spoke also of 'the object satirized disappearing in the poetry'.

'Disappearing' is just a little too strong. Many of the best jokes in the world are about—or against—fools and hypocrites; or at least against lapses into folly and hypocrisy. So the poetry of the matter retains an edge.

This may not define satire—a famously difficult thing to do; but it imposes a limit. One can say gravely that satire postulates an ideal condition of man or decency, and then despairs of it; and enjoys the despair, masochistically. But the joke must not be lost—the joke of statement, of sound, rhythm, form, vocabulary, rhyme, and surprise. Without the joke everything goes; and we may be left only with complaint, invective, or denunciation; all of which may be poetry, but of another kind. In making this selection from satire in English I have left out Marston, who is always spoken of in accounts of satire, because he uses words like a rumbling bully, without the least sparkle. I have not been too happy as well about his predecessor Skelton (who was certainly aware of those ancestral antipodes in satire, Horace and Juvenal), because Skelton's levity wears boots which are also rather thick:

> Your breath is strong and quick;
> You are an elder-stick;
> Ye wot what I think—
> At both ends ye stink.

To have narrowed my choice by too severe a definition would have been wrong, I think; and one thing I have done is to include, as well as the classics of satire, much that I would call satire of a milder levity, satire without rancour or bitterness which seems to contradict Byron's claim—instanced by him in Dryden, Pope, and Swift—that 'Satiric rhyme first sprang from selfish spleen'; satire of amusement directed

v

not at some shocking bishop or statesman, some corrupt judge or lord
mayor, some general or some toadying pretender to literary genius, not
at over-drinkers and under-thinkers and whoremasters, not at Scotchmen by Englishmen or at the English by the English, but at types who
stir less than indignation such as the squire and his wife in Prior's
Epitaph (No. 52) or Soame Jenyns's *Epistle to Lord Lovelace* (No. 87)
or Crabbe's vicar who found his way by a soothing sufferance (No.
109); satire of amusement also which is directed at conditions and
circumstances, at common states of mind or the clichés of sentimentalism.

Swift, grim enough elsewhere in his levity, satirizes the incon-
venience of squalid London under a sudden storm of rain (No. 55).
His little-known Dublin friend or acquaintance, John Winstanley,
makes what I call satire of milder levity against the pompously pathetic
passage from humble life to death, the bestowal of broken or worn-out
odds and ends by will (No. 63), or when he indulgently presents the
garret inhabited by an undergraduate at Trinity College (No. 64).
Tom Hood mildly satirizes hollyhock perennialism about sweet villages
by presenting in mockery a real village (No. 146):

> As for hollyoaks at the cottage doors, and honeysuckles
>   and jasmines, you may go and whistle;
> But the tailor's front garden grows two cabbages, a dock,
>   a ha'porth of pennyroyal, two dandelions and a thistle.

Tom Moore, earlier, is the grand master (the neglected master, too)
of this milder satire; which, mild or no, does now and then cut with a
half-concealed razor-blade. Read Tom Moore on Hum the Prince
Regent going to bed in Brighton Pavilion with 'His legs full of gout,
and his arms full of Hertford' (No. 127), or on tourists and pink
parasols among the pyramids or some Mrs Hopkins taking tea and
toast on the Great Wall of China (No. 129).

Epigrams I have left out, as a rule, with a notable exception in
Landor, who compressed his satirical impulse into couplet and
quatrain, and would have no showing if my rule against such satire
in miniature had been absolute. The inclusion of one satire, by Dr
Arbuthnot, Swift's friend, on that nasty job Colonel Chartres (No. 62)
may be questioned as prose among verse. I excuse myself by the
wonder of the first words, 'Here continueth to rot' and by the thought
that such measured prose on memorials of the time is a kind of
prose poetry, which in fact was often supplied by poets.

Remembering Eliot on the object satirized disappearing in the
poetry, I have confined notes chiefly to identification of those whose

celebrity has evaporated. Numbered notes are the author's own.

Spelling I have modernized (except in Scotch poems). Satire particularly demands quick comprehension, and all poetry must really be taken as an art of feeling, an art of life and not orthography. Surely we turn poetry into a museum of bygones if we preserve and project old spelling habits too rigorously (outside the necessary basic edition of each poet).

Names, if they are known, have been completed or filled in where blanks were left or dashes between initials. After all, when some satirist had yet another go at Castlereagh, that poetically most objurgated of statesmen, he did say to himself *Castlereagh*, as he composed, not *C dash dash dash H*.

Sub-titles to poems and extracts, with the exception of Nos. 144(i), 212(i) and (ii), are my own invention.

GEOFFREY GRIGSON

Broad Town
1979

CONTENTS

ix

CONTENTS

x

CONTENTS

xi

CONTENTS

CONTENTS

CONTENTS

xiv

CONTENTS

CONTENTS

xvi

CONTENTS

CONTENTS

ANONYMOUS

London Lickpenny

In London there I was bent,
I saw myself, where truth should be atteint,
Fast to Westminster ward I went
To a man of law, to make my complaint;
I said, 'For Mary's love, that holy saint,
Have pity on the poor that would proceed;
I would give silver, but my purse is faint:
For lack of money I may not speed.'

As I thrust throughout the throng
Among them all, my hood was gone;
Nathless I let not long
To King's Bench till I come.
Before a judge I kneeled anon,
I prayed him for God's sake he would take heed;
Full ruefully to him I gan make my moan:
'For lack of money I may not speed.'

Beneath him sat clerks, a great rout;
Fast they written by one assent;
There stood up one, and cried round about,
'Richard, Robert, and one of Kent!'
I wist not well what he meant,
He cried so thick there indeed;
There were strong thieves shamed and shent,
But they that lacked money might not speed.

Unto the Common Place I yowed thoo,
Where sat one with a silken hood;
I did him reverence as me ought to do,
I told him my case as well as I could,
And said all my goóds by nowrd and by sowde
I am defrauded with great falshed:
He would not give me a momme of his mouth;
For lack of money I may not speed.

shent] punished   yowed thoo] went then   nowrd, sowde] north, south
                    momme] mumble

I

Then I went me unto the Rollis,
Before the clerks of the Chancerie,
There were many *qui tollis*
But I heard no man speak of me;
Before them I kneeled upon my knee,
Showed them mine evidence and they began to read;
They said truer things might there never be—
But for lack of money I may not speed.

In Westminster Hall I found one
Went in a longe gown of ray;
I crouched, I kneeled before them anon,
For Mary's love, of help I gan them pray.
As he had been wroth, he voided away
Backward, his hand he gan me bid:
'I wot not what thou meanest,' gan he say,
'Lay down silver, or here thou may not speed.'

In all Westminster Hall I could find never a one
That for me would do, though I should die:
Without the doors were Flemings great wone,
Upon me fast gan to cry,
And said 'Master, what will ye copen or buy,
Fine felt hats, spectacles for to read
Of this gay gear?'—a great cause why
For lack of money I might not speed.

Then to Westminster gate I went.
When the sun was at high prime:
Cooks to me they took good intent,
Called me neare for to dine,
And proffered me good bread, ale and wine;
A fair cloth they began to spread,
Ribs of beef both fat and fine;
But for lack of money I might not speed.

---

many *qui tollis*]? many takers up of cases—from the Litany, *Agnus Dei, qui tollis peccata mundi* (Lamb of God, who takest away the sins of the world)   ray] striped cloth
great wone] very many   copen] buy   read of] estimate, inspect
high prime] nine in the morning

ANONYMOUS

Into London I gan me hie,
Of all the land it beareth the prize;
'Hot peascods!', one gan cry,
'Strawberry ripe!', and 'Cherry in the rice!'
One bad me come near and buy some spice,
Pepper and saffron they gan me bede,
Clove, grains, and flower of rice;
For lack of money I might not speed.

Then into Cheap I gan me drawn,
Where I saw stand much people;
One bad me come near, and buy fine cloth of lawn,
Paris thread, cotton and umple;
I said thereupon I could no skill,
I am not wont thereto indeed;
One bad me buy a hure, my head to hele:
For lack of money I might not speed.

Then went I forth by London Stone,
Throughout all Canywike Street;
Drapers to me they called anon,
Great cheap of cloth they gan me hete;
Then come there one and cried, 'Hot sheep's feet!'
'Rushes fair and green!' another gan to grete,
Both melwell and mackerel I gan meet,
But for lack of money I might not speed,

Then I hied me into Eastcheap;
One cried 'Ribs of beef, and many a pie!'
Pewter pots they clattered on a heap;
There was harp, pipe, and sawtry;
'Yea, by cock, nay, by cock' some began to cry;
Some sang of Jenken and Julian, to get themselves meed;
Full fain I would had of that minstrelsy,
But for lack of money I could not speed.

in the rice] on the bough   bede] offer
grains] a favourite medieval spice, Grains of Paradise, from Africa
umple] fine linen   I could no skill] I had no knowledge   hure] cap
hele] cover   Canywike Street] Cannon Street   cheap] bargain
hete] offer   melwell] cod

3

Into Cornhill anon I yode,
Where is much stolen gear among;
I saw where hunge mine own hood
That I had lost in Westminster among the throng!
Then I beheld it with looks full long;
I kenned it as well as I did my creed:
To buy mine own hood again methought it wrong,
But for lack of money I might not speed.

Then came the taverner, and took me by the sleeve.
And said 'Sir, a pint of wine would you assay?'
'Sir,' quod I, 'it may not grieve,
For a penny may do no more than it may.'
I drank a pint, and there for gan pay;
Sore a-hungered away I yede.
Farewell, London, Lickpenny, for one and ay!
For lack of money I may not speed.

Then I hied me to Billingsgate,
And cried, 'Wag, wag, go hence!'
I prayed a bargeman for God's sake,
That they would spare me mine expense.
He said, 'Rise up, man, and get thee hence!
What, weenist thou I will do on thee my alms deed?
Here scapeth no man beneath two pence!'
For lack of money I might not speed.

Then I conveyed me into Kent,
For of the law would I meddle no more;
Because no man to me would take intent,
I dight me to the plough, even as I did before.
Jesus save London, that in Bethlehem was bore!
And every true man of law God grant him soul's meed,
And they that be other, God their state restore,
For he that lacketh money, with them he shall not speed.

yode] went   'Wag, wag, go hence'] ? the customary cry for a ferry, or ferryman

4

JOHN SKELTON
?1460–1529

2   from *How the Doughty Duke of Albany like a
Coward Knight ran away shamefully with an
Hundred Thousand Tratling Scots and Faint-
hearted Frenchmen, beside the Water of Tweed* •

O YE wretched Scots,
Ye puant pisspots,
It shall be your lots
To be knit up with knots
Of halters and ropes
About your traitors' throats.
O Scots perjured,
Unhaply ured,
Ye may be assured
Your falsehood discured
It is and shall be, from the Scottish sea
Unto Gabione,
For ye be false each one,
False and false again,
Never true nor plain,
But fleery, flatter and feign,
And ever to remain
In wretched beggary
And maungy misery,
In lousy loathsomeness
And scabbed scorfiness,
And in abomination
Of all manner of nation,
Nation moost in hate,
Proud and poor of state:

puant] smelly   unhaply ured] unhappily fated   discured] made known
  Gabione] district in Persia round Gabae (Isfahan)   fleery] smile falsely

5

Twit, Scot, go keep thy den,
Mell not with English men.
Thou did nothing but bark
At the castell of Warke:
Twit, Scot, yet again once.
We shall break thy bones
And hang you upon poles
And burn you all to coals,
With twit, Scot, twit, Scot, twit.
Walk, Scot, go beg a bit
Of bread, at ilke man's heck.
The fiend, Scot, break thy neck.
Twit, Scot, again I say,
Twit, Scot of Galloway,
Twit, Scot, shake thee, dog, hey!
Twit, Scot, thou ran away.

We set not a fly
By your Duke of Albany.
We set not a prane
By such a drunken drane,
We set not a mite
By such a coward knight,
Such a proud palliard,
Such a skirgalliard,
Such a stark coward,
Such a proud poltroon,
Such a foul coistrown,
Such a doughty dagswain.
Send him to France again
To bring with him more brain
From King Francis of France.
God end them both mischance.
Ye Scots all the rabble,
Ye shall never be able
With us for to compare,
What though ye stamp and stare.
God send you sorrow and care.

mell] mix
ilke] every　　heck] hatch, half-hatch door　　prane] prawn
drane] drone　　palliard] straw-sleeper, tramp　　skirgalliard] rascal
coistrown] kitchen-boy　　dagswain] coarse coverlet

With us whenever ye mell
Yet we bear away the bell,
When ye cankered knaves
Must creep in to your caves
Your heads for to hide,
For you dare not abide.
  Sir Duke of Albany,
Right inconveniently
Ye rage and ye rave
And your worship deprave.
Not like Duke Hamilcar,
With the Romayns that made war,
Nor like his son Hannibal,
Nor like Duke Hasdrubal
Of Carthage in Afrike.
Yet somewhat ye be like
In some of their conditions
And their false seditions
And their dealing double
And their wayward trouble:
But yet they were bold
And manly manifold
Their enemies to assail
In plain field and battail.
  But ye and your hoost
Full of brag and boost
And full of waste wind,
How ye will bears bind,
And the devil down ding,
Yet ye dare do nothing
But leap away like frogs
And hide you under logs
Like pigs and like hogs.
What an army were ye?
Or what activity
Is in you beggars, brawls,
Full of scabs and scalls:
Of vermin and of lice
And of all manner vice?

---

bear away the bell] take the prize   your worship deprave] impair your honour
                brawls] brawlers   scalls] scaly eczemas

3

from *Colin Clout*
Doctor Bullatus and Dawpatus

DOCTORS that learned be
Nor bachelors of that faculty
That hath taken degree
In the universitie
Shall not be objected for me.

But Doctor Bullatus
Parum litteratus
Dominus doctoratus
At the Broad Gatus,
Doctor Dawpatus
And bachelor bacheleratus,
Drunken as a mouse
At the alehouse,
Taketh his pillion and his cap
At the good ale tap
For lack of good wine,
As wise as Robin swine
Under a notary's sign
Was made a divine,
As wise as Waltham's calf
Must preach a Godes half
In the pulpit solemnly,
More meet in the pillory,
For by Saint Hilary
He can nothing smatter
Of logic nor school matter,
Neither *syllogisare*
Nor of *enthymemare*,
Nor knoweth his elenches
Nor his predicamentes.

Bullatus] bombastic   *Parum litteratus*] insufficiently learned
Dominus doctoratus] cleric with a degree   Broad Gatus] Broadgates Hall (Oxford)
Dawpatus] with a jackdaw's pate   bacheleratus] with (only) a bachelor's degree
pillion] cap worn by doctors of divinity   a Godes half] on God's behalf
syllogisare] to syllogize   *enthymemare*] to draw conclusions from contraries
elenches] Aristotle's elenchs, sophisms   predicamentes] Aristotle's categories

And yet he will mell
To amend the Gospel
And will preach and tell
What they do in hell,
And he dare not well neven
What they do in heaven,
Nor how far Temple Bar is
From the Seven Starres.

4   from *Why Come ye not to Court*

Cardinal Wolsey in Hell

SUCH a prelate, I trow,
Were worthy to row
Thorow the straits Marocke
To the gibbet of Baldock.
He would dry up the streams
Of nine kinges' realms,
All rivers and wells,
All waters that swells,
For with us he so mells
That within England dwells,
I would he were somewhere els;
For else by and by
He will drink us so dry,
And suck us so nigh,
That men shall scantly
Have penny or halpenny.
God save his noble Grace,
And grant him a place
Endless to dwell
With the Devil of hell!
For and he were there
We necd never fear
Of the fiendes blake,
For I undertake
He would so brag and crake

mell] busy himself   amend] improve on   neven] speak of

4   Marocke] Morocco   mells] interferes
    crake] cry out harshly (as a corncrake)

That he would then make
The devils to quake,
To shudder and to shake,
Like a fire-drake,
And with a coal rake
Bruise them on a brake,
And bind them to a stake,
And set hell on fire,
At his own desire.
He is such a grim sire
And such a potestolate,
And such a potestate,
That he would break the brains
Of Lucifer in his chains,
And rule them each one
In Lucifer's trone.
I would he were gone.

WILLIAM DUNBAR
?1465–?1530

5   *The Amendis to the Telyouris and Sowtaris for the
Turnament maid on thame*

BETUIX twell houris and ellevin,
I dremed ane angell came fra Hevin
With plesand stevin sayand on hie,
Telyouris and Sowtaris, blist be ye.

In Hevin hie ordand is your place,
Aboif all sanctis in grit solace,
Nixt God grittest in dignitie:
Tailyouris and Sowtaris, blist be ye.

---

fire-drake] fiery dragon   brake] an iron cage   potestolate] magistrate
                    potestate] potentate   trone] throne

5   Telyouris and Sowtaris] tailors and shoemakers   stevin] voice

The caus to yow is nocht unkend,
That God mismakkis ye do amend,
Be craft and grit agilitie:
Tailyouris and Sowtaris, blist be ye.

Sowtaris, with schone weill maid and meit,
Ye mend the faltis of ill maid feit,
Quhairfoir to Hevin your saulis will fle;
Telyouris and Sowtaris, blist be ye.

Is nocht in all this fair a flyrok,
That hes upoun his feit a wyrok,
Knowll tais, nor mowlis in no degrie,
Bot ye can hyd thame: blist be ye.

And ye tailyouris, with weil maid clais
Can mend the werst maid man that gais,
And mak him semely for to se:
Telyouris and Sowtaris, blist be ye.

Thocht God mak ane misfassonit man,
Ye can him all schaip new agane,
And fassoun him bettir be sic thre:
Telyouris and Sowtaris, blist be ye.

Thocht a man haif a brokin bak,
Haif he a gude telyour, quhatt rak,
That can it cuver with craftis slie:
Telyouris and Sowtaris, blist be ye.

Off God grit kyndnes may ye clame,
That helpis his peple fra cruke and lame,
Supportand faltis with your supple:
Tailyouris and Sowtaris, blist be ye.

In erd ye kyth sic mirakillis heir,
In Hevin ye salbe sanctis full cleir,
Thocht ye be knavis in this cuntre:
Telyouris and Sowtaris, blist be ye.

meit] meet   flyrok] ? popinjay wyrok] corn
Knowll tais] knoll toes, hammer-toes mowlis] chilblains
be sic thre] three times   rak] matter kyth] display

SIR DAVID LYNDSAY

1490–1555

6   from *Ane Satyre of the Thrie Estaitis*

Robin Rome-Raker the Pardoner Parades his Treasures

MY patent pardouns ye may see,
Cum fra the Cane of Tartarie,
    Weill seald with oster-schellis.
Thocht ye have na contritioun,
Ye sall have full remissioun,
    With help of buiks and bellis.
Here is ane relict lang and braid,
Of Fine Macoull the richt chaft blaid,
    With teith and all togidder:
Of Colling's cow heir is ane horne;
For eating of Mackonnal's corne,
    Was slaine into Balquhidder.
Here is ane cord, baith great and lang,
Quhilk hangit Johne the Armistrang,
    Of gude hemp saft and sound:
Gude halie peopill, I stand for'd
Wha ever heis hangit with this cord
    Neids never to be dround.
The culum of Sanct Bridis kow,
The gruntill of Sanct Antonis sow,
    Quhilk buir his haly bell:
Quha ever he be heirs this bell clinck,
Gif me ane ducat for till drink,
    He sall never gang to hell,
Without he be of Beliell borne.
Maisters, trow ye that this be scorne?
    Cum win this pardoun, cum.
Quha luifis thair wyfis nocht with thair hart,
I have power them for till part.
    Me think yow deif and dum!

Cane] khan   Fine Macoull] the legendary hero Finn Mac Cool (Fingal)
    chaft] jaw   saft] soft   stand for'd] warrant   culum] gut
                        gruntill] snout

12

Hes nane of yow curst wickit wyfis,
That halds yow into sturt and stryfis?
  Cum tak my dispensatioun:
Of that cummer I sall mak yow quyte,
Howbeit your selfis be in the wyte,
  And mak ane fals narratioun.
Cum win the pardoun, now let se,
For meill, for malt or for monie,
  For cok, hen, guse or gryse.
Of relicts heir I haif ane hunder.
Quhy cum ye nocht? this is ane wonder.
  I trow ye be nocht wyse.

ANONYMOUS

7   *How the First Hielandman of God was made of ane*
       Horse Turd in Argyll as is said

         GOD and Sanct Peter
           Was gangand be the way
         Heich up in Argyll
           Where their gait lay.

         Sanct Peter said to God
           In a sport word,
         Can ye not mak a Hielandman
           Of this horse turd?

         God turn'd owre the horse turd
           With his pykit staff
         And up start a Hielandman
           Blak as ony draff.

         Quod God to the Hielandman,
           Where wilt thow now?
         I will doun in the Lawland, Lord,
           And there steill a cow.

sturt] violence   cummer] gossip, wife   wyte] wrong   gryse] piglet

7 sport] jesting   pykit] pointed   draff] rubbish

13

And thou steill a cow, cairle,
   Than they will hang thee.
What rack, Lord, of that,
   For anis mon I die.

God then he leuch
   And owre the dyke lap,
And out of his sheath
   His gully outgat.

Sanct Peter socht this gully
   Fast up and doun,
Yet could not find it
   In all that braid roun.

Now, quod God, here a marvel,
   How can this be,
That I suld want my gully,
   And we here bot three?

Humff, quod the Hielandman,
   And turn'd him about,
And at his plaid neuk
   The gully fell out.

Fy, quod Sanct Peter,
   Thou will never do weill,
And thou bot new made
   And sa soon gais to steill.

Umff, quod the Hielandman,
   And sware be yon kirk,
Sa lang as I may gear get to steill
   Will I never work.

anis] once   leuch] laughed   lap] leapt   gully] large knife
outgat] disappeared   fast] carefully   braid roun] space around
    his plaid neuk] corner of his plaid

SIR THOMAS WYATT
c. 1503–1542

8   *Of the Courtier's Life, Written to John Poyntz*

MINE own John Poyntz, since ye delight to know
   The cause why that homeward I me draw,
   And flee the press of courts whereso they go,
Rather than to live thrall, under the awe
   Of lordly looks, wrapped within my cloak,
   To will and lust learning to set a law;
It is not for because I scorn or mock
   The power of them, to whom fortune hath lent
   Charge over us, of right, to strike the stroke:
But true it is that I have always meant
   Less to esteem them than the common sort,
   Of outward things that judge in their intent,
Without regard what doth inward resort.
   I grant sometime that of glory the fire
   Doth touch my heart: me list not to report
Blame by honour and honour to desire.
   But how may I this honour now attain
   That cannot dye the colour black a liar?
My Poyntz, I cannot frame me tune to feign,
   To cloak the truth for praise without desert,
   Of them that list all vice for to retain.
I cannot honour them that sets their part
   With Venus and Bacchus all their life long;
   Nor hold my peace of them although I smart.
I cannot crouch nor kneel to do so great a wrong,
   To worship them, like God on earth alone,
   That are as wolves these seely lambs among.
I cannot with my words complain and moan
   And suffer nought; nor smart without complaint,
   Nor turn the word that from my mouth is gone.
I cannot speak and look like a saint,
   Use wiles for wit and make deceit a pleasure,
   And call craft counsel, for profit still to paint.

seely] innocent, happy

15

I cannot wrest the law to fill the coffer
  With innocent blood to feed myself fat,
  And do most hurt where most help I offer.
I am not he that can allow the state
  Of high Caesar and damn Cato to die,
  That with his death did scape out of the gate
From Caesar's hands (if Livy do not lie)
  And would not live where liberty was lost:
  So did his heart the commonweal apply.
I am not he such eloquence to boast,
  To make the crow singing as the swan,
  Nor call the lion of coward beasts the most
That cannot take a mouse as the cat can:
  And he that di'th for hunger of the gold
  Call him Alexander; and say that Pan
Passeth Apollo in music manifold;
  Praise Sir Thopas for a noble tale
  And scorn the story that the knight told.
Praise him for counsel that is drunk of ale;
  Grin when he laugheth that beareth all the sway,
  Frown when he frowneth and groan when he is pale;
On others' lust to hang both night and day:
  None of these points would ever frame in me;
  My wit is naught—I cannot learn the way.
And much the less of things which greater be,
  That asken help of colours of device
  To join the mean with each extremity,
With the nearest virtue to cloak alway the vice:
  And as to purpose likewise it shall fall,
  To press the virtue that it may not rise;
As drunkenness good fellowship to call;
  The friendly foe with his double face
  Say he is gentle and courtois therewithal;
And say that Favell hath a goodly grace
  In eloquence; and cruelty to name
  Zeal of justice and change in time and place;
And he that suffreth offence without blame
  Call him pitiful; and him true and plain
  That raileth reckless to every man's shame.

Sir Thopas] see *The Tale of Sir Thopas* in Chaucer's *Canterbury Tales*

Say he is rude that cannot lie and feign;
The lecher a lover; and tyranny
To be the right of a prince's reign.
I cannot, I! No, no, it will not be!
This is the cause that I could never yet
Hang on their sleeves that way as thou may'st see
A chip of chance more than a pound of wit.
This maketh me at home to hunt and to hawk
And in foul weather at my book to sit.
In frost and snow then with my bow to stalk,
No man doth mark whereso I ride or go;
In lusty leas at liberty I walk,
And of these news I feel nor weal nor woe,
Save that a clog doth hang yet at my heel:
No force for that, for it is ordered so,
That I may leap both hedge and dike full well.
I am not now in France to judge the wine,
With savoury sauce the delicates to feel;
Nor yet in Spain where one must him incline
Rather than to be, outwardly to seem.
I meddle not with wits that be so fine,
No Flanders' cheer letteth not my sight to deem
Of black and white, nor taketh my wit away
With beastliness they, beasts, do so esteem.
Nor I am not where Christ is given in prey
For money, poison and treason at Rome,
A common practice used night and day:
But here I am in Kent and Christendom
Among the muses where I read and rhyme;
Where if thou list, my Poyntz, for to come,
Thou shalt be judge how I do spend my time.

lusty] pleasant

BEN JONSON
1572–1637

9   *On Lieutenant Shift*

SHIFT, here, in town, not meanest among squires
That haunt Picked Hatch, Marsh Lambeth, and Whitefriars,
Keeps himself, with half a man, and defrays
The charge of that state with this charm, God pays.
By that one spell he lives, eats, drinks, arrays
Himself: his whole revenue is, God pays.
The quarter-day is come; the hostess says,
She must have money; he returns, God pays.
The tailor brings a suit home; he it 'ssays,
Looks o'er the bill, likes it; and says, God pays.
He steals to ordinaries; there he plays
At dice his borrowed money: which, God pays.
Then takes up fresh commodity, for days;
Signs to new bond, forfeits: and cries, God pays.
That lost, he keeps his chamber, reads Essays,
Takes physic, tears the papers: still God pays.
Or else by water goes, and so to plays;
Calls for his stool, adorns the stage: God pays.
To every cause he meets, this voice he brays:
His only answer is to all, God pays.
Not his poor cockatrice but he betrays
Thus: and for his lechery scores, God pays.
But see! th'old bawd hath served him in his trim,
Lent him a pocky whore. She hath paid him.

it (e)ssays] tries it on   cockatrice] tart   his trim] his own way

JOHN DONNE
1572–1631

10

from *Satire II*
The Poet turned Lawyer

SIR, though (I thank God for it) I do hate
Perfectly all this town, yet there's one state
In all ill things so excellently best
That hate, toward them, breeds pity towards the rest.
Though poetry indeed be such a sin
As I think that brings dearths, and Spaniards in,
Though like pestilence and old-fashioned love
Riddlingly it catch men, and doth remove
Never, till it be starved out, yet their state
Is poor, disarmed, like Papists, not worth hate.
One (like a wretch which at bar judged as dead,
Yet prompts him which stands next, and cannot read,
And saves his life) gives idiot actors means
(Starving himself) to live by his laboured scenes;
As in some organ puppets dance above
And bellows pant below, which them do move.
One would move love by rhythms, but witchcraft's charms
Bring not now their old fears, nor their old harms:
Rams and slings are now seely battery,
Pistolets are the best artillery.
And they who write to lords, rewards to get,
Are they not like fingers at doors for meat?
And they who write because all write, have still
That excuse for writing, and for writing ill.
But he is worst who (beggarly) doth chaw
Others' wits' fruits, and in his ravenous maw
Rankly digested, doth those things out-spew
As his own things; and they are his own, 'tis true,
For if one eat my meat, though it be known
The meat was mine, th'excrement is his own.
But these do me no harm, nor they which use
To outdo dildoes, and out-usure Jews;

---

seely] useless   pistolets] pistols, and also French and Spanish gold coins

To out-drink the sea, to out-swear the Litany;
Who with sins all kinds as familiar be
As confessors, and for whose sinful sake
Schoolmen new tenements in hell must make;
Whose strange sins canonists could hardly tell
In such commandment's large receipt they dwell.
But these punish themselves; the insolence
Of Coscus only breeds my just offence,
Whom time (which rots all, and makes botches pox,
And plodding on, must make a calf an ox)
Hath made a lawyer, which was, alas, of late
But a scarce poet. Jollier of this state
Than are new beneficed ministers, he throws
Like nets, or lime-twigs, wheresoever he goes
His title of barrister on every wench,
And woos in language of the pleas, and bench.
'A motion, lady.' 'Speak, Coscus.' 'I have been
In love ever since *tricesimo* of the Queen.
Continual claims I have made, injunctions got
To stay my rival's suit, that he should not
Proceed.' 'Spare me.' 'In Hilary term I went.
You said if I returned next size in Lent
I should be in remitter of your grace;
In the interim my letters should take place
Of affidavits'—words, words which would tear
The tender labyrinth of a soft maid's ear
More, more than ten Sclavonians scolding, more
Than when winds in our ruined abbeys roar.
When sick with poetry and possessed with muse
Thou wast, and mad, I hoped; but men which choose
Law practise for mere gain, bold soul, repute
Worse than imbrothelled strumpets prostitute.
Now like an owl-like watchman he must walk,
His hand still at a bill, now he must talk
Idly, like prisoners, which whole months will swear
That only suretyship hath brought them there,
And to every suitor lie in every thing,
Like a king's favourite, yea like a king.

---

a scarce poet] something of a poet   jollier] more stuck up, grander
tricesimo [anno] of the Queen] thirtieth [year] of the Queen's reign   size] assize
bill] weapon carried by constables of the watch

11

from *Satire III*

The Hill of Truth

SEEK true religion. O where? Mirreus
Thinking her unhoused here, and fled from us,
Seeks her at Rome; there, because he doth know
That she was there a thousand years ago,
He loves her rags so, as we here obey
The state-cloth where the Prince sat yesterday.
Crantz to such brave loves will not be enthralled,
But loves her only who at Geneva is called
Religion, plain, simple, sullen, young,
Contemptuous, yet unhandsome; as among
Lecherous humours, there is one that judges
No wenches wholesome but coarse country drudges.
Graius stays still at home here, and because
Some preachers, vile ambitious bawds, and laws
Still new like fashions, bid him think that she
Which dwells with us is only perfect, he
Embraceth her whom his godfathers will
Tender to him, being tender, as wards still
Take such wives as their guardians offer, or
Pay values. Careless Phrygius doth abhor
All, because all cannot be good, as one
Knowing some women whores, dare marry none.
Graccus loves all as one, and thinks that so
As women do in divers countries go
In divers habits, yet are still one kind,
So doth, so is religion; and this blind-
ness too much light breeds. But unmoved thou
Of force must one, and forced but one allow;
And the right. Ask thy father which is she,
Let him ask his. Though truth and falsehood be
Near twins, yet truth a little elder is;
Be busy to seek her; believe me this,
He's not of none, nor worst, that seeks the best.
To adore, or scorn an image, or protest,
May all be bad. Doubt wisely. In strange way
To stand inquiring right, is not to stray;

pay values] make equivalent payments

To sleep, or run wrong, is. On a huge hill,
Cragged, and steep, Truth stands, and he that will
Reach her, about must, and about must go,
And what the hill's suddenness resists, win so;
Yet strive so, that before age, death's twilight,
Thy soul rest, for none can work in that night.
To will implies delay, therefore now do.
Hard deeds the body's pains, hard knowledge too,
The mind's endeavours reach, and mysteries
Are like the sun, dazzling, yet plain to all eyes.
Keep the truth which thou hast found; men do not stand
In so ill case here that God hath with his hand
Signed kings blank charters to kill whom they hate,
Nor are they vicars, but hangmen to fate.
Fool and wretch, wilt thou let thy soul be tied
To mans' laws, by which she shall not be tried
At the last day? Oh, will it then boot thee
To say a Philip, or a Gregory,
A Harry, or a Martin taught thee this?
Is not this excuse for mere contraries
Equally strong? cannot both sides say so? .
That thou mayest rightly obey Power, her bounds know;
Those past, her nature, and name is changed; to be
Then humble to her is idolatry.
As streams are, Power is; those blest flowers that dwell
At the rough stream's calm head, thrive and do well,
But having left their roots, and themselves given
To the stream's tyrannous rage, alas, are driven
Through mills, and rocks, and woods, and at last, almost
Consumed in going, in the sea are lost:
So perish souls which more choose men's unjust
Power from God claimed, than God himself to trust.

Philip] Philip of Spain
Gregory] Pope Gregory XIII, who welcomed the Massacre of St. Bartholomew
Harry] Henry VIII   Martin] Martin Luther

12 *Satire IV*

WELL, I may now receive, and die: my sin
Indeed is great, but I have been in
A Purgatory, such as feared hell is
A recreation to, and scant map of this.
My mind neither with pride's itch, nor yet hath been
Poisoned with love to see, or to be seen;
I had no suit there, nor new suit to show,
Yet went to Court. But as Glaze which did go
To a Mass in jest, catched, was fain to disburse
The hundred marks, which is the statute's curse,
Before he 'scaped; so it pleased my destiny
(Guilty of my sin of going) to think me
As prone to all ill, and of good as forget-
ful, as proud, as lustful, and as much in debt,
As vain, as witless, and as false as they
Which dwell at Court, for once going that way.
   Therefore I suffered this: towards me did run
A thing more strange than on Nile's slime the sun
E'er bred, or all which into Noah's ark came—
A thing which would have posed Adam to name,
Stranger than seven antiquaries' studies,
Than Afric's monsters, Guiana's rarities.
Stranger than strangers; one who for a Dane
In the Danes' massacre had sure been slain,
If he had lived then, and without help dies
When next the 'prentices 'gainst strangers rise.
One whom the watch at noon lets scarce go by;
One to whom the examining Justice sure would cry
'Sir, by your priesthood tell me what you are'.
His clothes were strange, though coarse; and black, though bare;
Sleeveless his jerkin was, and it had been
Velvet, but 'twas, now (so much ground was seen)
Become tufftaffeta, and our children shall
See it plain rash awhile, then naught at all.
This thing hath travelled and (saith) speaks all tongues
And only knoweth what to all states belongs.

receive] receive the last sacrament
tufftaffeta] taffeta with a tufted nap   rash] a smooth fabric

Made of th' accents, and best phrase of all these,
He speaks one language. If strange meats displease,
Art can deceive, or hunger force my taste,
But pedants' motley tongue, soldiers' bombast,
Mountebanks' drug-tongue, nor the terms of law
Are strong enough preparatives to draw
Me to bear this: yet I must be content
With his tongue, in his tongue called complement,
In which he can win widows, and pay scores,
Make men speak treason, cozen subtlest whores,
Out-flatter favourites, or out-lie either
Jovius or Surius, or both together.
  He names me and comes to me; I whisper, 'God!
How have I sinned, that thy wrath's furious rod,
This fellow, chooseth me?' He saith, 'Sir,
I love your judgment: whom do you prefer
For the best linguist?' And I sillily
Said that I thought Calepine's dictionary.
'Nay, but of men, most sweet sir?' Beza then,
Some other Jesuits, and two reverend men
Of our two academies, I named. There
He stopped me, and said 'Nay, your Apostles were
Good pretty linguists, and so Panurge was;
Yet a poor gentleman all these may pass
By travel.' Then, as if he would have sold
His tongue, he praised it, and such wonders told
That I was fain to say 'If you have lived, sir,
Time enough to have been interpreter
To Babel's bricklayers, sure the Tower had stood.'
He adds, 'If of court life you knew the good,
You would leave loneness.' I said, 'Not alone
My loneness is. But Spartan's fashion,
To teach by painting drunkards, doth not taste
Now; Aretine's pictures have made few chaste;
No more can princes' courts, though there be few
Better pictures of vice, teach me virtue.'
He, like to a high-stretched lute-string, squeaked, 'O, sir,
'Tis sweet to talk of kings'. 'At Westminster',
Said I, 'the man that keeps the Abbey tombs,

---

drug-tongue] smooth talk
complement] in its two meanings of accomplishment and flattery
Jovius, Surius] Catholic historians   Beza] Protestant reformer and scholar

And for his price doth with whoever comes
Of all our Harries and our Edwards talk,
From king to king and all their kin can walk;
Your ears shall hear naught but kings, your eyes meet
Kings only; the way to it is King Street.'
He smacked, and cried 'He's base, mechanic, coarse;
So are all your Englishmen in their discourse.
Are not your Frenchmen neat?' 'Mine? As you see,
I have but one Frenchman—look, he follows me.'
'Certes they're neatly clothed; I of this mind am,
Your only wearing is your grogaram.'
'Not so, sir, I have more.' Under this pitch
He would not fly; I chaffed him. But, as itch
Scratched into smart, and as blunt iron ground
Into an edge, hurts worse, so I (fool) found
Crossing hurt me. To fit my sullenness
He to another key his style doth address,
And asks 'What news?' I tell of new plays.
He takes my hand: and, as a still which stays
A semibreve 'twixt each drop, he niggardly,
As loath to enrich me, so tells many a lie.
More than ten Holinsheds or Halls or Stows,
Of trivial household trash he knows. He knows
When the Queen frowned, or smiled, and he knows what
A subtle statesman may gather of that;
He knows who loves whom, and who by poison
Hastes to an office's reversion;
He knows who hath sold his land, and now doth beg
A licence old iron, boots, shoes and egg-
shells to transport. Shortly boys shall not play
At span-counter or blow-point but they pay
Toll to some courtier. And wiser than all us,
He knows what lady is not painted. Thus
He with home-meats tries me: I belch, spew, spit,
Look pale, and sickly, like a patient; yet
He thrusts on more. And, as if he undertook
To say Gallo-Belgicus without book,
Speaks of all states, and deeds, that have been since
The Spaniards came, to the loss of Amiens.

mechanic] vulgar
grogaram] coarse unfashionable fabric of gummed mohair and wool
Gallo-Belgicus] *Mercurius Gallobelgicus*, Latin chronicle of events 1587–94, published
at Cologne

Like a big wife at sight of loathed meat
Ready to travail, so I sigh and sweat
To hear this macaroon talk—in vain: for yet,
Either my humour, or his own to fit,
He like a privileged spy, whom nothing can
Discredit, libels now 'gainst each great man.
He names a price for every office paid;
He saith our wars thrive ill, because delayed;
That offices are entailed, and that there are
Perpetuities of them, lasting as far
As the last day; and that great officers
Do with the pirates share and Dunkirkers.
Who wastes in meat, in clothes, in horse, he notes;
Who loves whores, who boys, and who goats.
I, more amazed than Circe's prisoners when
They felt themselves turn beasts, felt myself then
Becoming traitor, and methought I saw
One of our giant statutes ope his jaw
To suck me in: for hearing him, I found
That (as burnt venomed lechers do grow sound
By giving others their sores) I might grow
Guilty, and he free. Therefore I did show
All signs of loathing; but since I am in,
I must pay mine and my forefathers' sin
To the last farthing. Therefore to my power
Toughly and stubbornly I bear this cross. But the hour
Of mercy now was come. He tries to bring
Me to pay a fine to 'scape his torturing,
And says, 'Sir, can you spare me?' I said 'Willingly'.
'Nay, sir, can you spare me a crown?' Thankfully I
Gave it, as ransom: but as fiddlers, still,
Though they be paid to be gone, yet needs will
Thrust one more jig upon you, so did he
With his long complemental thanks vex me.
But he is gone, thanks to his needy want,
And the prerogative of my crown. Scant
His thanks were ended, when I (which did see
All the court filled with more strange things than he)
Ran from hence with such, or more, haste than one
Who fears more actions, doth make from prison.

Dunkirkers] privateersmen operating from Dunkirk

At home in wholesome solitariness
My precious soul began the wretchedness
Of suitors at court to mourn, and a trance,
Like his who dreamt he saw hell, did advance
Itself on me: such men as he saw there,
I saw at court, and worse, and more. Low fear
Becomes the guilty, not the accuser: then
Shall I, none's slave, of high-born or raised men
Fear frowns? and, my mistress Truth, betray thee
To the huffing braggart, puffed nobility?
No, no: thou, which since yesterday hast been
Almost about the whole world, hast thou seen,
O sun, in all thy journey, vanity
Such as swells the bladder of our court? I
Think he which made your waxen garden, and
Transported it from Italy to stand
With us, at London, flouts our Presence: for
Just such gay painted things, which no sap nor
Taste have in them, ours are; and natural
Some of the stocks are, their fruits bastard all.
   'Tis ten o'clock and past: all whom the mews,
Balloon, tennis, diet or the stews
Had all the morning held, now the second
Time made ready, that day, in flocks are found
In the Presence—and I (God pardon me).
As fresh and sweet their apparels be, as be
The fields they sold to buy them. 'For a king
These hose are', cry the flatterers, and bring
Them next week to the Theatre to sell.
Wants reach all states: me seems they do as well
At stage, as court; all are players—whoe'er looks
(For themselves dare not go) o'er Cheapside books
Shall find their wardrobe's inventory. Now
The ladies come: as pirates, which do know
That there came weak ships fraught with cochineal,
The men board them; and praise, as they think, well
Their beauties, they the men's wits; both are bought.
Why good wits ne'er wear scarlet gowns I thought
This cause: these men men's wits for speeches buy,
And women buy all reds which scarlets dye.

balloon] game played with arm and air-ball
Presence] the royal chamber of presence

He called her beauty lime-twigs, her hair net;
She fears her drugs ill laid, her hair loose set.
Would not Heraclitus laugh to see Macrine,
From hat to shoe, himself at door refine,
As if the Presence were a moschite, and lift
His skirts and hose, and call his clothes to shrift,
Making them confess not only mortal
Great stains and holes in them, but venial
Feathers and dust, wherewith they fornicate;
And then by Durer's rules survey the state
Of his each limb, and with strings the odds try
Of his neck to his leg, and waist to thigh.
So in immaculate clothes, and symmetry
Perfect as circles—with such nicety
As a young preacher at his first time goes
To preach—he enters, and a lady which owes
Him not so much as goodwill, he arrests,
And unto her protests, protests, protests,
So much as at Rome would serve to have thrown
Ten Cardinals into the Inquisition;
And whispered 'By Jesu' so often that a
Pursuivant would have ravished him away
For saying of Our Lady's psalter. But 'tis fit
That they each other plague: they merit it.
But here comes Glorius that will plague them both,
Who, in the other extreme, only doth
Call a rough carelessness good fashion;
Whose cloak his spurs tear; whom he spits on
He cares not; his ill words do no harm
To him; he rusheth in, as if 'Arm, arm'
He meant to cry; and though his face be as ill
As theirs which in old hangings whip Christ, still
He strives to look worse, he keeps all in awe;
Jests like a licenced fool, commands like law.
　　Tired, now I leave this place, and but pleased so
As men which from gaols to execution go,
Go through the great chamber (why is it hung
With the seven deadly sins?). Being among
Those Ascaparts—men big enough to throw
Charing Cross for a bar, men that do know

Macrine] Macrinus, mentioned in Persius' *Satires*　　　moschite] mesquita, mosque
Ascaparts] Ascapart, giant in the romance of *Bevis of Hampton*

No token of worth but 'Queen's man', and fine
Living, barrels of beef, flagons of wine—
I shook like a spied spy. Preachers which are
Seas of wit and arts, you can, then dare
Drown the sins of this place, for, for me
Which am but a scarce brook, it enough shall be
To wash the stains away; although I yet
With Maccabees' modesty the known merit
Of my work lessen, yet some wise man shall,
I hope, esteem my writs canonical.

13   *Satire V*

THOU shalt not laugh in this leaf, Muse, nor they
Whom any pity harms. He which did lay
Rules to make courtiers (he being understood
May make good courtiers, but who courtiers good?)
Frees from the sting of jests all who in extreme
Are wretched or wicked: of these two a theme
Charity and liberty give me. What is he
Who officers' rage and suitors' misery
Can write, and jest? If all things be in all,
As I think, since all which were, are, and shall
Be, be made of the same elements,
Each thing, each thing implies or represents.
Then man is a world; in which officers
Are the vast ravishing seas; and suitors,
Springs, now full, now shallow, now dry, which to
That which drowns them, run. These self reasons do
Prove the world a man, in which officers
Are the devouring stomach, and suitors
The excrements, which they void. All men are dust;
How much worse are suitors, who to men's lust
Are made preys? O worse than dust, or worms' meat,
For they do eat you now, whose selves worms shall eat.
They are the mills which grind you, yet you are
The wind which drives them; and a wasteful war
Is fought against you, and you fight it; they
Adulterate law, and you prepare their way

---

12 Maccabees'] of the Books of Maccabees only *Maccabees* 1 and 2 were included in the
canon of the Bible by the Council of Trent

Like wittols; th'issue your own ruin is.
Greatest and fairest Empress, know you this?
Alas, no more than Thames' calm head doth know
Whose meads her arms drown, or whose corn o'erflow.
You, sir, whose righteousness she loves, whom I
By having leave to serve, am most richly
For service paid, authorized, now begin
To know and weed out this enormous sin.
O Age of rusty iron! Some better wit
Call it some worse name, if aught equal it—
The Iron Age that was when justice was sold; now
Injustice is sold dearer far! Allow
All demands, fees, and duties, gamesters, anon
The money which you sweat, and swear for, is gone
Into other hands: so controverted lands
Scape, like Angelica, the striver's hands.
If law be in the judge's heart, and he
Have no heart to resist letter, or fee,
Where wilt thou appeal? Power of the courts below
Flows from the first main head, and these can throw
Thee, if they suck thee in, to misery,
To fetters, halters. But if the injury
Steel thee to dare complain, alas, thou go'st
Against the stream, when upwards, when thou art most
Heavy and most faint; and in these labours they
'Gainst whom thou should'st complain, will in the way
Become great seas, o'er which, when thou shalt be
Forced to make golden bridges, thou shalt see
That all thy gold was drowned in them before.
All things follow their like, only who have may have more.
Judges are Gods; he who made and said them so
Meant not that men should be forced to them to go,
By means of angels. When supplications
We send to God, to Dominations,
Powers, Cherubims, and all Heaven's courts, if we
Should pay fees as here, daily bread would be
Scarce to kings; so 'tis. Would it not anger
A Stoic, a coward, yea a martyr,
To see a pursuivant come in, and call

---

wittols] fools   You, sir] Sir Thomas Egerton
Angelica] in Ariosto's *Orlando Furioso*, Angelica is striven for by Ferraù and Rinaldo

All his clothes, copes; books, primers; and all
His plate, chalices; and mistake them away,
And ask a fee for coming? Oh, ne'er may
Fair Law's white reverend name be strumpeted,
To warrant thefts: she is established
Recorder to destiny, on earth, and she
Speaks fate's words, and but tells us who must be
Rich, who poor, who in chairs, who in jails:
She is all fair, but yet hath foul long nails,
With which she scratcheth suitors. In bodies
Of men, so in Law, nails are th'extremities;
So officers stretch to more than Law can do,
As our nails reach what no else part comes to.
Why barest thou to yon officer? Fool, hath he
Got those goods for which erst men bared to thee?
Fool, twice, thrice, thou hast bought wrong, and now hungrily
Begg'st right; but that dole comes not till these die.
Thou had'st much, and law's Urim and Thummim try
Thou would'st for more; and for all hast paper
Enough to clothe all the great carrack's pepper.
Sell that, and by that thou much more shalt leese
Than Haman, when he sold his antiquities.
O wretch that thy fortunes should moralize
Aesop's fables, and make tales, prophecies.
Thou'rt the swimming dog whom shadows cozened,
And div'st, near drowning, for what's vanished.

---

great carrack's pepper] part of the cargo of the Portuguese carrack *Madre de Dios*
captured in 1592
leese] lose

JOSEPH HALL
1574–1656

14

from *Virgidemiae*

(i)
Lawyers and Clients

WHO doubts? The laws fell down from heaven's height
Like to some gliding star in winter's night.
Themis the scribe of God did long agone
Engrave them deep in during marble-stone,
And cast them down on this unruly clay,
That men might know to rule and to obey.
But now their characters depraved bin,
By them that would make gain of others' sin.
And now hath wrong so maistered the right
That they live best that on wrong's offal light.
So loathly fly that lives on galled wound,
And scabby festers inwardly unsound,
Feeds fatter with that poisonous carrion
Than they that haunt the healthy limbs alone.
Woe to the weal where many lawyers be,
For there is sure much store of maladie.
'Twas truly said, and truly was foreseen,
The fat kine are devoured of the lean.
Genus and Species long since barefoot went
Upon their ten toes in wild wonderment;
Whiles Father Bartoll on his foot-cloth rode
Upon high pavement gayly silver-strowed.
Each home-bred science percheth in the chair,
While sacred arts grovel on the groundsel bare.
Since peddling barbarisms gan be in request,
Nor classic tongues, nor learning found no rest.
The crouching client, with low-bended knee,

---

festers] ulcers
Genus and Species] two of the Five Predictables of logic, used as nicknames for humble
scholars
Father Bartoll] Bartolo of Sassoferrato, great Italian lawyer of the fourteenth century
foot-cloth] grandee's horse-cloth of velvet etc., hanging on either side to his feet
groundsel] door-sill

And many worships, and fair flattery,
Tells on his tale as smoothly as him list,
But still the lawyer's eye squints on his fist;
If that seem lined with a larger fee,
Doubt not the suit, the law is plain for thee.
Though must he buy his vainer hopes with price,
Disclout his crowns, and thank for his advice.
So have I seen in a tempestuous stour
Some breer-bush showing shelter from the shower
Unto the hopeful sheep, that fain would hide
His fleecy coat from that same angry tide.
The ruthless breer regardless of his plight
Lays hold upon the fleece he should acquite,
And takes advantage of the careless prey
That thought she in securer shelter lay.
The day is fair, the sheep would fare to feed;
The tyrant brier holds fast his shelter's meed,
And claims it for the fee of his defence;
So robs the sheep, in favour's fair pretence.

(ii)

The Time of Gold

Time was, and that was termed the time of Gold,
When world and time were young, that now are old
(When quiet Saturn swayed the mace of lead,
And pride was yet unborn, and yet unbred).
Time was, that whiles the autumn fall did last,
Our hungry sires gaped for the falling mast of the Dodonian oaks.
Could no unhusked acorn leave the tree,
But there was challenge made whose it might be.
And if some nice and lickerous appetite
Desired more dainty dish of rare delight,
They scaled the stored crab with clasped knee,
Till they had sated their delicious eye;
Or searched the hopeful thicks of hedgy rows,
For briary berries, or haws, or sourer sloes;
Or when they meant to fare the fin'st of all,
They licked oak-leaves besprent with honey fall.

stour] turmoil   breer] wild rose   acquite] set free
(ii)   delicious] sensuous

As for the thrice three-angled beech-nut shell,
Or chestnut's armed husk, and hid kernell,
No squire durst touch, the law would not afford,
Kept for the Court, and for the King's own board.
Their royal plate was clay, or wood, or stone:
The vulgar, save his hand, else had he none.
Their only cellar was the neighbour brook;
None did for better care, for better look.
Was then no plaining of the brewer's scape,
Nor greedy vintner mixed the strained grape.
The King's pavilion was the grassy green,
Under safe shelter of the shady treen.
Under each bank men laid their limbs along,
Not wishing any ease, not fearing wrong;
Clad with their own, as they were made of old,
Not fearing shame, not feeling any cold.
But when, by Ceres' housewifery and pain,
Men learned to bury the reviving grain,
And father Janus taught the new-found vine
Rise on the elm, with many a friendly twine,
And base desire bade men to delven low,
For needless metals, then 'gan mischief grow.
Then farewell, fairest age, the world's best days,
Thriving in ill as it in age decays.
Then crept in pride, and peevish covetise,
And men grew greedy, discordous and nice.
Now man, that erst hail-fellow was with beast,
Wox on to ween himself a god at least.
No airy fowl can take so high a flight,
Though she her daring wings in clouds have dight;
No fish can dive so deep in yielding sea,
Though Thetis' self should swear her safety;
Nor fearful beast can dig his cave so low,
All could he further than Earth's centre go;
As that the air, the earth, or ocean,
Should shield them from the gorge of greedy man.
Hath utmost Ind aught better than his own?
Then utmost Ind is near, and rife to gon.
O Nature! was the world ordained for nought,
But fill man's maw, and feed man's idle thought?

scape] trickery	covetise] covetousness	discordous] discordant
nice] difficult to please	wox on] grew	rife to gon] easy to go to

34

Thy grandsire's words savoured of thrifty leeks,
Or manly garlic; but thy furnace reeks
Hot steams of wine, and can aloof descry
The drunken draughts of sweet autumnity.
They naked went; or clad in ruder hide,
Or home-spun russet, void of foreign pride;
But thou canst mask in garish gaudery,
To suit a fool's far-fetched livery.
A French head joined to neck Italian;
Thy thighs from Germany, and breast fro Spain;
An Englishman in none, a fool in all,
Many in one, and one in severall.
Then men were men, but now the greater part
Beasts are in life, and women are in heart.
Good Saturn self, that homely emperor,
In proudest pomp was not so clad of yore,
As is the under-groom of the ostlery,
Husbanding it in work-day yeomanry.
Lo! the long date of those expired days,
Which the inspired Merlin's word foresays:
'When dunghill peasants shall be dight as kings,
Then one confusion another brings.'
Then farewell, fairest age, the world's best days,
Thriving in ill, as it in age decays.

(iii)
Quid placet ergo?

The sturdy ploughman doth the soldier see,
All scarfed with pied colours to the knee,
Whom Indian pillage hath made fortunate,
And now he gins to loathe his former state;
Now doth he inly scorn his Kendal green,
And his patched cockers now despised been.
Nor list he now go whistling to the car,
But sells his team and fettleth to the war.
O war to them that never tried thee sweet!

Husbanding it] doing farm work   yeomanry] yeoman's dress
(iii)   Kendal green] coarse green cloth woven in Kendal   cockers] gaitered boots
car] cart   fettleth to] prepares to go to

35

When his dead mate falls grovelling at his feet,
And angry bullets whistlen at his ear,
And his dim eyes see nought but death and drear;
O happy ploughman were thy weal well known;
O happy all estates except his own!
Some drunken rhymer thinks his time well spent,
If he can live to see his name in print;
Who when he is once fleshed to the press,
And see his handsel have such fair success,
Sung to the wheel, and sung unto the pail,
He sends forth thraves of ballads to the sale.
Nor then can rest; but volumes up bodged rhymes,
To have his name talked of in future times.
The brainsick youth that feeds his tickled ear
With sweet-sauced lies of some false traveller,
Which hath the *Spanish Decades* read awhile,
Or whetstone leasings of old Mandevile,
Now with discourses breaks his midnight sleep
Of his adventures through the Indian deep,
Of all their massy heaps of golden mine,
Or of the antique tombs of Palestine,
Or of Damascus' magic wall of glass,
Of Solomon his sweating piles of brass,
Of the bird Roc that bears an elephant;
Of mermaids that the southern seas do haunt;
Of headless men; of savage cannibals;
The fashion of their lives and governals;
What monstrous cities there erected be,
Cairo, or the City of the Trinity.
Now are they dunghill cocks that have not seen
The bordering Alps, or else the neighbour Rhene,
And now he plies the newsful Grasshopper,
Of voyages and ventures to enquire.

drunken rhymer] sidelong reference to the ballad writer William Elderton
handsel] first fruits   pail] milk pail   wheel] spinning wheel
thraves] sheaves, heaps
Spanish Decades] *The Decades of the newe worlde*, tr. 1555 from Peter Martyr's Latin
whetstone leasings] lies which win the proverbial whetstone for sharpening the liar's
tongue   mine] ore, metal   governals] rules of conduct
City of the Trinity] ? Alexandria
newsful Grasshopper] the Royal Exchange, surmounted by a grasshopper weather-vane

His land mortgaged, he sea-beat in the way
Wishes for home a thousand sithes a day;
And now he deems his home-bred fare as lief
As his parched biscuit, or his barrelled beef.
'Mongst all these stirs of discontented strife,
O let me lead an academic life,
To know much, and to think we nothing know;
Nothing to have, yet think we have enough,
In skill to want, and wanting seek for more,
In weal nor want, nor wish for greater store;
Envy, ye monarchs with your proud excess,
At our low sail, and our high happiness.

WILLIAM RANKINS
fl. 1588–1601

15   from *Satyrus Peregrinans*
In Westminster Hall

BY this time long-gowned Lumen walked abroad,
Under his girdle green-waxed labels hung,
Although his pace was slow, gold was his goad,
And as the pettifogger went, he sung,
His greased belt and the wax together clung:
He swore a mighty oath his writs were spoiled,
And by that means his client should be foiled.

I tracked his steps, and followed him aloof,
Weary with those mechanic mean deceits,
At last he entered to a spacious roof,
Where great men sat in high judicial seats,
And jugglers play at even and odd with feats:
As, Now, sir, it shall go with you today,
Tomorrow 'tis against you, you must pay.

sithes] times   low sail] humble living

15   green-waxed labels] parchment strips carrying the official seals of green wax attached to writs. The dishonest lawyer has detached them and tucked them under his gown   mechanic] base
spacious roof] Westminster Hall, which housed the law courts
even and odd] a guessing gambling game   feats] sleights, tricks

37

This hall, they say, is builded of such wood,
That cobwebs on the rafters are not spun,
By right the nature of these trees are good,
Yet there beheld I mighty spiders run,
And by their sucking little flies undone:
A thing most strange, that poisoned things must dwell,
Where nature scarce alloweth them a cell.

There stood Briareus with a hundred hands,
And every one was ready to receive,
As many sundry tongues, as seas have sands:
And when he said, The truth I do conceive,
Then meant the hell-hound soonest to deceive.
There saw I twelve good fellows called together,
That would forswear their father for a feather.

I saw the widow in a mourning weed,
Wringing her painful hands to get her right,
Th' oppressed soul tormented with more need,
And cruelty with scarlet clothed in spite,
As who should say, In blood is my delight.
Then thought I, Oh there is a Judge above
Will all this wrong with one true sentence move.

SAMUEL BUTLER
1612–1680

16   from *Hudibras*
(i)
The Religion of Sir Hudibras

FOR his religion it was fit
To match his learning and his wit:
'Twas Presbyterian true blue,
For he was of that stubborn crew
Of errant Saints, whom all men grant
To be the true Church Militant:

15   such wood] blessed oak from St. Patrick's Ireland, fatal to poisonous creatures

Such as do build their faith upon
The holy text of pike and gun;
Decide all controversies by
Infallible artillery;
And prove their doctrine orthodox
By apostolic blows and knocks;
Call fire and sword and desolation
A godly-thorough-Reformation,
Which always must be carried on,
And still be doing, never done:
As if religion were intended
For nothing else but to be mended.
A sect whose chief devotion lies
In odd perverse antipathies;
In falling out with that or this,
And finding somewhat still amiss:
More peevish, cross, and splenetick,
Than dog distract, or monkey sick.
That with more care keep holy-day
The wrong, than others the right way:
Compound for sins they are inclined to,
By damning those they have no mind to;
Still so perverse and opposite
As if they worshipped God for spite.
The selfsame thing they will abhor
One way, and long another for.
Free will they one way disavow,
Another, nothing else allow.
All piety consists therein
In them, in other men all sin.
Rather than fail, they will defy
That which they love most tenderly,
Quarrel with minced pies, and disparage
Their best and dearest friend, plum-porridge;
Fat pig and goose itself oppose,
And blaspheme custard through the nose.
Th'apostles of this fierce religion,
Like Mahomet's, were ass and widgeon,
To whom our Knight by fast instinct
Of wit and temper was so linkt,
As if hypocrisy and nonsense
Had got th'advowson of his conscience.

(ii)

The Tattling Gossip of the Newsheets

There is a tall long-sided dame,
(But wondrous light) ycleped Fame,
That like a thin chameleon boards
Herself on air, and eats your words:
Upon her shoulders wings she wears
Like hanging sleeves, lined through with ears,
And eyes, and tongues, as poets list,
Made good by deep mythologist.
With these, she through the welkin flies,
And sometimes carries truth, oft lies;
With letters hung like eastern pigeons,
And Mercuries of furthest regions;
Diurnals writ for regulation
Of lying, to inform the nation,
And by their public use to bring down
The rate of whetstones in the kingdom.
About her neck a packet-mail,
Fraught with advice, some fresh, some stale;
Of men that walked when they were dead,
And cows of monsters brought to bed:
Of hailstones big as pullets' eggs,
And puppies whelped with twice two legs:
A blazing star seen in the west,
By six or seven men at least.
Two trumpets she does sound at once,
But both of clean contrary tones.
But whether both with the same wind,
Or one before, and one behind,
We know not; only this can tell,
The one sounds vilely, th'other well;
And therefore vulgar authors name
Th'one Good, the other Evil Fame.

(iii)

Sir Hudibras courts the Lady

Quoth he, My faith as adamantine
As chains of destiny I'll maintain;
True as Apollo ever spoke,
Or oracle from heart of oak.
And if you'll give my flame but vent,
Now in close hugger-mugger pent,
And shine upon me but benignly
With that one, and that other pigsney,
The sun and day shall sooner part
Than love, or you, shake off my heart;
The sun that shall no more dispense
His own, but your bright influence.
I'll carve your name on barks of trees,
With true-love-knots, and flourishes,
That shall infuse eternal spring
And everlasting flourishing;
Drink ev'ry letter on't, in stum;
And make it brisk champagne become.
Where'er you tread your foot shall set
The primrose and the violet;
All spices, perfumes, and sweet powders,
Shall borrow from your breath their odours;
Nature her charter shall renew,
And take all lives of things from you;
The world depend upon your eye,
And when you frown upon it, die:
Only our loves shall still survive,
New worlds and natures to outlive,
And, like to heralds' moons, remain
All crescents, without change or wane.

Hold, hold, quoth she, no more of this;
Sir Knight, you take your aim amiss;
For you will find it a hard chapter
To catch me with poetic rapture,
In which your mastery of art
Doth shew itself, and not your heart:

pigsney] darling   stum] flat wine renewed with must

Nor will you raise in mine combustion
By dint of high heroic fustian.
She that with poetry is won
Is but a desk to write upon;
And what men say of her they mean
No more, than that on which they lean.

(iv)
The Saints

What makes a knave a child of God,
And one of us?—A livelihood.
What renders beating out of brains,
And murther godliness?—Great gains.
What's tender conscience?—'Tis a botch
That will not bear the gentlest touch,
But breaking out, dispatches more
Than the epidemical'st plague-sore.
What makes y'encroach upon our trade,
And damn all others?—To be paid.
What's orthodox, and true believing
Against a conscience?—A good living.
What makes rebelling against kings
A Good Old Cause?—Administ'rings.
What makes all doctrines plain and clear?
About two hundred pounds a year.
And that which was proved true before,
Prove false again? Two hundred more.
What makes the breaking of all oaths
A holy duty? Food, and clothes.
What laws and freedom, persecution?
B'ing out of pow'r and contribution.
What makes a church a den of thieves?
A Dean, a Chapter and white sleeves.
And what would serve if those were gone,
To make it orthodox? Our own.
What makes morality a crime,
The most notorious of the time?
Morality, which both the Saints,
And Wicked too, cry out against?
'Cause grace and virtue are within
Prohibited degrees of kin;

And therefore no true Saint allows,
They should be suffered to espouse;
For Saints can need no conscience
That with morality dispense;
As virtue's impious, when 'tis rooted
In nature only, and not imputed:
But why the Wicked should do so
We neither know, nor care to do.
What's liberty of conscience,
I' th' natural and genuine sense?
'Tis to restore with more security,
Rebellion to its ancient purity;
And Christian liberty reduce
To th' elder practice of the Jews:
For a large conscience is all one,
And signifies the same with none.

JOHN CLEVELAND
1613–1658

17   from *The Rebel Scot*

(i)

NATURE herself doth Scotchmen beasts confess,
Making their country such a wilderness,
A land that brings in question and suspense
God's omnipresence, but that CHARLES came thence;
But that Montrose and Crawford's loyal band
Attoned their sins, and christened half the land.
Nor is it all the nation hath these spots,
There is a Church as well as Kirk of Scots,
As in a picture, where the squinting paint
Shows fiend on this side, and on that side saint.
He that saw hell in's melancholy dream,
And in the twilight of his fancy's theme,
Scared from his sins, repented in a fright,
Had he viewed Scotland, had turned proselyte.
A land where one may pray with curst intent,

---

17   Crawford] Earl of Crawford, on the king's side in the Civil War

O may they never suffer banishment!
Had Cain been Scot, God would have changed his doom,
Not forced him wander, but confined him home.
Like Jews they spread, and as infection fly,
As if the Devil had ubiquity.
Hence 'tis, they live at rovers; and defy
This or that place, rags of geography.
They're citizens o' the world; they're all in all,
Scotland's a national epidemical.

(ii)

Lord! what a goodly thing is want of shirts!
How a Scotch stomach, and no meat, converts!
They wanted food and raiment; so they took
Religion for their seamstress and their cook.
Unmask them well, their honours and estate,
As well as conscience, are sophisticate.
Shrive but their titles, and their money poise,
A laird and twenty pence pronounced with noise,
When construed, but for a plain yeoman go,
And a good sober tuppence; and well so.
Hence then, you proud impostors, get you gone,
You Picts in gentry and devotion:
You scandal to the stock of verse! a race
Able to bring the gibbet in disgrace.
Hyperbolus by suffering did traduce
The ostracism, and shamed it out of use.
The Indian that heaven did forswear,
Because he heard the Spaniards were there,
Had he but known what Scots in hell had been,
He would Erasmus-like have hung between.
My Muse hath done. A voider for the nonce!
I wrong the Devil, should I pick the bones.

at rovers] everywhere, in no fixed place   (ii)   sophisticate] adulterated
            pence] twenty Scotch pence were worth two English pence
Hyperbolus] despised Athenian demagogue who ostracized (banished) himself when he
            hoped to have others banished   suffering] resorting to
Erasmus-like] 'They were wont to say that Erasmus was interpendent between Heaven
            and Hell' Aubrey, *Brief Lives*   voider] waste bin

That dish is his: for when the Scots decease,
Hell like their nation feeds on barnacles.
    A Scot, when from the gallows-tree got loose,
Drops into Styx, and turns a solan goose.

HENRY VAUGHAN
1621–1695

18   from *Juvenal's Tenth Satire Translated*
                Where Age doth hit

GIVE store of days, good Jove, give length of years,
Are the next vows; these with religious fears,
And constancy we pay; but what's so bad,
As a long, sinful age? what cross more sad
Than misery of years? how great an ill
Is that, which doth but nurse more sorrow still?
It blacks the face, corrupts, and dulls the blood,
Benights the quickest eye, distates the food,
And such deep furrows cuts i'the chequered skin
As in the old oaks of Tabraca are seen.
    Youth varies in most things; strength, beauty, wit,
Are several graces; but where age doth hit,
It makes no difference; the same weak voice,
And trembling ague in each member lies:
A general, hateful baldness, with a cursed
Perpetual pettishness; and which is worst,
A foul, strong flux of humours, and more pain
To feed, than if he were to nurse again.
So tedious to himself, his wife, and friends,
That his own sons, and servants, wish his end,
His taste, and feeling dies; and of that fire
The amorous lover burns in, no desire:
Or if there were, what pleasure could it be,
Where lust doth reign without ability?
Nor is this all, what matters it, where he
Sits in the spacious stage? who can nor see,
Nor hear what's acted, whom the stiller voice
Of spirited, wanton airs, or the loud noise
Of trumpets cannot pierce; whom thunder can

But scarce inform who enters, or what man
He personates, what 'tis they act, or say?
How many scenes are done? what time of day?
Besides that little blood, his carcass holds,
Hath lost its native warmth, and fraught with colds,
Catarrhs, and rheums, to thick, black jelly turns,
And never but in fits, and fevers burns;
Such vast infirmities, so huge a stock
Of sickness, and diseases to him flock,
That Hyppia ne'r so many lovers knew,
Nor wanton Maura; Physic never slew
So many patients, nor rich lawyers spoil
More wards, and widows; it were lesser toil
To number out what manors, and demesnes,
Licinius' razor purchased: one complains
Of weakness in the back, another pants
For lack of breath, the third his eyesight wants;
Nay some so feeble are, and full of pain,
That infant like they must be fed again.
These faint too at their meals; their wine they spill,
And like young birds, that wait the mother's bill
They gape for meat; but sadder far than this
Their senseless ignorance, and dotage is;
For neither they, their friends, nor servants know,
Nay those themselves begot, and bred up too
No longer now they'll own; for madly they
Proscribe them all, and what on the last day,
The misers cannot carry to the grave
For their past sins, their prostitutes must have.
　　But grant age lacked these plagues; yet must they see
As great, as many: frail mortality
In such a length of years, hath many falls,
And deads a life with frequent funerals.
The nimblest hour in all the span, can steal
A friend, or brother from's; there's no repeal
In death, or time; this day a wife we mourn,
Tomorrow's tears a son, and the next urn
A sister fills; long-livers have assigned
These curses still: that with a restless mind,
An age of fresh renewing cares they buy,
And in a tide of tears grow old and die.

ANDREW MARVELL
1621–1678

from *The Character of Holland*

HOLLAND, that scarce deserves the name of land,
As but the offscouring of the British sand,
And so much earth as was contributed
By English pilots when they heaved the lead,
Or what by th' ocean's slow alluvion fell
Of shipwrecked cockle and the mussel shell—
This indigested vomit of the sea
Fell to the Dutch by just propriety.
   Glad then, as miners that have found the ore,
They with mad labour fished the land to shore,
And dived as desperately for each piece
Of earth, as if 't had been of ambergris,
Collecting anxiously small loads of clay,
Less than what building swallows bear away,
Or than those pills which sordid beetles roll,
Transfusing into them their dunghill soul.
   How did they rivet, with gigantic piles,
Thorough the centre their new-catched miles,
And to the stake a struggling country bound,
Where barking waves still bait the forced ground,
Building their watery Babel far more high
To reach the sea, than those to scale the sky.
   Yet still his claim the injured ocean laid,
And oft at leap-frog o'er their steeples played,
As if on purpose it on land had come
To show them what's their *Mare Liberum.*
A daily deluge over them does boil;
The earth and water play at level-coil;
The fish ofttimes the burgher dispossessed,
And sat not as a meat but as a guest.
And oft the tritons and the sea nymphs saw
Whole shoals of Dutch served up for cabillau;

---

level-coil] game in which players shifted seats (*lever cul,* lift-bum)
cabillau] salt cod

Or as they over the new level ranged
For pickled herring, pickled *Heeren* changed.
Nature, it seemed, ashamed of her mistake,
Would throw their land away at duck and drake.
  Therefore necessity, that first made kings,
Something like government among them brings.
For as with pygmies, who best kills the crane,
Among the hungry, he that treasures grain,
Among the blind, the one-eyed blinkard reigns,
So rules among the drowned, he that drains.
Not who first sees the rising sun commands,
But who could first discern the rising lands.
Who best could know to pump an earth so leak,
Him they their Lord and country's Father speak.
To make a bank was a great plot of state;
Invent a shovel, and be magistrate.
Hence some small dyke-grave unperceived invades
The power, and grows, as 'twere, a King of Spades.
But for less envy some joint states endures,
Who look like a Commission of the Sewers.
For these Half-anders, half wet, and half dry,
Nor bear strict service, nor pure liberty.

20   from *The Last Instructions to a Painter*

(i)

Our Lady State

London, 4 September 1667

AFTER two sittings, now our Lady State
To end her picture does the third time wait.
But ere thou fall'st to work, first, Painter, see
If 't ben't too slight grown or too hard for thee.
Canst thou paint without colours? Then 'tis right:
For so we too without a fleet can fight.
Or canst thou daub a signpost, and that ill?
'Twill suit our great debauch and little skill.

---

19   leak] leaky
dyke-grave] official of the Court of Sewers in charge of sluices and dykes
Half-anders] i.e. not (W)hole-anders, Hollanders

Or hast thou marked how antic masters limn
The aly-roof with snuff of candle dim,
Sketching in shady smoke prodigious tools?
'Twill serve this race of drunkards, pimps, and fools.

(ii)

The King's Mistress, Lady Castlemaine

Paint Castlemaine in colours that will hold
(Her, not her picture, for she now grows old):
She through her lackey's drawers, as he ran,
Discerned love's cause and a new flame began.
Her wonted joys thenceforth and court she shuns,
And still within her mind the footman runs:
His brazen calves, his brawny thighs—the face
She slights—his feet shaped for a smoother race.
Poring within her glass she readjusts
Her looks, and oft-tried beauty now distrusts,
Fears lest he scorn a woman once assayed,
And now first wished she e'er had been a maid.
Great Love, how dost thou triumph and how reign,
That to a groom couldst humble her disdain!
Stripped to her skin, see how she stooping stands,
Nor scorns to rub him down with those fair hands,
And washing (lest the scent her crime disclose)
His sweaty hooves, tickles him 'twixt the toes.
But envious Fame, too soon, began to note
More gold in's fob, more lace upon his coat;
And he, unwary, and of tongue too fleet,
No longer could conceal his fortune sweet.
Justly the rogue was whipped in porter's den,
And Jermyn straight has leave to come again.

aly-roof] alehouse roof
(ii) Jermyn] the courtier Henry Jermyn, afterwards Lord Dover

(iii)
Charles the Second's Vision

Paint last the King, and a dead shade of night
Only dispersed by a weak taper's light,
And those bright gleams that dart along and glare
From his clear eyes, yet these too dark with care.
There, as in the calm horror all alone
He wakes, and muses of th' uneasy throne,
Raise up a sudden shape with virgin's face
(Though ill agree her posture, hour, or place),
Naked as born, and her round arms behind
With her own tresses, interwove and twined;
Her mouth locked up, a blind before her eyes,
Yet from beneath the veil her blushes rise,
And silent tears her secret anguish speak;
Her heart throbs and with very shame would break.
The object strange in him no terror moved:
He wondered first, then pitied, then he loved,
And with kind hand does the coy vision press
(Whose beauty greater seemed by her distress),
But soon shrunk back, chilled with her touch so cold,
And th' airy picture vanished from his hold.
In his deep thoughts the wonder did increase,
And he divined 'twas England or the Peace.

CHARLES COTTON
1630–1687

21   *The Litany*

I

FROM a ruler that's a curse,
And a government that's worse;
From a prince that rules by awe,
Whose tyrannic will's his law;
From an armed Council board,
And a sceptre that's a sword,
    Libera nos, etc.

II

From a kingdom, that from health
Sickens to a commonwealth;
From such peers as stain their blood,
And are neither wise, nor good;
From a gentry steeped in pots,
From unkennellers of plots,
    Libera nos, etc.

III

From a church without divines,
And a presbyter that whines;
From John Calvin, and his pupils,
From a sentence without scruples,
From a clergy without letters,
And a free state bound in fetters,
    Libera nos, etc.

IV

From the bustle of the town,
And the knavish tribe o' th' gown,
From long bills where we are debtors,
From bum-bailiffs, and their setters,
From the tedious city lectures,
And thanksgiving for protectors,
    Libera nos, etc.

V

From ill victuals when we dine,
And a tavern with ill wine;
From vile smoke in a short pipe,
And a landlord that will gripe,
From long reck'nings, and a wench
That claps in English; or in French,
    Libera nos, etc.

free state] republic   tribe o' th' gown] lawyers   setters] spies
lectures] discourses in church encouraged by the Puritans

VI

From demesnes whose barren soil
Ne'er produced the barley oil;
From a friend for nothing fit,
That nor courage has, nor wit;
From all liars, and from those
Who write nonsense verse or prose,
    Libera nos, etc.

VII

From a virgin that's no maid,
From a kicking, stumbling jade,
From false servants, and a scold,
From all women that are old,
From loud tongues that never lie,
And from a domestic spy;
    Libera nos, etc.

VIII

From a domineering spouse,
From a smoky, dirty house,
From foul linen, and the noise
Of young children, girls or boys,
From ill beds, and full of fleas,
From a wife with essences;
    Libera nos, etc.

IX

From trepans of wicked men,
From the interest of ten,
From rebellion, and the sense
Of a wounded conscience;
Lastly, from the poet's evil,
From His Highness, and the Devil,
    Libera nos, etc.

barley oil] strong drink   essences] perfumes   trepans] snares
the poet's evil] poverty

On Tobacco

WHAT horrid sin condemned the teeming Earth,
And cursed her womb with such a monstrous birth?
What crime, America, that Heav'n would please
To make thee mother of the world's disease?
In thy fair womb what accidents could breed,
What plague give root to this pernicious weed?
Tobacco! Oh, the very name doth kill,
And has already foxed my reeling quill;
I now could write libels against the King,
Treason, or blasphemy, or anything
'Gainst piety, and reason; I could frame
A panegyric to the Protector's name:
Such sly infection does the word infuse
Into the soul of ev'ry modest Muse.

What politic peregrine was't first could boast
He brought a pest into his native coast?
Th' abstract of poison in a stinking weed,
The spurious issue of corrupted seed;
Seed belched in earthquakes from the dark abyss,
Whose name a blot in nature's herbal is.
What drunken fiend taught Englishmen the crime,
Thus to puff out, and spawl away their time?
    Pernicious Weed (should not my Muse offend,
To say Heav'n made aught for a cruel end),
I should proclaim that thou created wert,
To ruin man's high, and immortal part.
The Stygian damp obscures our reason's eye,
Debauches wit, and makes invention dry;
Destroys the memory, confounds our care;
We know not what we do, or what we are:
Renders our faculties, and members lame
To ev'ry office of our country's claim.
Our life's a drunken dream devoid of sense,
And the best actions of our time offence.
Our health, diseases, lethargies, and rheum,
Our friendship's fire, and all our vows are fume.
Of late there's no such thing as wit, or sense,

peregrine] traveller   spawl] spit

53

Counsel, instruction or intelligence:
Discourse that should distinguish man from beast,
Is by the vapour of this weed supprest;
For what we talk is interrupted stuff,
The one half English, and the other puff;
Freedom and truth are things we do not know,
We know not what we say, or what we do:
We want in all, the understanding's light,
We talk in clouds, and walk in endless night.
    We smoke, as if we meant, concealed by spell,
To spy abroad, yet be invisible:
But no discovery shall the statesman boast,
We raise a mist wherein ourselves are lost,
A stinking shade, and whilst we pipe it thus,
Each one appears an *ignis fatuus.*
Courtier, and peasant, nay the madam nice
Is likewise fallen into the common vice,
We all in dusky error groping lie,
Robbed of our reasons, and the day's bright eye,
Whilst sailors from the main-top see our isle
Wrapped up in smoke, like the Aetnean pile.
    What nameless ill does its contagion shroud
In the dark mantle of this noisome cloud?
Sure 'tis the Devil; Oh, I know that's it,
Foh! How the sulphur makes me cough and spit!
'Tis he; or else some fav'rite fiend at least,
In all the mischief of his malice dressed;
Each deadly sin that lurks t'entrap the soul,
Does here concealed in curling vapours roll,
And for the body such an unknown ill,
As makes physicians' reading, and their skill:
One undistinguished pest made up of all
That men experienced do diseases call:
Coughs, asthmas, apoplexies, fevers, rheum,
All that kill dead, or lingeringly consume,
Folly, and madness, nay the plague, the pox;
And ev'ry fool wears a Pandora's box.
From that rich mine, the stupid sot doth fill,
Smokes up his liver, and his lungs, until
His reeking nostrils monstrously proclaim,
His brains, and bowels are consuming flame.
What noble soul would be content to dwell
In the dark lanthorn of a smoky cell?

To prostitute his body, and his mind,
To a debauch of such a stinking kind?
To sacrifice to Moloch, and to fry,
In such a base, dirty idolatry;
As if frail life, which of itself's too short,
Were to be whiffed away in drunken sport?
Thus, as if weary of our destined years,
We burn the thread so to prevent the shears.
 What noble end, can simple man propose
For a reward to his all-smoking nose?
His purposes are levelled sure amiss,
Where neither ornament, nor pleasure is.
What can he then design his worthy hire?
Sure 'tis t' inure him for eternal fire;
And thus his aim must admirably thrive,
In hopes of Hell, he damns himself alive.
 But my infected Muse begins to choke
In the vile stink of the increasing smoke,
And can no more in equal numbers chime,
Unless to sneeze, and cough, and spit in rhyme.
Half stifled now in this new time's disease,
She must *in fumo* vanish, and decease.
This is her fault's excuse, and her pretence,
This satire, perhaps, else had looked like sense.

JOHN DRYDEN
1631–1700

23   *Prologue to 'Amboyna, or, The Cruelties of the Dutch to the English Merchants'*

As needy gallants in the scriv'ners' hands
Court the rich knave that gripes their mortgaged lands,
The first fat buck of all the season's sent
And keeper takes no fee in compliment:
The dotage of some Englishmen is such
To fawn on those who ruin them, the Dutch.
They shall have all rather than make a war
With those who of the same religion are.
The Straits, the Guinea trade, the herrings too,
Nay, to keep friendship, they shall pickle you.
Some are resolved not to find out the cheat,
But cuckold-like, love him who does the feat:
What injuries soe'er upon us fall,
Yet still the same religion answers all.
Religion wheedled you to civil war,
Drew English blood, and Dutchmen now would spare:
Be gulled no longer, for you'll find it true,
They have no more religion, faith—than you;
Interest's the God they worship in their State,
And you, I take it, have not much of that.
Well monarchies may own religion's name,
But States are atheists in their very frame.
They share a sin, and such proportions fall
That like a stink, 'tis nothing to 'em all.
How they love England, you shall see this day:
No map shews Holland truer than our play:
Their pictures and inscriptions well we know;
We may be bold one medal more to show,
View then their falsehoods, rapine, cruelty,

States] republics

56

And think what once they were, they still would be:
But hope not either language, plot, or art,
'Twas writ in haste, but with an English heart.
And least hope wit; in Dutchmen that would be
As much improper as would honesty.

24   from *Prologue to 'The Spanish Friar'*

'TWERE well your judgments but in plays did range,
But ev'n your follies and debauches change
With such a whirl, the poets of your age
Are tired, and cannot score 'em on the stage,
Unless each vice in shorthand they indite,
Ev'n as notched prentices whole sermons write.
The heavy Hollanders no vices know
But what they used a hundred years ago:
Like honest plants, where they were stuck, they grow;
They cheat, but still from cheating sires they come;
They drink, but they were christ'ned first in mum.
Their patrimonial sloth the Spaniards keep,
And Philip first taught Philip how to sleep.
The French and we still change, but here's the curse,
They change for better, and we change for worse;
They take up our old trade of conquering,
And we are taking theirs, to dance and sing:
Our fathers did for change to France repair,
And they for change will try our English air.
As children, when they throw one toy away,
Straight a more foolish gugaw comes in play:
So we, grown penitent, on serious thinking,
Leave whoring, and devoutly fall to drinking.

25   *On Jacob Tonson, his Publisher*

WITH leering looks, bull-faced, and freckled fair,
With two left legs, and Judas-coloured hair,
With frowzy pores, that taint the ambient air.

---

24 notched] with hair cut short   mum] Brunswick beer

26   from *Absalom and Achitophel*

(i)

The False Achitophel, Lord Shaftesbury

SOME by their friends, more by themselves thought wise,
Opposed the pow'r, to which they could not rise.
Some had in courts been great, and thrown from thence,
Like fiends, were hardened in impenitence.
Some by their monarch's fatal mercy grown,
From pardoned rebels, kinsmen to the throne,
Were raised in pow'r and public office high:
Strong bands, if bands ungrateful men could tie.
   Of these the false Achitophel was first:
A name to all succeeding ages cursed.
For close designs, and crooked counsels fit;
Sagacious, bold, and turbulent of wit:
Restless, unfixed in principles and place;
In pow'r unpleased, impatient of disgrace.
A fiery soul, which working out its way,
Fretted the pigmy body to decay,
And o'er-informed the tenement of clay.
A daring pilot in extremity;
Pleased with the danger, when the waves went high
He sought the storms; but for a calm unfit,
Would steer too nigh the sands, to boast his wit.
Great wits are sure to madness near allied;
And thin partitions do their bounds divide:
Else why should he, with wealth and honour blest,
Refuse his age the needful hours of rest?
Punish a body which he could not please;
Bankrupt of life, yet prodigal of ease?
And all to leave, what with his toil he won,
To that unfeathered two-legged thing, a son;
Got, while his soul did huddled notions try;
And born a shapeless lump, like anarchy.
In friendship false, implacable in hate;
Resolved to ruin or to rule the State.
To compass this the triple bond he broke,
The pillars of the public safety shook,
And fitted Israel for a foreign yoke.
Then, seized with fear, yet still affecting fame,
Usurped a patriot's all-atoning name.

So easy still it proves in factious times,
With public zeal to cancel private crimes:
How safe is treason, and how sacred ill,
Where none can sin against the people's will:
Where crowds can wink, and so offence be known,
Since in another's guilt they find their own.
Yet fame deserved no enemy can grudge;
The statesman we abhor, but praise the judge.
In Israel's courts ne'er sat an Abbethdin
With more discerning eyes, or hands more clean:
Unbribed, unsought, the wretched to redress;
Swift of dispatch, and easy of access.
Oh, had he been content to serve the crown,
With virtues only proper to the gown;
Or had the rankness of the soil been freed
From cockle, that oppressed the noble seed:
David for him his tuneful harp had strung,
And Heav'n had wanted one immortal song.
But wild Ambition loves to slide, not stand;
And Fortune's ice prefers to Virtue's land.
Achitophel, grown weary to possess
A lawful fame, and lazy happiness,
Disdained the golden fruit to gather free,
And lent the crowds his arm to shake the tree.

(ii)

Zimri (the Duke of Buckingham)

A numerous host of dreaming Saints succeed,
Of the true old enthusiastic breed:
'Gainst form and order they their pow'r employ.
Nothing to build, and all things to destroy.
But far more numerous was the herd of such
Who think too little, and who talk too much.
These, out of mere instinct, they knew not why,
Adored their fathers' God, and property;
And, by the same blind benefit of fate,
The Devil and the Jebusite did hate:
Born to be saved, even in their own despite,

Abbethdin] Lord Chancellor (a Jewish title for a presiding judge)
(ii)   Jebusite] i.e. Papist

Because they could not help believing right.
Such were the tools, but a whole Hydra more
Remains, of sprouting heads too long to score;
In the first rank of these did Zimri stand:
A man so various, that he seemed to be
Not one, but all mankind's epitome.
Stiff in opinions, always in the wrong;
Was everything by starts, and nothing long,
But, in the course of one revolving moon,
Was chymist, fiddler, statesman, and buffoon;
Then all for women, painting, rhyming, drinking,
Besides ten thousand freaks that died in thinking.
Blest madman, who could every hour employ
With something new to wish, or to enjoy!
Railing and praising were his usual themes,
And both (to shew his judgment) in extremes:
So over violent, or over civil,
That every man, with him, was God or Devil.
In squand'ring wealth was his peculiar art:
Nothing went unrewarded, but desert.
Beggared by fools, whom still he found too late:
He had his jest, and they had his estate.
He laughed himself from court; then sought relief
By forming parties, but could ne'er be chief:
For, spite of him, the weight of business fell
On Absalom and wise Achitophel:
Thus wicked but in will, of means bereft,
He left not faction, but of that was left.

27   *Mac Flecknoe, or, A Satire upon the*
        True Blue Protestant Poet, T.S.

ALL human things are subject to decay,
And when fate summons, monarchs must obey:
This Flecknoe found, who, like Augustus, young
Was called to empire, and had governed long:
In prose and verse, was owned, without dispute,
Through all the realms of Nonsense, absolute.
This aged prince now flourishing in peace,
And blest with issue of a large increase,

26 Absalom] Duke of Monmouth   Achitophel] Lord Shaftesbury

Worn out with business, did at length debate
To settle the succession of the State:
And pond'ring which of all his sons was fit
To reign, and wage immortal war with wit,
Cried ''Tis resolved; for nature pleads that he
Should only rule, who most resembles me.
Shadwell alone my perfect image bears,
Mature in dulness from his tender years.
Shadwell alone, of all my sons, is he
Who stands confirmed in full stupidity.
The rest to some faint meaning make pretence,
But Shadwell never deviates into sense.
Some beams of wit on other souls may fall,
Strike through, and make a lucid interval;
But Shadwell's genuine night admits no ray,
His rising fogs prevail upon the day.
Besides, his goodly fabric fills the eye,
And seems designed for thoughtless majesty:
Thoughtless as monarch oaks that shade the plain,
And, spread in solemn state, supinely reign.
Heywood and Shirley were but types of thee,
Thou last great prophet of tautology.
Even I, a dunce of more renown than they,
Was sent before but to prepare thy way;
And coarsely clad in Norwich drugget came
To teach the nations in thy greater name.
My warbling lute, the lute I whilom strung,
When to King John of Portugal I sung,
Was but the prelude to that glorious day,
When thou on silver Thames didst cut thy way,
With well-timed oars before the royal barge,
Swelled with the pride of thy celestial charge;
And big with hymn, commander of an host,
The like was ne'er in Epsom blankets tossed.
Methinks I see the new Arion sail,
The lute still trembling underneath thy nail.
At thy well-sharpened thumb from shore to shore
The treble squeaks for fear, the basses roar:
Echoes from Pissing Alley Shadwell call,
And Shadwell they resound from Aston Hall.

Norwich drugget] coarse cloth from Norfolk, which was Shadwell's county
in Epsom blankets tossed] reference to the fate of a coxcomb character in
Shadwell's play *The Virtuoso*

About thy boat the little fishes throng,
As at the morning toast, that floats along.
Sometimes as prince of thy harmonious band
Thou wield'st thy papers in thy threshing hand.
St. André's feet ne'er kept more equal time,
Not ev'n the feet of thy own *Psyche's* rhyme;
Though they in number as in sense excel;
So just, so like tautology, they fell,
That, pale with envy, Singleton forswore
The lute and sword which he in triumph bore,
And vowed he ne'er would act Villerius more.'
Here stopped the good old sire; and wept for joy
In silent raptures of the hopeful boy.
All arguments, but most his plays, persuade,
That for anointed dulness he was made.
 Close to the walls which fair Augusta bind,
(The fair Augusta much to fears inclined,)
An ancient fabric raised t'inform the sight,
There stood of yore, and Barbican it hight:
A watch-tower once; but now, so fate ordains,
Of all the pile an empty name remains.
From its old ruins brothel-houses rise,
Scenes of lewd loves, and of polluted joys,
Where their vast courts the mother-strumpets keep,
And, undisturbed by watch, in silence sleep.
Near these a nursery erects its head,
Where queens are formed, and future heroes bred;
Where unfledged actors learn to laugh and cry,
Where infant punks their tender voices try,
And little Maximins the gods defy.
Great Fletcher never treads in buskins here,
Nor greater Jonson dares in socks appear;
But gentle Simkin just reception finds
Amidst this monument of vanished minds:
Pure clinches the suburbian Muse affords;
And Panton waging harmless war with words.

St. André] French dancer who performed in Shadwell's opera *Psyche* (1675)
Singleton] John Singleton, actor and royal musician
Villerius] character in Davenant's play *The Siege of Rhodes* Augusta] London
Maximin] ranting tyrant in Dryden's *Tyrannick Love* (1669)
Simkin] ? nickname of some simple-minded actor in farces
clinches] plays on words Panton] unidentified actor

Here Flecknoe, as a place to fame well known,
Ambitiously designed his Shadwell's throne;
For ancient Dekker prophesied long since,
That in this pile should reign a mighty prince,
Born for a scourge of wit, and flail of sense:
To whom true dulness should some *Psyches* owe,
But worlds of *Misers* from his pen should flow;
Humorists and *Hypocrites* it should produce,
Whole Raymond families, and tribes of Bruce.
Now Empress Fame had published the renown
Of Shadwell's coronation through the town.
Roused by report of Fame, the nations meet,
From near Bunhill, and distant Watling Street.
No Persian carpets spread th' imperial way,
But scattered limbs of mangled poets lay:
From dusty shops neglected authors come,
Martyrs of pies, and relics of the bum.
Much Heywood, Shirley, Ogleby there lay,
But loads of Shadwell almost choked the way.
Bilked stationers for yeomen stood prepared,
And Herringman was captain of the guard.
The hoary prince in majesty appeared,
High on a throne in his own labours reared.
At his right hand our young Ascanius sate,
Rome's other hope, and pillar of the State.
His brows thick fogs, instead of glories, grace,
And lambent dulness played around his face.
As Hannibal did to the altars come,
Sworn by his sire a mortal foe of Rome;
So Shadwell swore, nor should his vow be vain,
That he till death true dulness would maintain;
And in his father's right, and realm's defence,
Ne'er to have peace with wit, nor truce with sense.
The king himself the sacred unction made,
As king by office, and as priest by trade:
In his sinister hand, instead of ball,
He placed a mighty mug of potent ale;
Love's Kingdom to his right he did convey,
At once his sceptre, and his rule of sway;

Misers, Humorists, Hypocrites] Shadwell's plays included *The Miser* (1672), *The
Humorists* (1671) and a lost early play *The Hypocrite*
Raymond, Bruce] wits in plays by Shadwell
Herringman] Shadwell's publisher   *Love's Kingdom*] play by Flecknoe (1664)

Whose righteous lore the prince had practised young,
And from whose loins recorded *Psyche* sprung.
His temples last with poppies were o'er spread,
That nodding seemed to consecrate his head:
Just at that point of time, if fame not lie,
On his left hand twelve reverend owls did fly.
So Romulus, 'tis sung, by Tiber's brook,
Presage of sway from twice six vultures took.
Th' admiring throng loud acclamations make,
And omens of his future empire take.
The sire then shook the honours of his head,
And from his brows damps of oblivion shed
Full on the filial dulness: long he stood,
Repelling from his breast the raging god;
At length burst out this prophetic mood:
  'Heavens bless my son, from Ireland let him reign
To far Barbadoes on the western main;
Of his dominion may no end be known,
And greater than his father's be his throne.
Beyond *Love's Kingdom* let him stretch his pen!'
He paused, and all the people cried Amen.
Then thus continued he: 'My son, advance
Still in new impudence, new ignorance.
Success let others teach, learn thou from me
Pangs without birth, and fruitless industry.
Let *Virtuosos* in five years be writ;
Yet not one thought accuse thy toil of wit.
Let gentle George in triumph tread the stage,
Make Dorimant betray, and Loveit rage;
Let Cully, Cockwood, Fopling, charm the pit,
And in their folly shew the writer's wit.
Yet still thy fools shall stand in thy defence,
And justify their author's want of sense.
Let 'em be all by thy own model made
Of dulness, and desire no foreign aid;
That they to future ages may be known,
Not copies drawn, but issue of thy own.
Nay, let thy men of wit too be the same,
All full of thee, and differing but in name.

Virtuosos] Shadwell's play *The Virtuoso* (1676)
gentle George] nickname of the dramatist Sir George Etherege
Dorimant, Loveit, Cully, Cockwood, Fopling (Sir Fopling Flutter)] characters in plays
by Etherege

But let no alien Sedley interpose
To lard with wit thy hungry *Epsom* prose.
And when false flowers of rhetoric thou wouldst cull,
Trust nature, do not labour to be dull;
But write thy best, and top; and in each line,
Sir Formal's oratory will be thine.
Sir Formal, though unsought, attends thy quill,
And does thy northern dedications fill.
Nor let false friends seduce thy mind to fame,
By arrogating Jonson's hostile name.
Let father Flecknoe fire thy mind with praise,
And uncle Ogleby thy envy raise.
Thou art my blood, where Jonson has no part;
What share have we in nature or in art?
Where did his wit on learning fix a brand,
And rail at arts he did not understand?
Where made he love in Prince Nicander's vein,
Or swept the dust in *Psyche's* humble strain?
Where sold he bargains, whip-stitch, kiss my arse,
Promised a play and dwindled to a farce?
When did his Muse from Fletcher scenes purloin,
As thou whole Eth'rege dost transfuse to thine?
But so transfused as oil on waters flow,
His always floats above, thine sinks below.
This is thy province, this thy wondrous way,
New humours to invent for each new play:
This is that boasted bias of thy mind,
By which one way, to dulness, 'tis inclined,
Which makes thy writings lean on one side still,
And in all changes, that way bends thy will.
Nor let thy mountain-belly make pretence
Of likeness; thine's a tympany of sense.
A tun of man in thy large bulk is writ,
But sure thou'rt but a kilderkin of wit.
Like mine, thy gentle numbers feebly creep,
Thy tragic Muse gives smiles, thy comic sleep.
With whate'er gall thou sett'st thyself to write,
Thy inoffensive satires never bite.

Epsom prose] as in Shadwell's play *Epsom-Wells* (1673)
Sir Formal (Trife)] coxcomb in Shadwell's *Virtuoso*
Prince Nicander] character in Shadwell's *Psyche*
tympany] distension of the belly by wind
kilderkin] small cask (in contrast to large tun)

In thy felonious heart, though venom lies,
It does but touch thy Irish pen, and dies.
Thy genius calls thee not to purchase fame
In keen iambics, but mild anagram:
Leave writing plays, and choose for thy command
Some peaceful province in acrostic land.
There thou may'st wings display and altars raise,
And torture one poor word ten thousand ways.
Or if thou would'st thy different talents suit,
Set thy own songs, and sing them to thy lute.'
He said, but his last words were scarcely heard,
For Bruce and Longvil had a trap prepared,
And down they sent the yet declaiming bard.
Sinking he left his drugget robe behind,
Borne upwards by a subterranean wind.
The mantle fell to the young prophet's part,
With double portion of his father's art.

28 from *The Second Part of Absalom and Achitophel*

Doeg and Og, the Poets Settle and Shadwell

To make quick way I'll leap o'er heavy blocks,
Shun rotten Uzza as I would the pox
And hasten Og and Doeg to rehearse,
Two fools that crutch their feeble sense on verse;
Who by my Muse, to all succeeding times
Shall live in spite of their own dogg'rel rhymes.
   Doeg, though without knowing how or why,
Made still a blund'ring kind of melody;
Spurred boldly on, and dashed through thick and thin,
Through sense and nonsense, never out nor in;
Free from all meaning, whether good or bad,
And, in one word, heroically mad:
He was too warm on picking-work to dwell,
But faggoted his notions as they fell,
And if they rhymed and rattled all was well.
Spiteful he is not, though he wrote a satire,
For still there goes some thinking to ill-nature:
He needs no more than birds and beasts to think,
All his occasions are to eat and drink.

27   Bruce, Longvil] wits in Shadwell's *Virtuoso*

If he call rogue and rascal from a garret,
He means you no more mischief than a parrot:
The words for friend and foe alike were made,
To fetter 'em in verse is all his trade.
For almonds he'll cry whore to his own mother;
And call young Absalom King David's brother.
Let him be gallows-free by my consent,
And nothing suffer since he nothing meant;
Hanging supposes human soul and reason,
This animal's below committing treason:
Shall he be hanged who never could rebel?
That's a preferment for Achitophel.
The woman that committed buggery,
Was rightly sentenced by the law to die;
But 'twas hard fate that to the gallows led
The dog that never heard the statute read.
Railing in other men may be a crime,
But ought to pass for mere instinct in him;
Instinct he follows and no farther knows,
For to write verse with him is to transprose.
'Twere pity treason at his door to lay,
Who makes heaven's gate a lock to its own key:
Let him rail on, let his invective Muse
Have four and twenty letters to abuse,
Which if he jumbles to one line of sense,
Indict him of a capital offence.
In fireworks give him leave to vent his spite,
Those are the only serpents he can write;
The height of his ambition is we know
But to be master of a puppet show:
On that one stage his works may yet appear,
And a month's harvest keeps him all the year.
    Now stop your noses, readers, all and some,
For here's a tun of midnight work to come,
Og from a treason-tavern rolling home.
Round as a globe, and liquored ev'ry chink,
Goodly and great he sails behind his link.
With all this bulk there's nothing lost in Og,
For ev'ry inch that is not fool is rogue:
A monstrous mass of foul corrupted matter,

Absalom] Duke of Monmouth   King David] Charles II
        Achitophel] Lord Shaftesbury

67

As all the devils had spewed to make the batter.
When wine has given him courage to blaspheme,
He curses God, but God before cursed him;
And if man could have reason none has more,
That made his paunch so rich and him so poor.
With wealth he was not trusted, for Heav'n knew
What 'twas of old to pamper up a Jew;
To what would he on quail and pheasant swell,
That ev'n on tripe and carrion could rebel?
But though Heav'n made him poor, (with rev'rence speaking)
He never was a poet of God's making;
The midwife laid her hand on his thick skull,
With this prophetic blessing *Be thou dull*;
Drink, swear, and roar, forbear no lewd delight
Fit for thy bulk, do anything but write:
Thou art of lasting make like thoughtless men,
A strong nativity—but for the pen;
Eat opium, mingle arsenic in thy drink,
Still thou mayst live avoiding pen and ink.
I see, I see, 'tis counsel given in vain,
For treason botched in rhyme will be thy bane;
Rhyme is the rock on which thou art to wreck,
'Tis fatal to thy frame and to thy neck:
Why should thy metre good King David blast?
A psalm of his will surely be thy last.
Dar'st thou presume in verse to meet thy foes,
Thou whom the penny pamphlet foiled in prose?
Doeg, whom God for mankind's mirth has made,
O'ertops thy talent in thy very trade;
Doeg to thee, thy paintings are so coarse,
A poet is, though he's the poets' horse.
A double noose thou on thy neck dost pull,
For writing treason, and for writing dull;
To die for faction is a common evil,
But to be hanged for nonsense is the devil:
Hadst thou the glories of thy king expressed,
Thy praises had been satire at the best;
But thou in clumsy verse, unlicked, unpointed,
Hast shamefully defied the Lord's anointed:
I will not rake the dunghill of thy crimes,
For who would read thy life that reads thy rhymes?
But of King David's foes be this the doom,
May all be like the young man Absalom;

And for my foes may this their blessing be,
To talk like Doeg, and to write like thee.

29 from *The Hind and the Panther: The Third Part*

The Buzzard (*Gilbert Burnet*)

A PORTLY prince, and goodly to the sight,
He seemed a son of Anak for his height:
Like those whom stature did to crowns prefer;
Black-browed, and bluff, like Homer's Jupiter:
Broad-backed, and brawny built for love's delight,
A prophet formed to make a female proselyte.
A theologue more by need than genial bent,
By breeding sharp, by nature confident.
Int'rest in all his actions was discerned;
More learned than honest, more a wit than learned.
Or forced by fear, or by his profit led,
Or both conjoined, his native clime he fled:
But brought the virtues of his Heav'n along;
A fair behaviour, and a fluent tongue.
And yet with all his arts he could not thrive;
The most unlucky parasite alive.
Loud praises to prepare his paths he sent,
And then himself pursued his compliment:
But, by reverse of fortune chased away,
His gifts no longer than their author stay:
He shakes the dust against th' ungrateful race,
And leaves the stench of ordures in the place.
Oft has he flattered, and blasphemed the same,
For in his rage he spares no sov'reign's name:
The hero, and the tyrant change their style
By the same measure that they frown or smile:
When well received by hospitable foes,
The kindness he returns, is to expose:
For courtesies, though undeserved and great,
No gratitude in felon-minds beget,
As tribute to his wit the churl receives the treat.
His praise of foes is venomously nice,
So touched, it turns a virtue to a vice:
A Greek, and bountiful, forewarns us twice.
Sev'n sacraments he wisely does disown,
Because he knows Confession stands for one,

Where sins to sacred silence are conveyed,
And not for fear, or love, to be betrayed:
But he, uncalled, his patron to control,
Divulged the secret whispers of his soul:
Stood forth th'accusing Satan of his crimes,
And offered to the Moloch of the times.
Prompt to assail, and careless of defence,
Invulnerable in his impudence,
He dares the world, and eager of a name,
He thrusts about, and jostles into fame.
Frontless, and satire-proof he scours the streets,
And runs an Indian muck at all he meets.
So fond of loud report, that not to miss
Of being known (his last and utmost bliss)
He rather would be known for what he is.
  Such was, and is the captain of the test,
Though half his virtues are not here express't;
The modesty of fame conceals the rest.

30   from *Cymon and Iphigenia*

                 The Militia

  THE country rings around with loud alarms,
And raw in fields the rude militia swarms;
Mouths without hands; maintained at vast expense,
In peace a charge, in war a weak defence:
Stout once a month they march a blust'ring band,
And ever, but in times of need, at hand.
This was the morn when issuing on the guard,
Drawn up in rank and file they stood prepared
Of seeming arms to make a short essay,
Then hasten to be drunk, the business of the day.

31   from *Juvenal's Sixth Satire*

                    (i)
              In the Golden Age

IN Saturn's reign, at Nature's early birth,
There was that thing called chastity on earth;
When in a narrow cave, their common shade,
The sheep, their shepherds and their gods were laid:

When reeds and leaves, and hides of beasts were spread
By mountain huswives for their homely bed,
And mossy pillows raised, for the rude husband's head.
Unlike the niceness of our modern dames
(Affected nymphs with new affected names),
The Cynthias and the Lesbias of our years,
Who for a sparrow's death dissolve in tears,
Those first unpolished matrons, big and bold,
Gave suck to infants of gigantic mould;
Rough as their savage lords who ranged the wood,
And fat with acorns belched their windy food.
For when the World was buxom, fresh, and young,
Her sons were undebauched, and therefore strong;
And whether born in kindly beds of earth,
Or struggling from the teeming oaks to birth,
Or from what other atoms they begun,
No sires they had, or if a sire the Sun.
Some thin remains of chastity appeared
Ev'n under Jove, but Jove without a beard;
Before the servile Greeks had learned to swear
By heads of kings; while yet the bounteous year
Her common fruits in open plains exposed,
Ere thieves were feared, or gardens were enclosed.
At length uneasy Justice upwards flew,
And both the sisters to the stars withdrew;
From that old era whoring did begin,
So venerably ancient is the sin.
Adult'rers next invade the nuptial state,
And marriage-beds creaked with a foreign weight;
All other ills did Iron times adorn;
But whores and Silver in one age were born.
    Yet thou, they say, for marriage dost provide:
Is this an age to buckle with a bride?
They say thy hair the curling art is taught,
The wedding-ring perhaps already bought:
A sober man like thee to change his life!
What fury would possess thee with a wife?
Art thou of ev'ry other death bereft,
No knife, no ratsbane, no kind halter left
(For every noose compared to hers is cheap)?
Is there no city bridge from whence to leap?
Would'st thou become her drudge, who dost enjoy
A better sort of bedfellow, thy boy?

He keeps thee not awake with nightly brawls,
Nor with a begged reward thy pleasure palls;
Nor with insatiate heavings calls for more,
When all thy spirits were drained out before.
But still Ursidius courts the marriage bait,
Longs for a son, to settle his estate,
And takes no gifts though every gaping heir
Would gladly grease the rich old bachelor.
What revolution can appear so strange,
As such a lecher such a life to change?
A rank, notorious whoremaster, to choose
To thrust his neck into the marriage noose!
He who so often in a dreadful fright
Had in a coffer 'scaped the jealous cuckold's sight,
That he, to wedlock dotingly betrayed,
Should hope, in this lewd town, to find a maid!
The man's grown mad: to ease his frantic pain,
Run for the surgeon; breathe the middle vein;
But let a heifer with gilt horns be led
To Juno, Regent of the Marriage-bed,
And let him every deity adore,
If his new bride prove not an arrant whore,
In head and tail, and every other pore.
On Ceres' feast, restrained from their delight,
Few matrons, there, but curse the tedious night:
Few whom their fathers dare salute, such lust
Their kisses have, and come with such a gust.
With ivy now adorn thy doors, and wed;
Such is thy bride, and such thy genial bed.
Think'st thou one man is for one woman meant?
She sooner with one eye would be content.
    And yet, 'tis noised, a maid did once appear
In some small village, though fame says not where:
'Tis possible; but sure no man she found;
'Twas desert, all, about her father's ground:
And yet some lustful god might there make bold;
Are Jove and Mars grown impotent and old?
Many a fair nymph has in a cave been spread,
And much good love, without a feather-bed.

breathe] lance, open up

(ii)

The Book-learned Wife

But of all plagues, the greatest is untold,
The book-learned wife in Greek and Latin bold,
The critic-dame, who at her table sits,
Homer and Virgil quotes, and weights their wits;
And pities Dido's agonizing fits.
She has so far th'ascendant of the board,
The prating pedant puts not in one word,
The man of law is nonplussed, in his suit;
Nay every other female tongue is mute.
Hammers, and beating anvils, you would swear,
And Vulcan with his whole militia there.
Tabours and trumpets cease; for she alone
Is able to redeem the lab'ring moon.
Ev'n wit's a burthen, when it talks too long:
But she, who has no continence of tongue,
Should walk in breeches, and should wear a beard;
And mix among the philosophic herd.
O what a midnight curse has he, whose side
Is pestered with a mood and figure bride!
Let mine, ye Gods (if such must be my fate)
No logic learn, nor history translate;
But rather be a quiet, humble fool:
I hate a wife, to whom I go to school,
Who climbs the grammar-tree, distinctly knows
Where Noun, and Verb, and Participle grows,
Corrects her country neighbour; and, abed,
For breaking Priscian's, breaks her husband's head.
 The gawdy gossip, when she's set agog,
In jewels dressed, and at each ear a bob,
Goes flaunting out, and, in her trim of pride,
Think all she says or does, is justified.

mood and figure bride] one who is adept in the 'moods' and 'figures' of logic
breaking Priscian's [head]] violating the rules of grammar

CHARLES SACKVILLE,
EARL OF DORSET
1638–1706

32 *On Mr Edward Howard, upon his British Princes*

COME on, ye critics! Find one fault who dare,
For, read it backward like a witch's prayer,
'Twill do as well; throw not away your jests
On solid nonsense that abides all tests.
Wit, like tierce claret, when't begins to pall,
Neglected lies and's of no use at all;
But in its full perfection of decay,
Turns vinegar and comes again in play.
This simile shall stand in thy defence
'Gainst such dull rogues as now and then write sense.
He lies, dear Ned, who says thy brain is barren,
Where deep conceits, like vermin, breed in carren;
Thou hast a brain (such as thou hast) indeed—
On what else would thy worm of fancy feed?
Yet in a filbert I have often known
Maggots survive when all the kernel's gone.
Thy style's the same whatever be the theme,
As some digestions turn all meat to phlegm:
Thy stumbling, foundered jade can trot as high
As any other Pegasus can fly.
As skilful divers to the bottom fall
Sooner than those that cannot swim at all,
So in this way of writing without thinking
Thou hast a strange alacrity in sinking:
Thou writ'st below e'en thy own nat'ral parts
And with acquired dulness and new arts
Of studied nonsense tak'st kind readers' hearts.
So the dull eel moves nimbler in the mud
Than all the swift-finned racers of the flood.
Therefore, dear Ned, at my advice forbear
Such loud complaints 'gainst critics to prefer,
Since thou art turned an arrant libeller:
Thou sett'st thy name to what thyself dost write;
Did ever libel yet so sharply bite?

tierce claret] claret in tierces, 42-gallon casks   carren] carrion

SIR CHARLES SEDLEY
1639–1701

33   *To Nysus*

HOW shall we please this age? If in a song
We put above six lines, they count it long;
If we contract it to an epigram,
As deep the dwarfish poetry they damn;
If we write plays, few see above an act,
And those lewd masks, or noisy fops distract:
Let us write satire then, and at our ease
Vex th'ill-natured fools we cannot please.

34   from *The Happy Pair*
               Marriage and Money

WE mind not now the merits of our kind,
  Curious in gold, but to the persons blind.
The Man ne'er minds his love, for money still
  Is the base thirsted object of his will.
Upon condition of a promised store,
  He'll hug a thing that crawls upon all four.
Bring him an old rich corpse with grim death's head,
  He'll swear she's young, and her complexion red,
Of if you could bring one without a face,
  He'll praise her conqu'ring eyes, and charming grace.
The Woman too, by such affections led,
  Contemns the living, to embrace the dead,
And rather than not covet, basely bold,
  Would wed a coffin, were the hinges gold.
Nature's apostate, active youth she scorns,
  Will long for oxen, if you gild their horns.
Say he's deformed, has neither eyes nor nose,
  Nay nothing to bespeak him man but clothes,
Straight she replies he's rich, so passes down;
  There's nothing ugly but a poor baboon.
Thus might she clasp a loathsome toad in bed,
  Because he bears a pearl within his head,
And gilded pills, though bitter, may delight
  The liquorish lust of wav'ring appetite.

    34 passes down] goes down (well), is acceptable

ANONYMOUS

35 *Plain Dealing's Downfall*

LONG time Plain Dealing in the haughty town
Wand'ring about, though in threadbare gown,
At last unanimously was cried down.

When almost starved, she to the country fled,
In hopes, though meanly she should there be fed,
And tumble nightly on a pea-straw bed.

But Knav'ry knowing her intent, took post,
And rumoured her approach through every coast,
Vowing his ruin that should be her host.

Frighted at this, each rustic shut his door,
Bid her be gone, and trouble him no more,
For he that entertained her must be poor.

At this grief seized her, grief too great to tell,
When weeping, sighing, fainting, down she fell,
While Knavery, laughing, rung her passing bell.

JOHN WILMOT, EARL OF ROCHESTER
1647–1680

36 *Tunbridge Wells*

AT five this morn, when Phoebus raised his head
From Thetis' lap, I raised myself from bed,
And mounting steed, I trotted to the waters,
The rendezvous of fools, buffoons, and praters,
Cuckolds, whores, citizens, their wives and daughters.
 My squeamish stomach I with wine had bribed
To undertake the dose that was prescribed;
But turning head, a sudden cursed view

That innocent provision overthrew,
And without drinking, made me purge and spew.
From coach and six a thing unwieldy rolled,
Whose lumber, cart more decently would hold.
As wise as calf it looked, as big as bully,
But handled, proves a mere Sir Nicholas Cully;
A bawling fop, a natural Nokes, and yet
He dares to censure as if he had wit.
To make him more ridiculous, in spite
Nature contrived the fool should be a knight.
Though he alone were dismal sight enough,
His train contributed to set him off,
All of his shape, all of the selfsame stuff.
No spleen or malice need on them be thrown;
Nature had done the business of lampoon,
And in their looks their characters has shown.
　　Endeavouring this irksome sight to balk,
And a more irksome noise, their silly talk,
I silently slunk down t' th' Lower Walk.
But often when one would Charybdis shun,
Down upon Scylla 'tis one's fate to run,
For here it was my cursed luck to find
As great a fop, though of another kind,
A tall stiff fool that walked in Spanish guise:
The buckram puppet never stirred its eyes,
But grave as owl it looked, as woodcock wise.
He scorns the empty talking of this mad age,
And speaks all proverbs, sentences, and adage;
Can with as much solemnity buy eggs
As a cabal can talk of their intrigues;
Master o' th' Ceremonies, yet can dispense
With the formality of talking sense.
　　From hence unto the upper end I ran,
Where a new scene of foppery began.
A tribe of curates, priests, canonical elves,
Fit company for none besides themselves,
Were got together. Each his distemper told,
Scurvy, stone, strangury; some were so bold
To charge the spleen to be their misery,
And on that wise disease brought infamy.

Cully, Nokes] Sir Nicholas Cully, foolish character in Etherege's comedy *The Comical Revenge*, a part created by the actor James Nokes

But none had modesty enough t' complain
Their want of learning, honesty, and brain,
The general diseases of that train.
These call themselves ambassadors of heaven,
And saucily pretend commissions given;
But should an Indian king, whose small command
Seldom extends beyond ten miles of land,
Send forth such wretched tools in an ambassage,
He'd find but small effects of such a message.
Listening, I found the cob of all this rabble
Pert Bayes, with his importance comfortable.
He, being raised to an archdeaconry
By trampling on religion, liberty,
Was grown too great, and looked too fat and jolly,
To be disturbed with care and melancholy,
Though Marvell has enough exposed his folly.
He drank to carry off some old remains
His lazy dull distemper left in 's veins.
Let him drink on, but 'tis not a whole flood
Can give sufficient sweetness to his blood
To make his nature or his manners good.
    Next after these, a fulsome Irish crew
Of silly Macs were offered to my view.
The things did talk, but th' hearing what they said
I did myself the kindness to evade.
Nature has placed these wretches beneath scorn:
They can't be called so vile as they are born.
    Amidst the crowd next I myself conveyed,
For now were come, whitewash and paint being laid,
Mother and daughter, mistress and the maid,
And squire with wig and pantaloon displayed.
But ne'er could conventicle, play, or fair
For a true medley, with this herd compare.
Here lords, knights, squires, ladies and countesses,
Chandlers, mum-bacon women, sempstresses
Were mixed together, nor did they agree
More in their humours than their quality.

cob] male swan
Pert Bayes] Samuel Parker, Archdeacon of Canterbury, later Bishop of Oxford;
for his writings on the proper subservience of church to state Marvell satirized
him in *The Rehearsal Transposed*
mum-bacon women] ? bacon–mumbling women, country women

Here waiting for gallant, young damsel stood,
Leaning on cane, and muffled up in hood.
The would-be wit, whose business was to woo,
With hat removed and solemn scrape of shoe
Advanceth bowing, then genteelly shrugs,
And ruffled foretop into order tugs,
And thus accosts her: 'Madam, methinks the weather
Is grown much more serene since you came hither.
You influence the heavens; but should the sun
Withdraw himself to see his rays outdone
By your bright eyes, they would supply the morn,
And make a day before the day be born.'
With mouth screwed up, conceited winking eyes,
And breasts thrust forward, 'Lord, sir!' she replies.
'It is your goodness, and not my deserts,
Which makes you show this learning, wit, and parts.'
He, puzzled, bites his nail, both to display
The sparkling ring, and think what next to say,
And thus breaks forth afresh: 'Madam, egad!
Your luck at cards last night was very bad:
At cribbage fifty-nine, and the next show
To make the game, and yet to want those two.
God damn me, madam, I'm the son of a whore
If in my life I saw the like before!'
To peddler's stall he drags her, and her breast
With hearts and such like foolish toys he dressed;
And then, more smartly to expound the riddle
Of all his prattle, gives her a Scotch fiddle.
  Tired with this dismal stuff, away I ran
Where were two wives, with girl just fit for man—
Short-breathed, with pallid lips and visage wan.
Some curtsies past, and the old compliment
Of being glad to see each other, spent,
With hand in hand they lovingly did walk,
And one began thus to renew the talk:
'I pray, good madam, if it may be thought
No rudeness, what cause was it hither brought
Your ladyship?' She soon replying, smiled,
'We have a good estate, but have no child,
And I'm informed these wells will make a barren
Woman as fruitful as a cony warren.'

Scotch fiddle] indecent invitatory sign, moving one finger like a fiddle-bow

The first returned, 'For this cause I am come,
For I have no quietness at home.
My husband grumbles though we have got one,
This poor young girl, and mutters for a son.
And this is grieved with headache, pangs, and throes;
Is full sixteen, and never yet had *those*.'
She soon replied, 'Get her a husband, madam:
I married at that age, and ne'er had had 'em;
Was just like her. Steel waters let alone.
A back of steel will bring 'em better down.'
And ten to one but they themselves will try
The same means to increase their family.
Poor foolish fribble, who by subtlety
Of midwife, truest friend to lechery,
Persuaded art to be at pains and charge
To give thy wife occasion to enlarge
Thy silly head! For here walk Cuff and Kick,
With brawny back and legs and potent prick,
Who more substantially will cure thy wife,
And on her half-dead womb bestow new life.
From these the waters got the reputation
Of good assistants unto generation.
  Some warlike men were now got into th' throng,
With hair tied back, singing a bawdy song.
Not much afraid, I got a nearer view,
And 'twas my chance to know the dreadful crew.
They were cadets, that seldom can appear:
Damned to the stint of thirty pounds a year.
With hawk on fist, or greyhound led in hand,
The dogs and footboys sometimes they command.
But now, having trimmed a cast-off spavined horse,
With three hard-pinched-for guineas in their purse,
Two rusty pistols, scarf about the arse,
Coat lined with red, they here presume to swell:
This goes for captain, that for colonel.
So the Bear Garden ape, on his steed mounted,
No longer is a jackanapes accounted,
But is, by virtue of his trumpery, then
Called by the name of 'the young gentleman'.
  Bless me! thought I, what thing is man, that thus
In all his shapes, he is ridiculous?

steel waters] Tunbridge waters are impregnated with iron

Ourselves with noise of reason we do please
In vain: humanity's our worst disease.
Thrice happy beasts are, who, because they be
Of reason void, are so of foppery.
Faith, I was so ashamed that with remorse
I used the insolence to mount my horse;
For he, doing only things fit for his nature,
Did seem to me by much the wiser creature.

37   *Impromptu on Charles II*

GOD bless our good and gracious King,
     Whose promise none relies on;
Who never said a foolish thing,
     Nor ever did a wise one.

38   from *A Satire on Charles II*

RESTLESS he rolls about from whore to whore,
A merry monarch, scandalous and poor.

39   *A Satire against Mankind*

WERE I (who to my cost already am
One of those strange, prodigious creatures, man)
A spirit free to choose, for my own share,
What case of flesh and blood I pleased to wear,
I'd be a dog, a monkey, or a bear,
Or anything but that vain animal
Who is so proud of being rational.
    The senses are too gross, and he'll contrive
A sixth, to contradict the other five,
And before certain instinct, will prefer
Reason, which fifty times for one does err;
Reason, an *ignis fatuus* in the mind,
Which, leaving light of nature, sense, behind,
Pathless and dangerous wandering ways it takes
Through error's fenny bogs and thorny brakes;
Whilst the misguided follower climbs with pain
Mountains of whimseys, heaped in his own brain;
Stumbling from thought to thought, falls headlong down

Into doubt's boundless sea, where, like to drown,
Books bear him up awhile, and make him try
To swim with bladders of philosophy;
In hopes still to o'ertake th' escaping light,
The vapour dances in his dazzling sight
Till, spent, it leaves him to eternal night.
Then old age and experience, hand in hand,
Lead him to death, and make him understand,
After a search so painful and so long,
That all his life he has been in the wrong.
Huddled in dirt the reasoning engine lies,
Who was so proud, so witty, and so wise.
  Pride drew him in, as cheats their bubbles catch,
And made him venture to be made a wretch.
His wisdom did his happiness destroy,
Aiming to know that world he should enjoy.
And wit was his vain, frivolous pretence
Of pleasing others at his own expense,
For wits are treated just like common whores:
First they're enjoyed, and then kicked out of doors.
The pleasure past, a threatening doubt remains
That frights th' enjoyer with succeeding pains.
Women and men of wit are dangerous tools,
And ever fatal to admiring fools.
Pleasure allures, and when the fops escape,
'Tis not that they're beloved, but fortunate,
And therefore what they fear at heart, they hate.
  But now, methinks, some formal band and beard
Takes me to task. Come on, sir; I'm prepared.
  'Then, by your favour, anything that's writ
Against this gibing, jingling knack called wit
Likes me abundantly; but you take care
Upon this point, not to be too severe.
Perhaps my muse were fitter for this part,
For I profess I can be very smart
On wit, which I abhor with all my heart.
I long to lash it in some sharp essay,
But your grand indiscretion bids me stay
And turns my tide of ink another way.
  What rage ferments in your degenerate mind

bubbles] dupes, those who are 'bubbled'
formal band and beard] bearded cleric wearing Geneva bands like a Swiss Calvinist

To make you rail at reason and mankind?
Blest, glorious man! to whom alone kind heaven
An everlasting soul has freely given,
Whom his great Maker took such care to make
That from himself he did the image take
And this fair frame in shining reason dressed
To dignify his nature above beast;
Reason, by whose aspiring influence
We take a flight beyond material sense,
Dive into mysteries, then soaring pierce
The flaming limits of the universe,
Search heaven and hell, find out what's acted there,
And give the world true grounds of hope and fear.'
    Hold, mighty man, I cry, all this we know
From the pathetic pen of Ingelo,
From Patrick's *Pilgrim*, Sibbes' soliloquies,
And 'tis this very reason I despise:
This supernatural gift, that makes a mite
Think he's the image of the infinite,
Comparing his short life, void of all rest,
To the eternal and the ever blest;
This busy, puzzling stirrer-up of doubt
That frames deep mysteries, then finds 'em out,
Filling with frantic crowds of thinking fools
Those reverend bedlams, colleges and schools;
Borne on whose wings, each heavy sot can pierce
The limits of the boundless universe;
So charming ointments make an old witch fly
And bear a crippled carcass through the sky.
'Tis this exalted power, whose business lies
In nonsense and impossibilities,
This made a whimsical philosopher
Before the spacious world, his tub prefer,
And we have modern cloistered coxcombs who
Retire to think, 'cause they have nought to do.
    But thoughts are given for action's government;
Where action ceases, thought's impertinent.
Our sphere of action is life's happiness,

Ingelo] Dr Nathaniel Ingelo (?1621–1683), musician and writer
Patrick's *Pilgrim*] *The Parable of the Pilgrim* (1664) by Simon Patrick, cleric and later
bishop
Sibbes' soliloquies] sermons and meditations by the Puritan divine Richard Sibbes
(1577–1635)

And he who thinks beyond, thinks like an ass.
Thus, whilst against false reasoning I inveigh,
I own right reason, which I would obey:
That reason which distinguishes by sense
And gives us rules of good and ill from thence,
That bounds desires with a reforming will
To keep 'em more in vigour, not to kill.
Your reason hinders, mine helps to enjoy,
Renewing appetites yours would destroy.
My reason is my friend, yours is a cheat;
Hunger calls out, my reason bids me eat;
Perversely, yours your appetite does mock:
This asks for food, that answers, 'What's o'clock?'
This plain distinction, sir, your doubt secures:
'Tis not true reason I despise, but yours.

   Thus I think reason righted, but for man,
I'll ne'er recant; defend him if you can.
For all his pride and his philosophy,
'Tis evident beasts are, in their degree,
As wise at least, and better far than he.
Those creatures are the wisest who attain,
By surest means, the ends at which they aim.
If therefore Jowler finds and kills his hares
Better than Meres supplies committee chairs,
Though one's a statesman, th' other but a hound,
Jowler, in justice, would be wiser found.

   You see how far man's wisdom here extends;
Look next if human nature makes amends:
Whose principles most generous are, and just,
And to whose morals you would sooner trust.
Be judge yourself, I'll bring it to the test:
Which is the basest creature, man or beast?
Birds feed on birds, beasts on each other prey,
But savage man alone does man betray.
Pressed by necessity, they kill for food;
Man undoes man to do himself no good.
With teeth and claws by nature armed, they hunt
Nature's allowance, to supply their want.
But man, with smiles, embraces, friendship, praise,
Inhumanly his fellow's life betrays;

Meres] Sir Thomas Meres (1635–1715), M.P. who frequently chaired committees
of the House of Commons

With voluntary pains works his distress,
Not through necessity, but wantonness.
   For hunger or for love they fight and tear,
Whilst wretched man is still in arms for fear.
For fear he arms, and is of arms afraid,
By fear to fear successively betrayed;
Base fear, the source whence his best passions came:
His boasted honour, and his dear-bought fame;
That lust of power, to which he's such a slave,
And for the which alone he dares be brave;
To which his various projects are designed;
Which makes him generous, affable, and kind;
For which he takes such pains to be thought wise,
And screws his actions in a forced disguise,
Leading a tedious life in misery
Under laborious, mean hypocrisy.
Look to the bottom of his vast design,
Wherein man's wisdom, power, and glory join:
The good he acts, the ill he does endure,
'Tis all from fear, to make himself secure.
Merely for safety, after fame we thirst,
For all men would be cowards if they durst.
   And honesty's against all common sense:
Men must be knaves, 'tis in their own defence.
Mankind's dishonest; if you think it fair
Amongst known cheats to play upon the square,
You'll be undone.
Nor can weak truth your reputation save:
The knaves will all agree to call you knave.
Wronged shall he live, insulted o'er, oppressed,
Who dares be less a villain than the rest.
   Thus, sir, you see what human nature craves:
Most men are cowards, all men should be knaves.
The difference lies, as far as I can see,
Not in the thing itself, but the degree,
And all the subject matter of debate
Is only: Who's a knave of the first rate?

   All this with indignation have I hurled
At the pretending part of the proud world,
Who, swollen with selfish vanity, devise
False freedoms, holy cheats, and formal lies
Over their fellow slaves to tyrannize.

But if in Court so just a man there be
(In Court a just man, yet unknown to me)
Who does his needful flattery direct,
Not to oppress and ruin, but protect
(Since flattery, which way soever laid,
Is still a tax on that unhappy trade);
If so upright a statesman you can find,
Whose passions bend to his unbiased mind,
Who does his arts and policies apply
To raise his country, not his family,
Nor, whilst his pride owned avarice withstands,
Receives close bribes through friends' corrupted hands—
    Is there a churchman who on God relies,
Whose life, his faith and doctrine justifies?
Not one blown up with vain prelatic pride,
Who, for reproof of sins, does man deride,
Whose envious heart makes preaching a pretence,
With his obstreperous, saucy eloquence,
To chide at kings, and rail at men of sense;
None of that sensual tribe whose talents lie
In avarice, pride, sloth, and gluttony,
Who hunt good livings, but abhor good lives,
Whose lust exalted to that height arrives
They act adultery with their own wives,
And ere a score of years completed be,
Can from the lofty pulpit proudly see
Half a large parish their own progeny;
Nor doting bishop who would be adored
For domineering at the council board,
A greater fop in business at fourscore,
Fonder of serious toys, affected more,
Than the gay, glittering fool at twenty proves
With all his noise, his tawdry clothes, and loves;
    But a meek, humble man of honest sense,
Who, preaching peace, does practice continence;
Whose pious life's a proof he does believe
Mysterious truths, which no man can conceive.
If upon earth there dwell such God-like men,
I'll here recant my paradox to them,
Adore those shrines of virtue, homage pay,
And, with the rabble world, their laws obey.
    If such there be, yet grant me this at least:
Man differs more from man, than man from beast.

40 *The Disabled Debauchee*

As some brave admiral, in former war
 Deprived of force, but pressed with courage still,
Two rival fleets appearing from afar,
 Crawls to the top of an adjacent hill;

From whence, with thoughts full of concern, he views
 The wise and daring conduct of the fight,
Whilst each bold action to his mind renews
 His present glory and his past delight;

From his fierce eyes flashes of fire he throws,
 As from black clouds when lightning breaks away;
Transported, thinks himself amidst the foes,
 And absent, yet enjoys the bloody day;

So, when my days of impotence approach,
 And I'm by pox and wine's unlucky chance
Forced from the pleasing billows of debauch
 On the dull shore of lazy temperance,

My pains at least some respite shall afford
 While I behold the battles you maintain
When fleets of glasses sail about the board,
 From whose broadsides volleys of wit shall rain.

Nor let the sight of honourable scars,
 Which my too forward valour did procure,
Frighten new-listed soldiers from the wars:
 Past joys have more than paid what I endure.

Should any youth (worth being drunk) prove nice,
 And from his fair inviter meanly shrink,
'Twill please the ghost of my departed vice
 If, at my counsel, he repent and drink.

Or should some cold-complexioned sot forbid,
 With his dull morals, our bold night-alarms,
I'll fire his blood by telling what I did
 When I was strong and able to bear arms.

I'll tell of whores attacked, their lords at home;
 Bawds' quarters beaten up, and fortress won;
Windows demolished, watches overcome;
 And handsome ills by my contrivance done.

Nor shall our love-fits, Chloris, be forgot,
 When each the well-looked linkboy strove t' enjoy,
And the best kiss was the deciding lot
 Whether the boy fucked you, or I the boy.

With tales like these I will such thoughts inspire
 As to important mischief shall incline:
I'll make him long some ancient church to fire,
 And fear no lewdness he's called to by wine.

Thus, statesmanlike, I'll saucily impose,
 And safe from action, valiantly advise;
Sheltered in impotence, urge you to blows,
 And being good for nothing else, be wise.

41   *Upon Nothing*

NOTHING! thou elder brother even to Shade:
Thou hadst a being ere the world was made,
And well fixed, art alone of ending not afraid.

Ere Time and Place were, Time and Place were not,
When primitive Nothing Something straight begot;
Then all proceeded from the great united What.

Something, the general attribute of all,
Severed from thee, its sole original,
Into thy boundless self must undistinguished fall;

Yet Something did thy mighty power command,
And from thy fruitful Emptiness's hand
Snatched men, beasts, birds, fire, water, air, and land.

Matter, the wicked'st offspring of thy race,
By Form assisted, flew from thy embrace,
And rebel Light obscured thy reverend dusky face.

With Form and Matter, Time and Place did join;
Body, thy foe, with these did leagues combine
To spoil thy peaceful realm, and ruin all thy line;

But turncoat Time assists the foe in vain,
And bribed by thee, destroys their short-lived reign,
And to thy hungry womb drives back thy slaves again.

Though mysteries are barred from laic eyes,
And the divine alone with warrant pries
Into thy bosom, where the truth in private lies,

Yet this of thee the wise may truly say:
Thou from the virtuous nothing dost delay,
And to be part of thee the wicked wisely pray.

Great Negative, how vainly would the wise
Inquire, define, distinguish, teach, devise,
Didst thou not stand to point their blind philosophies!

Is or Is Not, the two great ends of Fate,
And True or False, the subject of debate,
That perfect or destroy the vast designs of state—

When they have racked the politician's breast,
Within thy bosom most securely rest,
And when reduced to thee, are least unsafe and best.

But Nothing, why does Something still permit
That sacred monarchs should in council sit
With persons highly thought at best for nothing fit,

While weighty Something modestly abstains
From princes' coffers, and from statesmen's brains,
And Nothing there like stately Nothing reigns?

Nothing! who dwellst with fools in grave disguise,
For whom they reverend shapes and forms devise,
Lawn sleeves and furs and gowns, when they like thee look wise:

French truth, Dutch prowess, British policy,
Hibernian learning, Scotch civility,
Spaniards' dispatch, Danes' wit are mainly seen in thee;

The great man's gratitude to his best friend,
Kings' promises, whores' vows—towards thee they bend,
Flow swiftly into thee, and in thee ever end.

ANONYMOUS

42   from *The Royal Angler*

Charles the Second

METHINKS I see our mighty monarch stand,
His pliant angle trembling in his hand,
Pleased with the sport, good man, nor does he know
His easy sceptre bends, and trembles so.
Fine representative, indeed, of God,
Whose sceptre's dwindled to a fishing-rod.
Such was Domitian in his Romans' eyes,
When his great Godship stooped to catching flies:
Bless us, what pretty sport have deities!
But see, he now does up from Datchet come,
Laden with spoils of slaughtered gudgeons home,
Nor is he warned by their unhappy fate,
But greedily he swallows every bait,
A prey to every kingfisher of state.
For how he gudgeons takes you have been taught,
Then listen now how he himself is caught.
So well, alas! the fatal bait is known,
Which Rowley does so greedily take down;
And howe'er weak and slender be the string,
Bait it with whore, and it will hold a King.

42   Rowley] Charles was nicknamed Rowley or Old Rowley after a notable stalli
in the royal stables

ALEXANDER RADCLIFFE
fl. 1669–1696

43   *As Concerning Man*

To what intent or purpose was Man made,
Who is by birth to misery betrayed?
Man in his tedious course of life runs through
More plagues than all the Land of Egypt knew.
Doctors, divines, grave disputations, puns,
Ill-looking citizens and scurvy duns;
Insipid squires, fat bishops, deans and chapters,
Enthusiasts, prophecies, new rants and raptures;
Pox, gout, catarrhs, old sores, cramps, rheums and aches;
Half-witted lords, double-chinned bawds with patches;
Illiterate courtiers, Chancery suits for life,
A teazing whore, and a more tedious wife;
Raw Inns of Court men, empty fops, buffoons,
Bullies, robust round aldermen, and clowns;
Gown-men which argue, and discuss, and prate,
And vent dull notions of a future state;
Sure of another world, yet do not know
Whether they shall be saved, or damned, or how.

　'Twere better then that Man had never been,
Than thus to be perplexed: *God save the Queen.*

　　patches] face patches, beauty patches　　　Gown-men] clergymen

91

JOHN OLDHAM
1653–1683

44

from *A Satire*

On Samuel Butler

On Butler who can think without just rage,
The glory, and the scandal of the age?
Fair stood his hopes, when first he came to town,
Met everywhere with welcomes of renown,
Courted, and loved by all, with wonder read,
And promise of princely favour fed;
But what reward for all had he at last,
After a life in dull expectance passed?
The wretch at summing up his misspent days
Found nothing left, but poverty, and praise;
Of all his gains by verse he could not save
Enough to purchase flannel, and a grave;
Reduced to want, he in due time fell sick,
Was fain to die, and be interred on tick;
And well might bless the fever that was sent,
To rid him hence, and his worse fate prevent.

45

from *A Satire Addressed to a Friend*

His Lordship's Chaplain

If you're so out of love with happiness,
To quit a college life and learned ease,
Convince me first, and some good reasons give,
What methods and designs you'll take to live;
For such resolves are needful in the case,
Before you tread the world's mysterious maze.
Without the premises, in vain you'll try
To live by systems of philosophy;
Your Aristotle, Cartes, and Le Grand,
And Euclid too, in little stead will stand.
    How many men of choice, and noted parts,

Well fraught with learning, languages, and arts,
Designing high preferment in their mind,
And little doubting good success to find,
With vast and tow'ring thoughts have flocked to town,
But to their cost soon found themselves undone,
Now to repent, and starve at leisure left,
Of misery's last comfort, hope, bereft?
　'These failed for want of good advice,' you cry,
'Because at first they fixed on no employ.'
Well then, let's draw the prospect, and the scene
To all advantage possibly we can.
The world lies now before you, let me hear
What course your judgment counsels you to steer;
Always considered, that your whole estate,
And all your fortune lies beneath your hat.
Were you the son of some rich usurer,
That starved and damned himself to make his heir,
Left nought to do, but to inter the sot,
And spend with ease what he with pains had got;
'Twere easy to advise how you might live,
Nor would there need instruction then to give.
But you, that boast of no inheritance,
Save that small stock, which lies within your brains,
Learning must be your trade, and therefore weigh
With heed, how you your game the best may play;
Bethink yourself awhile, and then propose
What way of life is fitt'st for you to choose.
　If you for orders and a gown design,
Consider only this, dear friend of mine,
The church is grown so overstocked of late,
That if you walk abroad, you'll hardly meet
More porters now than parsons in the street.
At every corner they are forced to ply
For jobs of hawkering divinity;
And half the number of the sacred herd
Are fain to stroll, and wander unpreferred.
　If this, or thoughts of such a weighty charge
Make you resolve to keep yourself at large,
For want of better opportunity,
A school must your next sanctuary be.
Go, wed some grammar-bridewell, and a wife,
And there beat Greek, and Latin for your life;
With birchen sceptre there command at will,

Greater than Busby's self, or Doctor Gill;
But who would be to the vile drudg'ry bound
Where there so small encouragement is found?
Where you for recompense of all your pains
Shall hardly reach a common fiddler's gains?
For when you've toiled, and laboured all you can,
To dung, and cultivate a barren brain,
A dancing master shall be better paid,
Though he instructs the heels, and you the head.
To such indulgence are kind parents grown,
That nought costs less in breeding than a son;
Nor is it hard to find a father now,
Shall more upon a setting-dog allow,
And with a freer hand reward the care
Of training up his spaniel, than his heir.
   Some think themselves exalted to the sky,
If they light in some noble family;
Diet, an horse, and thirty pounds a year,
Besides the advantage of his lordship's ear,
The credit of the business, and the state,
Are things that in a youngster's sense sound great.
Little the inexperienced wretch does know,
What slavery he oft must undergo,
Who, though in silken scarf and cassock dressed,
Wears but a gayer livery at best;
When dinner calls, the implement must wait,
With holy words to consecrate the meat,
But hold it for a favour seldom known,
If he be deigned the honour to sit down.
Soon as the tarts appear, Sir Crape, withdraw!
Those dainties are not for a spiritual maw;
Observe your distance, and be sure to stand
Hard by the cistern with your cap in hand;
There for diversion you may pick your teeth,
Till the kind voider comes for your relief.
For mere board wages such their freedom sell,
Slaves to an hour, and vassals to a bell;
And if th' enjoyment of one day be stole,

Busby] Richard Busby (1606–95) severe headmaster of Westminster School
Gill] Alexander Gill (1597–1642) friend of Milton and high master of St. Paul's
School, sacked for excessive flogging
voider] servant carrying round the voider or receptacle for left-over food

They are but prisoners out upon parole;
Always the marks of slavery remain,
And they, though loose, still drag about their chain.
    And where's the mighty prospect after all,
A chaplainship served up, and seven years' thrall?
The menial thing perhaps for a reward,
Is to some slender benefice preferred,
With this proviso bound, that he must wed
My lady's antiquated waiting maid,
In dressing only skilled, and marmalade.
    Let others, who such meannesses can brook,
Strike countenance to every great man's look;
Let those that have a mind, turn slaves to eat,
And live contented by another's plate;
I rate my freedom higher, nor will I
For food and raiment truck my liberty.
But, if I must to my last shifts be put,
To fill a bladder, and twelve yards of gut,
Rather with counterfeited wooden leg,
And my right arm tied up, I'll choose to beg;
I'll rather choose to starve at large, than be
The gaudiest vassal to dependency.
    'T has ever been the top of my desires,
The utmost height to which my wish aspires,
That Heav'n would bless me with a small estate,
Where I might find a close obscure retreat;
There, free from noise, and all ambitious ends,
Enjoy a few choice books, and fewer friends,
Lord of myself, accountable to none,
But to my conscience, and my God alone:
There live unthought of, and unheard of, die,
And grudge mankind my very memory.
But since the blessing is (I find) too great
For me to wish for, or expect of fate;
Yet, maugre all the spite of destiny,
My thoughts and actions are, and shall be free.

ANONYMOUS

46　　　　*An Acrostic on Wharton*

WHIG'S the first letter of his odious name;
Hypocrisy's the second of the same;
Anarchy's his darling; and his aim
Rebellion, discord, mutiny, and faction;
Tom, captain of the mob in soul and action;
O'ergrown in sin, cornuted, old, in debt,
Noll's soul and Ireton's live within him yet.

DANIEL DEFOE
?1660–1731

47　　　　from *The True-born Englishman*

(i)
The Breed Described

WHEREVER God erects a house of prayer,
The Devil always builds a chapel there,
And 'twill be found upon examination,
The latter has the largest congregation;
For ever since he first debauched the mind,
He made a perfect conquest of mankind.
With uniformity of service, he
Reigns with a general aristocracy.
No nonconforming sects disturb his reign,
For of his yoke there's very few complain.
He knows the genius and the inclination,
And matches proper sins for ev'ry nation.
He needs no standing-army government;
He always rules us by our own consent.
His laws are easy, and his gentle sway
Makes it exceeding pleasant to obey.

46 Wharton] Thomas Lord Wharton (1648–1715)

The list of his vicegerents and commanders
Outdoes your Caesars, or your Alexanders.
They never fail of his infernal aid,
And he's as certain n'er to be betrayed.
Through all the world they spread his vast command,
And Death's eternal empire is maintained.
They rule so politicly and so well,
As if they were Lords Justices of Hell,
Duly divided to debauch mankind,
And plant infernal dictates in his mind.

Pride, the First Peer, and President of Hell,
To his share Spain, the largest province, fell.
The subtile prince thought fittest to bestow
On these the golden mines of Mexico,
With all the silver mountains of Peru,
Wealth which would in wise hands the world undo,
Because he knew their genius was such,
Too lazy and too haughty to be rich,
So proud a people, so above their fate,
That if reduced to beg, they'll beg in state,
Lavish of money, to be counted brave,
And proudly starve, because they scorn to save.
Never was nation in the world before
So very rich, and yet so very poor.

Lust chose the torrid zone of Italy,
Where blood ferments in rapes and sodomy,
Where swelling veins o'erflow with livid streams,
With heat impregnate from Vesuvian flames,
Whose flowing sulphur forms infernal lakes,
And human body of the soil partakes.
There nature ever burns with hot desires,
Fanned with luxuriant air from subterranean fires.
Here undisturbed in floods of scalding lust
Th'Infernal King reigns with infernal gust.

Drunk'ness, the darling favourite of Hell,
Chose Germany to rule; and rules so well,
No subjects more obsequiously obey,
None please so well, or are so pleased as they.
The cunning artist manages so well,
He lets them bow to Heaven, and drink to Hell.

If but to wine and him they homage pay,
He cares not to what deity they pray,
What God they worship most, or in what way;
Whether by Luther, Calvin, or by Rome,
They sail for Heav'n, by wine he steers them home.

Ungoverned Passion settled first in France,
Where mankind lives in haste, and thrives by chance.
A dancing nation, fickle and untrue:
Have oft undone themselves, and others too:
Prompt the infernal dictates to obey,
And in Hell's favour none more great than they.

The Pagan World he blindly leads away,
And personally rules with arbitrary sway:
The mask thrown off, Plain Devil his title stands;
And what elsewhere he tempts, he there commands.
There with full gust th'ambition of his mind
Governs, as he of old in Heav'n designed.
Worshipped as God, his paynim altars smoke,
Imbrued with blood of those that him invoke.

The rest by deputies he rules as well,
And plants the distant colonies of Hell.
By them his secret power he maintains,
And binds the world in his infernal chains.

By Zeal the Irish, and the Russ by Folly,
Fury the Dane, the Swedes by Melancholy,
By stupid Ignorance the Muscovite,
The Chinese by a child of Hell, called Wit.
Wealth makes the Persian too effeminate,
And Poverty the Tartars desperate.
The Turks and Moors by Mah'met he subdues,
And God had giv'n him leave to rule the Jews.
Rage rules the Portuguese, and Fraud the Scotch;
Revenge the Pole, and Avarice the Dutch.

Satire, be kind, and draw a silent veil
Thy native England's vices to conceal;
Or if that task's impossible to do,
At least be just, and show her virtues too;
Too great the first, alas! the last too few.

England, unknown as yet, unpeopled lay;
Happy, had she remained so to this day,
And not to ev'ry nation been a prey.
Her open harbours, and her fertile plains,
The merchants' glory these, and those the swains',
To ev'ry barbarous nation have betrayed her,
Who conquer her as oft as they invade her.
So beauty guarded but by innocence,
That ruins her which should be her defence.

Ingratitude, a devil of black renown,
Possessed her very early for his own,
And ugly, surly, sullen, selfish spirit,
Who Satan's worst perfections does inherit,
Second to him in malice and in force,
All Devil without, and all within him worse.

He made her firstborn race to be so rude,
And suffered her to be so oft subdued,
By sev'ral crowds of wand'ring thieves o'errun,
Often unpeopled, and as oft undone;
While ev'ry nation that her pow'rs reduced,
Their languages and manners introduced;
From whose mixed relics our compounded breed,
By spurious generation does succeed,
Making a race uncertain and unev'n,
Derived from all the nations under Heav'n.

The Romans first with Julius Caesar came,
Including all the nations of that name,
Gauls, Greeks, and Lombards, and by computation,
Auxiliaries or slaves of ev'ry nation.
With Hengist, Saxons, Danes with Sueno came,
In search of plunder, not in search of fame.
Scots, Picts, and Irish from th'Hibernian shore:
And conqu'ring William brought the Normans o'er.

All these their barb'rous offspring left behind,
The dregs of armies, they, of all mankind;
Blended with Britons who before were here,
Of whom the Welsh have blessed the character.

From this amphibious ill-born mob began
That vain ill-natured thing, an Englishman.
The customs, surnames, languages, and manners,
Of all these nations are their own explainers,
Whose relics are so lasting and so strong
They have left a shibboleth upon our tongue;
By which with easy search you may distinguish
Your Roman-Saxon-Danish-Norman English.

The great invading Norman let us know
What conquerors in after-times might do.
To ev'ry musketeer[1] he brought to town,
He gave the lands which never were his own,
When first the English crown he did obtain
He did not send his Dutchmen home again.
No reassumptions in his reign were known,
Davenant might there have let his book alone.
No parliament his army could disband;
He raised no money, for he paid in land.
He gave his legions their eternal station,
And made them all freeholders of the nation.
He cantoned out the country to his men,
And ev'ry soldier was a denizen.
The rascals thus enriched, he called them *Lords*,
To please their upstart pride with new-made words;
And Doomsday Book his tyranny records.

And here begins the ancient pedigree
That so exalts our poor nobility:
'Tis that from some French trooper they derive,
Who with the Norman Bastard did arrive.
The trophies of the families appear;
Some show the sword, the bow, and some the spear,
Which their great ancestor, forsooth, did wear.
These in the Heralds' register remain,
Their noble, mean extraction to explain.
Yet who the hero was no man can tell,
Whether a drummer or a colonel.
The silent record blushes to reveal
Their undescended dark original.

---

[1] *or* archer

Davenant] Charles Davenant published in 1700 *A Discourse on Grants and Resumptions*, on Crown grants made in the past from forfeited estates

But grant the best, how came the change to pass,
A True-born Englishman of Norman race?
A Turkish horse can show more history,
To prove his well-descended family.
Conquest, as by the moderns 'tis expressed,
May give a title to the lands possessed,
But that the longest sword should be so civil,
To make a Frenchman English, that's the devil.

These are the heroes that despise the Dutch,
And rail at new-come foreigners so much,
Forgetting that themselves are all derived
From the most scoundrel race that ever lived,
A horrid medley of thieves and drones
Who ransacked kingdoms, and dispeopled towns.
The Pict and painted Briton, treach'rous Scot,
By hunger, theft, and rapine, hither brought,
Norwegian pirates, buccaneering Danes,
Whose red-haired offspring ev'rywhere remains,
Who joined with Norman-French compound the breed
From whence your True-born Englishmen proceed.

And lest by length of time it be pretended
The climate may this modern breed have mended,
Wise Providence, to keep us where we are,
Mixes us daily with exceeding care:
We have been Europe's sink, the jakes where she
Voids all her offal outcast progeny.
From our Fifth Henry's time the strolling bands
Of banished fugitives from neighb'ring lands
Have here a certain sanctuary found,
The eternal refuge of the vagabond,
Where in but half a common age of time,
Borr'wing new blood and manners from the clime,
Proudly they learn all mankind to contemn,
And all their race are True-born Englishmen.

Dutch, Walloons, Flemings, Irishmen and Scots
Vaudois and Valtolins, and Huguenots,
In good Queen Bess's charitable reign,
Supplied us with three hundred thousand men.
Religion, God we thank thee, sent them hither,
Priests, Protestants, the Devil and all together,

Of all professions, and of ev'ry trade,
All that were persecuted or afraid;
Whether for debt or other crimes they fled,
David of Hachilah was still their head.

The offspring of this miscellaneous crowd
Had not their new plantations long enjoyed,
But they grew Englishmen, and raised their votes
At foreign shoals of interloping Scots.
The Royal Branch from Pict-land did succeed,
With troops of Scots and scabs from North-by-Tweed,
The seven first years of his pacific reign
Made him and half his nation Englishmen.
Scots from the northern frozen banks of Tay,
With packs and plods came Whigging all away,
Thick as the locusts which in Egypt swarmed,
With pride and hungry hopes completely armed;
With native truth, diseases, and no money,
Plundered our Canaan of the milk and honey.
Here they grew quickly Lords and Gentlemen,
And all their race are True-born Englishmen.

The Civil Wars, the common purgative,
Which always use to make the nation thrive,
Made way for all that strolling congregation,
Which thronged in pious Charles's Restoration.
The royal refugee our breed restores
With foreign courtiers, and with foreign whores,
And carefully repeopled us again,
Throughout his lazy, long, lascivious reign.
With such a blest and True-born English fry,
As much illustrates our nobility.
A gratitude which will so black appear,
As future ages must abhor to hear,
When they look back on all that crimson flood,
Which streamed in Lindsey's and Carnarvon's blood,
Bold Strafford, Cambridge, Capel, Lucas, Lisle,

Hachilah] where David took refuge from Saul (I Samuel 23, 9–19)
Royal Branch] James I   plods] plaids
Lindsey, etc.] The earls of Lindsey and Carnarvon, killed in the Civil Wars; Earl
of Strafford, beheaded 1641; Earl of Cambridge, beheaded 1649; Lord Capel, beheaded
1649; Sir Charles Lucas and Sir George Lisle, royalists who were court-martialled
and shot 1648.

Who crowned in death his father's fun'ral pile;
The loss of whom, in order to supply
With True-born English nobility,
Six bastard dukes survive his luscious reign,
The labours of Italian Castlemaine,
French Portsmouth, Tabby Scot, and Cambrian,
Besides the num'rous bright and virgin throng,
Whose female glories shade them from my song.

This offspring, if one age they multiply,
May half the House with English peers supply.
There with true English pride they may contemn
Schomberg and Portland, new-made noblemen.

French cooks, Scotch pedlars, and Italian whores,
Were all made Lords, or Lords' progenitors.
Beggars and bastards by his new creation
Much multiplied the peerage of the nation;
Who will be all, ere one short age runs o'er,
As True-born Lords as those we had before.

Then to recruit the Commons he prepares,
And heal the latent breaches of the wars;
The pious purpose better to advance
H' invites the banished Protestants of France:
Hither for God's sake and their own they fled,
Some for religion came, and some for bread:
Two hundred thousand pair of wooden shoes,
Who, God be thanked, had nothing left to lose;
To Heav'n's great praise did for religion fly,
To make us starve our poor in charity.
In ev'ry port they plant their fruitful train,
To get a race of True-born Englishmen;
Whose children will, when riper years they see,
Be as ill-natured and as proud as we,
Call themselves English, foreigners despise,
Be surly like us all, and just as wise.

Countess of Castlemaine, Louise de Keroualle, Duchess of Portsmouth, Tabby Scot (Nell Gwyn), and Cambrian Lucy Walter] all fertile mistresses of Charles II

Thus from a mixture of all kinds began
That het'rogeneous thing, an Englishman,
In eager rapes, and furious lust begot
Betwixt a painted Briton and a Scot;
Whose gend'ring offspring quickly learnt to bow,
And yoke their heifers to the Roman plough,
From whence a mongrel half-bred race there came,
With neither name nor nation, speech or fame,
In whose hot veins new mixtures quickly ran,
Infused betwixt a Saxon and a Dane,
While their rank daughters, to their parents just,
Received all nations with promiscuous lust.
This nauseous brood directly did contain
The well-extracted blood of Englishmen.

Which medly cantoned in a heptarchy,
A rhapsody of nations to supply,
Among themselves maintained eternal wars,
And still the ladies loved the conquerors.

The Western Angles all the rest subdued,
A bloody nation, barbarous and rude,
Who by the tenure of the sword possessed
One part of Britain, and subdued the rest.
And as great things denominate the small,
The conqu'ring part gave title to the whole.
The Scot, Pict, Briton, Roman, Dane submit,
And with the English-Saxon all unite:
And these the mixture have so close pursued,
The very name and memory's subdued:
No Roman now, no Briton does remain;
Wales strove to separate, but strove in vain:
The silent nations undistinguished fall,
And Englishman's the common name for all.
Fate jumbled them together, God knows how;
Whate'er they were, they're True-born English now.

The wonder which remains is at our pride,
To value that which all wise men deride.
For Englishmen to boast of generation
Cancels their knowledge, and lampoons the nation.
A True-born Englishman's a contradiction,
In speech an irony, in fact a fiction,

A banter made to be a test of fools,
Which those that use it justly ridicules,
A metaphor invented to express
A man akin to all the universe.

For as the Scots, as learned men have said,
Throughout the world their wand'ring seed have spread,
So open-handed England, 'tis believed,
Has all the gleanings of the world received.

Some think of England 'twas our Saviour meant,
The Gospel should to all the world be sent:
Since when the blessed sound did hither reach
They to all nations might be said to preach.

'Tis well that virtue gives nobility,
Else God knows where we had our gentry,
Since scarce one family is left alive
Which does not from some foreigner derive.
Of sixty thousand English gentlemen,
Whose names and arms in registers remain,
We challenge all our heralds to declare
Ten families which English-Saxons are.

France justly boasts the ancient noble line
Of Bourbon, Montmorency, and Lorraine.
The Germans too their House of Austria show,
And Holland their invicible Nassau,
Lines which in heraldry were ancient grown
Before the name of Englishman was known.
Even Scotland too her elder glory shows,
Her Gordons, Hamiltons, and her Munros,
Douglas, Mackays, and Grahams, names well known
Long before ancient England knew her own.

But England, modern to the last degree,
Borrows or makes her own nobility,
And yet she boldly boasts of pedigree,
Repines that foreigners are put upon her,
And talks of her antiquity and honour.
Her Sackvilles, Savilles, Cecils, Delameres,
Mohuns and Montagues, Durases and Veres,
Not one have English names, yet all are English peers.

Your Houblons, Papillons, and Lethuilliers
Pass now for True-born English knights and squires,
And make good senate-members, or Lord Mayors.
Wealth, howsoever got, in England makes
Lords of mechanics, gentlemen of rakes.
Antiquity and birth are needless here;
'Tis impudence and money makes a peer.

   Innumerable city-knights we know,
From Bluecoat hospitals and Bridewell flow.
Dairymen and porters fill the City Chair,
And footboys magisterial purple wear.
Fate has but very small distinction set
Betwixt the counter and the coronet.
Tarpaulin lords, pages of high renown,
Rise up by poor mens' valour, not their own.
Great families of yesterday we show,
And Lords whose parents were the Lord knows who.

(ii)

The Temper of the Breed

The breed's described: Now, Satire, if you can,
Their temper show, for manners make the man.
Fierce as the Briton, as the Roman brave,
And less inclined to conquer than to save:
Eager to fight, and lavish of their blood,
And equally of fear and forecast void.
The Pict has made 'em sour, the Dane morose,
False from the Scot, and from the Norman worse.
What honesty they have, the Saxon gave them,
And that, now they grow old, begins to leave them.
The climate makes them terrible and bold;
And English beef their courage does uphold:
No danger can their daring spirit pall,
Always provided that their belly's full.

mechanics] workmen   Bluecoat hospitals] schools for charity children
Bridewell] house of correction off Fleet Street, in which abandoned children—'Bridewell
boys'—were housed and taught a trade
Tarpaulin lords] lords who were once 'tarpaulins' or lower-deck sailors

In close intrigues their faculty's but weak,
For gen'rally whate'er they know, they speak,
And often their own counsels undermine
By their infirmity, and not design.
From whence the learned say it does proceed
That English treason never can succeed:
For they're so open-hearted you may know
Their own most secret thoughts, and others too.

   The lab'ring poor, in spite of double pay,
Are saucy, mutinous, and beggarly:
So lavish of their money and their time,
That want of forecast is the nation's crime.
Good drunken company is their delight;
And what they get by day, they spend by night.
Dull thinking seldom does their heads engage,
But drink their youth away, and hurry on old age.
Empty of all good husbandry and sense;
And void of manners most, when void of pence.
Their strong aversion to behaviour's such,
They always talk too little, or too much.
So dull, they never take the pains to think;
And seldom are good-natured, but in drink.

   In English ale their dear enjoyment lies,
For which they'll starve themselves and families.
An Englishman will fairly drink as much
As will maintain two families of Dutch:
Subjecting all their labours to the pots,
The greatest artists are the greatest sots.

   The country poor do by example live;
The gentry lead them, and the clergy drive.
What may we not from such examples hope?
The landlord is their God, the priest their Pope.
A drunken clergy, and a swearing bench,
Has giv'n the reformation such a drench
As wise men think there is some cause to doubt,
Will purge good manners and religion out.

DANIEL DEFOE

(iii)
The True-born Englishman's Way to Heaven

In their religion they are so unev'n,
That each man goes his own by-way to Heav'n.
Tenacious of mistakes to that degree,
That ev'ry man pursues it sep'rately,
And fancies none can find the way but he,
So shy of one another they are grown
As if they strove to get to Heav'n alone.
Rigid and zealous, positive and grave,
And ev'ry grace, but charity, they have.
This makes them so ill-natured and uncivil
That all men think an Englishman the Devil.
  Surly to strangers, froward to their friend;
Submit to love with a reluctant mind,
Resolved to be ungrateful and unkind.
If by necessity reduced to ask,
The giver has the difficultest task,
For what's bestowed they awkwardly receive,
And always take less freely than they give.
The obligation is their highest grief;
And never love, where they accept relief.
So sullen in their sorrows that 'tis known
They'll rather die than their afflictions own;
And if relieved, it is too often true
That they'll abuse their benefactors too:
For in distress their haughty stomach's such,
They hate to see themselves obliged too much.
Seldom contented, often in the wrong;
Hard to be pleased at all, and never long.

(iv)
The Conclusion

Then let us boast of ancestors no more,
Or deeds of heroes done in days of yore,
In latent records of the ages past,
Behind the rear of time, in long oblivion placed.
For if our virtues must in lines descend,
The merit with the families would end,

108

And intermixtures would most fatal grow,
For vices would be hereditary too;
The tainted blood would, of necessity,
Involuntary wickedness convey.

Vice, like ill-nature, for an age or two
May seem a generation to pursue;
But virtue seldom does regard the breed;
Fools do the wise, and wise men fools succeed.

What is't to us, what ancestors we had?
If good, what better? or what worse, if bad?
Examples are for imitations set,
Yet all men follow virtue with regret.

Could but our ancestors retrieve their fate,
And see their offspring thus degenerate,
How we contend for birth and names unknown,
And build on their past actions, not our own,
They'd cancel records, and their tombs deface,
And openly disown the vile degenerate race:
For fame of families is all a cheat,
'Tis personal virtue only makes us great.

48   from *Reformation of Manners*

(i)

Old Venerable Jeph

YET Ostia boasts of her regeneration,
And tells us wondrous tales of reformation:
How against vice she has been so severe,
That none but Men of Quality may swear:
How public lewdness is expelled the nation,
That private whoring may be more in fashion;
How parish magistrates, like pious elves,
Let none be drunk a Sundays but themselves,
And hackney coachmen durst not ply the street
In sermon-time, till they had paid the state.
    These, Ostia, are the shams of reformation
With which thou mock'st thy Maker and the nation;

48 Ostia] i.e. London

While in thy streets unpunished there remain
Crimes which have yet insulted Heaven in vain,
Crimes which our satire blushes to review,
And sins thy sister Sodom never knew:
Superior lewdness crowns thy magistrates,
And vice grown grey usurps the reverend seats;
Eternal blasphemies and oaths abound,
And bribes among thy senators are found.
Old Venerable Jeph, with trembling air,
Ancient in sin, and Father of the Chair,
Forsook by vices he had loved so long,
Can now be vicious only with his tongue,
Yet talks of ancient lewdness with delight,
And loves to be the justice of the night.
On bawdy tales with pleasure he reflects,
And lewdly smiles at vices he corrects.
The feeble tottering magistrate appears
Willing to wickedness, in spite of years,
Struggles his age and weakness to resist,
And fain would sin, but nature won't assist.

(ii)

The London Sheriffs

Search all the Christian climes from pole to pole,
And match for sheriffs Sweetapple and Cole;
Equal in character and dignity,
This famed for justice, that for modesty:
By merit chosen for the chair of state,
This fit for Bridewell, that for Billingsgate;
That richly clad to grace the gaudy day
For which his father's creditors must pay:
This from the fluxing bagnio just dismissed,
Rides out to make himself the city jest.
From some lascivious dish-clout to the chair,
To punish lewdness and disorders there;
The brute he rides on would his crimes detest,

Jeph] Sir Robert Geffrey, rich merchant who had been Lord Mayor of London and
president of Bridewell
fluxing bagnio] bathing-house where customers were fluxed or purged, especially
with mercury for the pox

For that's the animal, and this the beast:
And yet some reformation he began;
For magistrates ne'er bear the sword in vain.
Expensive sinning always he declined,
To frugal whoring totally resigned:
His avarice his appetite oppressed,
Base like the man, and brutish like the lust:
Concise in sinning, nature's call supplied,
And in one act two vices gratified.

49   from *More Reformation*

The Reforming Fop

To sin's a vice in nature, and we find
All men to error and mistakes inclined,
And reprehension's not at all uncivil,
But to have rakes reprove us, that's the devil.
    Seaton, if such a thing this age can show,
Sets up for an instructing sober beau,
An air of gravity upon his brow,
And would be pious too, if he knew how;
His language decent, very seldom swears,
And never fails the playhouse, nor his prayers;
Vice seems to have been banished from his doors,
And very, very seldom whores.
    His brother fops he drags to church to pray,
And checks the ladies if they talk too gay;
But Seaton most unhappily has fixed
On two extremes which never can be mixed,
For it will all the power of art outdo
To join the new reformer and the beau.

SIR SAMUEL GARTH
1661–1719

50   from *The Dispensary*

(i)

The God of Sloth

How impotent a deity am I!
With godhead born, but cursed, that cannot die!
Through my indulgence mortals hourly share
A grateful negligence, and ease from care.
Lulled in my arms, how long have I withheld
The Northern Monarchs from the dusty field.
How have I kept the British fleet at ease,
From tempting the rough dangers of the seas.
Hibernia owns the mildness of my reign,
And my divinity's adored in Spain.
I swains to sylvan solitudes convey,
Where stretched on mossy beds they waste away,
In gentle inactivity, the day.
What marks of wondrous clemency I've shown,
Some Rev'rend Worthies of the Gown can own.
Triumphant Plenty, with a cheerful grace,
Basks in their eyes, and sparkles in their face.
How sleek their looks, how goodly is their mien,
When big they strut behind a double chin.
Each faculty in blandishments they lull,
Aspiring to be venerably dull.
No learn'd debates molest their downy trance,
Or discompose their pompous ignorance:
But undisturbed, they loiter life away,
So wither green, and blossom in decay.
Deep sunk in down, they, by my gentle care,
Avoid th'inclemencies of morning air,
And leave to tattered crape the drudgery of pray'r.

SIR SAMUEL GARTH

(ii)

Doctor Horoscope

This wight all mercenary projects tries,
And knows, that to be rich is to be wise.
By useful observations he can tell
The sacred charms that in true sterling dwell.
How gold makes a patrician of a slave,
A dwarf an Atlas, a Thersites brave.
It cancels all defects, and in their place
Finds sense in Brownlow, charms in Lady Grace.
It guides the fancy, and directs the mind;
No bankrupt ever found a fair one kind.

So truly Horoscope its virtue knows,
To this bright idol 'tis, alone, he bows;
And fancies that a thousand pound supplies
The want of twenty thousand qualities.

Long has he been of that amphibious fry,
Bold to prescribe, and busy to apply.
His shop the gazing vulgar's eyes employs
With foreign trinkets, and domestic toys.

Here, mummies lay most reverendly stale,
And there, the tortoise hung her coat o'mail;
Not far from some huge shark's devouring head
The flying fish their finny pinions spread.
Aloft in rows large poppy heads were strung,
And near a scaly alligator hung.
In this place, drugs in musty heaps decayed,
In that, dried bladders, and drawn teeth were laid.

An inner room receives the numerous shoals
Of such as pay to be reputed fools.
Globes stand by globes, volumes on volumes lie,
And planetary schemes amuse the eye.

Doctor Horoscope] Francis Bernard (1627–98), physician on the staff of St.
Bartholomew's Hospital, London

The sage, in velvet chair, here lolls at ease,
To promise future health for present fees.
Then, as from tripod, solemn shams reveals,
And what the stars know nothing of, foretells.

One asks, how soon Panthea may be won,
And longs to feel the marriage fetters on.
Others, convinced by melancholy proof,
Enquire when courteous Fates will strike 'em off.

Some, by what means they may redress the wrong,
When fathers the possession keep too long.
And some would know the issue of their cause,
And whether gold can sodder up its flaws.
Poor pregnant Lais his advice would have,
To lose by art what fruitful Nature gave:
And Portia old in expectation grown,
Laments her barren curse, and begs a son.
Whilst Iris his cosmetic wash would try,
To make her bloom revive, and lovers die.
Some ask for charms, and other philtres choose,
To gain Corinna, and their quartans lose.
Young Hylas, botched with stains too foul to name,
In cradle here renews his youthful frame:
Cloyed with desire, and surfeited with charms,
A hot-house he prefers to Julia's arms.
And old Lucullus would th'arcanum prove,
Of kindling in cold veins the sparks of love.

Bleak Envy these dull frauds with pleasure sees,
And wonders at the senseless mysteries.

die] achieve an orgasm
cradle] a sweating-tub for treatment of venereal disease

(iii)

Doctor Horoscope's Soliloquy

Oft has this planet rolled around the sun
Since to consult the skies I first begun:
Such my applause, so mighty my success,
I once thought my predictions more than guess.
But, doubtful as I am, I'll entertain
This faith, there can be no mistake in gain.
For the dull world most honour pay to those
Who on their understanding most impose.
First man creates, and then he fears the elf,
Thus others cheat him not, but he himself:
He loathes the substance, and he loves the show,
You'll hardly e'er convince a fool, he's so:
He hates realities, and hugs the cheat,
And still the only pleasure's the deceit.
So meteors flatter with a dazzling dye,
Which no existence has, but in the eye.
At distance prospects please us, but when near,
We find but desert rocks, and fleeting air.
From stratagem to stratagem we run,
And he knows most, who latest is undone.

Mankind one day serene and free appear;
The next, they're cloudy, sullen, and severe:
New passions, new opinions still excite,
And what they like at noon, despise at night:
They gain with labour what they quit with ease,
And health, for want of change, becomes disease.
Religion's bright authority they dare,
And yet are slaves to superstitious fear.
They counsel others, but themselves deceive,
And though they're cozened still, they still believe.

THOMAS BROWN

1663–1704

51   *An Epitaph upon that profound and learned*
Casuist, the late Ordinary of Newgate
[Mr Samuel Smith]

UNDER this stone
Lies a Reverend Drone,
To Tyburn well known;
Who preached against sin
With a terrible grin,
In which some may think, that he acted but oddly,
Since he lived by the wicked, and not by the godly.
In time of great need,
In case he were feed,
He'd teach one to read
Old pot-hooks and scrawls,
As ancient as Paul's:
But if no money came,
You might hang for old Sam,
And, foundered in psalter,
Be tied to a halter.
   This priest was well hung,
I mean with a tongue,
And bold sons of vice
Would disarm in a trice;
And draw tears from a flint,
Or the Devil was in't.
If a sinner came him nigh
With soul black as chimney,
And had but the sense
To give him the pence,
With a little church-paint
He'd make him a saint.
He understood physic,
And cured cough and phthisic,

Ordinary] the chaplain who prepared criminals for death

And, in short, all the ills
That we find in the bills,
With a sovereign balm,
The world calls a psalm.
Thus his Newgate birds once in the space of a moon,
Though they lived to no purpose, they died to some tune.
In death was his hope,
For he lived by a rope.
Yet this, by the way,
In his praise we may say,
That, like a true friend,
He his flock did attend,
Ev'n to the world's end,
And cared not to start
From sledge, or from cart,
Till he first saw them wear
Knots under their ear;
And merrily swing,
In a well twisted string.
But if any died hard,
And left no reward,
As I told you before,
He'd enhance their old score,
And kill them again
With his murd'ring pen.
Thus he kept sin in awe,
And supported the law;
But, oh! cruel fate!
So unkind, though I say't,
Last week, to our grief,
Grim Death, that old thief
Alas! and alack!
Had the boldness to pack
This old priest on his back,
And whither he's gone,
Is not certainly known,
But a man may conclude,
Without being rude,
That Orthodox Sam
His flock would not sham;
And to shew himself to 'em a pastor most civil,
As he led, so he followed 'em all to the Devil.

MATTHEW PRIOR
1664–1721

52 *An Epitaph*

INTERRED beneath this marble stone
Lie Saunt'ring Jack and Idle Joan.
While rolling threescore years and one
Did round this globe their courses run,
If human things went ill or well,
If changing empires rose or fell,
The morning passed, the evening came,
And found this couple still the same.
They walked and eat, good folks: what then?
Why then they walked and eat again:
They soundly slept the night away:
They did just nothing all the day:
And having buried children four,
Would not take pains to try for more.
Nor sister either had, nor brother:
They seemed just tallied for each other.

Their moral and economy
Most perfectly they made agree:
Each virtue kept its proper bound,
Nor trespassed on the other's ground.
Nor fame, nor censure they regarded:
They neither punished, nor rewarded.
He cared not what the footmen did:
Her maids she neither praised, nor chid:
So ev'ry servant took his course;
And bad at first, they all grew worse.
Slothful disorder filled his stable;
And sluttish plenty decked her table.
Their beer was strong; their wine was port;
Their meal was large; their grace was short.
They gave the poor the remnant-meat,
Just when it grew not fit to eat.

They paid the church and parish rate;
And took, but read not the receipt:
For which they claimed their Sunday's due,
Of slumb'ring in an upper pew.

No man's defects they sought to know;
So never made themselves a foe.
No man's good deeds did they commend;
So never raised themselves a friend.
Nor cherished they relations poor:
That might decrease their present store:
Nor barn nor house did they repair:
That might oblige their future heir.

They neither added, nor confounded:
They neither wanted, nor abounded.
Each Christmas they accompts did clear;
And wound their bottom round the year.
Nor tear, nor smile did they employ
At news of public grief, or joy.
When bells were rung, and bonfires made,
If asked, they ne'er denied their aid:
Their jug was to the ringers carried,
Whoever either died, or married.
Their billet at the fire was found,
Whoever was deposed, or crowned.

Nor good, nor bad, nor fools, nor wise,
They would not learn, nor could advise:
Without love, hatred, joy or fear,
They led—a kind of—as it were:
Nor wished, nor cared, nor laughed, nor cried:
And so they lived; and so they died.

wound their bottom round the year] used the balance for the year's expenses

53 *The Chameleon*

As the chameleon, who is known
To have no colours of his own;
But borrows from his neighbour's hue
His white or black, his green or blue;
And struts as much in ready light,
Which credit gives him upon sight
As if the rainbow were in tail
Settled on him, and his heirs male:
So the young Squire, when first he comes
From country school to Will's or Tom's;
And equally, in truth, is fit
To be a statesman, or a wit;
Without one notion of his own,
He saunters wildly up and down;
Till some acquaintance, good or bad,
Takes notice of a staring lad;
Admits him in among the gang:
They jest, reply, dispute, harangue:
He acts and talks, as they befriend him,
Smeared with the colours which they lend him.

Thus merely, as his fortune chances,
His merit, or his vice advances.

If haply he the sect pursues,
That read and comment upon news,
He takes up their mysterious face:
He drinks his coffee without lace.
This week his mimic tongue runs o'er
What they have said the week before.
His wisdom sets all Europe right;
And teaches Marlborough when to fight.

lace] a dash of spirits

Or if it be his fate to meet
With folks who have more wealth than wit,
He loves cheap port, and double bub;
And settles in the Hum-Drum Club.
He learns how stocks will fall or rise;
Holds poverty the greatest vice;
Thinks wit the bane of conversation;
And says, that learning spoils a nation.

But if, at first, he minds his hits,
And drinks champagne among the wits,
Five deep, he toasts the tow'ring lasses;
Repeats you verses wrote on glasses;
Is in the chair; prescribes the law;
And lies with those he never saw.

JONATHAN SWIFT
1667–1745

54

*A Satirical Elegy
on the Death of a Late Famous General*

HIS Grace! impossible! what dead!
Of old age too, and in his bed!
And could that Mighty Warrior fall?
And so inglorious, after all!
Well, since he's gone, no matter how,
The last loud trump must wake him now:
And, trust me, as the noise grows stronger,
He'd wish to sleep a little longer.
And could he be indeed so old
As by the newspapers we're told?
Threescore, I think, is pretty high;
'Twas time in conscience he should die.
This world he cumbered long enough;
He burnt his candle to the snuff;

54 a Late Famous General] The Duke of Marlborough

And that's the reason, some folks think,
He's left behind so great a stink.
Behold his funeral appears,
Nor widow's sighs, nor orphan's tears,
Wont at such times each heart to pierce,
Attend the progress of his hearse.
But what of that, his friends may say,
He had those honours in his day.
True to his profit and his pride,
He made them weep before he died.

Come hither, all ye empty things,
Ye bubbles raised by breath of kings;
Who float upon the tide of state,
Come hither, and behold your fate.
Let pride be taught by this rebuke,
How very mean a thing's a duke;
From all his ill-got honours flung,
Turned to that dirt from whence he sprung.

55   *A Description of a City Shower*

CAREFUL observers may foretell the hour
(By sure prognostics) when to dread a show'r.
While rain depends, the pensive cat gives o'er
Her frolics, and pursues her tail no more.
Returning home at night you find the sink
Strike your offended sense with double stink.
If you be wise, then go not far to dine,
You spend in coach hire more than save in wine.
A coming show'r your shooting corns presage;
Old aches throb, your hollow tooth will rage:
Saunt'ring in coffee-house is Dulman seen;
He damns the climate, and complains of spleen.

Meanwhile the South, rising with dabbled wings,
A sable cloud across the welkin flings;
That swilled more liquor than it could contain,
And like a drunkard gives it up again.

Brisk Susan whips her linen from the rope,
While the first drizzling show'r is born aslope:
Such is that sprinkling, which some careless quean
Flirts on you from her mop; but not so clean:
You fly, invoke the Gods; then turning, stop
To rail; she singing, still whirls on her mop.
Nor yet the dust had shunned the unequal strife,
But aided by the wind, fought still for life;
And wafted with its foe by vi'lent gust,
'Twas doubtful which was rain, and which was dust.
Ah! where must needy Poet seek for aid,
When dust and rain at once his coat invade?
Sole coat, where dust, cemented by the rain,
Erects the nap, and leaves a cloudy stain.

Now, in contiguous drops the flood comes down,
Threat'ning with deluge this devoted town.
To shops in crowds the daggled females fly,
Pretend to cheapen goods; but nothing buy.
The Templar spruce, while ev'ry spout's abroach,
Stays till 'tis fair, yet seems to call a coach.
The tucked-up Seamstress walks with hasty strides,
While streams run down her oiled umbrella's sides.
Here various kinds by various fortunes led,
Commence acquaintance underneath a shed.
Triumphant Tories, and desponding Whigs,
Forget their feuds, and join to save their wigs.
Boxed in a chair the Beau impatient sits,
While spouts run clatt'ring o'er the roof by fits;
And ever and anon with frightful din
The leather sounds; he trembles from within.
So, when Troy chair-men bore the wooden steed,
Pregnant with Greeks, impatient to be freed
(Those bully Greeks, who, as the moderns do,
Instead of paying chair-men, run them through),
Laocoön struck the outside with his spear,
And each imprisoned hero quaked for fear.

Now from all parts the swelling kennels flow,
And bear their trophies with them, as they go:
Filths of all hues and odours seem to tell
What streets they sailed from, by the sight and smell.
They, as each torrent drives with rapid force,
From Smithfield, or St. Pulchre's shape their course;
And in huge confluent join at Snow-Hill ridge,
Fall from the conduit prone to Holborn Bridge.
Sweepings from butcher's stall, dung, guts, and blood,
Drowned puppies, stinking sprats, all drenched in mud,
Dead cats, and turnip tops come tumbling down the flood.

56   *Phyllis; or, the Progress of Love*

DESPONDING Phyllis was endued
With ev'ry talent of a prude:
She trembled, when a man drew near;
Salute her, and she turned her ear;
If o'er against her you were placed,
She durst not look above your waist:
She'd rather take you to her bed,
Than let you see her dress her head:
In church you heard her through the crowd,
Repeat the absolution loud;
In church, secure behind her fan,
She durst behold that monster, Man:
There practised how to place her head,
And bit her lips, to make them red;
Or, on the mat devoutly kneeling,
Would lift her eyes up to the ceiling,
And heave her bosom, unaware,
For neighb'ring beaux to see it bare.

At length, a lucky lover came,
And found admittance to the dame.
Suppose all parties now agreed,
The writings drawn, the lawyer fee'd,
The vicar and the ring bespoke:
Guess, how could such a match be broke?
See then, what mortals place their bliss in!

55   kennels] open drains in the streets

Next morn, betimes, the bride was missing,
The mother screamed, the father chid;
Where can this idle wench be hid?
No news of Phyl! The bridegroom came,
And thought his bride had skulked for shame;
Because her father used to say,
The girl 'had such a bashful way'.

Now John, the butler, must be sent,
To learn the road that Phyllis went.
The groom was wished to saddle Crop;
For John must neither light, nor stop,
But find her wheresoe'er she fled,
And bring her back, alive or dead.

See here again, the Dev'l to do!
For, truly, John was missing too.
The horse and pillion both were gone!
Phyllis, it seems, was fled with John.

Old Madam, who went up to find
What papers Phyl had left behind,
A letter on the toilet sees,
To my much honoured Father—These
('Tis always done, romances tell us,
When daughters run away with fellows),
Filled with choicest commonplaces,
By others used in the like cases;
'That long ago, a fortune-teller
Exactly said what now befel her;
And in a glass had made her see
A serving-man of low degree.
It was her fate, must be forgiven,
For marriages were made in Heaven;
His pardon begged; but, to be plain,
She'd do 't, if 'twere to do again.
Thank God, 'twas neither shame nor sin;
For John was come of honest kin.
Love never thinks of rich and poor,
She'd beg with John from door to door.
Forgive her, if it be a crime,
She'll never do't another time.
She ne'er before in all her life

Once disobeyed him, maid nor wife.'
One argument she summed all up in,
'The thing was done, and past recalling;
And therefore hoped she should recover
His favour, when his passion's over!
She valued not what others thought her,
And was—his most obedient daughter.'

Fair maidens all, attend the Muse,
Who now the wand'ring pair pursues.
Away they rode in homely sort,
Their journey long, their money short;
The loving couple well bemired;
The horse and both the riders tired:
Their victuals bad, their lodging worse;
Phyl cried, and John began to curse;
Phyl wished, that she had strained a limb,
When first she ventured out with him:
John wished, that he had broke a leg,
When first for her he quitted Peg.

But what adventures more befel 'em,
The Muse hath now no time to tell 'em.
How Johnny wheedled, threatened, fawned,
Till Phyllis all her trinkets pawned:
How oft she broke her marriage vows,
In kindness, to maintain her spouse,
Till swains unwholesome spoiled the trade;
For now the surgeon must be paid,
To whom those perquisites are gone,
In Christian justice due to John.

When food and raiment now grew scarce,
Fate put a period to the farce,
And with exact poetic justice;
For John is landlord, Phyllis hostess:
They keep, at Staines, the Old Blue Boar,
Are cat and dog, and rogue and whore.

57   from *Verses Occasioned by the Sudden*
Drying up of St. Patrick's Well

The English in Ireland

[*St. Patrick speaks*]

WRETCHED Ierne! with what grief I see
The fatal changes Time hath wrought in thee.
The Christian rites I introduced in vain:
Lo! infidelity returned again.
Freedom and virtue in thy sons I found,
Who now in vice and slavery arc drowned.

By faith and prayer, this crozier in my hand,
I drove the venomed serpent from thy land;
The shepherd in his bower might sleep or sing,
Nor dread the adder's tooth, or scorpion's sting.

With omens oft I strove to warn thy swains,
Omens, the types of thy impending chains,
I sent the magpie from the British soil,
With restless beak thy blooming fruit to spoil;
To din thine ears with unharmonious clack,
And haunt thy holy walls in white and black.
What else are those thou see'st in bishop's gear,
Who crop the nurseries of learning here?
Aspiring, greedy, full of senseless prate,
Devour the church, and chatter to the state.

As you grew more degenerate and base,
I sent you millions of the croaking race,
Emblems of insects vile, who spread their spawn
Through all thy land in armour, fur and lawn;
A nauseous brood that fills your senate walls,
And in the chambers of your viceroy crawls.

On the Irish Club

YE paultry underlings of state,
Ye senators, who love to prate;
Ye rascals of inferior note,
Who, for a dinner, sell a vote;
Ye pack of pensionary peers,
Whose fingers itch for poets' ears;
Ye bishops far removed from saints,
Why all this rage? Why these complaints?
Why against printers all this noise?
This summoning of blackguard boys?
Why so sagacious in your guesses?
Your *effs* and *tees*, and *arrs*, and *esses*?
Take my advice; to make you safe,
I know a shorter way by half.
The point is plain: Remove the cause;
Defend your liberties and laws.
Be sometimes to your country true,
Have once the public good in view:
Bravely despise champagne at Court,
And choose to dine at home with port;
Let prelates, by their good behaviour,
Convince us they believe a Saviour;
Nor sell what they so dearly bought,
This country, now their own, for nought.
Ne'er did a true satiric muse
Virtue or innocence abuse;
And 'tis against poetic rules
To rail at men by nature fools:
But * * * * * * *
  * * * * * * * *

the Irish Club] the Irish House of Lords

59 *On Poetry: A Rhapsody*

ALL human race would fain be wits,
And millions miss, for one that hits.
Young's universal passion, Pride,
Was never known to spread so wide.
Say, Britain, could you ever boast
Three poets in an age at most?
Our chilling climate hardly bears
A sprig of bays in fifty years:
While ev'ry fool his claim alleges,
As if it grew in common hedges.
What reason can there be assigned
For this perverseness in the mind!
Brutes find out where their talents lie:
A bear will not attempt to fly:
A foundered horse will oft debate,
Before he tries a five-barred gate:
A dog by instinct turns aside,
Who sees the ditch too deep and wide,
But Man we find the only creature,
Who, led by folly, combats Nature:
Who, when she loudly cries, Forbear,
With obstinacy fixes there;
And, where his genius least inclines,
Absurdly bends his whole designs.

Not empire to the rising sun,
By valour, conduct, fortune won;
Not highest wisdom in debates
For framing laws to govern states;
Not skill in sciences profound,
So large to grasp the circle round;
Such heav'nly influence require,
As how to strike the Muses' lyre.

JONATHAN SWIFT

Not beggar's brat on bulk begot;
Not bastard of a pedlar Scot;
Not boy brought up to cleaning shoes,
The spawn of Bridewell or the stews;
Not infants dropped, the spurious pledges
Of gypsies litt'ring under hedges,
Are so disqualified by fate
To rise in church, or law, or state,
As he whom Phoebus in his ire
Hath blasted with poetic fire.

What hope of custom in the fair,
While not a soul demands your ware;
Where you have nothing to produce
For private life, or public use?
Court, city, country, wants you not;
You cannot bribe, betray, or plot.
For poets law makes no provision:
The wealthy have you in derision.
Of state affairs you cannot smatter;
Are awkward when you try to flatter.
Your portion, taking Britain round,
Was just one annual hundred pound;
Now not so much as in remainder,
Since Cibber brought in an attainder;
For ever fixed by right divine
(A monarch's right) on Grub Street line.

Poor starving bard, how small thy gains!
How unproportioned to thy pains!
And here a simile comes pat in:
Though chickens take a week to fatten,
The guests in less than half an hour,
Will more than half a score devour.
So, after toiling twenty days,
To earn a stock of pence and praise,
Thy labours grown the critics' prey,
Are swallowed o'er a dish of tea;
Gone, to be never heard of more;
Gone, where the chickens went before.

one annual hundred pound] stipend of the Poet Laureate
Cibber] Colley Cibber, playwright, appointed Poet Laureate 1730; Pope's victim in
The Dunciad

How shall a new attempter learn
Of diff'rent spirits to discern,
And how distinguish which is which,
The poet's vein or scribbling itch?
Then hear an old experienced sinner
Instructing thus a young beginner.

Consult yourself; and if you find
A powerful impulse urge your mind,
Impartial judge within your breast
What subject you can manage best;
Whether your genius most inclines
To satire, praise, or hum'rous lines;
To elegies in mournful tone,
Or prologue sent from hand unknown.
Then rising with Aurora's light,
The Muse invoked, sit down to write;
Blot out, correct, insert, refine,
Enlarge, diminish, interline:
Be mindful, when invention fails,
To scratch your head, and bite your nails.

Your poem finished, next your care
Is needful, to transcribe it fair.
In modern wit all printed trash is
Set off with num'rous breaks – and dashes –
To statesmen would you give a wipe,
You print it in italic type.
When letters are in vulgar shapes,
'Tis ten to one the wit escapes;
But when in CAPITALS expressed,
The dullest reader smokes a jest.
Or else perhaps he may invent
A better than the poet meant:
As learned commentators view
In Homer, more than Homer knew.

Your poem in its modish dress,
Correctly fitted for the press,

Convey by penny post to Lintot,
But let no friend alive look into't.
If Lintot thinks 'twill quit the cost,
You need not fear your labour lost;
And, how agreeably surprised
Are you to see it advertised!
The hawker shows you one in print,
As fresh as farthings from the mint:
The product of your toil and sweating;
A bastard of your own begetting.

    Be sure at Will's the following day,
Lie snug, to hear what critics say.
And if you find the general vogue
Pronounces you a stupid rogue;
Damns all your thoughts, as low and little;
Sit still, and swallow down your spittle.
Be silent as a politician,
For talking may beget suspicion:
Or praise the judgement of the town,
And help yourself to run it down.
Give up your fond paternal pride,
Nor argue on the weaker side:
For poems read without a name,
We justly praise, or justly blame:
And critics have no partial views,
Except they know whom they abuse.
And since you ne'er provoked their spite,
Depend upon't their judgment's right.
But if you blab you are undone;
Consider what a risk you run;
You lose your credit all at once;
The town will mark you for a dunce:
The vilest doggrel Grub Street sends,
Will pass for yours with foes and friends:
And you must bear the whole disgrace,
Till some fresh blockhead takes your place.

Lintot] Bernard Lintot (1675–1736), who published poems by Pope and others
Will's] Will's Coffee-house in Bow Street, frequented by wits and writers

Your secret kept, your poem sunk,
And sent in quires to line a trunk:
If still you be disposed to rhyme,
Or try your hand a second time:
Again you fail; yet safe's the word;
Take courage, and attempt a third.
But first with care employ your thoughts,
Where critics marked your former faults:
The trivial turns, the borrowed wit,
The similes that nothing fit;
The cant which every fool repeats,
Town jests, and coffee-house conceits:
Descriptions tedious, flat and dry,
And introduced the Lord knows why:
Or, where we find your fury set
Against the harmless alphabet;
On A's and B's your malice vent,
While readers wonder whom you meant;
A public or a private robber;
A statesman, or a South-Sea jobber.
A prelate, who no God believes;
A parliament, or den of thieves.
A pickpurse at the Bar or Bench;
A duchess, or a suburb wench.
Or oft when epithets you link,
In gaping lines to fill a chink;
Like stepping-stones to save a stride,
In streets where kennels are too wide:
Or like a heel-piece to support
A cripple with one foot too short:
Or like a bridge that joins a marish
To moorlands of a diff'rent parish.
So, have I seen ill-coupled hounds
Drag diff'rent ways in miry grounds.
So geographers in Afric maps
With savage pictures fill their gaps;
And o'er uninhabitable downs
Place elephants for want of towns.

kennels] open drains in the streets

But, though you miss your third essay,
You need not throw your pen away.
Lay now aside all thoughts of fame,
To spring more profitable game.
From party merit seek support;
The vilest verse thrives best at Court.
A pamphlet in Sir Bob's defence
Will never fail to bring in pence;
Nor be concerned about the sale,
He pays his workmen on the nail.

A prince the moment he is crowned,
Inherits ev'ry virtue round;
As emblems of the sov'reign pow'r,
Like other baubles of the Tow'r.
Is gen'rous, valiant, just and wise,
And so continues till he dies.
His humble senate this professes,
In all their speeches, votes, addresses.
But once you fix him in a tomb,
His virtues fade, his vices bloom;
And each perfection wrong imputed,
Is fully at his death confuted.
The loads of poems in his praise,
Ascending, make one fun'ral blaze.
As soon as you can hear his knell,
This god on earth turns devil in hell.
And, lo, his ministers of state,
Transformed to imps, his levee wait:
Where, in the scenes of endless woe,
They ply their former arts below:
And as they sail in Charon's boat,
Contrive to bribe the judge's vote.
To Cerberus they give a sop,
His triple-barking mouth to stop:
Or, in the iv'ry gate of dreams,
Project excise and South-Sea schemes;
Or hire their party-pamphleteers,
To set Elysium by the ears.

Then, Poet, if you mean to thrive,
Employ your Muse on kings alive;
With prudence gath'ring up a cluster
Of all the virtues you can muster:
Which formed into a garland sweet,
Lay humbly at your monarch's feet;
Who, as the odours reach his throne,
Will smile, and think 'em all his own:
For law and gospel both determine
All virtues lodge in royal ermine.
(I mean the oracles of both,
Who shall depose it upon oath).
Your garland in the foll'wing reign,
Change but the names, will serve again.

But, if you think this trade too base
(Which seldom is the dunce's case),
Put on the critic's brow, and sit
At Will's, the puny judge of wit.
A nod, a shrug, a scornful smile,
With caution used, may serve awhile.
Proceed no further in your part,
Before you learn the terms of art:
(For you can never be too far gone,
In all our modern critics' jargon).
Then talk with more authentic face,
Of Unities, in Time and Place.
Get scraps of Horace from your friends,
And have them at your fingers' ends.
Learn Aristotle's rules by rote,
And at all hazards boldly quote:
Judicious Rymer oft review:
With Dennis, and profound Bossu.
Read all the prefaces of Dryden,
For these our critics much confide in
(Though merely writ at first for filling,
To raise the volume's price, a shilling).

A forward critic often dupes us
With sham quotations Peri Hupsous:
And if we have not read Longinus,
Will magisterially outshine us.
Then lest with Greek he overrun ye,
Procure the book for love or money,
Translated from Boileau's translation,
And quote quotation on quotation.

At Will's you hear a poem read,
Where Battus from the table-head,
Reclining on his elbow-chair,
Gives judgment with decisive air.
To him the tribe of circling wits,
As to an oracle, submits.
He gives directions to the town,
To cry it up, or run it down
(Like courtiers, when they send a note,
Instructing members how to vote).
He sets the stamp of bad and good,
Though not a word be understood.
Your lesson learnt, you'll be secure
To get the name of connoisseur.
And when your merits once are known,
Procure disciples of your own.

For poets (you can never want 'em,
Spread through Augusta Trinobantum)
Computing by their pecks of coals,
Amount to just nine thousand souls.
These o'er their proper districts govern,
Of wit and humour, judges sov'reign.
In every street a City-bard
Rules like an alderman his ward.
His indisputed rights extend
Through all the lane, from end to end.
The neighbours round admire his shrewdness,
For songs of loyalty and lewdness.
Outdone by none in rhyming well,
Although he never learnt to spell.

Peri Hupsous] Longinus' treatise *On the Sublime*
Augusta Trinobantum] London (frequent in book imprints)

Two bord'ring wits contend for glory;
And one is Whig, and one is Tory.
And this, for epics claims the bays,
And that for elegiac lays.
Some famed for numbers soft and smooth,
By lovers spoke in Punch's booth.
And some as justly fame extols
For lofty lines in Smithfield drolls.
Bavius in Wapping gains renown,
And Maevius reigns o'er Kentish Town:
Tigellius placed in Phoebus' car
From Ludgate shines to Temple Bar.
Harmonious Cibber entertains
The Court with annual Birthday strains;
Whence Gay was banished in disgrace,
Where Pope will never show his face;
Where Young must torture his invention,
To flatter knaves, or lose his pension.

But these are not a thousandth part
Of jobbers in the poet's art,
Attending each his proper station,
And all in due subordination;
Through ev'ry alley to be found,
In garrets high, or under ground:
And when they join their pericranies,
Out skips a book of Miscellanies.

Hobbes clearly proves that ev'ry creature
Lives in a state of war by nature.
The greater for the smaller watch,
But meddle seldom with their match.
A whale of mod'rate size will draw
A shoal of herrings down his maw;
A fox with geese his belly crams;
A wolf destroys a thousand lambs.
But search among the rhyming race,
The brave are worried by the base.
If on Parnassus' top you sit,
You rarely bite, are always bit:
Each poet of inferior size
On you shall rail and criticize;
And try to tear you limb from limb,

While others do as much for him:
The vermin only tease and pinch
Their foes superior by an inch.
So, nat'ralists observe, a flea
Hath smaller fleas that on him prey,
And these have smaller yet to bite 'em,
And so proceed *ad infinitum*:
Thus ev'ry poet in his kind,
Is bit by him that comes behind;
Who, though too little to be seen,
Can tease, and gall, and give the spleen;
Call dunces, fools, and sons of whores,
Lay Grub Street at each other's doors:
Extol the Greek and Roman masters,
And curse our modern poetasters:
Complain, as many an ancient bard did,
How genius is no more rewarded:
How wrong a taste prevails among us;
How much our ancestors outsung us;
Can personate an awkward scorn
For those who are not poets born:
And all their brother dunces lash,
Who crowd the press with hourly trash.

O Grub Street! how I do bemoan thee,
Whose graceless children scorn to own thee.
Their filial piety forgot,
Deny their country like a Scot:
Though by their idiom and grimace,
They soon betray their native place:
Yet thou hast greater cause to be
Ashamed of them, than they of thee;
Degen'rate from their ancient brood,
Since first the Court allowed them food.

Remains a difficulty still,
To purchase fame by writing ill:
From Flecknoe down to Howard's time,
How few have reached the low sublime?
For when our highborn Howard died,
Blackmore alone his place supplied:
And lest a chasm should intervene,
When death had finished Blackmore's reign,

The leaden crown devolved to thee,
Great Poet of the Hollow Tree.
But, oh, how unsecure thy throne!
Ten thousand bards thy right disown:
They plot, to turn in factious zeal
Duncenia to a commonweal;
And with rebellious arms pretend
An equal priv'lege to descend.

In bulk there are not more degrees,
From elephants to mites in cheese,
Than what a curious eye may trace
In creatures of the rhyming race.
From bad to worse, and worse they fall,
But, who can reach to worst of all?
For though, in nature, depth and height
Are equally held infinite,
In poetry the height we know;
'Tis only infinite below.
For instance: when you rashly think,
No rhymer can like Welsted sink:
His merits balanced, you shall find,
The Laureate leaves him far behind.
Concannon, more aspiring bard,
Soars downwards, deeper by a yard:
Smart Jemmy Moore with vigour drops,
The rest pursue as thick as hops:
With heads to points the gulf they enter,
Linked perpendic'lar to the centre:
And as their heels belated rise,
Their heads attempt the nether skies.

O what indignity and shame
To prostitute the Muse's name,
By flatt'ring kings whom Heav'n designed
The plague and scourges of mankind,
Bred up in ignorance and sloth,
And ev'ry vice that nurses both.

Great Poet of the Hollow Tree] Lord Grimston (1683–1756), author of the play *The Lawyer's Fortune: or, Love in a Hollow Tree*

Fair Britain, in thy monarch blest,
Whose virtues bear the strictest test;
Whom never faction can bespatter,
Nor minister nor poet flatter.
What justice in rewarding merit!
What magnanimity of spirit!
What lineaments divine we trace
Through all his figure, mien and face!
Though Peace with olive bind his hands,
Confessed the conqu'ring hero stands.
Hydaspes, Indus, and the Ganges,
Dread from his arm impending changes.
From him the Tartar, and Chinese,
Short by the knees, intreat for Peace,
The consort of his throne and bed,
A perfect goddess born and bred:
Appointed sov'reign judge to sit
On learning, eloquence and wit.
Our eldest hope, divine Iulus
(Late, very late, O may he rule us).
What early manhood has he shown,
Before his downy beard was grown!
Then think what wonders will be done
By going on as he begun;
An heir for Britain to secure,
As long as sun and moon endure.

The remnant of the Royal Blood
Comes pouring on me like a flood.
Bright goddesses, in number five;
Duke William, sweetest prince alive.

Now sing the Minister of State,
Who shines alone, without a mate.
Observe with what majestic port
This Atlas stands to prop the Court;
Intent the public debts to pay,
Like prudent Fabius, by delay.
Thou great Vice-regent of the King,
Thy praises every Muse shall sing:

Bright goddesses, in number five] the five daughters of George II

In all affairs thou sole director,
Of wit and learning chief protector;
Though small the time thou hast to spare,
The Church is thy peculiar care.
Of pious prelates what a stock
You choose, to rule the sable flock!
You raise the honour of the peerage,
Proud to attend you at the steerage.
You dignify the noble race,
Content yourself with humbler place.
Now learning, valour, virtue, sense,
To titles give the sole pretence:
St. George beheld thee with delight
Vouchsafe to be an azure knight
When on thy breast and sides Herculean
He fixed the Star and String cerulean.

    Say, Poet, in what other nation
Shone ever such a constellation.
Attend ye Popes, and Youngs, and Gays,
And tune your harps, and strow your bays,
Your panegyrics here provide,
You cannot err on flatt'ry's side.
Above the stars exalt your style,
You still are low ten thousand mile.
On Lewis all his bards bestowed
Of incense many a thousand load;
But Europe mortified his pride,
And swore the fawning rascals lied:
Yet what the world refused to Lewis,
Applied to George exactly true is:
Exactly true! Invidious Poet!
'Tis fifty thousand times below it.

    Translate me now some lines, if you can,
From Virgil, Martial, Ovid, Lucan;
They could all pow'r in Heav'n divide,
And do no wrong to either side:
They teach you how to split a hair,
Give George and Jove an equal share.

Lewis] Louis XIV of France

141

Yet, why should we be laced so straight;
I'll give my monarch butter-weight.
And reason good; for many a year
Jove never intermeddled here:
Nor, though his priests be duly paid,
Did ever we desire his aid:
We now can better do without him,
Since Woolston gave us arms to rout him.

*****   *****
****   *Caetera desiderantur*   ****

60   *The Place of the Damned*

ALL folks who pretend to religion and grace,
Allow there's a Hell, but dispute of the place;
But if Hell may by logical rules be defined
The Place of the Damned—I'll tell you my mind.

Wherever the Damned do chiefly abound,
Most certainly there is Hell to be found;
Damned poets, damned critics, damned blockheads, damned knaves,
Damned senators bribed, damned prostitute slaves;
Damned lawyers and judges, damned lords and damned squires,
Damned spies and informers, damned friends and damned liars;
Damned villains corrupted in every station;
Damned time-serving priests all over the nation.
And into the bargain, I'll readily give ye,
Damned ignorant prelates, and counsellors privy.
Then let us no longer by parsons be flammed,
For we know by these marks the Place of the Damned:
And Hell to be sure is at Paris or Rome,
How happy for us, that it is not at home!

59 butter-weight] 18 ounces to the pound, i.e. good measure
Woolston] Thomas Woolston (1670–1733), freethinker, tried for blasphemy in 1729
after publishing his *Discourses on the Miracles of our Saviour*

61   *The Day of Judgment*

WITH a whirl of thought oppressed,
I sink from reverie to rest.
An horrid vision seized my head,
I saw the graves give up their dead.
Jove, armed with terrors, burst the skies,
And thunder roars, and light'ning flies!
Amazed, confused, its fate unknown,
The world stands trembling at his throne.
While each pale sinner hangs his head,
Jove, nodding, shook the heav'ns, and said,
'Offending race of human kind,
By nature, reason, learning, blind;
You who through frailty stepped aside,
And you who never fell—*through pride*;
You who in different sects have shammed,
And come to see each other damned
(So some folks told you, but they knew
No more of Jove's designs than you),
The world's mad business now is o'er,
And I resent these pranks no more.
I to such blockheads set my wit!
I damn such fools!—Go, go, you're bit.'

JOHN ARBUTHNOT
1667–1735

62   *Colonel Chartres*

HERE continueth to rot
The body of FRANCIS CHARTRES;
Who, with an INFLEXIBLE CONSTANCY and IMI-
MITABLE UNIFORMITY of life, PERSISTED,
In spite of AGE and INFIRMITIES,
In the practice of EVERY HUMAN VICE,
Excepting PRODIGALITY and HYPOCRISY:
His insatiable AVARICE exempted him from the first,
His matchless IMPUDENCE from the second.

Nor was he more singular in the undeviating *pravity
of his manners*, than successful in *accumulating*
WEALTH:

For, without TRADE or PROFESSION,
Without TRUST of PUBLICK MONEY,
And without BRIBE-WORTHY SERVICE,
He acquired, or more properly created,
A MINISTERIAL ESTATE.

He was the only person of his time
Who could CHEAT without the mask of HONESTY,
Retain his primeval MEANNESS when Possessed of
TEN THOUSAND a year;
And, having daily deserved the GIBBET for what he
did,
Was at last condemned to it for what he *could* not *do*.

O indignant reader!
Think not his life useless to mankind!
PROVIDENCE connived at his execrable designs,

To give to after-ages a conspicuous PROOF and
EXAMPLE
Of how small estimation is EXORBITANT WEALTH
in the sight of GOD, by bestowing it on the
most UNWORTHY of ALL MORTALS.

JOHN WINSTANLEY
?1678–1750

63   *A Last Will and Testament*

TO my dear wife,
My joy and life,
I freely now do give her
My whole estate,
With all my plate,
Being just about to leave her.

A tub of soap,
A long cart-rope,
A frying-pan and kettle;
  An ashes pail,
  A threshing flail,
An iron wedge and beetle.

Two painted chairs,
Nine warden pears,
A large old dripping platter;
  The bed of hay,
  On which I lay,
An old saucepan for butter.

A little mug,
A two-quart jug,
A bottle full of brandy;
  A looking-glass,
  To see your face,
You'll find it very handy.

A musket true
As ever flew,
A pound of shot, and wallet;
  A leather sash,
  My calabash,
My powder-horn, and bullet.

An old sword-blade,
A garden spade,
A hoe, a rake, a ladder;
  A wooden can,
  A close-stool pan,
A clyster-pipe, and bladder.

A greasy hat,
My old ram-cat,
A yard and half of linen;
  A pot of grease,
  A woollen fleece,
In order for your spinning.

A small toothcomb,
An ashen broom,
A candlestick, and hatchet;
   A coverlid,
   Striped down with red,
A bag of rags to patch it.

A ragged mat,
A tub of fat,
A book, put out by Bunyan,
   Another book,
   By Robin Rook,
A skein, or two, of spun yarn.

An old black muff,
Some garden stuff,
A quantity of borage;
   Some Devil's-weed,
   And burdock seed,
To season well your porridge.

A chafing-dish,
With one salt fish,
If I am not mistaken;
   A leg of pork,
   A broken fork,
And half a flitch of bacon.

A spinning-wheel,
One peck of meal;
A knife without a handle;
   A rusty lamp,
   Two quarts of samp,
And half a tallow candle.

My pouch and pipes,
Two oxen tripes,
An oaken dish well carved;
   My little dog,
   And spotted hog,
With two young pigs just starved.

samp] a gruel of ground maize

This is my store,
I have no more,
I heartily do give it;
  My days are spun,
  My life is done,
And so I think to leave it.

64   *An Inventory of the Furniture of a*
        Collegian's Chamber

Persicos edit puer apparatus
Horace

IMPRIMIS, there's a table blotted;
A tattered hanging all besnotted;
A bed of flocks, as we may rank it,
Reduced to rug, and half a blanket;
A tinder-box, as people tell us;
A broken-winded pair of bellows.
A pair of tongs, bought from a broker,
A fender, and a rusty poker.
A penny-pot, and bason, this
Designed for water, that for piss.
A trencher and a college-bottle
Riding on Locke, or Aristotle;
A smutty ballad, musty libel,
A Burgersdicius, and a Bible;
A prayer-book, he seldom handles;
Item, a pound of farthing candles.
A rusty fork, a blunted whittle,
To cut his table, and his vittle.
There is likewise a pair of breeches,
But patched, and fallen in the stitches.
Item, a surplice, not unmeeting
Either for chapel, or for sheeting,
Hung up in study very little,
Plaistered with cobwebs, ink, and spittle.

64   broker] rag-and-bone man, old iron man
              trencher] platter
college-bottle] ? wine-bottle with a Trinity College seal
Burgersdicius] a copy of Burgersdicius' *Logic* (Francis Burgersdyk, 1590–1629)
              whittle] large knife

With lofty prospect, all so pleasing,
And skylight window without glazing.
Item, if I am not mistaken,
A mouse-trap, with a bit of bacon,
A candlestick, without a snuffer,
Whereby his fingers often suffer;
And chairs a couple (I forgot 'em),
But each of them without a bottom.
A bottle-standish, pen unmended,
His INVENTORY thus is ended.

EDWARD YOUNG
1683–1765

65   from *Love of Fame, The Universal Passion*
(i)
The Love of Praise

THE love of praise, howe'er concealed by art,
Reigns, more or less, and glows, in ev'ry heart:
The proud, to gain it, toils on toils endure;
The modest shun it, but to make it sure.
O'er globes, and sceptres, now on thrones it swells,
Now, trims the midnight lamp in college cells.
'Tis Tory, Whig; it plots, prays, preaches, pleads,
Harangues in senates, squeaks in masquerades;
Here, to Swift's humour makes a bold pretence,
There, bolder, aims at Pultney's eloquence.
It aids the dancer's heel, the writer's head,
And heaps the plain with mountains of the dead;
Nor ends with life, but nods in sable plumes,
Adorns our hearse, and flatters on our tombs.
    What is not proud? The pimp is proud to see
So many like himself in high degree.
The whore is proud her beauties are the dread
Of peevish virtue, and the marriage-bed;
And the bribed cuckold, like crowned victims born
To slaughter, glories in his gilded horn.

64   bottle-standish] inkstand

Some go to church, proud humbly to repent.
And come back much more guilty than they went.
One way they look, another way they steer,
Pray to the gods, but would have mortals hear,
And when their sins they set sincerely down,
They'll find that their religion has been one.

(ii)
'Thy Books are Furniture'

With what, O Codrus! is thy fancy smit?
The flow'r of learning, and the bloom of wit.
Thy gaudy shelves with crimson bindings glow,
And Epictetus is a perfect beau.
How fit for thee, bound up in crimson too,
Gilt, and, like them, devoted to the view!
Thy books are furniture. Methinks 'tis hard
That science should be purchased by the yard,
And Tonson, turned upholsterer, send home
The gilded leather to fit up thy room.
    If not to some peculiar ends designed,
Study's the specious trifling of the mind,
Or is at best a secondary aim,
A chase for sport alone, and not for game.
If so, sure they who the mere volume prize
But love the thicket where the quarry lies.
    On buying books Lorenzo long was bent,
But found at length that it reduced his rent.
His farms were flown, when lo! a sale comes on,
A choice collection! what is to be done?
He sells his last, for he the whole will buy,
Sells ev'n his house; nay, wants whereon to lie,
So high the generous ardour of the man
For Romans, Greeks, and Orientals ran.
When terms were drawn, and brought him by the clerk,
Lorenzo signed the bargain—with his mark.
Unlearned men of books assume the care
As eunuchs are the guardians of the fair.
    Not in his authors' liveries alone
Is Codrus' erudite ambition shown:
Editions various, at high prices bought,
Inform the world what Codrus would be thought,

And to this cost another must succeed
To pay a sage, who says that he can read,
Who titles knows, and indexes has seen,
But leaves to Chesterfield what lies between,
Of pompous books who shuns the proud expense,
And humbly is contented with their sense.

(iii)
The Beau

These all their care expend on outward show
For wealth and fame; for fame alone, the beau.
Of late at White's was young Florello seen!
How blank his look! how discomposed his mien!
So hard it proves in grief sincere to feign!
Sunk were his spirits, for his coat was plain.
Next day his breast regained its wonted peace,
His health was mended with a silver lace.
A curious artist, long inured to toils
Of gentler sort, with combs, and fragrant oils,
Whether by chance, or by some god inspired,
So touched his curls, his mighty soul was fired.
The well-swoln ties an equal homage claim,
And either shoulder has its share of fame;
His sumptuous watch-case, though concealed it lies,
Like a good conscience, solid joy supplies.
He only thinks himself (so far from vain!)
Stanhope in wit, in breeding Deloraine.
Whene'er, by seeming chance, he throws his eye
On mirrors that reflect his Tyrian dye,
With how sublime a transport leaps his heart!
But fate ordains that dearest friends must part.
In active measures, brought from France, he wheels,
And triumphs, conscious of his learned heels.
So have I seen, on some bright summer's day,
A calf of genius, debonair and gay,
Dance on the bank, as if inspired by fame,
Fond of the pretty fellow in the stream.
Morose is sunk with shame, whene'er surprised
In linen clean, or peruke undisguised.
No sublunary chance his vestments fear,
Valued, like leopards, as their spots appear.

A famed surtout he wears, which once was blue,
And his foot swims in a capacious shoe.
One day his wife (for who can wives reclaim?)
Levelled her barb'rous needle at his fame;
But open force was vain; by night she went,
And while he slept, surprised the darling rent.
Where yawned the frieze is now become a doubt,
And glory, at one entrance, quite shut out.[1]

He scorns Florello, and Florello him;
This hates the filthy creature; that the prim.
Thus, in each other, both these fools despise
Their own dear selves, with undiscerning eyes,
Their methods various, but alike their aim:
The sloven and the fopling are the same.

Ye Whigs and Tories! thus it fares with you,
When party rage too warmly you pursue;
Then both club nonsense, and impetuous pride,
And folly joins whom sentiments divide.
You vent your spleen, as monkeys, when they pass,
Scratch at the mimic monkey in the glass,
While both are one: and henceforth be it known,
Fools of both sides shall stand for fools alone.

'But who art thou?' methinks Florello cries:
'Of all thy species art thou only wise?'
Since smallest things can give our sins a twitch,
As crossing straws retard a passing witch,
Florello, thou my monitor shalt be;
I'll conjure thus some profit out of thee.
O THOU myself! abroad our counsels roam,
And, like ill husbands, take no care at home.
Thou too art wounded with the common dart,
And love of fame lies throbbing at thy heart,
And what wise means to gain it hast thou chose?
Know, fame and fortune both are made of prose.
Is thy ambition sweating for a rhyme,
Thou unambitious fool, at this late time?
While I a moment name, a moment's past,
I'm nearer death in this verse, than the last.
What then is to be done? Be wise with speed;
A fool at forty is a fool indeed.

[1] Milton

(iv)
The Legislature

See commons, peers, and ministers of state,
In solemn council met, and deep debate!
What Godlike enterprise is taking birth?
What wonder opens on th' expecting earth?
'Tis done! with loud applause the council rings!
Fixed is the fate of whores and fiddle-strings!

(v)
Britannia's Daughters

Britannia's daughters, much more fair than nice,
Too fond of admiration, lose their price;
Worn in the public eye, give cheap delight
To throngs, and tarnish to the sated sight:
As unreserved, and beauteous, as the sun,
Through every sign of vanity they run,
Assemblies, parks, coarse feasts in City halls,
Lectures, and trials, plays, committees, balls,
Wells, bedlams, executions, Smithfield scenes,
And fortune-tellers' caves, and lions' dens,
Taverns, exchanges, bridewells, drawing-rooms,
Instalments, pillories, coronations, tombs,
Tumblers, and funerals, puppet-shows, reviews,
Sales, races, rabbits, and (still stranger!) pews.

66   from *Epistles to Mr Pope*
The Black Militia

THESE labouring wits, like paviours, mend our ways,
With heavy, huge, repeated, flat, essays,
Ram their coarse nonsense down, though ne'er so dull,
And hem at every thump upon your skull.
These staunch-bred writing hounds begin the cry,
And honest folly echoes to the lie.
O how I laugh, when I a blockhead see
Thanking a villain for his probity,

(v)   instalments] installations, as of the Lord Mayor

Who stretches out a most respectful ear,
With snares for woodcocks in his holy leer.
It tickles through my soul to hear the cock's
Sincere encomium on his friend the fox,
Sole patron of his liberties and rights!
While graceless Reynard listens—till he bites.
　　As when the trumpet sounds, th'o'erloaded state
Discharges all her poor and profligate,
Crimes of all kinds dishonoured weapons wield,
And prisons pour their filth into the field,
Thus nature's refuse, and the dregs of men,
Compose the black militia of the pen.

JOHN GAY
1685–1732

67　　　*To my ingenious and worthy friend*
　　　　William Lowndes, Esq.
Author of that celebrated treatise in folio, called the
'Land-tax Bill'

WHEN poets print their works, the scribbling crew
Stick the bard o'er with bays, like Christmas pew;
Can meagre Poetry such fame deserve?
Can Poetry, that only writes to starve?
And shall no laurel deck that famous head,
In which the senate's annual law is bred?
That hoary head, which greater glory fires,
By nobler *ways* and *means* true fame acquires.
O had I Vergil's force to sing the man,
Whose learned line can millions raise *per ann.*
Great Lowndes his praise should swell the trump of fame,
And Rapes and Wapentakes resound his name.
　　If the blind poet gained a long renown
By singing ev'ry Grecian chief and town,
Sure Lowndes his prose much greater fame requires,
Which sweetly counts five thousand knights and squires,
Their seats, their cities, parishes and shires.

---

ways and *means*] the parliamentary term was also the motto of the family of
　　William Lowndes, who was Secretary to the Treasury

Thy copious preamble so smoothly runs
Taxes no more appear like legal duns,
Lords, knights, and squires th'assessor's power obey,
We read with pleasure, though with pain we pay.
  Ah why did Coningsby thy works defame?
That author's long harangue betrays his name;
After his speeches can his pen succeed?
Though forced to hear, we're not obliged to read.
  Under what science shall thy works be read?
All know thou wert not poet born and bred;
Or dost thou boast th'historian's lasting pen,
Whose annals are the *Acts* of worthy men?
No. Satire is thy talent; and each lash
Makes the rich miser tremble o'er his cash;
What on the drunkard can be more severe,
Than direful taxes on his ale and beer?
  Ev'n Button's wits are nought compared to thee,
Who ne'er were known or praised but o'er his tea,
While thou through Britain's distant isle shall spread,
In ev'ry hundred and division read.
Critics in classics oft interpolate,
But ev'ry word of thine is fixed as fate:
And where's your author boasts a longer date?
Poets of old had such a wondrous power,
That with their verses they could raise a tower;
But in thy prose a greater force is found;
What poet ever raised ten thousand pound?
Cadmus, by sowing dragon's teeth, we read,
Raised a vast army from the pois'nous seed,
Thy labours, Lowndes, can greater wonders do,
Thou raisest armies, and canst pay them too.
Truce with thy dreaded pen; thy annals cease;
Why need we armies when the land's in peace?
Soldiers are perfect devils in their way,
When once they're raised, they're cursed hard to lay.

Button] proprietor of Button's Coffee-house near Covent Garden

WILLIAM DIAPER
?1686–1717

68   from *Brent: A Poem to*
Thomas Palmer Esq.

(i)

Too Much Moisture

HAPPY are you, whom Quantock overlooks,
Blessed with keen healthy air, and crystal brooks;
While wretched we the baneful influence mourn
Of cold Aquarius, and his weeping urn.
Eternal mists their dropping curse distill
And drizzly vapours all the ditches fill:
The swampy land's a bog, the fields are seas
And too much moisture is the grand disease.
Here every eye with brackish rheum o'erflows
And a fresh drop still hangs at every nose.
Here the winds rule with uncontested right,
The wanton Gods at pleasure take their flight;
No sheltering hedge, no tree, or spreading bough
Obstruct their course, but unconfined they blow;
With dewy wings they sweep the wat'ry meads
And proudly trample o'er the bending reeds.
We are to north, and southern blasts exposed,
Still drowned by one, or by the other frozed.
Though Venice boast, Brent is as famed a seat,
For here we live in seas, and sail through every street;
And this great privilege we farther gain,
We never are obliged to pray for rain.
And 'tis as fond to wish for sunny days,
For though the God of light condense his rays
And try his pow'r, we must in water lie;
The marsh will still be such, and Brent will ne'er be dry.

Sure this is nature's gaol for rogues designed;
Whoever lives in Brent, must live confined.
Moated around, the water is our fence;
None comes to us, and none can go from hence;
But should a milder day invite abroad
To wade through mire, and wallow in the mud,
Some envious rhine will quickly thwart the road;
And then a small round twig is all your hopes,
You pass not bridges, but you dance on ropes.

All dogs here take the water, and we find
No creature but of an amphibious kind:
Rabbits with ducks, and geese here sail with hens,
And all for food must paddle in the fens;
Nay when provision fails, the hungry mouse
Will fear no pool to reach a neighb'ring house.
The good old hen clucks boldly through the stream
And chicken newly hatched assay to swim.
All have a moorish taste, cow, sheep, and swine,
Eat all like frog, and savour of the rhine.
Bread is our only sauce, a barley cake
Hard as your cheese, and as your trencher black.
Our choicest drink (and that's the greatest curse)
Is but bad water made by brewing worse;
Better to taste the ditch, pure, and unmixed,
Than when to more unwholsome ale bewitched.

To him that hath is alway given more
And a new stock supplies the rising store.
Not only rain from bounteous heaven descends,
But th'ocean with an after-flood befriends;
For nature this as a relief designs
To salt the stinking water of the rhines;
As when of late enraged Neptune sware
Brent was his own, part of his lawful share;
He said, and held his trident o'er the plain,
And soon the waves assert their ancient claim,
They scorn the shore, and o'er the marshes sound,
And mudwall cotts are levelled with the ground;
Though the coarse buildings are so humbly low
That when the house is fall'n, you hardly know.

rhine] a dyke (on Sedgemoor)

Buried we are alive; the spacious dome
Has like the grave but one poor scanty room,
Neither so large, or lofty as a tomb.
Thus, as in th'Ark, here in one common sty
Men and their fellow-brutes with equal honour lie.

(ii)

The Rude Men of Brent

Had mournful Ovid been to Brent condemned,
His Tristibus he would more movingly have penned.
Gladly he would have changed his miry slough
For colder Pontus, and the Scythian snow.
The Getes were not so barbarous a race,
As the grim natives of this motley place,
Of reason void, and thought, whom instinct rules,
Yet will be rogues though nature meant 'em fools,
A strange half-human, and ungainly brood,
Their speech uncouth, as are their manners rude;
When they would seem to speak the mortals roar
As loud as waves contending with the shore;
Their widened mouths into a circle grow,
For all their vowels are but A and O.
The beasts have the same language, and the cow
After her owner's voice is taught to low;
The lamb to baw, as doth her keeper, tries,
And puppies learn to howl from children's cries.

Some think us honest, but through this belief,
That where all steal, there no one is a thief.
Rogues of all kinds you may at leisure choose;
One finds a horse, another fears the noose
And humbly is content to take the shoes.

It never yet could be exactly stated
What time of th'year this ball was first created.
Some plead for summer, but the wise bethought 'em
That th'earth like other fruits was ripe in autumn;
While gayer wits the vernal bloom prefer,
And think the smiling world did first appear
In th'youthful glory of the budding year.

. But the bleak Knoll, and all the marshes round
(A sort of chaos, and unfinished ground)
Were made in winter, one may safely swear,
For winter is the only season there.

Of four prime elements all things below
By various mixtures were composed, but now
(At least with us) they are reduced to two.
The daily want of fire our chimneys mourn,
Cow-dung and turf may smoke, but never burn.
Water and earth are all that Brent can boast,
The air in mists and dewy steams is lost;
We live on fogs, and in this moory sink
When we are thought to breathe, we rather drink.

It's said the world at length in flames must die
And thus interred in its own ashes lie.
If any part shall then remain entire
And be excepted from that common fire,
Sure 'twas this wat'ry spot that nature meant,
For though the world be burned, this never will be Brent.[1]

ANONYMOUS

69 *The Vicar of Bray*

IN good King Charles's golden days,
When loyalty no harm meant,
A furious High Church man I was,
And so I gained preferment.
Unto my flock I daily preached,
'Kings are by God appointed,
And damned are those who dare resist,
Or touch the Lord's Anointed.'
And this is law, I will maintain
Unto my dying day, Sir,
That whatsoever king shall reign,
I will be Vicar of Bray, Sir!

[1] An old word for burnt.

When royal James possessed the crown,
   And Popery grew in fashion,
The penal laws I hooted down,
   And read the Declaration:
The Church of Rome I found would fit
   Full well my constitution,
And I had been a Jesuit,
      But for the Revolution.
         And this is law, etc.

When William our deliverer came
   To heal the nation's grievance,
I turned the cat in pan again,
   And swore to him allegiance:
Old principles I did revoke,
   Set conscience at a distance,
Passive obedience is a joke,
      A jest is non-resistance.
         And this is law, etc.

When glorious Anne became our Queen,
   The Church of England's glory,
Another face of things was seen,
   And I became a Tory:
Occasional conformists base
   I damned, and moderation,
And thought the Church in danger was,
      From such prevarication.
         And this is law, etc.

When George in pudding time came o'er,
   And moderate men looked big, Sir,
My principles I changed once more.
   And so became a Whig, Sir:
And thus preferment I procured
   From our Faith's Great Defender,
And almost every day abjured
      The Pope and the Pretender.
         And this is law, etc.

in pudding time] at the right or lucky moment

The illustrious House of Hanover,
　　And Protestant Succession,
To these I lustily will swear,
　　Whilst they can keep possession:
For in my faith and loyalty
　　I never once will falter,
But George my lawful King shall be,
　　Except the times should alter.
　　　And this is law, etc.

ANONYMOUS

70　　　　　*The Poet's Prayer*

If e'er in thy sight I found favour, Apollo,
Defend me from all the disasters which follow:
From the knaves and the fools, and the fops of the time,
From the drudges in prose, and the triflers in rhyme:
From the patchwork and toils of the royal sack-bibber,
Those dead birthday odes, and the farces of Cibber:
From servile attendance on men in high places,
Their worships, and honours, and lordships, and graces:
From long dedications to patrons unworthy,
Who hear and receive, but will do nothing for thee:
From being caressed to be left in the lurch,
The tool of a party, in state or in church:
From dull thinking blockheads, as sober as Turks,
And petulant bards who repeat their own works:
From all the gay things of a drawing-room show,
The sight of a belle and the smell of a beau:
From busy backbiters, and tattlers and carpers,
And scurvy acquaintance of fiddlers and sharpers:
From old politicians, and coffee-house lectures,
The dreams of a chemist, and schemes of projectors:
From the fears of a gaol, and the hopes of a pension,
The tricks of a gamester, and oath of an ensign:
From shallow freethinkers in taverns disputing,
Nor ever confuted, nor ever confuting:
From the constant good fare of another man's board,
My lady's broad hints, and the jests of my lord;

From hearing old chemists prelecting *de oleo*,
And reading of Dutch commentators in folio:
From waiting, like Gay, whole years at Whitehall:
From the pride of gay wits, and the envy of small,
From very fine ladies with very fine incomes,
Which they finely lay out on fine toys and fine trincums:
From the pranks of ridottos and court masquerades,
The snares of young jilts, and the spite of old maids:
From a saucy dull stage, and submitting to share
In an empty third night with a beggarly play'r:
From Curl and such printers as would have me curst
To write second parts, let who will write the first:
From all pious patriots, who would to their best,
Put on a new tax, and take off an old test:
From the faith of informers, the fangs of the law,
And the great rogues, who keep all the lesser in awe:
From a poor country cure, that living interment,
With a wife and no prospect of any preferment:
From scribbling for hire, when my credit is sunk,
To buy no new coat, and to line an old trunk:
From squires, who divert us with jokes at their tables
Of hounds in their kennels, and nags in their stables:
From the nobles and commons, who bound in strict league are
To subscribe for no book, yet subscribe to Heidegger:
From the cant of fanatics, the jargon of schools,
The censures of wise men, and praises of fools:
From critics who never read Latin or Greek,
And pedants, who boast they read both all the week:
From borrowing wit, to repay it like Budgell.
Or lending, like Pope, to be paid by a cudgel:
If ever thou didst, or wilt ever befriend me,
From these, and such evils, Apollo, defend me;
And let me be rather but honest with no wit,
Than a noisy nonsensical half-witted poet.

Heidegger] J. J. Heidegger (?1659–1749), partner with Handel in the Haymarket
Theatre; promoter of masquerades and ridottos
Budgell] Eustace Budgell (1686–1737), pamphleteer and contributor to the *Spectator*

HENRY CAREY
?1687–1743

71   *Namby-Pamby*
A Panegyric on the New Versification
Addressed to Ambrose Philips, Esq.

Naughty Paughty Jack-a-Dandy,
Stole a Piece of Sugar Candy
From the Grocer's Shoppy-Shop,
And away did hoppy-hop.

ALL ye poets of the age,
All ye witlings of the stage,
Learn your jingles to reform,
Crop your numbers to conform.
Let your little verses flow
Gently, sweetly, row by row;
Let the verse the subject fit,
Little subject, little wit.
Namby-Pamby is your guide,
Albion's joy, Hibernia's pride.
Namby-Pamby, pilly-piss,
Rhimy-pimed on Missy Miss
Tartaretta Tartaree,
From the navel to the knee;
That her father's gracy-grace
Might give him a placey place.

He no longer writes of Mammy
Andromache and her lammy,
Hanging-panging at the breast
Of a matron most distressed.
Now the venal poet sings
Baby clouts and baby things,
Baby dolls and baby houses,
Little misses, little spouses,
Little playthings, little toys,
Little girls and little boys.
As an actor does his part,

162

So the nurses get by heart
Namby-Pamby's little rhymes,
Little jingles, little chimes,
To repeat to missy-miss,
Piddling ponds of pissy-piss;
Cracking-packing like a lady,
Or bye-bying in the crady.
Namby-Pamby's doubly mild,
Once a man, and twice a child;
To his hanging sleeves restored,
Now he foots it like a lord;
Now he pumps his little wits,
Shitting writes, and writing shits,
All by little tiny bits.
And methinks I hear him say,
Boys and girls, come out to play!
Moon does shine as bright as day.

Now my Namby-Pamby's found
Sitting on the friar's ground,
Picking silver, picking gold;
Namby-Pamby's never old.
Bally-cally, they begin,
Namby-Pamby still keeps in.
Namby-Pamby is no clown.
London Bridge is broken down:
Now he courts the gay ladee,
Dancing o'er the Lady-Lee.
Now he sings of Lick-spit Liar,
Burning in the brimstone fire;
Liar, liar! Lick-spit, Lick,
Turn about the candlestick!
Now he sings of Jacky Horner,
Sitting in the chimney corner,
Eating of a Christmas pie,
Putting in his thumb, O fie!
Putting in, O fie! his thumb,
Pulling out, O strange, a plum.
Now he plays at Stee-Staw-Stud,
Sticking apples in the mud;
When 'tis turned to Stee-Staw-Stire,
Then he sticks them in the mire,
Now he acts the grenadier,

Calling for a pot of beer.
Where's his money? He's forgot;
Get him gone, a drunken sot.
Now a cock-horse does he ride,
And anon on timber stride.
See and Saw, and Sacch'ry Down,
London is a gallant town!
Now he gathers riches in,
Thicker, faster, pin by pin;
Pins apiece to see his show,
Boys and girls flock row by row;
From their clothes the pins they take,
Risk a whipping for his sake;
From their clothes the pins they pull
To fill Namby's cushion full.
So much wit at such an age
Does a genius great presage;
Second childhood gone and past,
Should he prove a man at last,
What must second manhood be
In a child so bright as he.

Guard him, ye poetic pow'rs,
Watch his minutes, watch his hours;
Let your tuneful nine inspire him;
Let the poets, one and all,
To his genius victims fall.

ALEXANDER POPE
1688–1744

72   from *The Wife of Bath her Prologue,*
from Chaucer
Wives

IF poor (you say) she drains her husband's purse;
If rich, she keeps her priest, or something worse;
If highly born, intolerably vain;
Vapours and pride by turns possess her brain;
Now gaily mad, now sourly splenetick,
Freakish when well, and fretful when she's sick.

If fair, then chaste she cannot long abide,
By pressing youth attacked on ev'ry side.
If foul, her wealth the lusty lover lures,
Or else her wit some fool-gallant procures,
Or else she dances with becoming grace,
Or shape excuses the defects of face.
There swims no goose so gray, but, soon or late,
She finds some honest gander for her mate.
    Horses (thou say'st), and asses, men may try,
And ring suspected vessels ere they buy,
But wives, a random choice, untried they take;
They dream in courtship, but in wedlock wake.
Then, nor till then, the veil's removed away,
And all the woman glares in open day.

73   from *The Rape of the Lock*
                          Hampton Court

CLOSE by those meads for ever crowned with flow'rs,
Where Thames with pride surveys his rising tow'rs,
There stands a structure of majestic frame,
Which from the neighb'ring Hampton takes its name.
Here Britain's statesmen oft the fall foredoom
Of foreign tyrants, and of nymphs at home;
Here thou, great Anna! whom three realms obey,
Dost sometimes counsel take—and sometimes tea.
    Hither the heroes and the nymphs resort,
To taste awhile the pleasures of a court;
In various talk th'instructive hours they passed,
Who gave the ball, or paid the visit last:
One speaks the glory of the British Queen,
And one describes a charming Indian screen;
A third interprets motions, looks, and eyes;
At ev'ry word a reputation dies.
Snuff, or the fan, supply each pause of chat,
With singing, laughing, ogling, and all that.
    Meanwhile declining from the noon of day,
The Sun obliquely shoots his burning ray;
The hungry judges soon the sentence sign,
And wretches hang that jurymen may dine;
The merchant from th'Exchange returns in peace,
And the long labours of the toilette cease.

from *An Essay on Criticism*

(i)

Plain Fools

SOME are bewildered in the maze of Schools,
And some made coxcombs Nature meant but fools.
In search of wit these lose their common sense,
And then turn critics in their own defence.
Each burns alike, who can, or cannot write,
Or with a rival's or an eunuch's spite.
All fools have still an itching to deride,
And fain would be upon the laughing side:
If Maevius scribble in Apollo's spite,
There are, who judge still worse than he can write.
  Some have at first for wits, then poets passed,
Turned critics next, and proved plain fools at last;
Some neither can for wits nor critics pass,
As heavy mules are neither horse nor ass.
Those half-learned witlings, num'rous in our isle
As half-formed insects on the banks of Nile;
Unfinished things one knows not what to call,
Their generation's so equivocal:
To tell 'em, would a hundred tongues require,
Or one vain wit's, that might a hundred tire.

(ii)

The Servile Herd

  Some ne'er advance a judgment of their own,
But catch the spreading notion of the town;
They reason and conclude by precedent,
And own stale nonsense which they ne'er invent.
Some judge of authors' names, not works, and then
Nor praise nor blame the writings, but the men.
Of all this servile herd the worst is he
That in proud dullness joins with quality,
A constant critic at the Great Man's board,
To fetch and carry nonsense for my Lord.
What woeful stuff this madrigal would be,
In some starved hackney sonneteer, or me?

But let a Lord once own the happy lines,
How the wit brightens! How the style refines!
Before his sacred name flies ev'ry fault,
And each exalted stanza teems with thought!
　The vulgar thus through imitation err;
As oft the learned by being singular;
So much they scorn the crowd, that if the throng
By chance go right, they purposely go wrong;
So schismatics the plain believers quit,
And are but damned for having too much wit.
　Some praise at morning what they blame at night;
But always think the last opinion right.
A Muse by these is like a mistress used,
This hour she's idolized, the next abused,
While their weak heads, like towns unfortified,
'Twixt sense and nonsense daily change their side.

(iii)
The Bookful Blockhead

　Such shameless bards we have; and yet 'tis true,
There are as mad, abandoned critics too.
The bookful blockhead, ignorantly read,
With loads of learned lumber in his head,
With his own tongue still edifies his ears,
And always list'ning to himself appears.
All books he reads, and all he reads assails,
From Dryden's fables down to Durfey's tales,
With him, most authors steal their works, or buy;
Garth did not write his own *Dispensary*.
Name a new play, and he's the poet's friend,
Nay showed his faults—but when would poets mend?
No place so sacred from such fops is barred,
Nor is Paul's Church more safe than Paul's Churchyard:
Nay, fly to altars; there they'll talk you dead;
For fools rush in where angels fear to tread.

(iii)　(St.) Paul's Churchyard] traditional centre of the London trade in books

75 from *An Epistle to Dr Arbuthnot*

(i)

Atticus

THE bard whom pilf'red pastorals renown,
Who turns a Persian tale for half a crown,
Just writes to make his barrenness appear,
And strains from hard-bound brains eight lines a year:
He, who still wanting though he lives on theft,
Steals much, spends little, yet has nothing left:
And he, who now to sense, now nonsense leaning,
Means not, but blunders round about a meaning:
And he, whose fustian's so sublimely bad,
It is not poetry, but prose run mad:
All these my modest satire bad translate,
And owned that nine such poets made a Tate.
How did they fume, and stamp, and roar, and chafe!
And swear, not Addison himself was safe.
    Peace to all such! but were there one whose fires
True genius kindles, and fair fame inspires,
Blest with each talent and each art to please,
And born to write, converse, and live with ease:
Should such a man, too fond to rule alone,
Bear, like the Turk, no brother near the throne,
View him with scornful, yet with jealous eyes,
And hate for arts that caused himself to rise,
Damn with faint praise, assent with civil leer,
And without sneering, teach the rest to sneer;
Willing to wound, and yet afraid to strike,
Just hint a fault, and hesitate dislike;
Alike reserved to blame, or to commend,
A tim'rous foe, and a suspicious friend,
Dreading ev'n fools, by flatterers besieged,
And so obliging that he ne'er obliged;
Like Cato, give his little senate laws,
And sit attentive to his own applause;
While wits and Templars ev'ry sentence raise,
And wonder with a foolish face of praise.
Who but must laugh, if such a man there be?
Who would not weep, if Atticus were he!

Atticus] Addison

(ii)

The Patron

Proud, as Apollo on his forked hill,
Sate full-blown Bufo, puffed by ev'ry quill;
Fed with soft dedication all day long,
Horace and he went hand in hand in song.
His library (where busts of poets dead
And a true Pindar stood without a head)
Received of wits an undistinguished race,
Who first his judgment asked, and then a place:
Much they extolled his pictures, much his seat,
And flattered ev'ry day, and some days eat:
Till grown more frugal in his riper days,
He paid some bards with port, and some with praise,
To some a dry rehearsal was assigned,
And others (harder still) he paid in kind.
Dryden alone (what wonder?) came not nigh,
Dryden alone escaped this judging eye:
But still the great have kindness in reserve,
He helped to bury whom he helped to starve.

(iii)

Sporus

Let Sporus tremble—'What? that thing of silk,
Sporus, that mere white curd of ass's milk?
Satire or sense alas! can Sporus feel?
Who breaks a butterfly upon a wheel?'
Yet let me flap this bug with gilded wings,
This painted child of dirt that stinks and stings;
Whose buzz the witty and the fair annoys,
Yet wit ne'er tastes, and beauty ne'er enjoys,
So well-bred spaniels civilly delight
In mumbling of the game they dare not bite.
Eternal smiles his emptiness betray,
As shallow streams run dimpling all the way.
Whether in florid impotence he speaks,
And, as the prompter breathes, the puppet squeaks;

(iii)   Sporus] Lord Hervey

Or at the ear of Eve, familiar toad,
Half froth, half venom, spits himself abroad,
In puns, or politics, or tales, or lies,
Or spite, or smut, or rhymes, or blasphemies.
His wit all see-saw between *that* and *this*,
Now high, now low, now Master up, now Miss,
And he himself one vile antithesis.
Amphibious thing! that acting either part,
The trifling head, or the corrupted heart!
Fop at the toilet, flatt'rer at the board,
Now trips a Lady, and now struts a Lord.
Eve's tempter thus the rabbins have expressed,
A cherub's face, a reptile all the rest;
Beauty that shocks you, parts that none will trust,
Wit that can creep, and pride that licks the dust.

76   from *Epistle to a Lady:*
Of the Characters of Women

(i)
Cloe

'YET Cloe sure was formed without a spot—'
Nature in her then erred not, but forgot.
'With ev'ry pleasing, ev'ry prudent part,
Say, what can Cloe want?'—she wants a heart.
She speaks, behaves, and acts just as she ought;
But never, never, reached one gen'rous thought.
Virtue she finds too painful an endeavour,
Content to dwell in decencies for ever.
So very reasonable, so unmoved,
As never yet to love, or to be loved.
She, while her lover pants upon her breast,
Can mark the figures on an Indian chest;
And when she sees her friend in deep despair,
Observes how much a chintz exceeds mohair.
Forbid it Heav'n, a favour or a debt
She e'er should cancel—but she may forget.
Safe is your secret still in Cloe's ear;
But none of Cloe's shall you ever hear.

Of all her dears she never slandered one,
But cares not if a thousand are undone.
Would Cloe know if you're alive or dead?
She bids her footman put it in her head.
Cloe is prudent—would you too be wise?
Then never break your heart when Cloe dies.

(ii)
The Ghosts of Beauty

Men, some to bus'ness, some to pleasure take;
But ev'ry woman is at heart a rake:
Men, some to quiet, some to public strife;
But ev'ry lady would be queen for life.
   Yet mark the fate of a whole sex of queens!
Pow'r all their end, but beauty all the means.
In youth they conquer, with so wild a rage,
As leaves them scarce a subject in their age:
For foreign glory, foreign joy, they roam;
No thought of peace or happiness at home.
But wisdom's triumph is well-timed retreat,
As hard a science to the Fair as Great!
Beauties, like tyrants, old and friendless grown,
Yet hate to rest, and dread to be alone,
Worn out in public, weary ev'ry eye,
Nor leave one sigh behind them when they die.
   Pleasures the sex, as children birds, pursue,
Still out of reach, yet never out of view,
Sure, if they catch, to spoil the toy at most,
To covet flying, and regret when lost:
At last, to follies youth could scarce defend,
'Tis half their age's prudence to pretend;
Ashamed to own they gave delight before,
Reduce to feign it, when they give no more:
As hags hold sabbaths, less for joy than spite,
So these their merry, miserable night;
Still round and round the ghosts of beauty glide,
And haunt the places where their honour died.

(ii)   night] night-time party

See how the world its veterans rewards!
A youth of frolics, an old age of cards,
Fair to no purpose, artful to no end,
Youth without lovers, old without a friend,
A fop their passion, but their prize a sot,
Alive, ridiculous, and dead, forgot!

77 from *Epistle to Richard Boyle, Earl of Burlington*

At Timon's Villa

AT Timon's villa let us pass a day,
Where all cry out, 'What sums are thrown away!'
So proud, so grand, of that stupendous air,
Soft and Agreeable come never there.
Greatness, with Timon, dwells in such a draught
As brings all Brobdignag before your thought.
To compass this, his building is a town,
His pond an ocean, his parterre a down:
Who must but laugh, the Master when he sees,
A puny insect, shiv'ring at a breeze!
Lo, what huge heaps of littleness around!
The whole, a laboured quarry above ground.
Two Cupids squirt before, a lake behind
Improves the keenness of the northern wind.
His gardens next your admiration call,
On ev'ry side you look, behold the wall!
No pleasing intricacies intervene,
No artful wildness to perplex the scene;
Grove nods at grove, each alley has a brother,
And half the platform just reflects the other.
The suff'ring eye inverted nature sees,
Trees cut to statues, statues thick as trees,
With here a fountain, never to be played,
And there a summer-house, that knows no shade;
Here Amphitrite sails through myrtle bow'rs;
There gladiators fight, or die, in flow'rs;
Unwatered see the drooping sea-horse mourn,
And swallows roost in Nilus' dusty urn.

My Lord advances with majestic mien,
Smit with the mighty pleasure, to be seen:
But soft—by regular approach—not yet—
First through the length of yon hot terrace sweat,
And when up ten steep slopes you've dragged your thighs,
Just at his study door he'll bless your eyes.

His study! with what authors is it stored?
In books, not authors, curious is my Lord;
To all their dated backs he turns you round,
These Aldus printed, those Du Suëil has bound.
Lo some are vellum, and the rest as good
For all his Lordship knows, but they are wood.
For Locke or Milton 'tis in vain to look,
These shelves admit not any modern book.

And now the chapel's silver bell you hear,
That summons you to all the pride of pray'r:
Light quirks of music, broken and uneven,
Make the soul dance upon a jig to Heaven.
On painted ceiling you devoutly stare,
Where sprawl the saints of Verrio or Laguerre,
On gilded clouds in fair expansion lie,
And bring all Paradise before your eye.
To rest, the cushion and soft Dean invite,
Who never mentions Hell to ears polite.

But hark! the chiming clocks to dinner call;
A hundred footsteps scrape the marble hall:
The rich buffet well-coloured serpents grace,
And gaping Tritons spew to wash your face.
Is this a dinner? this a genial room?
No, 'tis a temple, and a hecatomb.
A solemn sacrifice, performed in state,
You drink by measure, and to minutes eat.
So quick retires each flying course, you'd swear
Sancho's dread Doctor and his wand were there.
Between each act the trembling salvers ring,
From soup to sweet-wine, and God bless the King.
In plenty starving, tantalized in state,
And complaisantly helped to all I hate,

Treated, caressed, and tired, I take my leave,
Sick of his civil pride from morn to eve;
I curse such lavish cost, and little skill,
And swear no day was ever passed so ill.

78   from *The First Satire of
the Second Book of Horace Imitated*

   Pope. There are (I scarce can think it, but am told)
There are to whom my satire seems too bold,
Scarce to wise Peter complaisant enough,
And something said of Chartres much too rough.
The lines are weak, another's pleased to say,
Lord Fanny spins a thousand such a day.
Tim'rous by nature, of the rich in awe,
I come to council learned in the law,
You'll give me, like a friend doth sage and free,
Advice; and (as you use) without a fee.
   Friend. I'd write no more.
               Pope. Not write? but then I *think*,
And for my soul I cannot sleep a wink.
I nod in company, I wake at night,
Fools rush into my head, and so I write.
   Friend. You could not do a worse thing for your life.
Why, if the nights seem tedious—take a wife;
Or rather truly, if your point be rest,
Lettuce and cowslip wine; *probatum est.*
But talk with Celsus, Celsus will advise
Hartshorn, or something that shall close your eyes.
Or if you needs must write, write Caesar's praise:
You'll gain at least a knighthood, or the bays.

wise Peter] Peter Walker, rich attorney and moneylender to the great
Chartres] Colonel Francis Chartres, rake and rapist (see No. 62)

79   from *The First Epistle of the First*
Book of Horace Imitated

The People

WELL, if a King's a lion, at the least
The People are a many-headed beast:
Can they direct what measures to pursue,
Who know themselves so little what to do?
Alike in nothing but one lust of gold,
Just half the land would buy, and half be sold:
Their country's wealth our mightier misers drain,
Or cross, to plunder provinces, the main:
The rest, some farm the poor-box, some the pews;
Some keep assemblies, and would keep the stews;
Some with fat bucks on childless dotards fawn;
Some win rich widows by their chine and brawn;
While with the silent growth of ten per cent,
In dirt and darkness hundreds stink content.

80   from *The Second Satire of*
the First Book of Horace

WITH all a woman's virtues but the pox,
Fufidia thrives in money, land, and stocks:
For int'rest, ten per cent her constant rate is;
Her body? hopeful heirs may have it gratis.
She turns her very sister to a job,
And, in the happy minute, picks your fob:
Yet starves herself, so little her own friend,
And thirsts and hungers only at one end:
A self-tormentor, worse than (in the play)
The wretch, whose av'rice drove his son away.
But why all this? I'll tell you, 'tis my theme:
'Women and fools are always in extreme.'
Rufa's at either end a common shore,
Sweet Moll and Jack are civet-cat and boar:
Nothing in nature is so lewd as Peg,
Yet, for the world, she would not show her leg!

80   Fufidia] Lady Mary Wortley Montagu   job] act of fornication
common shore] open sewer

While bashful Jenny, ev'n at morning prayer,
Spreads her fore-buttocks to the navel bare.
But diff'rent taste in diff'rent men prevails,
And one is fired by heads, and one by tails;
Some feel no flames but at the court or ball,
And others hunt white aprons in the Mall.
　My Lord of London, chancing to remark
A noted Dean much busied in the Park,
'Proceed (he cried) proceed, my reverend brother,
'Tis *fornicatio simplex*, and no other:
Better than lust for boys, with Pope and Turk,
Or others' spouses, like my Lord of York.'

81　　　　　　from *Epilogue to the Satires*

(i)

VIRTUE may choose the high or low degree,
'Tis just alike to Virtue, and to me;
Dwell in a monk, or light upon a king,
She's still the same, beloved, contented thing.
Vice is undone, if she forgets her birth,
And stoops from angels to the dregs of earth:
But 'tis the fall degrades her to a whore;
Let Greatness own her, and she's mean no more:
Her birth, her beauty, crowds and courts confess,
Chaste matrons praise her, and grave bishops bless:
In golden chains the willing world she draws,
And hers the Gospel is, and hers the laws:
Mounts the tribunal, lifts her scarlet head,
And sees pale Virtue carted in her stead!
Lo! at the wheels of her triumphal car,
Old England's Genius, rough with many a scar,
Dragged in the dust! his arms hang idly round,
His flag inverted trails along the ground!
Our youth, all liveried o'er with foreign gold,
Before her dance; behind her crawl the old!

81　Greatness own her] as exemplified in Walpole and his mistress Molly Skerrett
carted] taken round in a cart, a punishment for bawds, tarts and unfaithful wives

See thronging millions to the pagod run,
And offer country, parent, wife, or son!
Hear her black trumpet through the land proclaim,
That 'Not to be corrupted is the shame'.
In soldier, churchman, patriot, man in pow'r,
'Tis av'rice all, ambition is no more!
See, all our nobles begging to be slaves!
See, all our fools aspiring to be knaves!
The wit of cheats, the courage of a whore,
Are what ten thousand envy and adore.
All, all look up, with reverential awe,
On crimes that scape, or triumph o'er the law:
While Truth, Worth, Wisdom, daily they decry—
'Nothing is sacred now but Villany.'

(ii)

Friend. Spare then the person, and expose the vice.
Pope. How Sir! not damn the sharper, but the dice?
Come on then, Satire! gen'ral, unconfined,
Spread thy broad wing, and souse on all the kind.
Ye statesmen, priests, of one religion all!
Ye tradesmen vile, in army, court, or hall!
Ye rev'rend atheists!—*Friend.* Scandal! name them, Who?
   Pope. Why that's the thing you bid me not to do.
Who starved a sister, who foreswore a debt,
I never named—the town's enquiring yet.
The pois'ning dame—*Friend.* You mean—*Pope.* I don't.—*Friend.*
   You do.
   Pope. See! now I keep the secret, and not you.
The bribing statesman—*Friend.* Hold! too high you go.
   Pope. The bribed elector—*Friend.* There you stoop too low.
   Pope. I fain would please you, if I knew with what:
Tell me, which knave is lawful game, which not?
Must great offenders, once escaped the crown,
Like royal harts, be never more run down?
Admit your law to spare the knight requires,
As beasts of nature may we hunt the squires?
Suppose I censure—you know what I mean—
To save a bishop, may I name a dean?
   Friend. A dean, Sir? no: his fortune is not made,
You hurt a man that's rising in his trade.

Pope. If not the tradesman who set up today,
Much less the prentice who tomorrow may.
Down, down, proud Satire! though a realm be spoiled,
Arraign no mightier thief than wretched Wild,
Or if a court or country's made a job,
Go drench a pickpocket, and join the mob.
    But Sir, I beg you, for the love of vice!
The matter's weighty, pray consider twice:
Have you less pity for the needy cheat,
The poor and friendless villain, than the great?
Alas! the small discredit of the bribe
Scarce hurts the lawyer, but undoes the scribe.
Then better sure it charity becomes
To tax directors, who (thank God) have plums;
Still better, ministers; or if the thing
May pinch ev'n there—why lay it on a king.
    Friend. Stop! stop!
                  Pope. Must Satire, then, not rise nor fall?
Speak out, and bid me blame no rogues at all.

(iii)

Pope. Ask you what provocation I have had?
The strong antipathy of good to bad.
When Truth or Virtue an affront endures,
Th'affront is mine, my friend, and should be yours.
Mine, as a foe professed to false pretence,
Who think a coxcomb's honour like his sense;
Mine, as a friend to ev'ry worthy mind;
And mine as Man, who feel for all mankind.
    Friend. You're strangely proud.
                 Pope. So proud, I am no slave:
So impudent, I own myself no knave:
So odd, my country's ruin makes me grave.
Yes, I am proud; I must be proud to see
Men not afraid of God, afraid of me:
Safe from the Bar, the Pulpit, and the Throne,
Yet touched and shamed by Ridicule alone.
    O sacred weapon! left for Truth's defence,
Sole dread of Folly, Vice, and Insolence!

Wild] Jonathan Wild, thief and fence, hanged 1725

To all but Heav'n-directed hands denied,
The Muse may give thee, but the Gods must guide.
Rev'rent I touch thee! but with honest zeal;
To rouse the watchmen of the public weal,
To Virtue's work provoke the tardy Hall,
And goad the prelate slumb'ring in his stall.

    Ye tinsel insects! whom a court maintains,
That counts your beauties only by your stains,
Spin all your cobwebs o'er the eye of day!
The Muse's wing shall brush you all away:
All his Grace preaches, all his Lordship sings,
All that makes saints of Queens, and gods of Kings,
All, all but Truth, drops dead-born from the press,
Like the last Gazette, or the last Address.

82   from *The Dunciad*

(i)

THE Mighty Mother, and her son who brings
The Smithfield Muses to the ear of kings,
I sing. Say you, her instruments the great!
Called to this work by Dulness, Jove, and Fate;
You by whose care, in vain decried and cursed,
Still Dunce the second reigns like Dunce the first;
Say how the Goddess bade Britannia sleep,
And poured her spirit o'er the land and deep.

    In eldest times, e'er mortals writ or read,
E'er Pallas issued from the Thund'rer's head,
Dulness o'er all possessed her ancient right,
Daughter of Chaos and eternal Night:
Fate in their dotage this fair idiot gave,
Gross as her sire, and as her mother grave,
Laborious, heavy, busy, bold, and blind,
She ruled, in native anarchy, the mind.

    Still her old empire to restore she tries,
For, born a goddess, Dulness never dies.

    O thou! whatever title please thine ear,
Dean, Drapier, Bickerstaff, or Gulliver!
Whether thou choose Cervantes' serious air,
Or laugh and shake in Rab'lais' easy chair,

---

81 Hall] Westminster Hall, which was the High Court of Justice

Or praise the court, or magnify mankind,
Or thy grieved country's copper chains unbind;
From thy Bœotia though her pow'r retires,
Mourn not, my SWIFT, at aught our realm acquires,
Here pleased behold her mighty wings outspread
To hatch a new Saturnian Age of Lead.
Close to those walls where Folly holds her throne,
And laughs to think Monroe would take her down,
Where o'er the gates, by his famed father's hand
Great Cibber's brazen, brainless brothers stand;
One cell there is, concealed from vulgar eye,
The Cave of Poverty and Poetry.
Keen, hollow winds howl through the bleak recess,
Emblem of music caused by emptiness.
Hence bards, like Proteus long in vain tied down,
Escape in monsters, and amaze the town.
Hence miscellanies spring, the weekly boast
Of Curl's chaste press, and Lintot's rubric post:
Hence hymning Tyburn's elegiac lines,
Hence journals, medleys, merc'ries, magazines:
Sepulchral lies, our holy walls to grace,
And New Year Odes, and all the Grub Street race.
In clouded majesty here Dulness shone;
Four guardian Virtues, round, support her throne:
Fierce champion Fortitude, that knows no fears
Of hisses, blows, or want, or loss of ears:
Calm Temperance, whose blessings those partake
Who hunger, and who thirst for scribbling sake:
Prudence, whose glass presents th'approaching jail:
Poetic Justice, with her lifted scale,
Where, in nice balance, truth with gold she weighs,
And solid pudding against empty praise.
Here she beholds the Chaos dark and deep,
Where nameless somethings in their causes sleep,
Till genial Jacob, or a warm Third Day,
Call forth each mass, a poem, or a play:

Monroe] James Monro, physician in charge of Bedlam
brainless brothers] figures of Raving and Melancholy Madness over Bedlam gateway,
carved by Caius Cibber, father of 'Great Cibber', the Poet Laureate.
rubric post] Lintot the publisher 'usually adorn'd his shop with Titles in red letters'
merc(e)ries] mercer's wares
Jacob] Jacob Tonson, publisher of Swift, Dryden, Pope, etc.
Third Day] day when takings of a play went to the playwright

How hints, like spawn, scarce quick in embryo lie,
How new-born nonsense first is taught to cry,
Maggots half-formed in rhyme exactly meet,
And learn to crawl upon poetic feet.
Here one poor word an hundred clenches makes,
And ductile dulness new meanders takes;
There motley Images her fancy strike,
Figures ill paired, and Similies unlike.
She sees a mob of Metaphors advance,
Pleased with the madness of the mazy dance:
How Tragedy and Comedy embrace;
How Farce and Epic get a humbled race;
How Time himself stands still at her command,
Realms shift their place, and Ocean turns to land.
Here gay Description Egypt glads with show'rs,
Or gives to Zembla fruits, to Barca flow'rs;
Glitt'ring with ice here hoary hills are seen,
There painted valleys of eternal green,
In cold December fragrant chaplets blow,
And heavy harvests nod beneath the snow.
  All these, and more, the cloud-compelling Queen
Beholds through fogs, that magnify the scene.
She, tinselled o'er in robes of varying hues,
With self-applause her wild creation views;
Sees momentary monsters rise and fall,
And with her own fool's colours gilds them all.

(ii)

  Next bidding all draw near on bended knees,
The Queen confers her titles and degrees.
Her children first of more distinguished sort,
Who study Shakespeare at the Inns of Court,
Impale a glow-worm, or vertù profess,
Shine in the dignity of F.R.S.
Some, deep Freemasons, join the silent race
Worthy to fill Pythagoras's place:
Some botanists, or florists at the least,
Or issue members of an annual feast.

(i)   clench] a play on words

Nor passed the meanest unregarded, one
Rose a Gregorian, one a Gormogon.
The last, not least in honour or applause,
Isis and Cam made Doctors of her Laws.
　　Then blessing all, 'Go children of my care!
To practice now from theory repair.
All my commands are easy, short and full:
My sons! be proud, be selfish, and be dull.
Guard my prerogative, assert my throne:
This nod confirms each privilege your own.
The Cap and Switch be sacred to his Grace;
With Staff and Pumps the Marquis leads the race;
From stage to stage the licensed Earl may run,
Paired with his fellow charioteer the Sun;
The learned Baron butterflies design,
Or draw to silk Arachne's subtile line;
The Judge to dance his brother sergeant call;
The Senator to cricket urge the ball;
The Bishop stow (pontific luxury!)
An hundred souls of turkey in a pie;
The sturdy Squire to Gallic masters stoop,
And drown his lands and manors in a soup.
Others import yet nobler arts from France,
Teach Kings to fiddle, and make Senates dance.
Perhaps more high some daring son may soar,
Proud to my list to add one monarch more;
And notably conscious, Princes are but things
Born for First Ministers, as slaves for kings,
Tyrant supreme! shall three estates command,
And MAKE ONE MIGHTY DUNCIAD OF THE LAND!'
　　More she had spoke, but yawned—All Nature nods:
What mortal can resist the yawn of Gods?
Churches and chapels instantly it reached
(St. James's first, for leaden Gilbert preached),
Then catched the schools; the Hall scarce kept awake;
The Convocation gaped, but could not speak:
Lost was the Nation's sense, nor could be found,
While the long solemn unison went round:
Wide, and more wide, it spread o'er all the realm;
Ev'n Palinurus nodded at the helm:

Gregorian, Gormogon] The Gregorians and the Gormogons were two fraternities called
into being by the early eighteenth-century revival of Freemasonry
leaden Gilbert] John Gilbert, Bishop of Llandaff, later Archbishop of York

The vapour mild o'er each committee crept;
Unfinished treaties in each office slept;
And chiefless armies dozed out the campaign;
And navies yawned for orders on the main.
   O Muse! relate (for you can tell alone,
Wits have short memories, and dunces none)—
Relate, who first, who last resigned to rest;
Whose heads she partly, whose completely blest;
What charms could faction, what ambition lull,
The venal quiet, and entrance the dull;
Till drowned was Sense, and Shame, and Right, and Wrong—
O sing, and hush the nations with thy song!

               *   *   *

   In vain, in vain—the all-composing hour
Resistless falls: The Muse obeys the Pow'r.
She comes! she comes! the sable throne behold
Of Night primeval, and of Chaos old!
Before her, fancy's gilded clouds decay,
And all its varying rainbows die away.
Wit shoots in vain its momentary fires,
The meteor drops, and in a flash expires.
As one by one, at dread Medea's strain,
The sick'ning stars fade off th'ethereal plain,
As Argus' eyes by Hermes' wand oppressed,
Closed one by one to everlasting rest,
Thus at her felt approach, and secret might,
Art after art goes out, and all is night.
See skulking Truth to her old cavern fled,
Mountains of casuistry heaped o'er her head!
Philosophy, that leaned on Heav'n before,
Shrinks to her second cause, and is no more.
Physic of Metaphysic begs defence,
And Metaphysic calls for aid on Sense!
See Mystery to Mathematics fly!
In vain! they gaze, turn giddy, rave, and die.
Religion blushing veils her sacred fires,
And unawares Morality expires.
Nor public flame, nor private, dares to shine;
Nor human spark is left, nor glimpse divine!
Lo! thy dread empire, CHAOS! is restored;
Light dies before thy uncreating word:
Thy hand, great Anarch! lets the curtain fall;
And Universal Darkness buries all.

RICHARD SAVAGE

?1697–1743

83   from *The Bastard*

IN gayer hours, when high my fancy ran,
The muse, exulting, thus her lay began.
    Blessed be the Bastard's birth! through wond'rous ways,
He shines eccentric like a comet's blaze.
No sickly fruit of faint compliance he;
He! stamped in nature's mint of ecstasy!
He lives to build, not boast, a gen'rous race,
No tenth transmitter of a foolish face.
His daring hope no sire's example bounds;
His firstborn lights no prejudice confounds.
He, kindling from within, requires no flame;
He glories in a Bastard's glowing name.
    Born to himself, and no possession led,
In freedom fostered, and by fortune fed,
Nor guides, nor rules, his sov'reign choice control,
His body independent, as his soul.
Loosed to the world's wide range—enjoined no aim,
Prescribed no duty, and assigned no name,
Nature's unbounded son, he stands alone,
His heart unbiassed, and his mind his own.

84   from *The Progress of a Divine*

NOW in the patron's mansion see the wight,
Factious for power—a Son of Levi right!
Servile to squires, to vassals proud his mien,
As codex to inferior clergy seen.
He flatters till you blush, but when withdrawn,
'Tis his to·slander, as 'twas his to fawn.
He pumps for secrets, pries o'er servants' ways,
And, like a meddling priest, can mischief raise,
And from such mischief thus can plead desert:
''Tis all my patron's int'rest at my heart.'
Deep in his mind all wrongs from others live;
None more need pardon, and none less forgive.

At what does next his erudition aim?
To kill the footed and the feathered game.
Then this apostle, for a daintier dish,
With line, or net, shall plot the fate of fish.
In kitchen what the cookmaid calls a cot;
In cellar, with the butler brother sot.
Here too he corks, in brewhouse hops the beer;
Bright in the hall, his parts at whisk appear,
Dext'rous to pack, yet at all cheats exclaiming,
The priest has av'rice, av'rice itch of gaming,
And gaming fraud—but fair he strikes the ball,
And at the plain of billiards pockets all.
At tables now!— But oh, if gammoned there,
The startling echoes learn, like him, to swear!
Though ne'er at authors, in the study, seen,
At bowls, sagacious masters of the green.
A connoisseur, as cunning as a fox,
To bet on racers, or on battling cocks;
To preach o'er beer, in boroughs to procure
Voters, to make the squire's election sure:
For this, where clowns stare, gape, and grin, and bawl,
Free to buffoon his function to 'em all.
When the clod Justice some horse-laugh would raise,
Foremost the dullest of dull jokes to praise;
To say, or unsay, at his patron's nod;
To do the will of all—save that of God.
   His int'rest the most servile part he deems,
Yet much he sways, where much to serve he seems:
He sways his patron, rules the lady most,
And as he rules the lady, rules the roast.
   Old tradesmen must give way to new—his aim
Extorted poundage, once the steward's claim.
Tenants are raised; or, as his pow'r increases,
Unless they fine to him, renew no leases.
Thus tradesmen, servants, tenants, none are free;
Their loss and murmur are his gain and glee.
   Lux'ry he loves; but, like a priest of sense,
Ev'n lux'ry loves not at his own expense.
Though harlot passions wanton with his will,
Yet av'rice is his wedded passion still.

---

cot] a man who meddles in women's work, especially in the kitchen

See him with napkin, o'er his band, tucked in,
While the rich grease hangs glist'ning on his chin,
Or, as the dew from Aaron's beard declines,
Ev'n to his garment hem soft-trickling shines!
He feeds, and feeds, swills soup, and sucks up marrow,
Swills, sucks, and feeds, till lech'rous as a sparrow.
Thy pleasure, Onan, now no more delights,
The lone amusement of his chaster nights.
He boasts (let ladies put him to the test!)
Strong back, broad shoulders, and a well-built chest.
With stiff'ning nerves, now steals he sly away,
Alert, warm, chuckling, ripe for am'rous play;
Ripe to caress the lass he once thought meet
At church to chide, when penanced in a sheet.
He pants, the titillating joy to prove,
The fierce, short sallies of luxurious love.
Not fair Cadière and confessor than they,
In straining transport, more lascivious lay.
Conceives her womb, while each so melts, and thrills?
He plies her now with love, and now with pills.
No more falls penance, clothed in shame, upon her;
These kill her embryo, and preserve her honour.

85   from *The Authors of the Town*

FIRST, let me view what noxious nonsense reigns,
While yet I loiter on prosaic plains.
If pens impartial active annals trace,
Others, with secret hist'ry, truth deface:
Views, and reviews, and wild memoirs appear,
And slander darkens each recorded year.
Each Prince's death to poison they apply,
No Royal Mortals sure by nature die,
Fav'rites or kindred artful deaths create,
A father, brother, son, or wife is fate.
In a past reign was formed a secret league,
Some ring, or letter, now reveals th'intrigue:
A certain Earl a certain Queen enjoys,

---

84 Cadière] not long before Savage wrote his poem the world was entertained by
the scandal of Catherine Cadière's pregnancy by her Jesuit confessor and his attempt
to conceal matters by putting her away in a nunnery

A certain subject fair her peace destroys;
The jealous Queen a vengeful art assumes,
And scents her rival's gloves with dire perfumes.
Queens, with their ladies, work unseemly things,
And boys grow dukes, when catamites to kings.
A lying monk on miracles refines,
And vengeance glares from violated shrines.

 Thus slander o'er the dead one's fame prevails,
And easy minds imbibe romantic tales.
Thus from feigned facts a false reflection flows,
And by tradition superstition grows.

 Next, pamphleteers a trade licentious drive,
Like wrangling lawyers, they by discord thrive.
If Hancock proves cold water's virtue clear,
His rival prints a treatise on warm beer.
If next inoculation's art spreads wide
(An art that mitigates infection's tide),
Loud pamphleteers 'gainst innovation cry
'Let nature work—'Tis natural to die.'

 If heav'n-born wisdom, gazing nature through,
Through nature's optics forms religion's view,
Priestcraft opposes demonstration's aid,
And with dark myst'ry dignifies her trade.

 If ruin rushes o'er a statesman's sway,
Scribblers, like worms, on tainted grandeur prey.
While a poor felon waits th'impending stroke,
Voracious scribes like hov'ring ravens croak.
In their dark quills a dreary insult lies,
Th'offence lives recent, though th'offender dies;
In his last words they suck his parting breath,
And gorge on his loathed memory after death.

 Wretches like these no satire would chastise,
But follies here to ruthless insult rise;
Distinguished insult taints a nation's fame,
And various vice deserves a various shame.

SOAME JENYNS
1704–1787

from *The Modern Fine Gentleman*

After the Grand Tour

JUST broke from school, pert, impudent, and raw,
Expert in Latin, more expert in taw,
His Honour posts o'er Italy and France,
Measures St. Peter's dome, and learns to dance.
Thence, having quick through various countries flown,
Gleaned all their follies, and exposed his own,
He back returns, a thing so strange all o'er,
As never ages past produced before;
A monster of such complicated worth,
As no one single clime could e'er bring forth;
Half atheist, papist, gamester, bubble, rook,
Half fiddler, coachman, dancer, groom, and cook.
Next, because business is now all the vogue,
And who'd be quite polite must be a rogue,
In parliament he purchases a seat,
To make the accomplished gentleman complete.
There safe in self-sufficient impudence,
Without experience, honesty, or sense,
Unknowing in her int'rest, trade, or laws,
He vainly undertakes his country's cause:
Forth from his lips, prepared at all to rail,
Torrents of nonsense burst, like bottled ale,
Though shallow, muddy; brisk, though mighty dull;
Fierce without strength; o'erflowing, though not full.

bubble] dupe   rook] cheat

87 from *An Epistle written in the Country to the right honourable the Lord Lovelace, then in town*

September 1735

IN days, my Lord, when mother Time,
Though now grown old, was in her prime,
When Saturn first began to rule,
And Jove was hardly come from school,
How happy was a country life!
How free from wickedness and strife!
Then each man lived upon his farm,
And thought and did no mortal harm;
On mossy banks fair virgins slept,
As harmless as the flocks they kept;
Then love was all they had to do,
And nymphs were chaste, and swains were true.
　　But now, whatever poets write,
I'm sure the case is altered quite:
Virtue no more in rural plains,
Or innocence, or peace remains;
But vice is in the cottage found,
And country girls are oft unsound;
Fierce party rage each village fires,
With wars of justices and squires;
Attorneys, for a barley straw,
Whole ages hamper folks in law,
And ev'ry neighbour's in a flame
About their rates, or tithes, or game:
Some quarrel for their hares and pigeons,
And some for diff'rence in religions:
Some hold their parson the best preacher,
The tinker some a better teacher;
These to the Church they fight for strangers,
Have faith in nothing but her dangers;
While those, a more believing people,
Can swallow all things—but a steeple.
　　But I, my Lord, who, as you know,
Care little how these matters go,
And equally detest the strife
And usual joys of country life,
Have by good fortune little share

Of its diversions, or its care;
For seldom I with squires unite,
Who hunt all day and drink all night;
Nor reckon wonderful inviting
A quarter-sessions, or cock-fighting:
But then no farm I occupy
With sheep to rot, and cows to die;
Nor rage I much, or much despair,
Though in my hedge I find a snare;
Nor view I, with due admiration,
All the high honours here in fashion;
The great commissions of the quorum,
Terrors to all who come before 'em;
Militia scarlet edged with gold,
Or the white staff high sheriffs hold;
The representative's caressing,
The judge's bow, the bishop's blessing;
Nor can I feel my soul delight
In the dull feast of neighb'ring knight,
Who, if you send three days before,
In white gloves meets you at the door,
With superfluity of breeding
First makes you sick, and then with feeding:
Or if with ceremony cloyed,
You would next time such plagues avoid,
And visit without previous notice,
'John, John, a coach!—I can't think who 'tis,'
My lady cries, who spies your coach,
Ere you the avenue approach:
'Lord, how unlucky!—washing day!
And all the men are in the hay!'
Entrance to gain is something hard,
The dogs all bark, the gates are barred;
The yard's with lines of linen crossed,
The hall door's locked, the key is lost:
These difficulties are all o'ercome,
We reach at length the drawing-room;
Then there's such trampling overhead,
Madam you'd swear was brought to bed;
Miss in a hurry bursts her lock,
To get clean sleeves to hide her smock;
The sevants run, the pewter clatters,
My lady dresses, calls and chatters;

The cook-maid raves for want of butter,
Pigs squeak, fowls scream, and green geese flutter.
Now after three hours tedious waiting,
On all our neighbours' faults debating,
And having nine times viewed the garden,
In which there's nothing worth a farthing,
In comes my lady, and the pudden:
'You will excuse, sir,—on a sudden'—
Then, that we may have four and four,
The bacon, fowls, and cauliflow'r
Their ancient unity divide,
The top one graces, one each side;
And by and by, the second course
Comes lagging like a distanced horse;
A salver then to church and king;
The butler sweats, the glasses ring;
The cloth removed, the toasts go round,
Bawdy and politics abound;
And as the knight more tipsy waxes,
We damn all ministers and taxes.
At last the ruddy sun quite sunk,
The coachman tolerably drunk,
Whirling o'er hillocks, ruts, and stones,
Enough to dislocate one's bones,
We home return, a wondrous token
Of Heaven's kind care, with limbs unbroken.

88   from *The Modern Fine Lady*

FOR love no time has she, or inclination,
Yet must coquet it for the sake of fashion;
For this she listens to each fop that's near,
Th' embroidered colonel flatters with a sneer,
And the cropped ensign nuzzles in her car.
But with most warmth her dress and airs inspire
Th' ambtious bosom of the landed Squire,
Who fain would quit plump Dolly's softer charms
For withered lean Right Honourable arms;
He bows with reverence at her sacred shrine,
And treats her as if sprung from race divine,
Which she returns with insolence and scorn,
Nor deigns to smile on a plebeian born.

Ere long by friends, by cards, and lovers crossed,
Her fortune, health, and reputation lost;
Her money gone, yet not a tradesman paid,
Her fame, yet she still damned to be a maid,
Her spirits sink, her nerves are so unstrung,
She weeps,[1] if but a handsome thief is hung:
By mercers, lacemen, mantua-makers pressed,
But most for ready cash for play distressed,
Where can she turn?—The Squire must all repair,
She condescends to listen to his pray'r,
And marries him at length in mere despair.

But soon th'endearments of a husband cloy,
Her soul, her frame incapable of joy:
She feels no transport in the bridal-bed,
Of which so oft sh' has heard, so much has read;
Then vexed, that she should be condemned alone
To seek in vain this philosophic stone,
To abler tutors she resolves t'apply,
A prostitute from curiosity:
Hence men of ev'ry sort, and ev'ry size,
Impatient for heav'n's cordial drop, she tries;
The fribbling beau, the rough unwieldy clown,
The ruddy templar newly on the town,
Th'Hibernian captain of gigantic make,
The brimful parson, and th'exhausted rake.

But still malignant fate her wish denies,
Cards yield superior joys, to cards she flies,
All night from rout to rout her chairmen run,
Again she plays, and is again undone.

---

[1] Some of the brightest eyes were at this time in tears for one Maclean, condemned for a robbery on the highway.

89   *Dr Johnson*

HERE lies poor Johnson. Reader! have a care,
Tread lightly, lest you rouse a sleeping bear.
Religious, moral, generous and humane,
He was, but self-conceited, rude, and vain:
Ill-bred, and overbearing in dispute,
A scholar and a Christian, yet a brute.
Would you know all his wisdom and his folly,
His actions, sayings, mirth, and melancholy,
Boswell and Thrale, retailers of his wit,
Will tell you how he wrote, and talked, and spit.

SAMUEL JOHNSON
1709–1784

90   from *London: A Poem in Imitation of the
Third Satire of Juvenal*

BY numbers here from shame or censure free,
All crimes are safe, but hated poverty.
This, only this, the rigid law pursues,
This, only this, provokes the snarling Muse;
The sober trader at a tattered cloak,
Wakes from his dream, and labours for a joke;
With brisker air the silken courtiers gaze,
And turn the varied taunt a thousand ways.
Of all the griefs that harass the distressed,
Sure the most bitter is a scornful jest;
Fate never wounds more deep the gen'rous heart,
Than when a blockhead's insult points the dart.

Has Heaven reserved, in pity to the poor,
No pathless waste, or undiscovered shore?

No secret island in the boundless main?
No peaceful desert yet unclaimed by Spain?
Quick let us rise, the happy seats explore,
And bear oppression's insolence no more.
This mournful truth is ev'rywhere confessed,
Slow rises worth, by poverty depressed:
But here more slow, where all are slaves to gold,
Where looks are merchandise, and smiles are sold,
Where won by bribes, by flatteries implored,
The groom retails the favours of his lord.

91   from *The Vanity of Human Wishes: The
Tenth Satire of Juvenal Imitated*

(i)
Delusive Fortune

UNNUMBERED suppliants crowd preferment's gate,
Athirst for wealth, and burning to be great;
Delusive fortune hears th' incessant call,
They mount, they shine, evaporate, and fall.
On ev'ry stage the foes of peace attend,
Hate dogs their flight, and insult mocks their end.
Love ends with hope, the sinking statesman's door
Pours in the morning worshipper no more;
For growing names the weekly scribbler lies,
To growing wealth the dedicator flies,
From every room descends the painted face,
That hung the bright palladium of the place,
And smoked in kitchens, or in auctions sold,
To better features yields the frame of gold;
For now no more we trace in ev'ry line
Heroic worth, benevolence divine:
The form distorted justifies the fall,
And detestation rids th'indignant wall.

(ii)
The Scholar's Life

When first the college rolls receive his name,
The young enthusiast quits his ease for fame;
Through all his veins the fever of renown
Burns from the strong contagion of the gown;
O'er Bodley's dome his future labours spread,
And Bacon's mansion trembles o'er his head;
Are these thy views? Proceed, illustrious youth,
And virtue guard thee to the throne of truth,
Yet should thy soul indulge the gen'rous heat,
Till captive science yields her last retreat;
Should reason guide thee with her brightest ray,
And pour on misty doubt resistless day;
Should no false kindness lure to loose delight,
Nor praise relax, nor difficulty fright;
Should tempting novelty thy cell refrain,
And sloth effuse her opiate fumes in vain;
Should beauty blunt on fops her fatal dart,
Nor claim the triumphs of a lettered heart;
Should no disease thy torpid veins invade,
Nor melancholy phantoms haunt thy shade;
Yet hope not life from grief or danger free,
Nor think the doom of man reversed for thee:
Deign on the passing world to turn thine eyes,
And pause awhile from letters to be wise;
There mark what ills the scholar's life assail,
Toil, envy, want, the patron, and the jail.

92   *A Short Song of Congratulation*

LONG-EXPECTED one-and-twenty,
Lingering year at last is flown:
Pomp and pleasure, pride and plenty,
Great Sir John, are all your own.

Loosened from the minor's tether,
Free to mortgage or to sell,
Wild as wind, and light as feather,
Bid the slaves of thrift farewell.

Call the Betties, Kates, and Jennies,
Every name that laughs at care;
Lavish of your grandsire's guineas,
Show the spirit of an heir.

All that prey on vice and folly
Joy to see their quarry fly;
Here the gamester light and jolly,
There the lender grave and sly.

Wealth, Sir John, was made to wander,
Let it wander as it will;
See the jockey, see the pander,
Bid them come and take their fill.

When the bonny blade carouses,
Pockets full, and spirits high,
What are acres? What are houses?
Only dirt, or wet or dry.

If the guardian or the mother
Tell the woes of wilful waste,
Scorn their counsel, scorn their pother:
You can hang or drown at last!

EDWARD MOORE
1712–1757

93

To the Right Hon.
Henry Pelham
The Humble Petition of the Worshipful Company of
POETS AND NEWSWRITERS

SHEWETH,
That your Honour's petitioners (dealers in rhymes,
And writers of scandal for mending the times)
By losses in business and England's well doing
Are sunk in their credit and verging on ruin.
  That these their misfortunes they humbly conceive
Arise not from dullness, as some folks believe,
But from rubs in their way which your Honour has laid,
And want of materials to carry on trade.
  That they always had formed high conceits of their use,
And meant their last breath should go out in abuse;
But now (and they speak it with sorrow and tears)
Since your Honour has sat at the helm of affairs
No party will join them, no faction invite,
To heed what they say or to read what they write;
Sedition, and Tumult, and Discord, are fled,
And Slander scarce ventures to lift up her head –
In short, public business is so carried on
That their country is saved and the patriots undone.
  To perplex them still more, and sure famine to bring,
(Now satire has lost both its truth and its sting)
If in spite of their natures they bungle at praise
Your Honour regards not, and nobody pays.
  Your petitioners therefore most humbly entreat
(As the times will allow and your Honour thinks meet)
That measures be changed, and some cause of complaint
Be immediately furnished to end their restraint.
Their credit thereby and their trade to retrieve,
That again they may rail and the nation believe.

Or else (if your wisdom shall deem it all one)
Now the Parliament's rising and business is done,
That your Honour would please at this dangerous crisis
To take to your bosom a few private vices,
By which your petitioners haply might thrive,
And keep both themselves and contention alive.

In compassion, good Sir! give them something to say,
And your Honour's petitioners ever shall pray.

WILLIAM WHITEHEAD
1715–1785

94   from *A Charge to the Poets*

IF nature prompts you, or if friends persuade,
Why, write; but ne'er pursue it as a trade.
And seldom publish: manuscripts disarm
The censor's frown, and boast an added charm,
Enhance their worth by seeming to retire,
For what but few can prate of, all admire.
Who trade in verse, alas, as rarely find
The public grateful, as the Muses kind.
From constant feasts like sated guests we steal,
And tired of tickling lose all power to feel.
'Tis novelty we want; with that in view
We praise stale matter, so the bard be new;
Or from known bards with ecstasy receive
Each pert new whim they almost blush to give.
A life of writing, unless wond'rous short,
No wit can brave, no genius can support.
Some soberer province for your business choose,
Be that your helmet, and your plume the muse.
Through fame's long rubric, down from Chaucer's time,
Few fortunes have been raised by lofty rhyme.
And, when our toils success no longer crowns,
What shelter find we from a world in frowns?
O'er each distress, which vice or folly brings,
Though charity extend her healing wings,

No Maudlin hospitals are yet assigned
For slipshod muses of the vagrant kind;
Where anthems might succeed to satires keen,
And hymns of penitence to songs obscene.
   What refuge then remains?—with gracious grin
Some practised bookseller invites you in,
Where luckless luckless bards, condemned to court the town,
(Not for their parents' vices, but their own!)
Write gay conundrums with an aching head,
Or earn by defamation daily bread,
Or friendless, shirtless, penniless complain,
Not of the world's, but 'Cælia's cold disdain'.
   Lords of their workhouse, see the tyrants sit
Brokers in books, and stockjobbers in wit,
Beneath whose lash, obliged to write or fast,
Our confessors and martyrs breathe their last!
   And can ye bear such insolence?—away,
For shame; plough, dig, turn pedlars, drive the dray;
With minds indignant each employment suits,
Our fleets want sailors, and our troops recruits;
And many a dirty street, on Thames's side,
Is yet by stool and brush unoccupied.

OLIVER GOLDSMITH

1730–1774

95   from *Epilogue to 'The Sister'*

Lud! what a group the motley scene discloses!
False wits, false wives, false virgins and false spouses:
Statesmen with bridles on; and, close beside 'em,
Patriots, in party-coloured suits, that ride 'em.
There Hebes, turned of fifty, try once more
To raise a flame in Cupids of threescore.
These in their turn, with appetites as keen,
Deserting fifty, fasten on fifteen.
Miss, not yet full fifteen, with fire uncommon,
Flings down her sampler, and takes up the woman:
The little urchin smiles and spreads her lure,
And tries to kill ere she's got power to cure.

Thus 'tis with all—their chief and constant care
Is to seem everything but what they are.
Yon broad, bold, angry spark, I fix my eye on,
Who seems to have robbed his vizor from the lion,
Who frowns, and talks, and swears, with round parade,
Looking, as who should say, *Damme! who's afraid?*
Strip but his vizor off, and sure I am
You'll find his lionship a very lamb.
Yon politician, famous in debate,
Perhaps, to vulgar eyes, bestrides the state;
Yet, when he deigns his real shape to assume,
He turns old woman and bestrides a broom.
Yon patriot, too, who presses on your sight,
And seems to every gazer all in white,
If with a bribe his candour you attack,
He bows, turns round, and whip – the man's a black!

96   from *The Deserted Village*

(i)

ILL fares the land, to hastening ill a prey,
Where wealth accumulates and men decay:
Princes and lords may flourish or may fade;
A breath can make them, as a breath has made;
But a bold peasantry, their country's pride,
When once destroyed, can never be supplied.

A time there was, ere England's griefs began,
When every rood of ground maintained its man;
For him light labour spread her wholesome store,
Just gave what life required, but gave no more:
His best companions, innocence and health;
And his best riches, ignorance of wealth.

But times are altered; trade's unfeeling train
Usurp the land and dispossess the swain;
Along the lawn, where scattered hamlets rose,
Unwieldy wealth and cumbrous pomp repose;
And every want to opulence allied,
And every pang that folly pays to pride.

These gentle hours that plenty bade to bloom,
Those calm desires that asked but little room,
Those healthful sports that graced the peaceful scene,
Lived in each look and brightened all the green;
These, far departing, seek a kinder shore,
And rural mirth and manners are no more.

(ii)

Yes! let the rich deride, the proud disdain,
These simple blessings of the lowly train;
To me more dear, congenial to my heart,
One native charm, than all the gloss of art.
Spontaneous joys, where Nature has its play,
The soul adopts, and owns their firstborn sway;
Lightly they frolic o'er the vacant mind,
Unenvied, unmolested, unconfined.
But the long pomp, the midnight masquerade,
With all the freaks of wanton wealth arrayed—
In these, ere triflers half their wish obtain,
The toiling pleasure sickens into pain;
And, even while fashion's brightest arts decoy,
The heart distrusting asks if this be joy.

Ye friends to truth, ye statesmen, who survey
The rich man's joy increase, the poor's decay,
'Tis yours to judge, how wide the limits stand
Between a splendid and a happy land.
Proud swells the tide with loads of freighted ore,
And shouting Folly hails them from her shore;
Hoards even beyond the miser's wish abound,
And rich men flock from all the world around.
Yet count our gains! This wealth is but a name
That leaves our useful products still the same.
Not so the loss. The man of wealth and pride
Takes up a space that many poor supplied;
Space for his lake, his park's extended bounds,
Space for his horses, equipage, and hounds:
The robe that wraps his limbs in silken sloth
Has robbed the neighbouring fields of half their growth;
His seat, where solitary sports are seen,
Indignant spurns the cottage from the green:

Around the world each needful product flies,
For all the luxuries the world supplies;
While thus the land adorned for pleasure all
In barren splendour feebly waits the fall.
As some fair female unadorned and plain,
Secure to please while youth confirms her reign,
Slights every borrowed charm that dress supplies,
Nor shares with art the triumph of her eyes;
But when those charms are past, for charms are frail,
When time advances, and when lovers fail,
She then shines forth, solicitous to bless,
In all the glaring impotence of dress.
Thus fares the land by luxury betrayed:
In nature's simplest charms at first arrayed,
But verging to decline, its splendours rise,
Its vistas strike, its palaces surprise;
While, scourged by famine from the smiling land
The mournful peasant leads his humble band,
And while he sinks, without one arm to save,
The country blooms – a garden and a grave.

WILLIAM COWPER
1731–1800

97   *Sweet Meat has Sour Sauce*
        or, the Slave-Trader in the Dumps

A TRADER I am to the African shore,
But since that my trading is like to be o'er,
I'll sing you a song that you ne'er heard before,
        Which nobody can deny, deny,
        Which nobody can deny.

When I first heard the news it gave me a shock,
Much like what they call an electrical knock,
And now I am going to sell off my stock,
        Which nobody, &c.

'Tis a curious assortment of dainty regales,
To tickle the negroes with when the ship sails,
Fine chains for the neck, and a cat with nine tails,
      Which nobody, &c.

Here's supple-jack plenty, and store of rat-tan,
That will wind itself round the sides of a man,
As close as a hoop round a bucket or can,
      Which nobody, &c.

Here's padlocks and bolts, and screw for the thumbs,
That squeeze them so lovingly till the blood comes,
They sweeten the temper like comfits or plums,
      Which nobody, &c.

When a negro his head from his victuals withdraws,
And clenches his teeth and thrusts out his paws,
Here's a notable engine to open his jaws,
      Which nobody, &c.

Thus going to market, we kindly prepare
A pretty black cargo of African ware,
For what they must meet with when they get there,
      Which nobody, &c.

'Twould do your heart good to see 'em below
Lie flat on their backs all the way as we go,
Like sprats on a gridiron, scores in a row,
      Which nobody, &c.

But ah! if in vain I have studied an art
So gainful to me, all boasting apart,
I think it will break my compassionate heart,
      Which nobody, &c.

For oh! how it enters my soul like an awl!
This pity, which some people self-pity call,
Is sure the most heart-piercing pity of all,
      Which nobody, &c.

So this is my song, as I told you before;
Come buy off my stock, for I must no more
Carry Caesars and Pompeys to Sugar-cane shore,
        Which nobody can deny, deny,
        Which nobody can deny.

98   from *Tirocinium: or, A Review of Schools*

(i)
'Our public hives of puerile resort'

WOULD you your son should be a sot or dunce,
Lascivious, headstrong; or all these at once;
That, in good time, the stripling's finished taste
For loose expense and fashionable waste
Should prove your ruin and his own at last,
Train him in public with a mob of boys,
Childish in mischief only and in noise,
Else of a mannish growth, and five in ten
In infidelity and lewdness men.
There shall he learn, ere sixteen winters old,
That authors are most useful pawned or sold;
That pedantry is all that schools impart,
But taverns teach the knowledge of the heart;
There waiter Dick, with Bacchanalian lays,
Shall win his heart, and have his drunken praise,
His counsellor and bosom friend shall prove,
And some street-pacing harlot his first love.

(ii)
Mounting the church-ladder

The father, who designs his babe a priest,
Dreams him episcopally such at least;
And, while the playful jockey scours the room
Briskly, astride upon the parlour broom,
In fancy sees him more superbly ride
In coach with purple lined, and mitres on its side.
Events improbable and strange as these,
Which only a parental eye foresees,
A public school shall bring to pass with ease.
But how! resides such virtue in that air
As must create an appetite for pray'r?

And will it breathe into him all the zeal
That candidates for such a prize should feel,
To take the lead and be the foremost still
In all true worth and literary skill?
  'Ah, blind to bright futurity, untaught
The knowledge of the world, and dull of thought!
Church-ladders are not always mounted best
By learned clerks and Latinists professed.
Th' exalted prize demands an upward look,
Not to be found by poring on a book.
Small skill in Latin, and still less in Greek,
Is more than adequate to all I seek.
Let erudition grace him or not grace,
I give the bauble but the second place;
His wealth, fame, honours, all that I intend,
Subsist and centre in one point—a friend!
A friend, whate'er he studies or neglects,
Shall give him consequence, heal all defects.
His intercourse with peers, and sons of peers—
There dawns the splendour of his future years;
In that bright quarter his propitious skies
Shall blush betimes, and there his glory rise.
Your Lordship, and *Your Grace!* what school can teach
A rhet'ric equal to those parts of speech?
What need of Homer's verse or Tully's prose,
Sweet interjections! if he learn but those?
Let rev'rend churls his ignorance rebuke,
Who starve upon a dog's-eared Pentateuch,
The parson knows enough who knows a duke.'

(iii)
Bred at the Public Schools

  To you, then, tenants of life's middle state,
Securely placed between the small and great,
Whose character, yet undebauched, retains
Two-thirds of all the virtue that remains,
Who wise yourselves, desire your sons should learn
Your wisdom and your ways—to you I turn.
Look round you on a world perversely blind;
See what contempt is fall'n on human kind;
See wealth abused, and dignities misplaced,

Great titles, offices, and trusts disgraced,
Long lines of ancestry, renowned of old,
Their noble qualities all quenched and cold;
See Bedlam's closeted and handcuffed charge
Surpassed in frenzy by the mad at large;
See great commanders making war a trade,
Great lawyers, lawyers without study made;
Churchmen, in whose esteem their blest employ
Is odious, and their wages all their joy,
Who, far enough from furnishing their shelves
With gospel lore, turn infidel themselves;
See womanhood despised, and manhood shamed
With infamy too nauseous to be named,
Fops at all corners, lady-like in mien,
Civeted fellows, smelt ere they are seen;
Else coarse and rude in manners, and their tongue
On fire with curses, and with nonsense hung,
Now flushed with drunk'ness, now with whoredom pale,
Their breath a sample of last night's regale;
See volunteers in all the vilest arts,
Men well endowed of honourable parts,
Designed by nature wise, but self-made fools;
All these, and more like these, were bred at schools!
And, if it chance, as sometimes chance it will,
That, though school-bred, the boy be virtuous still,
Such rare exceptions, shining in the dark,
Prove, rather than impeach, the just remark;
As here and there a twinkling ray descried
Serves but to show how black is all beside.

CHARLES CHURCHILL
1731–1764

99   from *The Prophecy of Famine*
(i)
The Insulted Scot

OFT have I heard thee mourn the wretched lot
Of the poor, mean, despised, insulted Scot,
Who, might calm reason credit idle tales,
By rancour forged where prejudice prevails,
Or starves at home, or practises, through fear
Of starving, arts which damn all conscience here.
When scribblers, to the charge by int'rest led,
The fierce *North-Briton* foaming at their head,
Pour forth invectives, deaf to candour's call,
And, injured by one alien, rail at all;
On northern Pisgah when they take their stand,
To mark the weakness of that Holy Land,
With needless truths their libels to adorn,
And hang a nation up to public scorn,
Thy gen'rous soul condemns the frantic rage,
And hates the faithful, but ill-natured, page.

The Scots are poor, cries surly English pride;
True is the charge, nor by themselves denied.
Are they not then in strictest reason clear,
Who wisely come to mend their fortunes here?
If by low supple arts successful grown,
They sapped our vigour to increase their own,
If, mean in want, and insolent in pow'r,
They only fawned, more surely to devour,
Roused by such wrongs should Reason take alarm,
And e'en the Muse for public safety arm;
But if they own ingenuous virtue's sway,
And follow where true honour points the way,
If they revere the hand by which they're fed,
And bless the donors for their daily bread,
Or by vast debts of higher import bound,
Are always humble, always grateful found,

If they, directed by Paul's holy pen,
Become discreetly all things to all men,
That all men may become all things to them,
Envy may hate, but justice can't condemn.
'Into our places, states, and beds they creep'.
They've sense to get, what we want sense to keep.

(ii)

Jockey and Sawney

Two boys, whose birth beyond all question springs
From great and glorious, though forgotten, kings,
Shepherds of Scottish lineage, born and bred
On the same bleak and barren mountain's head,
By niggard nature doomed on the same rocks
To spin out life, and starve themselves and flocks,
Fresh as the morning, which, enrobed in mist,
The mountain top with usual dulness kissed,
Jockey and Sawney to their labours rose;
Soon clad I ween, where nature needs no clothes,
Where, from their youth enured to winter skies,
Dress and her vain refinements they despise.

Jockey, whose manly high-boned cheeks to crown
With freckles spotted flamed the golden down,
With mickle art, could on the bagpipes play,
E'en from the rising to the setting day;
Sawney as long without remorse could bawl
Home's madrigals, and ditties from Fingal.
Oft at his strains, all natural though rude,
The Highland Lass forgot her want of food,
And, whilst she scratched her lover into rest,
Sunk pleased, though hungry, on her Sawney's breast.

Far as the eye could reach, no tree was seen,
Earth, clad in russet, scorned the lively green.
The plague of locusts they secure defy,
For in three hours a grasshopper must die.
No living thing, whate'er its food, feasts there,
But the chameleon, who can feast on air.
No birds, except as birds of passage, flew,
No bee was known to hum, no dove to coo.
No streams as amber smooth, as amber clear,

Were seen to glide, or heard to warble here.
Rebellion's spring, which through the country ran,
Furnished, with bitter draughts, the steady clan.
No flow'rs embalmed the air, but one white rose,
Which, on the tenth of June, by instinct blows,
By instinct blows at morn, and when the shades
Of drizzly eve prevail, by instinct fades.

  One, and but one poor solitary cave,
Too sparing of her favours, nature gave;
That one alone (hard tax on Scottish pride)
Shelter at once for man and beast supplied.
Their snares without entangling briers spread,
And thistles, armed against th' invader's head,
Stood in close ranks all entrance to oppose,
Thistles now held more precious than the rose.
All creatures, which, on nature's earliest plan,
Were formed to loath, and to be loathed by man,
Which owed their birth to nastiness and spite,
Deadly to touch, and hateful to the sight,
Creatures, which, when admitted in the ark,
Their Saviour shunned, and rankled in the dark,
Found place within; marking her noisome road
With poison's trail, here crawled the bloated toad;
There webs were spread of more than common size,
And half-starved spiders preyed on half-starved flies;
In quest of food, efts strove in vain to crawl;
Slugs, pinched with hunger, smeared the slimy wall;
The cave around with hissing serpents rung;
On the damp roof unhealthy vapour hung,
And famine, by her children always known,
As proud as poor, here fixed her native throne.

  Here, for the sullen sky was overcast,
And summer shrunk beneath a wintry blast,
A native blast, which, armed with hail and rain,
Beat unrelenting on the naked swain,
The boys for shelter made; behind, the sheep,
Of which those shepherds every day take keep,
Sickly crept on, and, with complainings rude,
On nature seemed to call, and bleat for food.

white rose] Jacobites wore the white rose on 10 June, the birthday of
the Young Pretender

100   from *The Author*

(i)

WHEN with much pains this boasted learning's got,
'Tis an affront to those who have it not.
In some it causes hate, in others fear,
Instructs our foes to rail, our friends to sneer.
With prudent haste the worldly-minded fool,
Forgets the little which he learned at school;
The elder brother, to vast fortunes born,
Looks on all science with an eye of scorn;
Dependent breth'ren the same features wear,
And younger sons are stupid as the heir.
In senates, at the bar, in church and state,
Genius is vile, and learning out of date.
Is this—O death to think! is this the land
Where merit and reward went hand in hand,
Where heroes, parent-like, the poet viewed?—
By whom they saw their glorious deeds renewed;
Where poets, true to honour, tuned their lays,
And by their patrons sanctified their praise?
Is this the land, where, on our Spencer's tongue,
Enamoured of his voice, Description hung;
Where Johnson rigid gravity beguiled,
Whilst Reason through her critic fences smiled;
Where Nature list'ning stood, whilst Shakespeare played,
And wondered at the work herself had made?
Is this the land, where, mindful of her charge
And office high, fair Freedom walked at large;
Where, finding in our laws a sure defence,
She mocked at all restraints, but those of sense;
Where, health and honour trooping by her side,
She spread her sacred empire far and wide;
Pointed the way, affliction to beguile,
And bade the face of sorrow wear a smile,
Bade those, who dare obey the gen'rous call,
Enjoy her blessings, which God meant for all?
Is this the land, where, in some tyrant's reign,
When a weak, wicked ministerial train,
The tools of pow'r, the slaves of int'rest, planned
Their country's ruin, and with bribes unmanned
Those wretches, who, ordained in freedom's cause,

Gave up our liberties, and sold our laws;
When pow'r was taught by meanness where to go,
Nor dared to love the virtue of a foe;
When, like a lep'rous plague, from the foul head
To the foul heart her sores Corruption spread,
Her iron arm when stern Oppression reared,
And Virtue, from her broad base shaken, feared
The scourge of Vice; when, impotent and vain,
Poor Freedom bowed the neck to slav'ry's chain;
Is this the land, where, in those worst of times,
The hardy poet raised his honest rhymes
To dread rebuke, and bade controlment speak
In guilty blushes on the villain's cheek,
Bade pow'r turn pale, kept mighty rogues in awe,
And made them fear the Muse, who feared not law?

(ii)
    Gods! with what pride I see the titled slave,
Who smarts beneath the stroke which Satire gave,
Aiming at ease, and with dishonest art
Striving to hide the feelings of his heart!
How do I laugh, when, with affected air,
(Scarce able through despite to keep his chair,
Whilst on his trembling lip pale anger speaks,
And the chafed blood flies mounting to his cheeks)
He talks of conscience, which good men secures
From all those evil moments guilt endures,
And seems to laugh at those, who pay regard
To the wild ravings of a frantic bard.
'Satire, whilst envy and ill-humour sway
The mind of man, must always make her way,
Nor to a bosom, with discretion fraught,
Is all her malice worth a single thought.
The wise have not the will, nor fools the pow'r
To stop her headstrong course; within the hour,
Left to herself, she dies; opposing strife
Gives her fresh vigour, and prolongs her life.
All things her prey, and ev'ry man her aim,
I can no patent for exemption claim,
Nor would I wish to stop that harmless dart
Which plays around, but cannot wound my heart:
Though pointed at myself, be Satire free;
To her 'tis pleasure, and no pain to me.'

Dissembling wretch! hence to the Stoic school,
And there amongst thy breth'ren play the fool,
There, unrebuked, these wild, vain doctrines preach;
Lives there a man, whom Satire cannot reach?
Lives there a man, who calmly can stand by,
And see his conscience ripped with steady eye?
When Satire flies abroad on falsehood's wing,
Short is her life indeed, and dull her sting;
But when to truth allied, the wound she gives
Sinks deep, and to remotest ages lives.
When in the tomb thy pampered flesh shall rot,
And e'en by friends thy mem'ry be forgot,
Still shalt thou live, recorded for thy crimes,
Live in her page, and stink to after-times.

101   from *The Ghost*

Pomposo [Dr Johnson]

POMPOSO (insolent and loud,
Vain idol of a scribbling crowd,
Whose very name inspires an awe,
Whose ev'ry word is sense and law,
For what his greatness hath decreed,
Like laws of Persia and of Mede,
Sacred through all the realm of wit,
Must never of repeal admit;
Who, cursing flatt'ry, is the tool
Of ev'ry fawning flatt'ring fool;
Who wit with jealous eye surveys,
And sickens at another's praise;
Who, proudly seized of learning's throne,
Now damns all learning but his own;
Who scorns those common wares to trade in,
Reas'ning, Convincing, and Persuading,
But makes each sentence current pass
With Puppy, Coxcomb, Scoundrel, Ass;
For 'tis with *him* a certain rule,
The folly's proved, when he calls fool;

Who, to increase his native strength,
Draws words, six syllables in length,
With which, assisted with a frown
By way of club, he knocks us down;
Who 'bove the vulgar dares to rise,
And sense of decency defies,
For this same decency is made
Only for bunglers in the trade;
And, like the cobweb laws, is still
Broke through by great ones when they will)—
Pomposo, with strong sense supplied,
Supported, and confirmed by pride,
His comrades' terrors to beguile,
Grinned horribly a ghastly smile:
Features so horrid, were it light,
Would put the Devil himself to flight.

102   from *Night. An Epistle to Robert Lloyd*

SPECTATORS only on this bustling stage,
We see what vain designs mankind engage.
Vice after vice with ardour they pursue,
And one old folly brings forth twenty new.
Perplexed with trifles through the vale of life,
Man strives 'gainst man, without a cause for strife;
Armies embattled meet, and thousands bleed,
For some vile spot which cannot fifty feed.
Squirrels for nuts contend, and, wrong or right,
For the world's empire kings ambitious fight.
What odds?—*to us* 'tis all the self-same thing,
A nut, a world, a squirrel, and a king.

101   grinned, etc.] Death 'grinnd horrible a gastly smile', in Milton's *Paradise Lost*,
2.846

103   from *The Times*

An Heir

Is a son born into this world of woe?
In never ceasing streams let sorrow flow,
Be from that hour the house with sables hung,
Let lamentations dwell upon thy tongue,
E'en from the moment that he first began
To wail and whine, let him not see a man.
Lock, lock him up, far from the public eye,
Give him no opportunity to buy,
Or to be bought; B——, though rich, was sold,
And gave his body up to shame for gold.

    Let it be bruited all about the town,
That he is coarse, indelicate, and brown,
An antidote to lust, his face deep scarred
With the smallpox, his body maimed and marred,
Eat up with the king's evil, and his blood,
Tainted throughout, a thick and putrid flood,
Where dwells corruption, making him all o'er,
From head to foot, a rank and running sore.
Should'st thou report him as by nature made,
He is undone, and by thy praise betrayed;
Give him out fair, lechers in number more,
More brutal and more fierce, than thronged the door
Of Lot in Sodom, shall to thine repair,
And force a passage, though a God is there.

    Let him not have one servant that is male;
Where lords are baffled, servants oft prevail.
Some vices they propose, to all agree;
H—— was guilty, but was M—— free?

    Give him no tutor—throw him to a punk,
Rather than trust his morals to a monk—
Monks we all know—we, who have lived at home,
From fair report, and travellers, who roam,
More feelingly—nor trust him to the gown,
'Tis oft a covering in this vile town
For base designs, ourselves have lived to see
More than one parson in the pillory.

Should he have brothers (image to thy view
A scene, which, though not public made, is true)
Let not one brother be to t'other known,
Nor let his father sit with him alone.

Be all his servants female, young, and fair,
And if the pride of nature spur thy heir
To deeds of venery, if, hot and wild,
He chance to get some score of maids with child,
Chide, but forgive him; whoredom is a crime,
Which, more at this, than any other time,
Calls for indulgence, and, 'mongst such a race,
To have a bastard is some sign of grace.

104   from *The Duellist*

On William Warburton, Bishop of Gloucester

THE first (entitled to the place
Of honour both by gown and grace)
Who never let occasion slip
To take right hand of fellowship,
And was so proud, that should he meet
The Twelve Apostles in the street,
He'd turn his nose up at them all,
And shove his Saviour from the wall;
Who was so mean (meanness and pride
Still go together side by side)
That he would cringe, and creep, be civil,
And hold a stirrup for the Devil,
If in a journey to his mind,
He'd let him mount, and ride behind;
Who basely fawned through all his life,
For patrons first, then for a wife,
Wrote dedications which must make
The heart of ev'ry Christian quake,
Made one man equal to, or more
Than God, then left him as before
His God he left, and drawn by pride,
Shifted about to t'other side)

104   one man] William Pitt

Was by his sire a parson made,
Merely to give the boy a trade,
But he himself was thereto drawn
By some faint omens of the Lawn,
And on the truly Christian plan
To make himself a gentleman,
A title, in which form arrayed him,
Though Fate ne'er thought on't when she made him.

The Oaths he took, 'tis very true,
But took them, as all wise men do,
With an intent, if things should turn,
Rather to temporize, than burn.
Gospel and loyalty were made
To serve the purposes of trade,
Relgion's are but paper ties,
Which bind the fool, but which the wise,
Such idle notions far above,
Draw on and off, just like a glove;
All gods, all kings (let his great aim
Be answered) were to him the same.

A curate first, he read and read,
And laid in, whilst he should have fed
The souls of his neglected flock,
Of reading such a mighty stock,
That he o'ercharged the weary brain
With more than she could well contain,
More than she was with spirits fraught
To turn, and methodize to thought,
And which, like ill-digested food,
To humours turned, and not to blood.
Brought up to London, from the plow
And pulpit, how to make a bow
He tried to learn, he grew polite,
And was the poets' parasite.
With wits conversing (and wits then
Were to be found 'mongst noblemen)
He caught, or would have caught the flame,
And would be nothing, or the same;
He drank with drunkards, lived with sinners,
Herded with infidels for dinners,
With such an emphasis and grace

Blasphemed, that Potter kept not pace;
He, in the highest reign of noon,
Bawled bawdry songs to a psalm tune,
Lived with men infamous and vile,
Trucked his salvation for a smile,
To catch their humour caught their plan,
And laughed at God to laugh with Man,
Praised them, when living, in each breath,
And damned their mem'ries after death.

To prove his faith, which all admit
Is at least equal to his wit,
And make himself a man of note,
He in defence of Scripture wrote;
So long he wrote, and long about it,
That e'en believers 'gan to doubt it,
He wrote too of the inward light,
Though no one knew how he came by't,
And of that influencing grace,
Which in his life ne'er found a place;
He wrote too of the Holy Ghost,
Of whom, no more than of a post
He knew, nor, should an angel show him,
Would he or know, or choose to know him.

Next (for he knew 'twixt ev'ry science
There was a natural alliance)
He wrote, t'advance his Maker's praise,
Comments on rhymes, and notes on plays,
And with an all-sufficient air
Placed himself in the critic's chair,
Usurped o'er reason full dominion,
And governed merely by opinion.
At length dethroned, and kept in awe
By one plain simple man of law,
He armed dead friends, to vengeance true,
T'abuse the man they never knew.

Potter] Thomas Potter, dissolute wit and politician, a friend of Warburton's
Comments on rhymes, and notes on plays] Warburton edited Pope and misedited
Shakespeare
one plain, simple man of law] when the barrister Thomas Edwards exposed Warburton's
editing of Shakespeare, Warburton added to his edition of Pope's *Dunciad* an offensive
note attacking Edwards

Examine strictly all mankind,
Most characters are mixed we find,
And vice and virtue take their turn
In the same breast to beat and burn.
Our priest was an exception here,
Nor did one spark of grace appear,
Not one dull, dim spark in his soul;
Vice, glorious vice possessed the whole,
And, in her service truly warm,
He was in sin most uniform.

Injurious Satire, own at least
One snivelling virtue in the Priest,
One snivelling virtue which is placed,
They say, in or about the waist,
Called Chastity; the prudish dame
Knows it at large by virtue's name.
To this his wife (and in these days
Wives seldom without reason praise)
Bears evidence—then calls her child,
And swears that Tom was vastly wild.

Ripened by a long course of years,
He great and perfect now appears.
In shape scarce of the human kind;
A man, without a manly mind;
No husband, though he's truly wed;
Though on his knees a child is bred,
No father; injured, without end
A foe; and, though obliged, no friend;
A heart, which virtue ne'er disgraced;
A head, where learning runs to waste;
A gentleman well-bred, if breeding
Rests in the article of reading;
A man of this world, for the next
Was ne'er included in his text;
A judge of genius, though confest
With not one spark of genius blest;
Amongst the first of critics placed,
Though free from every taint of taste;

No father] the paternity of Warburton's son was ascribed to Thomas Potter

A Christian without faith or works,
As he would be a Turk 'mongst Turks;
A great divine, as lords agree,
Without the least divinity;
To crown all, in declining age,
Inflamed with church and party rage,
Behold him, full and perfect quite,
A false saint, and true hypocrite.

105   *The Dedication*

HEALTH to great Gloucester—from a man unknown,
Who holds thy health as dearly as his own,
Accept this greeting—nor let modest fear
Call up one maiden blush—I mean not here
To wound with flatt'ry—'tis a villain's art,
And suits not with the frankness of my heart.
Truth best becomes an Orthodox divine,
And, spite of hell, that character is mine;
To speak e'en bitter truths I cannot fear;
But truth, my Lord, is panegyric here.

Health to great Gloucester—nor, through love of ease,
Which all priests love, let this address displease.
I ask no favour, not one note I crave,
And, when this busy brain rests in the grave,
(For till that time it never can have rest)
I will not trouble you with one bequest.
Some humbler friend, my mortal journey done,
More near in blood, a nephew or a son,
In that dread hour executor I'll leave;
For I, alas! have many to receive,
To give but little—to great Gloucester health;
Nor let thy true and proper love of wealth
Here take a false alarm—in purse though poor,
In spirit I'm right proud, nor can endure
The mention of a bribe—thy pocket's free,
I, though a dedicator, scorn a fee.
Let thy own offspring all thy fortunes share;
I would not Allen rob, nor Allen's heir.

Gloucester] Churchill's posthumous *Sermons* were, ironically, dedicated to William
Warburton, Bishop of Gloucester.
Allen] Ralph Allen—Pope's friend, of Prior Park, Bath. Warburton married his niece

Think not, a thought unworthy thy great soul,
Which pomps of this world never could control,
Which never offered up at power's vain shrine,
Think not that pomp and power can work on mine.
'Tis not thy name, though that indeed is great,
'Tis not the tinsel trumpery of state,
'Tis not thy title, doctor though thou art,
'Tis not thy mitre, which hath won my heart.
State is a farce, names are but empty things,
Degrees are bought, and, by mistaken kings,
Titles are oft misplaced; mitres, which shine
So bright in other eyes, are dull in mine,
Unless set off by virtue; who deceives
Under the sacred sanction of lawn sleeves;
Enhances guilt, commits a double sin;
So fair without, and yet so foul within.
'Tis not thy outward form, thy easy mien,
Thy sweet complacency, thy brow serene,
Thy open front, thy love-commanding eye,
Where fifty Cupids, as in ambush, lie,
Which can from sixty to sixteen impart
The force of love, and point his blunted dart;
'Tis not thy face, though that by nature's made
An index to thy soul, though there displayed
We see thy mind at large, and through thy skin
Peeps out that courtesy which dwells within;
'Tis not thy birth—for that is low as mine,
Around our heads no lineal glories shine—
But what is birth, when, to delight mankind,
Heralds can make those arms they cannot find;
When thou art to thyself, thy sire unknown,
A whole, Welsh genealogy alone?
No, 'tis thy inward man, thy proper worth,
Thy right just estimation here on earth,
Thy life and doctrine uniformly joined,
And flowing from that wholesome source thy mind,
Thy known contempt of persecution's rod,
Thy charity for man, thy love of God,
Thy faith in Christ, so well approved 'mongst men,
Which now give life, and utterance to my pen.
Thy virtue, not thy rank, demands my lays;
'Tis not the bishop, but the saint I praise.

Raised by that theme, I soar on wings more strong,
And burst forth into praise withheld too long.

   Much did I wish, e'en whilst I kept those sheep,
Which, for my curse, I was ordained to keep;
Ordained, alas! to keep through need, not choice,
Those sheep which never heard their shepherd's voice,
Which accents of rebuke could never bear,
Nor would have heeded Christ, had Christ been there;
Those sheep, which my good father (on his bier
Let filial duty drop the pious tear)
Kept well, yet starved himself, e'en at that time,
Whilst I was pure, and innocent of rhyme,
Whilst, sacred dullness ever in my view,
Sleep at my bidding crept from pew to pew,
Much did I wish, though little could I hope,
A friend in him, who was the friend of Pope.

   His hand, said I, my youthful steps shall guide,
And lead me safe where thousands fall beside;
His temper, his experience shall control,
And hush to peace the tempest of my soul;
His judgment teach me, from the critic school,
How not to err, and how to err by rule;
Instruct me, mingling profit with delight,
Where Pope was wrong, where Shakespeare was not right;
Where they are justly praised, and where through whim,
How little's due to them, how much to him.
Raised 'bove the slavery of common rules,
Of commonsense, of modern, ancient schools,
Those feelings banished, which mislead us all,
Fools as we are, and which we nature call,
He, by his great example, might impart
A better something, and baptize it art;
He, all the feelings of my youth forgot,
Might show me what is taste, by what is not;
By him supported, with a proper pride,
I might hold all mankind as fools beside;
He (should a world, perverse and peevish grown,
Explode his maxims, and assert their own)
Might teach me, like himself, to be content,
And let their folly be their punishment;

Might, like himself, teach his adopted son,
'Gainst all the world, to quote a Warburton.

    Fool that I was, could I so much deceive
My soul with lying hopes; could I believe
That he, the servant of his maker sworn,
The servant of his Saviour, would be torn
From their embrace, and leave that dear employ,
The cure of souls, his duty and his joy,
For toys like mine, and waste his precious time,
On which so much depended, for a rhyme?
Should he forsake the task he undertook,
Desert his flock, and break his past'ral crook?
Should he (forbid it Heav'n) so high in place,
So rich in knowledge, quit the work of grace,
And, idly wand'ring o'er the Muses' hill,
Let the salvation of mankind stand still?

    Far, far be that from thee—yes, far from thee
Be such revolt from grace, and far from me
The will to think it—guilt is in the thought.
Not so, not so, hath Warburton been taught,
Not so learned Christ—recall that day, well-known,
When (to maintain God's honour—and his own)
He called blasphemers forth. Methinks I now
See stern rebuke enthroned on his brow,
And armed with tenfold terrors—from his tongue,
Where fiery zeal, and Christian fury hung,
Methinks I hear the deep-toned thunders roll,
And chill with horror every sinner's soul.
In vain they strive to fly—flight cannot save,
And Potter trembles even in his grave.
With all the conscious pride of innocence,
Methinks I hear him, in his own defence,
Bear witness to himself, whilst all men knew,
By gospel rules, his witness to be true.

Potter] Thomas Potter, said to have been intimate with Bishop Warburton's wife.

O glorious man, thy zeal I must commend,
Though it deprived me of my dearest friend.
The real motives of thy anger known,
Wilkes must the justice of that anger own;
And, could thy bosom have been bared to view,
Pitied himself, in turn had pitied you.

Bred to the law, you wisely took the gown,
Which I, like Demas, foolishly laid down.
Hence double strength our Holy Mother drew;
Me she got rid of, and made prize of you.
I, like an idle truant, fond of play,
Doting on toys, and throwing gems away,
Grasping at shadows, let the substance slip;
But you, my Lord, renounced attorneyship
With better purpose, and more noble aim,
And wisely played a more substantial game.
Nor did Law mourn, blessed in her younger son,
For Mansfield does what Gloucester would have done.

Doctor, Dean, Bishop, Gloucester, and *My Lord*,
If haply these high titles may accord
With thy meek spirit, if the barren sound
Of pride delights thee, to the topmost round
Of fortune's ladder got, despise not one,
For want of smooth hypocrisy undone,
Who, far below, turns up his wond'ring eye,
And, without envy, sees thee placed so high,
Let not thy brain (as brains less potent might)
Dizzy, confounded, giddy with the height,
Turn round, and lose distinction, lose her skill
And wonted pow'rs of knowing good from ill,
Of sifting truth from falsehood, friends from foes;
Let Gloucester well remember, how he rose,
Nor turn his back on men who made him great;
Let him not, gorged with pow'r, and drunk with state,
Forget what once he was, though now so high;
How low, how mean, and full as poor as I.

Cetera desunt.

Demas] Paul's Second Epistle to Timothy 4.10—'For Demas hath forsaken me.'
Mansfield] Lord Mansfield, Lord Chief Justice and one of Warburton's patrons.

ROBERT LLOYD
1733–1764

106   from *A Familiar Epistle to J.B. Esq*

MARK yon round parson, fat and sleek,
Who preaches only once a week,
Whom claret, sloth, and ven'son join
To make an orthodox divine;
Whose holiness receives its beauty
From income large, and little duty;
Who loves the pipe, the glass, the smock,
And keeps—a curate for his flock.
The world obsequious to his nod
Shall hail this oily man of God,
While the poor priest, with half a score
Of prattling infants at his door,
Whose sober wishes ne'er regale
Beyond the homely jug of ale,
Is hardly deemed companion fit
For men of wealth, or men of wit,
Though learn'd perhaps and wise as he
Who signs with staring S.T.P.
And full of sacerdotal pride
Lays God and duty both aside.

'This curate, say you, learn'd and wise!
Why does not then this curate rise?'

This curate then, at forty-three,
(Years which become a curacy)
At no great mart of letters bred,
Had strange odd notions in his head,
That parts, and books, and application
Furnished all means of education;
And that a pulpiteer should know
More than his gaping flock below;
That learning was not got with pain
To be forgotten all again;

S.T.P.] Sanctac Theologiae Professor—Doctor of Divinity

That Latin words, and rumbling Greek,
However charming sounds to speak,
Apt or unapt in each quotation,
Were insults on a congregation,
Who could not understand one word
Of all the learned stuff they heard;
That something more than preaching fine
Should go to make a sound divine;
That church and pray'r, and holy Sunday
Were no excuse for sinful Monday;
That pious doctrine, pious life,
Should make both one, as man and wife.

    Thinking in this uncommon mode,
So out of all the priestly road,
What man alive can e'er suppose,
Who marks the way Preferment goes,
That she should ever find her way
To this poor curate's house of clay?

    Such was the priest, so strangely wise!
He could not bow—how should he rise?
Learned he was, and deeply read,
But what of that?—not duly bred.
For he had sucked no grammar rules
From royal founts, or public schools,
Nor gained a single corn of knowledge
From that vast granary—a college.
A granary, which food supplies
To vermin of uncommon size.

    Aye, now indeed the matter's clear,
There is a mighty error here.
A public school's the place alone,
Where talents may be duly known.
It has, no doubt, its imperfections,
But then, such friendships! such connections!
The parent, who has formed his plan,
And in his child considered man,
What is his grand and golden rule,
'Make your connections, child, at school,
Mix with your equals, fly inferiors,
But follow closely your superiors,

On them your ev'ry hope depends,
Be prudent, Tom, get useful friends;
And therefore like a spider wait,
And spin your web about the great.
If my Lord's genius wants supplies,
Why—you must make his exercise.
Let the young marquis take your place,
And bear a whipping for his Grace.
Suppose (such things may happen once)
The nobles wits, and you the dunce,
Improve the means of education,
And learn commodious adulation.
Your master scarcely holds it sin,
He chucks his Lordship on the chin,
And would not for the world rebuke,
Beyond a pat, the schoolboy duke.
The pastor there, of—what's the place?—
With smiles eternal in his face,
With dimpling cheek, and snowy hand,
That shames the whiteness of his band,
Whose mincing dialect abounds
In hums and hahs, and half-formed sounds;
Whose elocution, fine and chaste,
Lays his *commainds* with judgment *vaist*,
And lest the company should hear,
Whispers his nothings in your ear—
Think you 'twas zeal, or virtue's care
That placed the smirking Doctor there?
No—'twas connections formed at school
With some rich wit, or noble fool,
Obsequious flattery, and attendance,
A wilful, useful, base dependence;
A supple bowing of the knees
To any human God you please.
(For true good breeding's so polite,
'Twould call the very Devil white).'

EVAN LLOYD
1734–1776

107

from *The Methodist*

THE Sons of War sometimes are known
To fight with weapons not their own,
Ceasing the sword of steel to wield,
They take religion's sword and shield.

Every Mechanic will commence
Orator, without mood or tense.
Pudding is pudding still, they know,
Whether it has a plum or no;
So, though the preacher has no skill,
A sermon is a sermon still.

The Bricklayer throws his trowel by,
And now builds mansions in the sky;
The Cobbler, touched with holy pride,
Flings his old shoes and last aside,
And now devoutly sets about
Cobbling of souls that ne'er wear out;
The Baker, now a poacher grown,
Finds man lives not by bread alone,
And now his customers he feeds
With pray'rs, with sermons, groans and creeds;
The Tinman, mov'd by warmth within,
Hammers the Gospel, just like tin;
Weavers inspir'd their shuttles leave,
Sermons, and flimsy hymns to weave;
Barbers unreaped will leave the chin,
To trim, and shave the man within;
The Waterman forgets his wherry,
And opens a celestial ferry;
The Brewer, bit by frenzy's grub,
The mashing for the preaching tub
Resigns, those waters to explore,
Which if you drink, you thirst no more;
The Gard'ner, weary of his trade,
Tired of the mattock, and the spade,

227

Changed to apostle in a trice,
Waters the plants of paradise;
The Fishermen no longer set
For fish the meshes of their net,
But catch, like Peter, men of sin,
For catching is to take them in.

JOHN WOLCOT ('PETER PINDAR')
1738–1819

108   *The Apple Dumplings and a King*

ONCE on a time, a Monarch, tired with whooping,
    Whipping and spurring,
    Happy in worrying
A poor, defenceless, harmless buck
(The horse and rider wet as muck),
From his high confidence and wisdom stooping,
    Entered, through curiosity, a cot
Where sat a poor Old Woman and her pot.

The wrinkled, blear-eyed, good old granny,
In this same cot, illumed by many a cranny,
    Had finished apple dumplings for her pot.
In tempting row the naked dumplings lay,
When, lo! the Monarch, in his usual way,
Like lightning spoke: 'What's this? what's this? what? what?'

Then, taking up a dumpling in his hand,
His eyes with admiration did expand,
    And oft did Majesty the dumpling grapple:
''Tis monstrous, monstrous hard indeed,' he cried:
'What makes it, pray, so hard?'—The dame replied,
    Low curtseying, 'Please your Majesty, the apple.'—

'Very astonishing indeed! strange thing!'
(Turning the dumpling round, rejoined the King),
    ''Tis most extraordinary then, all this is;
    It beats Pinetti's conjuring all to pieces:
Strange I should never of a dumpling dream!
But, Goody, tell me where, where, where's the seam?'

'Sir, there's no seam,' quoth she, 'I never knew
That folks did apple dumplings sew.'—
'No!' cried the staring Monarch with a grin:
'How, how the devil got the apple in?'

On which the dame the curious scheme revealed
By which the apple lay so sly concealed;
　　Which made the Solomon of Britain start;

Who to the Palace with full speed repaired,
And Queens and Princesses so beauteous scared,
　　All with the wonders of the dumpling art.
There did he labour one whole week, to show
　　The wisdom of an apple dumpling maker;
And, lo! so deep was Majesty in dough,
　　The Palace seemed the lodging of a baker.

GEORGE CRABBE
1754–1832

109　　　　　　from *The Borough*
The Vicar

WHERE ends our chancel in a vaulted space,
Sleep the departed vicars of the place;
Of most, all mention, memory, thought are past—
But take a slight memorial of the last.
　　To what famed college we our Vicar owe,
To what fair county, let historians show.
Few now remember when the mild young man,
Ruddy and fair, his Sunday-task began;
Few live to speak of that soft soothing look
He cast around, as he prepared his book;
It was a kind of supplicating smile,
But nothing hopeless of applause, the while;
And when he finished, his corrected pride
Felt the desert, and yet the praise denied.
Thus he his race began, and to the end
His constant care was, no man to offend;

No haughty virtues stirred his peaceful mind,
Nor urged the priest to leave the flock behind;
He was his Master's soldier, but not one
To lead an army of his martyrs on:
Fear was his ruling passion; yet was love,
Of timid kind, once known his heart to move;
It led his patient spirit where it paid
Its languid offerings to a listening maid;
She, with her widowed mother, heard him speak,
And sought awhile to find what he would seek.
Smiling he came, he smiled when he withdrew,
And paid the same attention to the two;
Meeting and parting without joy or pain,
He seemed to come that he might go again.
The wondering girl, no prude, but something nice,
At length was chilled by his unmelting ice;
She found her tortoise held such sluggish pace,
That she must turn and meet him in the chase.
This not approving, she withdrew till one
Came who appeared with livelier hope to run;
Who sought a readier way the heart to move,
Than by faint dalliance of unfixing love.
  Accuse me not that I approving paint
Impatient hope or love without restraint;
Or think the passions, a tumultuous throng,
Strong as they are, ungovernably strong;
But is the laurel to the soldier due,
Who cautious comes not into danger's view?
What worth has virtue by desire untried,
When Nature's self enlists on duty's side?
  The married dame in vain assailed the truth
And guarded bosom of the Hebrew youth;
But with the daughter of the Priest of On
The love was lawful, and the guard was gone;
But Joseph's fame had lessened in our view,
Had he, refusing, fled the maiden too.
  Yet our good priest to Joseph's praise aspired,
As once rejecting what his heart desired;
'I am escaped,' he said, when none pursued;
When none attacked him, 'I am unsubdued';

'Oh pleasing pangs of love,' he sang again,
Cold to the joy, and stranger to the pain.
Ev'n in his age would he address the young,
'I too have felt these fires, and they are strong';
But from the time he left his favourite maid,
To ancient females his devoirs were paid;
And still they miss him after morning prayer;
Nor yet successor fills the Vicar's chair,
Where kindred spirits in his praise agree,
A happy few, as mild and cool as he—
The easy followers in the female train,
Led without love, and captives without chain.
    Ye lilies male! think (as your tea you sip,
While the town small-talk flows from lip to lip;
Intrigues half-gathered, conversation-scraps,
Kitchen-cabals, and nursery-mishaps)
If the vast world may not some scene produce,
Some state, where your small talents might have use.
Within seraglios you might harmless move,
'Mid ranks of beauty, and in haunts of love;
There from too daring man the treasures guard,
An easy duty, and its own reward;
Nature's soft substitutes, you there might save
From crime the tyrant, and from wrong the slave.
    But let applause be dealt in all we may:
Our priest was cheerful, and in season gay;
His frequent visits seldom failed to please;
Easy himself, he sought his neighbour's ease.
To a small garden with delight he came,
And gave successive flowers a summer's fame;
These he presented with a grace his own
To his fair friends, and made their beauties known,
Not without moral compliment: how they
'Like flowers were sweet, and must like flowers decay'.
    Simple he was, and loved the simple truth,
Yet had some useful cunning from his youth;
A cunning never to dishonour lent,
And rather for defence than conquest meant;
'Twas fear of power, with some desire to rise,
But not enough to make him enemies;

He ever aimed to please; and to offend
Was ever cautious; for he sought a friend;
Yet for the friendship never much would pay,
Content to bow, be silent, and obey,
And by a soothing suff'rance find his way.
  Fiddling and fishing were his arts; at times
He altered sermons, and he aimed at rhymes;
And his fair friends, not yet intent on cards,
Oft he amused with riddles and charades.
  Mild were his doctrines, and not one discourse
But gained in softness what it lost in force:
Kind his opinions; he would not receive
An ill report, nor evil act believe;
'If true, 'twas wrong; but blemish great or small
Have all mankind; yea, sinners are we all.'
  If ever fretful thought disturbed his breast,
If aught of gloom that cheerful mind oppressed,
It sprang from innovation; it was then
He spake of mischief made by restless men,
Not by new doctrines: never in his life
Would he attend to controversial strife;
For sects he cared not; 'They are not of us,
Nor need we, brethren, their concerns discuss;
But 'tis the change, the schism at home I feel;
Ills few perceive, and none have skill to heal:
Not at the altar our young brethren read
(Facing their flock) the decalogue and creed;
But at their duty, in their desks they stand,
With naked surplice, lacking hood and band:
Churches are now of holy song bereft,
And half our ancient customs changed or left;
Few sprigs of ivy are at Christmas seen,
Nor crimson berry tips the holly's green;
Mistaken choirs refuse the solemn strain
Of ancient Sternhold, which from ours amain
Comes flying forth, from aisle to aisle about,
Sweet links of harmony and long drawn out.'
  These were to him essentials; all things new
He deemed superfluous, useless, or untrue;
To all beside indifferent, easy, cold,
Here the fire kindled, and the woe was told.

Habit with him was all the test of truth,
'It must be right: I've done it from my youth.'
Questions he answered in as brief a way,
'It must be wrong—it was of yesterday.'
    Though mild benevolence our priest possessed,
'Twas but by wishes or by words expressed:
Circles in water, as they wider flow,
The less conspicuous in their progress grow;
And when at last they touch upon the shore,
Distinction ceases, and they're viewed no more.
His love, like that last circle, all embraced,
But with effect that never could be traced.
    Now rests our Vicar. They who knew him best
Proclaim his life t' have been entirely rest—
Free from all evils which disturb his mind
Whom studies vex and controversies blind.
    The rich approved—of them in awe he stood;
The poor admired—they all believed him good;
The old and serious of his habits spoke;
The frank and youthful loved his pleasant joke;
Mothers approved a safe contented guest,
And daughters one who backed each small request:
In him his flock found nothing to condemn;
Him sectaries liked—he never troubled them;
No trifles failed his yielding mind to please,
And all his passions sunk in early ease;
Nor one so old has left this world of sin,
More like the being that he entered in.

ANONYMOUS

110   *To the Marquis of Graham on his Marriage*

WITH joy Britannia sees her fav'rite goose
Fast bound and pinioned in the nuptial noose;
Presaging fondly from so fair a mate
A brood of goslings, cackling in debate.

WILLIAM BLAKE
1757–1827

III   *Orator Prigg*

I ASKED my dear friend, Orator Prigg,
'What's the first part of oratory?' He said 'A great wig.'
'And what is the second?' Then dancing a jig
And bowing profoundly he said, 'A great wig.'
'And what is the third?' Then he snored like a pig.
And puffing his cheeks he replied 'A great wig.'

112   *The Little Vagabond*

DEAR mother, dear mother, the church is cold,
But the alehouse is healthy and pleasant and warm;
Besides I can tell where I am used well,
Such usage in heaven will never do well.

But if at the church they would give us some ale,
And a pleasant fire our souls to regale,
We'd sing and we'd pray all the livelong day,
Nor ever once wish from the church to stray.

Then the parson might preach, and drink, and sing,
And we'd be as happy as birds in the spring;
And modest Dame Lurch, who is always at church,
Would not have bandy children, nor fasting, nor birch.

And God, like a father rejoicing to see
His children as pleasant and happy as he,
Would have no more quarrel with the Devil or the barrel,
But kiss him, and give him both drink and apparel.

ROBERT BURNS
1759–1796

Holy Willie's Prayer—

And send the Godly in a pet to pray—
                                        POPE.

Argument.

Holy Willie was a rather oldish bachelor elder in the parish of
Mauchline, and much and justly famed for that polemical chattering
which ends in tippling orthodoxy, and for that spiritualized bawdry
which refines to liquorish devotion. In a sessional process with a gentleman in Mauchline, a Mr Gavin Hamilton, Holy Willie, and his priest,
father Auld, after full hearing in the Presbytery of Ayr, came off but
second best; owing partly to the oratorical powers of Mr Robt. Aiken,
Mr Hamilton's counsel; but chiefly to Mr Hamilton's being one of the
most irreproachable and truly respectable characters in the country.
On losing his process, the Muse overheard him at his devotions as
follows—

O THOU that in the heavens does dwell!
Wha, as it pleases best thysel,
Sends ane to heaven and ten to hell,
            A' for thy glory!
And no for ony gude or ill
            They've done before thee.—

I bless and praise thy matchless might,
When thousands thou has left in night,
That I am here before thy sight,
            For gifts and grace,
A burning and a shining light
            To a' this place.—

What was I, or my generation,
That I should get such exaltation?
I, wha deserved most just damnation,
            For broken laws
Sax thousand years ere my creation,
            Thro' Adam's cause!

235

When from my mother's womb I fell,
Thou might hae plunged me deep in hell,
To gnash my gooms, and weep, and wail,
   In burning lakes,
Where damned devils roar and yell
   Chained to their stakes.—

Yet I am here, a chosen sample,
To shew thy grace is great and ample:
I'm here, a pillar o' thy temple
   Strong as a rock,
A guide, a ruler and example
   To a' thy flock.—

O Lord thou kens what zeal I bear,
When drinkers drink, and swearers swear,
And singin' there, and dancin' here,
   Wi' great an' sma';
For I am keepet by thy fear,
   Free frae them a'.—

But yet—O Lord—confess I must—
At times I'm fashed wi' fleshly lust;
And sometimes too, in warldly trust
   Vile Self gets in;
But thou remembers we are dust,
   Defiled wi' sin.—

O Lord—yestreen—thou kens—wi' Meg—
Thy pardon I sincerely beg!
O may't ne'er be a living plague,
   To my dishonor!
And I'll ne'er lift a lawless leg
   Again upon her.—

Fashed] vexed

Besides, I farther maun avow,
Wi' Leezie's lass, three times—I trow—
But Lord, that Friday I was fou
      When I cam near her;
Or else, thou kens, thy servant true
      Wad never steer her.—

Maybe thou lets this fleshy thorn
Buffet thy servant e'en and morn,
Lest he o'er proud and high should turn,
      That he's sae gifted;
If sae, thy hand maun e'en be borne
      Untill thou lift it.—

Lord bless thy Chosen in this place,
For here thou has a chosen race:
But God, confound their stubborn face,
      And blast their name,
Wha bring thy rulers to disgrace
      And open shame.—

Lord mind Gaun Hamilton's deserts!
He drinks, and swears, and plays at cartes,
Yet has sae mony taking arts
      Wi' Great and Sma',
Frae God's ain priest the people's hearts
      He steals awa.—

And when we chastened him therefore,
Thou kens how he bred sic a splore,
And set the warld in a roar
      O' laughin at us:
Curse thou his basket and his store,
      Kail and potatoes.—

Lord hear my earnest cry and prayer
Against that Presbytry of Ayr!
Thy strong right hand, Lord, make it bare
      Upon their heads!
Lord visit them, and dinna spare,
      For their misdeeds!

fou] full, i.e. drunk   steer] stir   splore] commotion

O Lord my God, that glib-tongued Aiken!
My very heart and flesh are quaking
To think how I sat, sweating, shaking,
   And pissed wi' dread,
While Auld wi' hingin lip gaed sneaking
   And hid his head!

Lord, in thy day o' vengeance try him!
Lord, visit him that did employ him!
And pass not in thy mercy by them,
   Nor hear their prayer;
But for thy people's sake destroy them,
   And dinna spare!

But Lord, remember me and mine
Wi' mercies temporal and divine!
That I for grace and gear may shine,
   Excelled by nane!
And a' the glory shall be thine!
   AMEN! AMEN!

114 from *A Dedication to G**** H******* Esq*

Sound Believing

MORALITY, thou deadly bane,
Thy tens of thousands thou hast slain!
Vain is his hope, whase stay an' trust is
In moral mercy, truth and justice!

 No—stretch a point to catch a plack;
Abuse a brother to his back;
Steal thro' the winnock frae a whore,
But point the rake that taks the door;
Be to the poor like onie whunstane,
And haud their noses to the grunstane;
Ply ev'ry art o' legal thieving;
No matter—stick to sound believing.

114 plack] farthing winnock] window whunstane] whinstone

Learn three-mile pray'rs, an' half-mile graces,
Wi' weel spread looves, an' lang, wry faces;
Grunt up a solemn, lengthened groan,
And damn a' parties but your own;
I'll warrant then, ye're nae deceiver,
A steady, sturdy, staunch believer.

115   *The Holy Fair**

A robe of seeming truth and trust
    Hid crafty Observation;
And secret hung, with poisoned crust,
    The dirk of Defamation:
A mask that like the gorget showed,
    Dye-varying, on the pigeon;
And for a mantle large and broad,
    He wrapt him in Religion.
                        Hypocrisy a-la-Mode.

UPON a simmer Sunday morn,
    When Nature's face is fair,
I walked forth to view the corn,
    An' snuff the callor air:
The rising sun, owre Galston muirs,
    Wi' glorious light was glintan;
The hares were hirplan down the furrs,
    The lav'rocks they were chantan
                Fu' sweet that day.

As lightsomely I glowred abroad,
    To see a scene sae gay,
Three hizzies, early at the road,
    Cam skelpan up the way.
Twa had manteeles o' dolefu' black,
    But ane wi' lyart lining;
The third, that gaed a wee aback,
    Was in the fashion shining
                Fu' gay that day.

looves] palms of the hand

115   * *Holy Fair*] a common phrase in the West of Scotland for a sacramental occasion
                callor] cool   hirplan] hobbling
            furrs] ploughlands   glowred] gazed
        hizzies] hussies, girls   skelpan] hurrying
                lyart] mottled

The twa appeared like sisters twin,
  In features, form an' claes;
Their visage—withered, lang an' thin,
  An' sour as onie slaes:
The third cam up, hap-step-an'-loup,
  As light as onie lambie,—
An' wi' a curchie low did stoop,
  As soon as e'er she saw me,
        Fu' kind that day.

Wi' bonnet aff, quoth I, 'Sweet lass,
  I think ye seem to ken me;
I'm sure I've seen that bonie face,
  But yet I canna name ye.—'
Quo' she, an' laughan as she spak,
  An' taks me by the hands,
'Ye, for my sake, hae gien the feck
  Of a' the ten commands
        A screed some day.

'My name is FUN—your cronie dear,
  The nearest friend ye hae;
An' this is SUPERSTITION here,
  An' that's HYPOCRISY:
I'm gaun to ********* holy fair,
  To spend an hour in daffin;
Gin ye'll go there, yon runkled pair,
  We will get famous laughin
        At them this day.'

Quoth I, 'With a' my heart, I'll do 't;
  I'll get my Sunday sark on,
An' meet you on the holy spot;
  Faith we'se hae fine remarkin!'
Then I gaed hame, at crowdie-time,
  An' soon I made me ready;
For roads were clad, frae side to side,
  Wi' monie a weary body,
        In droves that day.

the feck] the most   daffin] fun   runkled] wrinkled   sark] shirt
        crowdie-time] breakfast time, porridge time

240

Here, farmers gash, in ridin graith,
  Gaed hoddan by their cotters;
There, swankies young, in braw braid-claith,
  Are springan owre the gutters.
The lasses, skelpan barefit, thrang,
  In silks an' scarlets glitter;
Wi' sweet-milk cheese, in mony a whang,
  An' farls, baked wi' butter,
        Fu' crump that day.

When by the plate we set our nose,
  Weel heaped up wi' ha'pence,
A greedy glowr Black-bonnet throws,
  An' we maun draw our tippence.
Then in we go to see the show,
  On ev'ry side they're gath'ran;
Some carryan dails, some chairs an' stools,
  An' some are busy bleth'ran
        Right loud that day.

Here, stands a shed to fend the show'rs,
  An' screen our countra Gentry;
There, Racer-Jess, an' twathree whores,
  Are blinkan at the entry:
Here sits a raw o' tittlan jads,
  Wi' heaving breasts an' bare neck;
An' there, a batch o' wabster lads,
  Blackguarding frae K*******ck
        For fun this day.

Here, some are thinkan on their sins,
  An' some upo' their claes;
Ane curses feet that fyled his shins,
  Anither sighs an' prays:
On this hand sits a Chosen swatch,
  Wi' screwed-up, grace-proud faces;
On that, a set o' chaps, at watch,
  Thrang winkan on the lasses
        To chairs that day.

gash] chat   graith] gear   hoddan] jogging   skelpan] hurrying
whang] wedge   farls] oatcake quarters   crump] dry and crisp
glowr] stare   Black-bonnet] elder wearing the Covenanter's black bonnet
draw] pull out   dails] deals, planks   tittlan jads] whispering jades
wabster] weaver   fyled] soiled   swatch] sample

O happy is that man, an' blest!
  Nae wonder that it pride him!
Whase ain dear lass, that he likes best,
  Comes clinkan down beside him!
Wi' arm reposed on the chair back,
  He sweetly does compose him;
Which, by degrees, slips round her neck,
  An's loof upon her bosom
          Unkend that day.

Now a' the congregation o'er,
  Is silent expectation;
For Sawnie speels the holy door,
  Wi' tidings o' damnation:
Should Hornie, as in ancient days,
  'Mang sons o' God present him,
The vera sight o' Sawnie's face,
  To's ain het hame had sent him
          Wi' fright that day.

Hear how he clears the points o' Faith
  Wi' rattlin an' thumpin!
Now meekly calm, now wild in wrath,
  He's stampan, an' he's jumpan!
His lengthened chin, his turned up snout,
  His eldritch squeel an' gestures,
O how they fire the heart devout,
  Like cantharidian plaisters
          On sic a day!

But hark! the tent has changed its voice;
  There's peace an' rest nae langer;
For a' the real judges rise,
  They canna sit for anger.
Smith opens out his cauld harangues,
  On *practice* and on *morals*;
An' aff the godly pour in thrangs,
  To gie the jars an' barrels
          A lift that day.

loof] palm (of hand)   speels] climbs   het] hot
     tent] open air pulpit

What signifies his barren shine,
  Of *moral pow'rs* an' *reason*;
His English style, an' gesture fine,
  Are a' clean out o' season.
Like SOCRATES or ANTONINE,
  Or some auld pagan heathen,
The *moral man* he does define,
  But ne'er a word o' *faith* in
      That's right that day.

In guid time comes an antidote
  Against sic poosioned nostrum;
For Peebles, frae the water-fit,
  Ascends the holy rostrum:
See, up he's got the Word o' God,
  An' meek an' mim has viewed it,
While COMMON-SENSE has taen the road,
  An' aff, an' up the Cowgate
      Fast, fast that day.

Wee Miller niest, the guard relieves,
  An' Orthodoxy raibles,
Tho' in his heart he weel believes,
  An' thinks it auld wives' fables:
But faith! the birkie wants a manse,
  So, cannilie he hums them;
Altho' his carnal wit an' sense
  Like hafflins-wise o'ercomes him
      At times that day.

Now, butt an' ben, the change-house fills,
  Wi' yill-caup commentators:
Here's crying out for bakes an' gills,
  An' there, the pint-stowp clatters;
While thick an' thrang, an' loud an' lang,
  Wi' *Logic*, an' wi' *Scripture*,
They raise a din, that, in the end,
  Is like to breed a rupture
      O' wrath that day.

poosioned] poisoned   water-fit] waters-foot, mouth of a stream
mim] affectedly modest   raibles] gabbles   birkie] smart chap
hafflins-wise] half   butt an' ben] front and back   change-house] alehouse
yill-caup] ale bowl   bakes] biscuits   gills] gills of ale
pint-stowp] pint measure

Leeze me on Drink! it gies us mair
 Than either school or colledge:
It kindles wit, it waukens lear,
 It pangs us fou o' knowledge.
Be't whisky-gill or penny-wheep,
 Or onie stronger potion,
It never fails, on drinkin deep,
 To kittle up our notion,
  By night or day.

The lads an' lasses, blythely bent
 To mind baith *saul* an' *body*,
Sit round the table, weel content,
 An' steer about the toddy.
On this ane's dress, an' that ane's leuk,
 They're makin observations;
While some are cozie i' the neuk,
 An' forming assignations
  To meet some day.

But now the Lord's ain trumpet touts,
 Till a' the hills are rairan,
An' echos back return the shouts,
 Black Russel is na spairan:
His piercin words, like highlan swords,
 Divide the joints an' marrow;
His talk o' Hell, whare devils dwell,
 Our vera 'Sauls does harrow'
  Wi' fright that day.

A vast, unbottomed, boundless pit,
 Filled fou o' lowan brunstane.
Whase raging flame, an' scorching heat,
 Wad melt the hardest whunstane!
The half-asleep start up wi' fear,
 An' think they hear it roaran,
When presently it does appear,
 'Twas but some neebor snoran
  Asleep that day.

leeze me on] pleased am I with
lear] learning   pangs] stuffs   penny-wheep] small beer at 1*d*. a bottle
  kittle up] excite   notion] understanding
 lowan] burning   brunstane] brimstone   whunstane] whinstone

'Twad be owre lang a tale to tell,
　　How monie stories past,
An' how they crouded to the yill,
　　When they were a' dismist:
How drink gaed round, in cogs an' caups,
　　Amang the furms an' benches;
An' cheese an' bread, frae women's laps,
　　Was dealt about in lunches,
　　　　　　An' dawds that day

In comes a gausie, gash guidwife,
　　An' sits down by the fire,
Syn draws her kebbuck an' her knife;
　　The lasses they are shyer.
The auld guidmen, about the grace,
　　Frae side to side they bother,
Till some ane by his bonnet lays,
　　An' gies them't, like a tether,
　　　　　　Fu' lang that day.

Wae sucks! for him that gets nae lass,
　　Or lasses that hae naething!
Sma' need has he to say a grace,
　　Or melvie his braw claething!
O wives be mindfu', ance yoursel,
　　How bonie lads ye wanted,
An' dinna, for a kebbuck-heel,
　　Let lasses be affronted
　　　　　　On sic a day!

Now clinkumbell, wi' rattlan tow,
　　Begins to jow an' croon;
Some swagger hame, the best they dow,
　　Some wait the afternoon.

yill] ale　　　　cogs] wooden mugs　　　lunches] big slices　　　dawds] hunks
　　　gausie] fine　　　gash] neat　　　kebbuck] cheese
tether] rope　　　wae sucks] alas　　　melvie] spill meal on
　　clinkumbell] bell making a clinking sound　　　tow] rope
　　　　jow] ring　　　croon] boom　　　dow] can

At slaps the billies halt a blink,
   Till lasses strip their shoon:
Wi' *faith* an' *hope*, an' *love* an' drink,
   They're a' in famous tune
       For crack that day.

How monie hearts this day converts,
   O' sinners and o' lasses!
Their hearts o' stane, gin night are gane
   As saft as ony flesh is.
There's some are fou o' *love divine*;
   There's some are fou o' *brandy*;
An' monie jobs that day begin,
   May end in *houghmagandie*
       Some ither day.

RICHARD PORSON
1759–1808

116   *The Mutual Congratulations*
of the Poets Anna Seward
and Hayley

Miss Seward:
Tuneful poet, Britain's glory,
   Mr Hayley, that is you.

Hayley:
Ma'am, you carry all before you,
   Trust me, Lichfield Swan, you do.

Miss Seward:
Ode, didactic, epic, sonnet,
   Mr Hayley, you're divine.

Hayley:
Ma'am, I'll take my oath upon it,
   You yourself are all the Nine.

---

115   slaps] gaps (e.g. in a hedge)   billies] fellows   blink] moment
           crack] talk   *houghmagandie*] fornication

ROBERT SOUTHEY
1774–1843
and
SAMUEL TAYLOR COLERIDGE
1772–1834

117   *The Devil's Thoughts*

FROM his brimstone bed at break of day,
  A walking the Devil is gone,
To look at his snug little farm the Earth,
  And see how his stock went on.

Over the hill and over the dale,
  And he went over the plain,
And backward and forward he swished his long tail,
  As a gentleman swishes his cane.

He saw a lawyer killing a viper
  On a dunghill beside his stable;
'Oh—oh,' quoth he, for it put him in mind
  Of the story of Cain and Abel.

An apothecary on a white horse
  Rode by on his vocation;
And the Devil thought of his old friend
  Death, in the Revelation.

He went into a rich bookseller's shop,
  Quoth he, 'We are both of one college!
For I sate myself, like a cormorant, once
  Hard by the tree of Knowledge.'[1]

---

[1] This anecdote is related by that most interesting of the Devil's Biographers, Mr John Milton, in his *Paradise Lost*, and we have here the Devil's own testimony to the truth and accuracy of it.

He saw a turnkey in a trice
   Handcuff a troublesome blade—
'Nimbly,' quoth he, 'do the fingers move
   If a man be but used to his trade.'

He saw the same turnkey unfettering a man
   With but little expedition,
And he laughed, for he thought of the long debates
   On the Slave Trade Abolition.

As he went through Cold-Bath Fields he looked
   At a solitary cell—
And the Devil was pleased, for it gave him a hint
   For improving the prisons of Hell.

He past a cottage with a double coach-house,
   A cottage of gentility,
And he grinned at the sight, for his favourite vice
   Is pride that apes humility.

He saw a pig right rapidly
   Adown the river float,
The pig swam well, but every stroke
   Was cutting his own throat.

Old Nicholas grinned, and swished his tail
   For joy and admiration—
And he thought of his daughter, Victory,
   And her darling babe, Taxation.

He met an old acquaintance
   Just by the Methodist meeting;
She held a consecrated flag,
   And the Devil nods a greeting.

She tipped him the wink, then frowned and cried,
   'Avaunt! my name's Religion.'
And turned to Mr ——
   And leered like a lovesick pigeon.

General ——'s burning face
  He saw with consternation,
And back to Hell his way did take,
For the Devil thought by a slight mistake,
  It was General Conflagration.

WALTER SAVAGE LANDOR
1775–1864

118   *The Georges*

GEORGE the First was always reckoned
Vile, but viler George the Second;
And what mortal ever heard
Any good of George the Third?
When from earth the Fourth descended
(God be praised!) the Georges ended.

119   *Bourbons*

ISABELLA spits at Spain,
  Bomba strips and scourges Naples:
Are there not then where they reign
  Addled eggs or rotten apples?

Treadmills, pillories, humbler stocks!
  Ye repeat your lessons yet.
Halters, gibbets, axes, blocks!
  Your old textbook ye forget.

Men have often heard the thunder
  Roll at random; where, O where
Rolls it now? I smell it under
  That fat priest in that foul chair.

119   fat priest] Pope Pius IX

249

Never was there poet wanting
　　Where the lapdog licks the throne;
Lauds and hymns we hear them chanting,
　　Shame if I were mute alone!

Let me then your deeds rehearse,
　　Gem of kings and flower of queens!
Though I may but trail a verse
　　Languider than Lamartine's.

120　　　　　　*A Case at Sessions*

YESTERDAY, at the Sessions held in Buckingham,
The Reverend Simon Shutwood, famed for tucking ham
And capon into his appointed maw,
Gravely discussed a deadly breach of law,
And then committed to the county jail
(After a patient hearing) William Flail:
　　For that he, Flail, one day last week,
　　Was seen maliciously to sneak
　　And bend his body by the fence
　　Of his own garden, and from thence
　　Abstract, out of a noose, a hare,
　　Which he unlawfully found there,
　　Against the peace (as may be seen
　　In Burn and Blackstone) of the Queen.
　　He, questioned thereupon, in short,
　　Could give no better reason for't
　　Than that his little boys and he
　　Did often in the morning see
　　Said hare, and sundry other hares,
　　Nibbling on certain herbs of theirs.
　　Teddy, the seventh of the boys,
　　Counted twelve rows, fine young savoys,
　　Bit to the ground by them, and out
　　Of ne'er a plant a leaf to sprout:
　　And Sam, the youngest lad, did think
　　He saw a couple at a pink.

Lamartine] as a royalist, Lamartine had been decorated by Charles X of France and
　　　　　had written a poem on his grand coronation

'Come!' cried the Reverend, 'Come, confess!'
Flail answered, 'I will do no less.
Puss we did catch; Puss we did eat;
It was her turn to give the treat.
Nor overmuch was there for eight o' us
With a half-gallon o' potatoes:
Eight; for our Prue lay sick abed,
And poor dear Bessy with the dead.'
'We can not listen to such idle words,'
The Reverend cried: 'The hares are all my Lord's.
Have you no more, my honest friend, to say
Why we should not commit you, and straightway?'
    Whereat Will Flail
    Grew deadly pale,
And cried, 'If you are so severe on me,
An ignorant man, and poor as poor can be,
O Mister Shutwood! what would you have done
If you had caught God's blessed only Son,
When he broke off (in land not His they say)
That ear of barley on the Sabbath-day?
Sweet Jesus! in the prison he had died,
And never for our sins been crucified.'
With the least gouty of two doeskin feet
The Reverend stamped, then cried in righteous heat,
   'Constable! take that man downstairs,
   He quotes the Scripture and eats hares.'

121   *Idle Words*

    THEY say that every idle word
    Is numbered by the Omniscient Lord.
    O Parliament! 'tis well that He
    Endureth for Eternity,
    And that a thousand Angels wait
    To write them at thy inner gate.

122   *The Heart's Abysses*

TRIUMPHANT Demons stand, and Angels start,
To see the abysses of the human heart.

123   *The Scribblers*

WHY should the scribblers discompose
Our temper? would we look like those?
There are some curs in every street
Who snarl and snap at all they meet:
The taller mastiff deems it aptest
To lift a leg and play the baptist.

124   *A Foreign Ruler*

HE says, *My reign is peace*, so slays
    A thousand in the dead of night.
Are you all happy now? he says,
    And those he leaves behind cry *quite*.
He swears he will have no contention,
    And sets all nations by the ears;
He shouts aloud, *No intervention*!
    Invades, and drowns them all in tears.

125   *A Quarrelsome Bishop*

To hide her ordure, claws the cat;
You claw, but not to cover that.
Be decenter, and learn at least
One lesson from the cleanlier beast.

THOMAS MOORE
1779–1852

126   *To Sir Hudson Lowe*

SIR Hudson Lowe, Sir Hudson *Low*,
(By name, and ah! by nature so)
  As thou art fond of persecutions,
Perhaps thou'st read, or heard repeated,
How Captain Gulliver was treated,
  When thrown among the Lilliputians.

They tied him down—these little men did—
And having valiantly ascended
  Upon the Mighty Man's protuberance,
They did so strut!—upon my soul,
It must have been extremely droll
  To see their pigmy pride's exuberance!

And how the doughty mannikins
Amused themselves with sticking pins,
  And needles in the great man's breeches:
And how some *very* little things
That passed for Lords, on scaffoldings
  Got up, and worried him with speeches.

Alas, alas! that it should happen
To mighty men to be caught napping!—
  Though different, too, these persecutions;
For Gulliver, *there*, took the nap,
While, *here* the *Nap*, oh sad mishap,
  Is taken by the Lilliputians!

Sir Hudson Lowe] Governor of St Helena, criticized for his treatment of
Napoleon

127   *Fum and Hum, the Two Birds of Royalty*

To the Editor of the Morning Chronicle.

Sir,
   In order to explain the following Fragment,
it is necessary to refer your readers to a
late florid description of the Pavilion at
Brighton, in the apartments of which we are
told, 'FUM, The Chinese Bird of Royalty'
is a principal ornament.
                    I am, Sir, yours, etc.
                              MUM.

ONE day the Chinese Bird of Royalty, FUM,
Thus accosted our own Bird of Royalty, HUM,
In that palace or china-shop (Brighton, which is it?)
Where FUM had just come to pay HUM a short visit.—
Near akin are these birds, though they differ in nation
(The breed of the HUMS is as old as creation);
Both, full-crawed Legitimates—both, birds of prey,
Both, cackling and ravenous creatures, half way
'Twixt the goose and the vulture, like Lord CASTLEREAGH.
While FUM deals in Mandarins, Bonzes, Bohea,
Peers, Bishops, and Punch, HUM, are sacred to thee!
So congenial their tastes, that, when FUM first did light on
The floor of that grand China-warehouse at Brighton,
The lanterns, and dragons, and things round the dome
Were so like what he left, 'Gad,' says FUM, 'I'm at home.'—
And when, turning, he saw Bishop LEGGE, 'Zooks, it is,'
Quoth the bird, 'Yes—I know him—a Bonze, by his phyz—
And that jolly old idol he kneels to so low
Can be none but our round-about godhead, fat Fo!'
It chanced at this moment, th'Episcopal Prig
Was imploring the PRINCE to dispense with his wig'[1]
Which the bird, overhearing, flew high o'er his head,
And some TOBIT-like marks of his patronage shed,

---

[1] In consequence of an old promise, that he should be allowed to wear his own hair,
whenever he might be elevated to a Bishopric by his Royal Highness.

Legge] Edward Legg, Bishop of Oxford

Which so dimmed the poor Dandy's idolatrous eye,
That, while FUM cried 'Oh Fo!' all the court cried 'Oh fie!'

But, a truce to digression;— these Birds of a feather
Thus talked, t'other night, on State matters together
(The PRINCE just in bed, or about to depart for't,
His legs full of gout, and his arms full of HERTFORD);
'I say, HUM,' says FUM—FUM, of course, spoke Chinese,
But, bless you, that's nothing—at Brighton one sees
Foreign lingoes and Bishops *translated* with ease—
'I say, HUM, how fares it with royalty now?
Is it *up*? is it *prime*? is it *spooney*—or how?'
(The bird had just taken a flash-man's degree
Under BARRYMORE, YARMOUTH, and young Master LEE)
'As for us in Pekin'—here, a dev'l of a din
From the bed-chamber came, where that long Mandarin,
CASTLEREAGH (whom FUM calls the *Confusius* of Prose),
Was rehearsing a speech upon Europe's repose
To the deep, double bass of the fat Idol's nose.

(*Nota bene*—his Lordship and LIVERPOOL come,
In collateral lines, from the old Mother HUM,
CASTLEREAGH a HUM-bug—LIVERPOOL a HUM-drum).
The speech being finished, out rushed CASTLEREAGH,
Saddled HUM in a hurry, and, whip, spur, away,
Through the regions of air, like a Snip on his hobby,
Ne'er paused, till he lighted in St. Stephen's lobby.)

Hertford] the Marchioness of Hertford, the Prince Regent's mistress, and mother
of Lord Yarmouth   *up*] done for   *prime*] well thought of
spooney] thought to be silly (all words of flash-man's slang)
Yarmouth] Lord Yarmouth, dissipated friend of the Prince Regent, later Marquis of
Hertford, on whom Thackeray modelled the Marquis of Steyne in *Vanity Fair*
Snip on his hobby] tailor on his hobby-horse

128   from *The Fudge Family in Paris*

Letter II
From Phil. Fudge, Esq., to the Lord Viscount Castlereagh

Paris

AT length, my Lord, I have the bliss
To date to you a line from this
'Demoralized' metropolis;
Where, by plebeians low and scurvy,
The throne was turned quite topsy-turvy,
And kingship, tumbled from its seat,
'Stood prostrate' at the people's feet;
Where (still to use your Lordship's tropes)
The *level* of obedience *slopes*
Upward and downward, as the *stream*
Of *hydra* faction *kicks the beam*!
Where the poor palace changes masters
     Quicker than a snake its skin,
And LOUIS is rolled out on castors,
     While BONEY'S borne on shoulders in:
But where, in every change, no doubt,
     One special good your Lordship traces,
That 'tis the *Kings* alone turn out,
     The *Ministers* still keep their places.

How oft, dear Viscount CASTLEREAGH,
I've thought of thee upon the way,
As in my *job* (what place could be
More apt to wake a thought of thee?)—
Or, oftener far, when gravely sitting
Upon my dicky (as is fitting
For him who writes a Tour, that he
May more of men and manners see),
I've thought of thee and of thy glories,
Thou guest of Kings, and King of Tories!
Reflecting how thy fame has grown
     And spread, beyond man's usual share,
At home, abroad, till thou art known,
     Like Major Semple, everywhere!

Semple] James Semple, adventurer in the American and French wars, imprisoned for
fraud

THOMAS MOORE

And marv'lling with what pow'rs of breath
Your Lordship, having speeched to death
Some hundreds of your fellow-men,
Next speeched to Sovereigns' ears—and when
All Sovereigns else were dozed, at last
Speeched down the Sovereign of Belfast.
Oh! 'mid the praises and the trophies
Thou gain'st from Morosophs and Sophis;
'Mid all the tributes to thy fame,
    There's *one* thou should'st be chiefly pleased at—
That Ireland gives her snuff thy name,
    And CASTLEREAGH'S the thing now sneezed at!

But hold, my pen!—a truce to praising—
    Though even your Lordship will allow
The theme's temptations are amazing;
    But time and ink run short, and now,
(As *thou* wouldst say, my guide and teacher
    In these gay metaphoric fringes)
I must *embark* into the *feature*
    On which this letter chiefly *hinges*;—
My Book, the Book that is to prove—
And *will* (so help ye Sprites above,
That sit on clouds, as grave as judges,
Watching the labours of the FUDGES!)
Will prove that all the world, at present,
Is in a state extremely pleasant;
That Europe—thanks to royal swords
    And bay'nets, and the Duke commanding—
Enjoys a peace which, like the Lord's,
    Passeth all human understanding:
That France prefers her go-cart King
    To such a coward scamp as BONEY;
Though round, with each a leading-string,
    There standeth many a Royal crony,
For fear the chubby, tottering thing
    Should fall, if left there *loney-poney*;
That England, too, the more her debts,
The more she spends, the richer gets;
And that the Irish, grateful nation!
    Remember when by *thee* reigned over,

Sovereign of Belfast] title of the chief magistrate of the city
Morosoph] foolish pedant (Rabelais's *morosophe*)   Sophi] potentate

And bless thee for their flagellation,
  As HELOISA did her lover!
That Poland, left for Russia's lunch
  Upon the sideboard, snug reposes:
While Saxony's as pleased as Punch,
  And Norway 'on a bed of roses!'
That, as for some few million souls,
  Transferred by contract, bless the clods!
If half were strangled—Spaniards, Poles,
  And Frenchmen—'twouldn't make much odds,
So Europe's goodly Royal ones
Sit easy on their sacred thrones;
So FERDINAND embroiders gaily,
And LOUIS eats his *salmi*, daily;
So time is left to EMPEROR SANDY
To be *half* Caesar and *half* Dandy;
And GEORGE the REGENT (who'd forget
The doughtiest chieftain of the set?)
Hath wherewithal for trinkets new,
  For dragons, after Chinese models,
And chambers where Duke Ho and Soo
  Might come and nine times knock their noddles!—
All this my Quarto'll prove—much more
Than Quarto ever proved before:
In reas'ning with the *Post* I'll vie,
My facts the *Courier* shall supply,
My jokes VANSITTART, POLE my sense,
And thou, sweet Lord, my eloquence!

My Journal, penned by fits and starts,
  On BIDDY'S back or BOBBY'S shoulder
.(My son, my Lord, a youth of parts,
  Who longs to be a small place-holder),
Is—though *I* say't, that shouldn't say—
Extremely good; and, by the way,
One extract from it—*only* one—
To show its spirit, and I've done.
  JUL. THIRTY-FIRST. Went, after snack,
    To the Cathedral of St. Denny;
  Sighed o'er the Kings of ages back,

Ferdinand] Ferdinand VII of Spain   Sandy] Alexander I of Russia
Vansittart] Nicholas Vansittart, Chancellor of the Exchequer
Pole] William Wellesley-Pole, cabinet minister

And—gave the old concierge a penny!
(MEM.—Must see *Rheims*, much famed, 'tis said,
For making Kings and gingerbread.)
Was shown the tomb where lay, so stately,
A little Bourbon, buried lately,
Thrice high and puissant, we were told,
Though only twenty-four hours old!
Hear this, thought I, ye Jacobins:
Ye Burdetts, tremble in your skins!
If Royalty, but aged a day,
Can boast such high and puissant sway,
What impious hand its pow'r would fix,
Full fledged and wigged, at fifty-six!'

The argument's quite new, you see,
And proves exactly Q.E.D.
So now, with duty to the REGENT,
I am, dear Lord,
        Your most obedient,
              P.F.

Hôtel Breteuil, Rue Rivoli.
Neat lodgings—rather dear for me;
But BIDDY said she thought 'twould look
Genteeler thus to date my Book;
And BIDDY's right—besides, it curries
Some favour with our friends at MURRAY'S,
Who scorn what any man can say,
That dates from Rue St. Honoré!

129   from *Rhymes on the Road*

Extract IX

                     Venice
AND is there then no earthly place,
   Where we can rest, in dream Elysian,
Without some cursed, round English face,
   Popping up near, to break the vision?

128   Burdett] Sir Francis Burdett, reformer and opponent of the French war

'Mid northern lakes, 'mid southern vines,
   Unholy cits we're doomed to meet;
Nor highest Alps nor Apennines
   Are sacred from Threadneedle Street!

If up the Simplon's path we wind,
Fancying we leave this world behind,
Such pleasant sounds salute one's ear
As—'Baddish news from 'Change, my dear—
The Funds—(phew, curse this ugly hill)—
Are lowering fast—(what, higher still?)—
And—(zooks, we're mounting up to heaven!)—
Will soon be down to sixty-seven.'

Go where we may—rest where we will,
Eternal London haunts us still.
The trash of Almack's or Fleet Ditch—
And scarce a pin's head difference *which*—
Mixes, though ev'n to Greece we run,
With every rill from Helicon!
And, if this rage for travelling lasts,
If Cockneys, of all sects and castes,
Old maidens, aldermen, and squires,
Will leave their puddings and coal fires,
To gape at things in foreign lands,
No soul among them understands;
If Blues desert their coteries,
To show off 'mong the Wahabees;
If neither sex nor age controls,
   Nor fear of Mamelukes forbids
Young ladies, with pink parasols,
   To glide among the Pyramids—

Why, then, farewell all hope to find
A spot, that's free from London-kind!

Who knows, if to the West we roam,
But we may find some *Blue* 'at home'
    Among the *Blacks* of Carolina—
Or, flying to the Eastward, see
Some Mrs Hopkins, taking tea
    And toast upon the Wall of China!

130   *Copy of an Intercepted Despatch*
From His Excellency Don Strepitoso
Diabolo, Envoy Extraordinary to
His Satanic Majesty

St. James's Street, July 1, 1826

GREAT Sir, having just had the good luck to catch
    An official young Demon, preparing to go,
Ready booted and spurred, with a black-leg despatch
    From the Hell here, at Crockford's, to *our* Hell, below—

I write these few lines to your Highness Satanic,
    To say that, first having obeyed your directions,
And done all the mischief I could in 'the Panic',
    My next special care was to help the Elections.

Well knowing how dear were those times to thy soul,
    When ev'ry good Christian tormented his brother,
And caused, in thy realm, such a saving of coal,
    From all coming down, ready grilled by each other;

Remembering, besides, how it pained thee to part
    With the Old Penal Code—that *chef-d'oeuvre* of Law,
In which (though to own it too modest thou art)
    We could plainly perceive the fine touch of thy claw;

I thought, as we ne'er can those good times revive,
    (Though Eldon, with help from your Highness would try),
'Twould still keep a taste for Hell's music alive,
    Could we get up a thund'ring No-Popery cry;—

That yell which, when chorused by laics and clerics,
  So like is to *ours*, in its spirit and tone,
That I often nigh laugh myself into hysterics,
  To think that Religion should make it her own.

So, having sent down for th' original notes
  Of the chorus, as sung by your Majesty's choir,
With a few pints of lava, to gargle the throats
  Of myself and some others, who sing it 'with fire',

Thought I, 'if the Marseillois Hymn could command
  Such audience, though yelled by a *Sans-culotte* crew,
What wonders shall *we* do, who've men in our band,
  That not only wear breeches, but petticoats too.'

Such *then* were my hopes; but with sorrow, your Highness,
  I'm forced to confess—be the cause what it will,
Whether fewness of voices, or hoarseness, or shyness—
  Our Beelzebub Chorus has gone off but ill.

The truth is, no placeman now knows his right key,
  The Treasury pitch-pipe of late is so various;
And certain *base* voices, that looked for a fee
  At the *York* music-meeting, now think it precarious.

Even some of our Reverends *might* have been warmer—
  Though one or two capital roarers we've had;
Doctor Wise is, for instance, a charming performer,
  And *Huntingdon* Maberley's yell was not bad!

Altogether, however, the thing was not hearty;—
  Even Eldon allows we got on but so so;
And when next we attempt a No-Popery party,
  We *must*, please your Highness, recruit *from below*.

But, hark, the young Black-leg is cracking his whip—
  Excuse me, Great Sir—there's no time to be civil;
The next opportunity shan't be let slip,
  But, till then,
              I'm, in haste, your most dutiful
                                        DEVIL

THOMAS MOORE

131   *A Pastoral Ballad. By John Bull*

'*Dublin, March 12, 1827*. Friday, after the arrival of the packet bringing the account of the deafeat of the Catholic Question, in the House of Commons, orders were sent to the Pigeon House to forward 5,000,000 rounds of musket-ball cartridge to the different garrisons round the country.' *Freeman's Journal*

I have found out a gift for my Erin,
    A gift that will surely content her;—
Sweet pledge of a love so endearing!
    Five millions of bullets I've sent her.

She asked me for Freedom and Right,
    But ill she her wants understood;—
Ball cartridges morning and night,
    Is a dose that will do her more good.

There is hardly a day of our lives
    But we read, in some amiable trials,
How husbands make love to their wives
    Through the medium of hemp and of phials.

One thinks, with his mistress or mate
    A good halter is sure to agree—
That love-knot which early and late,
    I have tried, my dear Erin, on thee.

While *another*, whom Hymen has blessed
    With a wife that is not over placid,
Consigns the dear charmer to rest,
    With a dose of the best Prussic acid.

Thus, Erin! my love do I show—
    Thus quiet thee, mate of my bed!
And, as poison and hemp are too slow,
    Do thy business with bullets instead.

Should thy faith in my medicine be shaken,
    Ask Rawdon, that mildest of saints,
He'll tell thee, lead, inwardly taken,
    Alone can remove thy complaints;

That, blest as thou art in thy lot,
    Nothing's wanted to make it more pleasant
But being hanged, tortured, and shot,
    Much oftener than thou art at present.

Even Wellington's self hath averred,
    Thou art yet but half sabred and hung,
And I loved him the more when I heard
    Such tenderness fall from his tongue.

So take the five millions of pills,
    Dear partner, I herewith inclose;
'Tis the cure that all quacks for thy ills,
    From Cromwell to Eldon, propose.

And you, ye brave bullets that go,
    How I wish that, before you set out,
The *Devil* of the Freischutz could know
    The good work you are going about.

For he'd charm ye, in spite of your lead,
    Into such supernatural wit,
That you'd all of you know, as you sped,
    Where a bullet of sense *ought* to hit.

132   *The Cherries. A Parable*

(Written during the late discussion on the Test and Corporation Acts)

    SEE those cherries, how they cover
        Yonder sunny garden wall:
    Had they not that network over,
        Thieving birds would eat them all.

131   Rawdon] Francis Rawdon-Hastings, Lord Hastings: general, governor of Bengal,
           subjugator of central India

So, to guard our posts and pensions,
  Ancient sages wove a net,
Through whose holes, of small dimensions,
  Only *certain* knaves can get.

Shall we then this network widen?
  Shall we stretch these sacred holes,
Through which, even already, slide in
  Lots of small dissenting souls?

'God forbid!' old *Testy* crieth;
  'God forbid!' so echo I;
Every ravenous bird that flieth
  Then would at our cherries fly.

Ope but half an inch or so,
  And, behold, what bevies break in;
Here, some cursed old Popish crow
  Pops his long and lickerish beak in;

Here, sly Arians flock unnumbered,
  And Socinians, slim and spare,
Who, with small belief encumbered,
  Slip in easy any where;

Methodists, of birds the aptest,
  Where there's *pecking* going on;
And that water-fowl, the Baptist—
  All would share our fruits anon;

Ev'ry bird, of ev'ry city,
  That, for years, with ceaseless din,
Hath reversed the starling's ditty,
  Singing out 'I can't get *in*.'

'God forbid!' old *Testy* snivels;
  'God forbid!' I echo too;
Rather may ten thousand devils
  Seize the whole voracious crew!

If less costly fruit won't suit 'em,
  Hips and haws, and such like berries,
Curse the corm'rants! stone 'em, shoot 'em,
  Any thing—to save our cherries.

133   *Tory Pledges*

I PLEDGE myself through thick and thin,
  To labour still, with zeal devout,
To get the Outs, poor devils, in,
  And turn the Ins, the wretches, out.

I pledge myself, though much bereft
  Of ways and means of ruling ill,
To make the most of what are left,
  And stick to all that's rotten still.

Though gone the days of place and pelf,
  And drones no more take all the honey,
I pledge myself to cram myself
  With all I can of public money.

To quarter on that social purse
  My nephews, nieces, sisters, brothers,
Nor, so *we* prosper, care a curse
  How much 'tis at th' expense of others.

I pledge myself, whenever Right
  And Might on any point divide,
Not to ask which is black or white,
  But take, at once, the strongest side.

For instance, in all tithe discussions,
  I'm *for* the reverend encroachers:—
I loathe the Poles, applaud the Russians,—
  Am *for* the squires, *against* the poachers.

Betwixt the Corn-Lords and the Poor
  I've not the slightest hesitation—
The People *must* be starved, t' insure
  The Land its due remuneration.

I pledge myself to be no more
　　With Ireland's wrongs beprosed or shammed,—
I vote her grievances a *bore*,
　　So she may suffer, and be damned.

Or if she kick, let it console us,
　　We still have plenty of red coats,
To cram the Church, that general bolus,
　　Down any giv'n amount of throats.

I dearly love the Frankfort Diet,
　　Think newspapers the worst of crimes;
And would, to give some chance of quiet,
　　Hang all the writers of The Times;

Break all their correspondents' bones,
　　All authors of 'Reply', 'Rejoinder',
From the Anti-Tory, Colonel Jones,
　　To the Anti-Suttee, Mr Poynder.

Such are the Pledges I propose;
　　And though I can't now offer gold,
There's many a way of buying those
　　Who've but the taste for being sold.

So here's, with three times three hurrahs,
　　A toast, of which you'll not complain,—
'Long life to jobbing; may the days
　　Of Peculation shine again!'

Frankfort Diet] the repressive Diet of the German Federation which met at
Frankfurt
Colonel Jones] Colonel L. G. Jones (1779–1839) celebrated for his radical
letters to *The Times*
Poynder] John Poynder (1779–1849), evangelical lawyer who campaigned against
suttee, abolished in 1829

134 *Scene from a Play, acted at Oxford, called
'Matriculation'*

[*Boy discovered at a table, with the Thirty-Nine Articles before him.—
Enter the Rt. Rev. Doctor Phillpots.*]

Doctor P.: THERE, my lad, lie the Articles—(*Boy begins to count
them*) just thirty-nine—
No occasion to count—you've now only to sign.
At Cambridge, where folks are less High-church than we,
The whole Nine-and-Thirty are lumped into Three.
Let's run o'er the items; there's Justification,
Predestination, and Supererogation,
Not forgetting Salvation and Creed Athanasian,
Till we reach, at last, Queen Bess's Ratification.
That's sufficient—now, sign—having read quite enough,
You 'believe in the full and true meaning thereof,' (*Boy stares*)
Oh, a mere form of words, to make things smooth and brief—
A commodious and short make-believe of belief,
Which our Church has drawn up, in a form thus articular,
To keep out, in general, all who're particular.
But what's the boy doing? what! reading all through,
And my luncheon fast cooling!—this never will do.
Boy (*poring over the Articles*)—Here are points which—pray,
Doctor, what's 'Grace of Congruity?'
Doctor P. (*sharply*)—You'll find out, young sir, when you've more
ingenuity.
At present, by signing, you pledge yourself merely,
Whate'er it may be, to believe it sincerely.
Both in *dining* and *signing* we take the same plan—
First, swallow all down, then digest—as we can.
Boy (*still reading*)—I've to gulp, I see, St. Athanasius's Creed,
Which, I'm told, is a very tough morsel indeed;
As he damns—
Doctor P. (*aside*)—Ay, and so would *I*, willingly, too,
All confounded particular young boobies, like you.
This comes of Reforming!—all's o'er with our land,
When people won't stand what they can't *under*stand;
Nor perceive that our ever-revered Thirty-Nine
Were made, not for men to *believe*, but to *sign*.
[*Exit Dr. P. in a passion.*

Phillpots] Bishop of Exeter, and noted reactionary in politics and church affairs

EBENEZER ELLIOTT
1781–1849

Drone v. Worker

How God speeds the tax-bribed plough,
    Fen and moor declare, man;
Where once fed the poor man's cow,
    Acres drives his share, man.
But he did not *steal* the fen,
    Did not *steal* the moor, man;
If he feeds on starving men,
    Still he loves the poor, man.
Hush! he bullies State and Throne,
    Quids them in his jaw, man;
Thine and mine he calls *his own;*
    Acres' lie is law, man.
Acres eats his tax on bread,
    Acres loves the plough, man;
Acres' dogs are better fed,
    Beggar's slave! than thou, man.
Acres' feeder pays his debts,
    Waxes thin and pale, man,
Harder works and poorer gets,
    Pays his debts in jail, man.
Acres in a palace lives,
    While his feeder pines, man;
Palaced beggar ne'er forgives
    Dog on whom he dines, man.
Acres' feeder, beggared, begs,
    Treadmilled rogue is he, man;
Scamp! he deals in pheasants' eggs;
    Hangs on gallows-tree, man!
Who would be a useful man?
    Who sell cloth or hats, man?
Who make boiler or mend pan?
    Who keep Acres' brats, man?
Better ride, and represent;
    Better borough tools, man;
Better sit in pauperment;

Better Corn-Law fools, man.
Why not right the plundered poor?
    Why not use our *own*, man?
Plough the seas and *not* the moor?
    Why not pick a bone, man!
Lo! the merchant builds huge mills;
    Bread-taxed thinks and sighs, man!
Thousand mouths and bellies fills;
    Bread-taxed breaks and dies, man!
Thousand mouths and bellies then,
    Bread-taxed, writhe and swear, man:
England once bred honest men—
    Bread-taxed, Burke and Hare, man!
Hark ye! millions soon may pine,
    Starving millions curse, man!
Desperate millions long to dine
    A-la-Burke, and worse, man!
What will then remain to eat?
    Who be eaten then, man?
'Few may part, though many meet,'
    At Famine's Feast, ye ken, man.

136   from *The Splendid Village*

VILLAGE! thy butcher's son, the steward now,
Still bears the butcher on his burly brow.
Oft with his sire he deigns to ride and stare;
And who like them, at market or at fair?
King of the Inn, he takes the highest place,
And carves the goose, and grimly growls the grace.
There in the loud debate, with might—with might,
Still speaks he last, and conquers still the right;
Red as a lobster, vicious as his horse,
That, like its master, worships fraud and force,
And if the stranger 'scape its kick or bite,
Low'rs its vexed ears, and screams for very spite.
'He hath enough, thank God, to wear and eat;
He gives no alms'—not e'en his putrid meat;
'But keeps his cab, whips beggars from his door,
Votes for my Lord, and hates the *thankless* poor.'

THOMAS LOVE PEACOCK
1785–1866

137   *Rich and Poor; or Saint and Sinner*

THE poor man's sins are glaring;
In the face of ghostly warning
  He is caught in the fact
  Of an overt act—
Buying greens on Sunday morning.

The rich man's sins are hidden
In the pomp of wealth and station;
  And escape the sight
  Of the children of light,
Who are wise in their generation.

The rich man has a kitchen,
And cooks to dress his dinner;
  The poor who would roast
  To the baker's must post,
And thus becomes a sinner.

The rich man has a cellar,
And a ready butler by him;
  The poor must steer
  For his pint of beer
Where the saint can't choose but spy him.

The rich man's painted windows
Hide the concerts of the quality;
  The poor can but share
  A cracked fiddle in the air,
Which offends all sound morality.

The rich man is invisible
In the crowd of his gay society;
  But the poor man's delight
  Is a sore in the sight,
And a stench in the nose of piety.

271

THOMAS LOVE PEACOCK

The rich man has a carriage
Where no rude eye can flout him;
The poor man's bane
Is a third-class train,
With the daylight all about him.

The rich man goes out yachting,
Where sanctity can't pursue him;
The poor goes afloat
In a fourpenny boat,
Where the bishop groans to view him.

GEORGE GORDON NOEL, LORD BYRON
1788–1824

138   from *English Bards and Scotch Reviewers*
(i)
Lord and Lady Holland

ILLUSTRIOUS Holland! hard would be his lot,
His hirelings mentioned, and himself forgot!
Holland, with Henry Petty at his back,
The whipper-in and huntsman of the pack.
Blest be the banquets spread at Holland House,
Where Scotchmen feed, and critics may carouse!
Long, long beneath that hospitable roof
Shall Grub Street dine, while duns are kept aloof.
See honest Hallam lay aside his fork,
Resume his pen, review his Lordship's work,
And, grateful for the dainties on his plate,
Declare his landlord can at least translate!
Dunedin! view thy children with delight,
They write for food—and feed because they write:
And lest, when heated with the unusual grape,
Some glowing thoughts should to the press escape,
And tinge with red the female reader's cheek,
My lady skims the cream of each critique;
Breathes o'er the page her purity of soul,
Reforms each error, and refines the whole.

272

(ii)

On Thomas Maurice's poem 'Richmond Hill'

As Sisyphus against the infernal steep
Rolls the huge rock whose motions ne'er may sleep,
So up thy hill, ambrosial Richmond, heaves
Dull Maurice all his granite weight of leaves:
Smooth, solid monuments of mental pain!
The petrifactions of a plodding brain,
That, ere they reach the top, fall lumbering back again.

139   from *The Age of Bronze*

Rent, Rent, Rent!

ALAS, the country! how shall tongue or pen
Bewail her now *un*country gentlemen?
The last to bid the cry of warfare cease,
The first to make a malady of peace.
For what were all these country patriots born?
To hunt, and vote, and raise the price of corn?
But corn, like every mortal thing, must fall,
Kings, conquerors, and markets most of all.
And must ye fall with every ear of grain?
Why would you trouble Buonaparté's reign?
He was your great Triptolemus; his vices
Destroyed but realms, and still maintained your prices;
He amplified to every lord's content
The grand agrarian alchemy, high *rent*.
Why did the tyrant stumble on the Tartars,
And lower wheat to such desponding quarters?
Why did you chain him on yon isle so lone?
The man was worth much more upon his throne.
True, blood and treasure boundlessly were spilt,
But what of that? the Gaul may bear the guilt;
But bread was high, the farmer paid his way,
And acres told upon the appointed day.
But where is now the goodly audit ale?
The purse-proud tenant, never known to fail?
The farm which never yet was left on hand?
The marsh reclaimed to most improving land?
The impatient hope of the expiring lease?

The doubling rental? What an evil's peace!
In vain the prize excites the ploughman's skill,
In vain the Commons pass their patriot bill;
The *landed interest*—(you may understand
The phrase much better leaving out the *land*)—
The land self-interest groans from shore to shore,
For fear that plenty should attain the poor.
Up, up again, ye rents! exalt your notes,
Or else the ministry will lose their votes,
And patriotism, so delicately nice,
Her loaves will lower to the market price;
For ah! 'the loaves and fishes', once so high,
Are gone—their oven closed, their ocean dry,
And nought remains of all the millions spent,
Excepting to grow moderate and content.
They who are not so, *had* their turn—and turn
About still flows from Fortune's equal urn;
Now let their virtue be its own reward,
And share the blessings which themselves prepared.
See these inglorious Cincinnati swarm,
Farmers of war, dictators of the farm;
Their ploughshare was the sword in hireling hands,
Their fields manured by gore of other lands;
Safe in their barns, these Sabine tillers sent
Their brethren out to battle—why? for rent!
Year after year they voted cent. per cent.,
Blood, sweat, and tear-wrung millions—why? for rent!
They roared, they dined, they drank, they swore they meant
To die for England—why then live?—for rent!
The peace has made one general malcontent
Of these high-market patriots; war was rent!
Their love of country, millions all misspent,
How reconcile? by reconciling rent!
And will they not repay the treasures lent?
No: down with everything, and up with rent!
Their good, ill, health, wealth, joy, or discontent,
Being, end, aim, religion—rent, rent, rent! .

from *The Waltz*

Hail, Spirit-stirring Waltz

MUSE of the many-twinkling feet! whose charms
Are now extended up from legs to arms;
Terpsichore!—too long misdeemed a maid—
Reproachful term—bestowed but to upbraid—
Henceforth in all the bronze of brightness shine,
The least a vestal of the virgin Nine.
Far be from thee and thine the name of prude;
Mocked, yet triumphant; sneered at, unsubdued;
Thy legs must move to conquer as they fly,
If but thy coats are reasonably high;
Thy breast—if bare enough—requires no shield;
Dance forth—*sans armour* thou shalt take the field,
And own—impregnable to *most* assaults,
Thy not too lawfully begotten 'Waltz'.

  Hail, nimble nymph! to whom the young hussar,
The whiskered votary of waltz and war,
His night devotes, despite of spur and boots;
A sight unmatched since Orpheus and his brutes:
Hail, spirit-stirring Waltz!—beneath whose banners
A modern hero fought for modish manners;
On Hounslow's heath to rival Wellesley's fame,
Cocked—fired—and missed his man—but gained his aim;
Hail, moving Muse! to whom the fair one's breast
Gives all it can, and bids us take the rest.
Oh! for the flow of Busby, or of Fitz,
The latter's loyalty, the former's wits,
To 'energize the object I pursue',
And give both Belial and his dance their due!

  Imperial Waltz! imported from the Rhine
(Famed for the growth of pedigrees and wine),
Long be thine import from all duty free,
And hock itself be less esteemed than thee;
In some few qualities alike—for hock
Improves our cellar—*thou* our living stock.
The head to hock belongs—thy subtler art
Intoxicates alone the heedless heart:
Through the full veins thy gentler poison swims,
And wakes to wantonness the willing limbs.

Oh, Germany! how much to thee we owe,
As heaven-born Pitt can testify below,
Ere cursed confederation made thee France's,
And only left us thy damned debts and dances!
Of subsidies and Hanover bereft,
We bless thee still—for George the Third is left!
Of kinds the best—and last, not least in worth,
For graciously begetting George the Fourth.
To Germany, and highnesses serene,
Who owe us millions—don't we owe the queen?
To Germany, what owe we not besides?
So oft bestowing Brunswickers and brides;
Who paid for vulgar, with her royal blood,
Drawn from the stem of each Teutonic stud:
Who sent us—so be pardoned all her faults—
A dozen dukes, some kings, a queen—and Waltz.

141   from *The Vision of Judgment*
(i)
A Royal Candidate for Heaven

SAINT Peter sat by the celestial gate:
 His keys were rusty, and the lock was dull,
So little trouble had been given of late;
 Not that the place by any means was full,
But since the Gallic era 'eighty-eight'
 The devils had ta'en a longer, stronger pull,
And 'a pull altogether', as they say
At sea—which drew most souls another way.

The angels all were singing out of tune,
 And hoarse with having little else to do,
Excepting to wind up the sun and moon,
 Or curb a runaway young star or two,
Or wild colt of a comet, which too soon
 Broke out of bounds o'er the ethereal blue,
Splitting some planet with its playful tail,
As boats are sometimes by a wanton whale.

The guardian seraphs had retired on high,
  Finding their charges past all care below;
Terrestrial business filled nought in the sky
  Save the recording angel's black bureau;
Who found, indeed, the facts to multiply
  With such rapidity of vice and woe,
That he had stripped off both his wings in quills,
And yet was in arrear of human ills.

His business so augmented of late years,
  That he was forced, against his will, no doubt,
(Just like those cherubs, earthly ministers,)
  For some resource to turn himself about
And claim the help of his celestial peers,
  To aid him ere he should be quite worn out
By the increased demand for his remarks;
Six angels and twelve saints were named his clerks.

This was a handsome board—at least for heaven;
  And yet they had even then enough to do,
So many conquerors' cars were daily driven,
  So many kingdoms fitted up anew;
Each day too slew its thousands six or seven,
  Till at the crowning carnage, Waterloo,
They threw their pens down in divine disgust—
The page was so besmeared with blood and dust.

This by the way; 'tis not mine to record
  What angels shrink from: even the very devil
On this occasion his own work abhorred,
  So surfeited with the infernal revel:
Though he himself had sharpened every sword,
  It almost quenched his innate thirst of evil.
(Here Satan's sole good work deserves insertion—
'Tis, that he has both generals in reversion.)

Let's skip a few short years of hollow peace,
  Which peopled earth no better, hell as wont,
And heaven none—they form the tyrant's lease,
  With nothing but new names subscribed upon't;
'Twill one day finish: meantime they increase,
  'With seven heads and ten horns', and all in front,
Like Saint John's foretold beast; but ours are born
Less formidable in the head than horn.

In the first year of freedom's second dawn
   Died George the Third; although no tyrant, one
Who shielded tyrants, till each sense withdrawn
   Left him nor mental nor external sun:
A better farmer ne'er brushed dew from lawn,
   A worse king never left a realm undone!
He died—but left his subjects still behind,
One half as mad—and t'other no less blind.

He died!—his death made no great stir on earth;
   His burial made some pomp; there was profusion
Of velvet, gilding, brass, and no great dearth
   Of aught but tears—save those shed by collusion.
For these things may be bought at their true worth;
   Of elegy there was the due infusion—
Bought also; and the torches, cloaks, and banners,
Heralds, and relics of old Gothic manners,

Formed a sepulchral melodrame. Of all
   The fools who flocked to swell or see the show,
Who cared about the corpse? The funeral
   Made the attraction, and the black the woe.
There throbbed not there a thought which pierced the pall;
   And when the gorgeous coffin was laid low,
It seemed the mockery of hell to fold
The rottenness of eighty years in gold.

So mix his body with the dust! It might
   Return to what it *must* far sooner, were
The natural compound left alone to fight
   Its way back into earth, and fire, and air;
But the unnatural balsams merely blight
   What nature made him at his birth, as bare
As the mere million's base unmummied clay—
Yet all his spices but prolong decay.

He's dead—and upper earth with him has done;
   He's buried; save the undertaker's bill,
Or lapidary scrawl, the world is gone
   For him, unless he left a German will;
But where's the proctor who will ask his son?
   In whom his qualities are reigning still,
Except that household virtue, most uncommon,
Of constancy to a bad, ugly woman.

'God save the king!' It is a large economy
   In God to save the like; but if he will
Be saving, all the better; for not one am I
   Of those who think damnation better still:
I hardly know too if not quite alone am I
   In this small hope of bettering future ill
By circumscribing, with some slight restriction,
The eternity of hell's hot jurisdiction.

I know this is unpopular; I know
   'Tis blasphemous; I know one may be damned
For hoping no one else may e'er be so;
   I know my catechism; I know we are crammed
With the best doctrines till we quite o'erflow;
   I know that all save England's church have shammed,
And that the other twice two hundred churches
And synagogues have made a *damned* bad purchase.

God help us all! God help me too! I am,
   God knows, as helpless as the devil can wish,
And not a whit more difficult to damn
   Than is to bring to land a late-hooked fish,
Or to the butcher to purvey the lamb;
   Not that I'm fit for such a noble dish
As one day will be that immortal fry
Of almost every body born to die.

Saint Peter sat by the celestial gate,
   And nodded o'er his keys; when, lo! there came
A wondrous noise he had not heard of late—
   A rushing sound of wind, and stream, and flame;
In short, a roar of things extremely great,
   Which would have made aught save a saint exclaim;
But he, with first a start and then a wink,
Said, 'There's another star gone out, I think!'

But ere he could return to his repose,
   A cherub flapped his right wing o'er his eyes—
At which Saint Peter yawned, and rubbed his nose:
   'Saint porter,' said the angel, 'prithee rise!'
Waving a goodly wing, which glowed, as glows
   An earthly peacock's tail, with heavenly dyes:
To which the saint replied, 'Well, what's the matter?
Is Lucifer come back with all this clatter?'

'No,' quoth the cherub; George the Third is dead.'
    'And who *is* George the Third?' replied the apostle:
'*What George? what Third?*' 'The king of England,' said
    The angel. 'Well! he won't find kings to jostle
Him on his way; but does he wear his head?
    Because the last we saw here had a tustle,
And ne'er would have got into heaven's good graces,
Had he not flung his head in all our faces.

'He was, if I remember, king of France;
    That head of his, which could not keep a crown
On earth, yet ventured in my face to advance
    A claim to those of martyrs—like my own:
If I had had my sword, as I had once
    When I cut ears off, I had cut him down;
But having but my keys, and not my brand,
I only knocked his head from out his hand.

'And then he set up such a headless howl,
    That all the saints came out and took him in;
And there he sits by St. Paul, cheek by jowl;
    That fellow Paul—the parvenu! The skin
Of Saint Bartholomew, which makes his cowl
    In heaven, and upon earth redeemed his sin
So as to make a martyr, never sped
Better than did this weak and wooden head.

'But had it come up here upon its shoulders,
    There would have been a different tale to tell:
The fellow-feeling in the saints beholders
    Seems to have acted on them like a spell;
And so this very foolish head heaven solders
    Back on its trunk: it may be very well,
And seems the custom here to overthrow
Whatever has been wisely done below.'

The angel answered, 'Peter! do not pout:
    The king who comes has head and all entire,
And never knew much what it was about—
    He did as doth the puppet—by its wire,
And will be judged like all the rest, no doubt:
    My business and your own is not to enquire
Into such matters, but to mind our cue—
Which is to act as we are bid to do.'

While thus they spake, the angelic caravan,
   Arriving like a rush of mighty wind,
Cleaving the fields of space, as doth the swan
   Some silver stream (say Ganges, Nile, or Inde,
Or Thames, or Tweed), and 'midst them an old man
   With an old soul, and both extremely blind,
Halted before the gate, and in his shroud
Seated their fellow-traveller on a cloud.

(ii)
Laureate Southey's Presumption

AT length with jostling, elbowing, and the aid
   Of cherubim appointed to that post,
The devil Asmodeus to the circle made
   His way, and looked as if his journey cost
Some trouble. When his burden down he laid,
   'What's this?' cried Michael; 'why, 'tis not a ghost?'
'I know it,' quoth the incubus; 'but he
Shall be one, if you leave the affair to me.

'Confound the renegado! I have sprained
   My left wing, he's so heavy; one would think
Some of his works about his neck were chained.
   But to the point; while hovering o'er the brink
Of Skiddaw (where as usual it still rained),
   I saw a taper, far below me, wink,
And stooping, caught this fellow at a libel—
No less on history than the Holy Bible.

'The former is the devil's scripture, and
   The latter yours, good Michael; so the affair
Belongs to all of us, you understand.
   I snatched him up just as you see him there,
And brought him off for sentence out of hand:
   I've scarcely been ten minutes in the air—
At least a quarter it can hardly be:
I dare say that his wife is still at tea.'

Here Satan said, 'I know this man of old,
   And have expected him for some time here;

A sillier fellow you will scarce behold,
　Or more conceited in his petty sphere:
But surely it was not worth while to fold
　Such trash below your wing, Asmodeus dear:
We had the poor wretch safe (without being bored
With carriage) coming of his own accord.

'But since he's here, let's see what he has done.'
　'Done!' cried Asmodeus, 'he anticipates
The very business you are now upon,
　And scribbles as if head clerk to the Fates.
Who knows to what his ribaldry may run,
　When such an ass as this, like Balaam's, prates?'
'Let's hear,' quoth Michael, 'what he has to say;
You know we're bound to that in every way.'

Now the bard, glad to get an audience, which
　By no means often was his case below,
Began to cough, and hawk, and hem, and pitch
　His voice into that awful note of woe
To all unhappy hearers within reach
　Of poets when the tide of rhyme's in flow;
But stuck fast with his first hexameter,
Not one of all whose gouty feet would stir.

But ere the spavined dactyls could be spurred
　Into recitative, in great dismay
Both cherubim and seraphim were heard
　To murmur loudly through their long array;
And Michael rose ere he could get a word
　Of all his foundered verses under way,
And cried, 'For God's sake stop, my friend! 'twere best—
Non Di, non homines—you know the rest.'

A general bustle spread throughout the throng,
　Which seemed to hold all verse in detestation;
The angels had of course enough of song
　When upon service; and the generation
Of ghosts had heard too much in life, not long
　Before, to profit by a new occasion;
The monarch, mute till then, exclaimed, 'What! what!
Pye come again? No more—no more of that!'

The tumult grew; an universal cough
Convulsed the skies, as during a debate,
When Castlereagh has been up long enough
  (Before he was first minister of state,
I mean—the *slaves hear now*); some cried 'Off, off!'
  As at a farce; till, grown quite desperate,
The bard Saint Peter prayed to interpose
(Himself an author) only for his prose.

The varlet was not an ill-favoured knave;
  A good deal like a vulture in the face,
With a hook nose and a hawk's eye, which gave
  A smart and sharper-looking sort of grace
To his whole aspect, which, though rather grave,
  Was by no means so ugly as his case;
But that indeed was hopeless as can be,
Quite a poetic felony '*de se*'.

Then Michael blew his trump, and stilled the noise
  With one still greater, as is yet the mode
On earth besides; except some grumbling voice,
  Which now and then will make a slight inroad
Upon decorous silence, few will twice
  Lift up their lungs when fairly overcrowed;
And now the bard could plead his own bad cause,
With all the attitudes of self-applause.

He said—(I only give the heads)—he said,
  He meant no harm in scribbling; 'twas his way
Upon all topics; 'twas, besides, his bread,
  Of which he buttered both sides; 'twould delay
Too long the assembly (he was pleased to dread),
  And take up rather more time than a day,
To name his works—he would but cite a few—
'Wat Tyler'—'Rhymes on Blenheim'—'Waterloo'.

He had written praises of a regicide;
  He had written praises of all kings whatever;
He had written for republics far and wide,
  And then against them bitterer than ever:
For pantisocracy he once had cried
  Aloud, a scheme less moral than 'twas clever;
Then grew a hearty anti-jacobin—
Had turned his coat—and would have turned his skin.

He had sung against all battles, and again
   In their high praise and glory; he had called
Reviewing 'the ungentle craft', and then
   Become as base a critic as e'er crawled—
Fed, paid, and pampered by the very men
   By whom his muse and morals had been mauled:
He had written much blank verse, and blanker prose,
And more of both than anybody knows.

He had written Wesley's life:—here turning round
   To Satan, 'Sir, I'm ready to write yours,
In two octavo volumes, nicely bound,
   With notes and preface, all that most allures
The pious purchaser; and there's no ground
   For fear, for I can choose my own reviewers:
So let me have the proper documents,
That I may add you to my other saints.'

Satan bowed, and was silent. 'Well, if you,
   With amiable modesty, decline
My offer, what says Michael? There are few
   Whose memoirs could be rendered more divine.
Mine is a pen of all work; not so new
   As it was once, but I would make you shine
Like your own trumpet. By the way, my own
Has more of brass in it, and is as well blown.

'But talking about trumpets, here's my Vision!
   Now you shall judge, all people; yes, you shall
Judge with my judgment, and by my decision
   Be guided who shall enter heaven or fall.
I settle all these things by intuition,
   Times present, past, to come, heaven, hell, and all,
Like King Alfonso. When I thus see double,
I save the Deity some worlds of trouble.'

He ceased, and drew forth an MS.; and no
   Persuasion on the part of devils, or saints,
Or angels, now could stop the torrent; so
   He read the first three lines of the contents;
But at the fourth, the whole spiritual show
   Had vanished, with variety of scents,
Ambrosial and sulphureous, as they sprang,
Like lightning, off from his 'melodious twang'.

Those grand heroics acted as a spell;
   The angels stopped their ears and plied their pinions;
The devils ran howling, deafened, down to hell;
   The ghosts fled, gibbering, for their own dominions—
(For 'tis not yet decided where they dwell,
   And I leave every man to his opinions);
Michael took refuge in his trump—but, lo!
His teeth were set on edge, he could not blow!

Saint Peter, who has hitherto been known
   For an impetuous saint, upraised his keys,
And at the fifth line knocked the poet down;
   Who fell like Phaeton, but more at ease,
Into his lake, for there he did not drown;
   A different web being by the Destinies
Woven for the Laureate's final wreath, whene'er
Reform shall happen either here or there.

He first sank to the bottom—like his works,
   But soon rose to the surface—like himself;
For all corrupted things are buoyed like corks,
   By their own rottenness, light as an elf,
Or wisp that flits o'er a morass: he lurks,
   It may be, still, like dull books on a shelf,
In his own den, to scrawl some 'Life' or 'Vision',
As Welborn says—'the devil turned precisian'.

As for the rest, to come to the conclusion
   Of this true dream, the telescope is gone
Which kept my optics free from all delusion,
   And showed me what I in my turn have shown;
All I saw farther, in the last confusion,
   Was, that King George slipped into heaven for one;
And when the tumult dwindled to a calm,
I left him practising the hundredth psalm.

142   *Beppo: A Venetian Story*

'Tis known, at least it should be, that throughout
    All countries of the Catholic persuasion,
Some weeks before Shrove Tuesday comes about,
    The people take their fill of recreation,
And buy repentance, ere they grow devout,
    However high their rank, or low their station,
With fiddling, feating, dancing, drinking, masking,
And other things which may be had for asking.

The moment night with dusky mantle covers
    The skies (and the more duskily the better),
The time less liked by husbands than by lovers
    Begins, and prudery flings aside her fetter;
And gaiety on restless tiptoe hovers,
    Giggling with all the gallants who beset her;
And there are songs and quavers, roaring, humming,
Guitars, and every other sort of strumming.

And there are dresses splendid, but fantastical,
    Masks of all times and nations, Turks and Jews,
And harlequins and clowns, with feats gymnastical,
    Greeks, Romans, Yankee-doodles, and Hindoos;
All kinds of dress, except the ecclesiastical,
    All people, as their fancies hit, may choose,
But no one in these parts may quiz the clergy—
Therefore take heed, ye Freethinkers! I charge ye.

You'd better walk about begirt with briars,
    Instead of coat and smallclothes, than put on
A single stitch reflecting upon friars,
    Although you swore it only was in fun;
They'd haul you o'er the coals, and stir the fires
    Of Phlegethon with every mother's son,
Nor say one mass to cool the cauldron's bubble
That boiled your bones, unless you paid them double.

But saving this, you may put on whate'er
   You like by way of doublet, cape, or cloak,
Such as in Monmouth Street, or in Rag Fair,
   Would rig you out in seriousness or joke;
And even in Italy such places are,
   With prettier name in softer accents spoke,
For, bating Covent Garden, I can hit on
No place that's called 'Piazza' in Great Britain.

This feast is named the Carnival, which being
   Interpreted, implies 'farewell to flesh':
So called, because the name and thing agreeing,
   Through Lent they live on fish both salt and fresh.
But why they usher Lent with so much glee in,
   Is more than I can tell, although I guess
'Tis as we take a glass with friends at parting,
In the stage-coach or packet, just at starting.

And thus they bid farewell to carnal dishes,
   And solid meats, and highly spiced ragouts,
To live for forty days on ill-dressed fishes,
   Because they have no sauces to their stews;
A thing which causes many 'poohs' and 'pishes',
   And several oaths (which would not suit the Muse),
From travellers accustomed from a boy
To eat their salmon, at the least, with soy;

And therefore humbly I would recommend
   'The curious in fish-sauce', before they cross
The sea, to bid their cook, or wife, or friend,
   Walk or ride to the Strand, and buy in gross
(Or if set out beforehand, these may send
   By any means least liable to loss)
Ketchup, Soy, Chili-vinegar, and Harvey,
Or by the Lord! a Lent will well nigh starve ye;

That is to say, if your religion's Roman,
   And you at Rome would do as Romans do,
According to the proverb—although no man,
   If foreign, is obliged to fast; and you
If Protestant, or sickly, or a woman,
   Would rather dine in sin on a ragout—
Dine and be damned! I don't mean to be coarse,
But that's the penalty, to say no worse.

Of all the places where the Carnival
    Was most facetious in the days of yore,
For dance, and song, and serenade, and ball,
    And masque, and mime, and mystery, and more
Than I have time to tell now, or at all,
    Venice the bell from every city bore,—
And at the moment when I fix my story,
That sea-born city was in all her glory.

They've pretty faces yet, those same Venetians,
    Black eyes, arched brows, and sweet expressions still;
Such as of old were copied from the Grecians,
    In ancient arts by moderns mimicked ill;
And like so many Venuses of Titian's
    (The best's at Florence—see it, if ye will),
They look when leaning over the balcony,
Or stepped from out a picture by Giorgione,

Whose tints are truth and beauty at their best;
    And when you to Manfrini's palace go,
That picture (howsoever fine the rest)
    Is loveliest to my mind of all the show;
It may perhaps be also to *your* zest,
    And that's the cause I rhyme upon it so:
'Tis but a portrait of his son, and wife,
And self; but *such* a woman! love in life!

Love in full life and length, not love ideal,
    No, nor ideal beauty, that fine name,
But something better still, so very real,
    That the sweet model must have been the same;
A thing that you would purchase, beg, or steal,
    Were't not impossible, besides a shame:
The face recalls some face, as 'twere with pain,
You once have seen, but ne'er will see again.

One of those forms which flit by us, when we
    Are young, and fix our eyes on every face;
And, oh! the loveliness at times we see
    In momentary gliding, the soft grace,
The youth, the bloom, the beauty which agree,
    In many a nameless being we retrace,
Whose course and home we knew not, nor shall know,
Like the lost Pleiad seen no more below.

I said that like a picture by Giorgione
    Venetian women were, and so they *are*,
Particularly seen from a balcony
    (For beauty's sometimes best set off afar),
And there, just like a heroine of Goldoni,
    They peep from out the blind, or o'er the bar;
And truth to say, they're mostly very pretty,
And rather like to show it, more's the pity!

For glances beget ogles, ogles sighs,
    Sighs wishes, wishes words, and words a letter,
Which flies on wings of light-heeled Mercuries,
    Who do such things because they know no better;
And then, God knows what mischief may arise,
    When love links two young people in one fetter,
Vile assignations, and adulterous beds,
Elopements, broken vows, and hearts, and heads.

Shakespeare described the sex in Desdemona
    As very fair, but yet suspect in fame,
And to this day from Venice to Verona
    Such matters may be probably the same,
Except that since those times was never known a
    Husband whom mere suspicion could inflame
To suffocate a wife no more than twenty,
Because she had a 'cavalier servente'.

Their jealousy (if they are ever jealous)
    Is of a fair complexion altogether,
Not like that sooty devil of Othello's,
    Which smothers women in a bed of feather,
But worthier of these much more jolly fellows,
    When weary of the matrimonial tether
His head for such a wife no mortal bothers,
But takes at once another, or another's.

Didst ever see a Gondola? For fear
    You should not, I'll describe it you exactly:
'Tis a long covered boat that's common here,
    Carved at the prow, built lightly, but compactly,
Rowed by two rowers, each called 'gondolier',
    It glides along the water looking blackly.
Just like a coffin clapped in a canoe,
Where none can make out what you say or do.

And up and down the long canals they go,
　And under the Rialto shoot along,
By night and day, all paces, swift or slow,
　And round the theatres, a sable throng,
They wait in their dusk livery of woe—
　But not to them do woeful things belong,
For sometimes they contain a deal of fun,
Like mourning coaches when the funeral's done.

But to my story. 'Twas some years ago,
　It may be thirty, forty, more or less,
The Carnival was at its height, and so
　Were all kinds of buffoonery and dress;
A certain lady went to see the show,
　Her real name I know not, nor can guess,
And so we'll call her Laura, if you please,
Because it slips into my verse with ease.

She was not old, nor young, nor at the years
　Which certain people call a '*certain age*',
Which yet the most uncertain age appears,
　Because I never heard, nor could engage
A person yet by prayers, or bribes, or tears,
　To name, define by speech, or write on page,
The period meant precisely by that word—
Which surely is exceedingly absurd.

Laura was blooming still, had made the best
　Of time, and time returned the compliment
And treated her genteelly, so that, dressed,
　She looked extremely well where'er she went;
A pretty woman is a welcome guest,
　And Laura's brow a frown had rarely bent;
Indeed, she shone all smiles, and seemed to flatter
Mankind with her black eyes for looking at her.

She was a married woman; 'tis convenient,
　Because in Christian countries 'tis a rule
To view their little slips with eyes more lenient;
　Whereas if single ladies play the fool
(Unless within the period intervenient
　A well-timed wedding makes the scandal cool),
I don't know how they ever can get over it,
Except they manage never to discover it.

Her husband sailed upon the Adriatic,
   And made some voyages, too, in other seas,
And when he lay in quarantine for pratique
   (A forty days' precaution 'gainst disease),
His wife would mount, at times, her highest attic,
   For thence she could discern the ship with ease:
He was a merchant trading to Aleppo,
His name Giuseppe, called more briefly, Beppo.

He was a man as dusky as a Spaniard,
   Sunburnt with travel, yet a portly figure;
Though coloured, as it were, within a tanyard,
   He was a person both of sense and vigour—
A better seaman never yet did man yard;
   And she, although her manners showed no rigour,
Was deemed a woman of the strictest principle,
So much as to be thought almost invincible.

But several years elapsed since they had met;
   Some people thought the ship was lost, and some
That he had somehow blundered into debt,
   And did not like the thought of steering home;
And there were several offered any bet,
   Or that he would, or that he would not come;
For most men (till by losing rendered sager)
Will back their own opinions with a wager.

'Tis said that their last parting was pathetic,
   As partings often are, or ought to be.
And their presentiment was quite prophetic,
   That they should never more each other see,
(A sort of morbid feeling, half poetic,
   Which I have known occur in two or three)
When kneeling on the shore upon her sad knee
He left this Adriatic Ariadne.

And Laura waited long, and wept a little,
   And thought of wearing weeds, as well she might;

pratique] license for ship to enter harbour after quarantine

She almost lost all appetite for victual,
   And could not sleep with ease alone at night;
She deemed the window-frames and shutters brittle
   Against a daring housebreaker or sprite,
And so she thought it prudent to connect her
With a vice-husband, *chiefly* to *protect her.*

She chose, (and what is there they will not choose,
   If only you will but oppose their choice?)
Till Beppo should return from his long cruise,
   And bid once more her faithful heart rejoice,
A man some women like, and yet abuse—
   A coxcomb was he by the public voice;
A Count of wealth, they said, as well as quality,
And in his pleasures of great liberality.

And then he was a Count, and then he knew
   Music, and dancing, fiddling, French and Tuscan;
The last not easy, be it known to you,
   For few Italians speak the right Etruscan.
He was a critic upon operas, too,
   And knew all niceties of sock and buskin;
And no Venetian audience could endure a
Song, scene, or air, when he cried 'seccatura!'

His 'bravo' was decisive, for that sound
   Hushed 'Academie' sighed in silent awe;
The fiddlers trembled as he looked around,
   For fear of some false note's detected flaw;
The prima donna's tuneful heart would bound,
   Dreading the deep damnation of his 'bah!'
Soprano, basso, even the contra-alto,
Wished him five fathom under the Rialto.

He patronized the Improvisatori,
   Nay, could himself extemporize some stanzas,
Wrote rhymes, sang songs, could also tell a story,
   Sold pictures, and was skilful in the dance as
Italians can be, though in this their glory
   Must surely yield the palm to that which France has;
In short, he was a perfect cavaliero,
And to his very valet seemed a hero.

Then he was faithful too, as well as amorous;
  So that no sort of female could complain,
Although they're now and then a little clamorous,
  He never put the pretty souls in pain;
His heart was one of those which most enamour us,
  Wax to receive, and marble to retain:
He was a lover of the good old school,
Who still become more constant as they cool.

No wonder such accomplishments should turn
  A female head, however sage and steady—
With scarce a hope that Beppo could return,
  In law he was almost as good as dead, he
Nor sent, nor wrote, nor showed the least concern,
  And she had waited several years already;
And really if a man won't let us know
That he's alive, he's *dead*, or should be so.

Besides, within the Alps, to every woman,
  (Although, God knows, it is a grievous sin.)
'Tis, I may say, permitted to have *two* men;
  I can't tell who first brought the custom in,
But 'Cavalier Serventes' are quite common,
  And no one notices or cares a pin;
And we may call this (not to say the worst)
A *second* marriage which corrupts the *first*.

The word was formerly a 'Cicisbeo',
  But *that* is now grown vulgar and indecent;
The Spaniards call the person a '*Cortejo*',
  For the same mode subsists in Spain, though recent;
In short, it reaches from the Po to Teio,
  And may perhaps at last be o'er the sea sent:
But Heaven preserve Old England from such courses!
Or what becomes of damage and divorces?

However, I still think, with all due deference
  To the fair *single* part of the creation,
That married ladies should preserve the preference
  In *tête-à-tête* or general conversation—
And this I say without peculiar reference
  To England, France, or any other nation—
Because they know the world, and are at ease,
And being natural, naturally please.

'Tis true, your budding Miss is very charming,
  But shy and awkward at first coming out,
So much alarmed, that she is quite alarming,
  All Giggle, Blush; half Pertness, and half Pout;
And glancing at *Mamma*, for fear there's harm in
  What you, she, it, or they, may be about,
The nursery still lisps out in all they utter—
Besides, they always smell of bread and butter.

But 'Cavalier Servente' is the phrase
  Used in politest circles to express
This supernumerary slave, who stays
  Close to the lady as a part of dress,
Her word the only law which he obeys,
  His is no sinecure, as you may guess;
Coach, servants, gondola, he goes to call,
And carries fan and tippet, gloves and shawl.

With all its sinful doings, I must say,
  That Italy's a pleasant place to me,
Who love to see the sun shine every day,
  And vines (not nailed to walls) from tree to tree
Festooned, much like the back scene of a play,
  Or melodrame, which people flock to see,
When the first act is ended by a dance
In vineyards copied from the south of France.

I like on autumn evenings to ride out,
  Without being forced to bid my groom be sure
My cloak is round his middle strapped about,
  Because the skies are not the most secure;
I know too that, if stopped upon my route,
  Where the green alleys windingly allure,
Reeling with grapes red waggons choke the way—
In England 'twould be dung, dust, or a dray.

I also like to dine on becaficas,
  To see the sun set, sure he'll rise tomorrow,
Not through a misty morning twinkling weak as
  A drunken man's dead eye in maudlin sorrow,
But with all Heaven t'himself; the day will break as
  Beauteous as cloudless, nor be forced to borrow
That sort of farthing candlelight which glimmers
Where reeking London's smoky cauldron simmers.

I love the language, that soft bastard Latin,
   Which melts like kisses from a female mouth,
And sounds as if it should be writ on satin,
   With syllables which breathe of the sweet South,
And gentle liquids gliding all so pat in,
   That not a single accent seems uncouth,
Like our harsh northern whistling, grunting guttural,
Which we're obliged to hiss, and spit, and sputter all.

I like the women too (forgive my folly),
   From the rich peasant cheek of ruddy bronze,
And large black eyes that flash on you a volley
   Of rays that say a thousand things at once,
To the high dama's brow, more melancholy,
   But clear, and with a wild and liquid glance,
Heart on her lips, and soul within her eyes,
Soft as her clime, and sunny as her skies.

Eve of the land which still is Paradise!
   Italian beauty! didst thou not inspire
Raphael, who died in thy embrace, and vies
   With all we know of Heaven, or can desire,
In what he hath bequeathed us!—in what guise,
   Though flashing from the fervour of the lyre,
Would *words* describe thy past and present glow,
While yet Canova can create below?

'England! with all thy faults I love thee still.'
   I said at Calais, and have not forgot it;
I like to speak and lucubrate my fill;
   I like the government (but that is not it);
I like the freedom of the press and quill;
   I like the Habeas Corpus (when we've got it);
I like a parliamentary debate,
Particularly when 'tis not too late;

I like the taxes, when they're not too many;
   I like a seacoal fire, when not too dear;
I like a beef-steak, too, as well as any;
   Have no objection to a pot of beer;
I like the weather, when it is not rainy,
   That is, I like two months of every year,
And so God save the Regent, Church, and King!
Which means that I like all and everything.

Our standing army, and disbanded seamen,
   Poor's rate, Reform, my own, the nation's debt,
Our little riots just to show we are free men,
   Our trifling bankruptcies in the Gazette,
Our cloudy climate, and our chilly women,
   All these I can forgive, and those forget,
And greatly venerate our recent glories,
And wish they were not owing to the Tories.

But to my tale of Laura—for I find
   Digression is a sin, that by degrees
Becomes exceeding tedious to my mind,
   And, therefore, may the reader too displease—
The gentle reader, who may wax unkind,
   And caring little for the author's ease,
Insist on knowing what he means, a hard
And hapless situation for a bard.

Oh that I had the art of easy writing
   What should be easy reading! could I scale
Parnassus, where the Muses sit inditing
   Those pretty poems never known to fail,
How quickly would I print (the world delighting)
   A Grecian, Syrian, or Assyrian tale;
And. sell you, mixed with western sentimentalism,
Some samples of the finest Orientalism!

But I am but a nameless sort of person,
   (A broken dandy lately on my travels)
And take for rhyme, to hook my rambling verse on,
   The first that Walker's Lexicon unravels,
And when I can't find that, I put a worse on,
   Not caring as I ought for critics' cavils;
I've half a mind to tumble down to prose,
But verse is more in fashion—so here goes.

The Count and Laura made their new arrangement,
   Which lasted, as arrangements sometimes do,
For half a dozen years without estrangement;
   They had their little differences, too;
Those jealous whiffs, which never any change meant;
   In such affairs there probably are few
Who have not had this pouting sort of squabble,
From sinners of high station to the rabble.

But, on the whole, they were a happy pair,
    As happy as unlawful love could make them;
The gentleman was fond, the lady fair,
    Their chains so slight, 'twas not worth while to break them;
The world beheld them with indulgent air;
    The pious only wished 'the devil take them!'
He took them not; he very often waits,
And leaves old sinners to be young ones' baits.

But they were young: Oh! what without our youth
    Would love be! What would youth be without love!
Youth lends it joy, and sweetness, vigour, truth,
    Heart, soul, and all that seems as from above;
But, languishing with years, it grows uncouth—
    One of few things experience don't improve,
Which is, perhaps, the reason why old fellows
Are always so preposterously jealous.

It was the Carnival, as I have said
    Some six and thirty stanzas back, and so
Laura the usual preparations made,
    Which you do when your mind's made up to go
Tonight to Mrs Boehm's masquerade,
    Spectator, or partaker in the show;
The only difference known between the cases
Is—*here*, we have six weeks of 'varnished faces'.

Laura, when dressed, was (as I sang before)
    A pretty woman as was ever seen,
Fresh as the Angel o'er a new inn door,
    Or frontispiece of a new magazine,
With all the fashions which the last month wore,
    Coloured, and silver paper leaved between
That and the title-page, for fear the press
Should soil with parts of speech the parts of dress.

They went to the Ridotto; 'tis a hall
    Where people dance, and sup, and dance again;
Its proper name, perhaps, were a masqued ball,
    But that's of no importance to my strain;
'Tis (on a smaller scale) like our Vauxhall,
    Excepting that it can't be spoilt by rain;
The company is 'mixed' (the phrase I quote is
As much as saying they're below your notice);

For a 'mixed company' implies that, save
   Yourself and friends, and half a hundred more,
Whom you may bow to without looking grave,
   The rest are but a vulgar set, the bore
Of public places, where they basely brave
   The fashionable stare of twenty score
Of well-bred persons, called *'The World'*; but I,
Although I know them, really don't know why.

This is the case in England; at least was
   During the dynasty of Dandies, now
Perchance succeeded by some other class
   Of imitated imitators: how
Irreparably soon decline, alas!
   The demagogues of fashion: all below
Is frail; how easily the world is lost
By love, or war, and now and then by frost!

Crushed was Napoleon by the northern Thor,
   Who knocked his army down with icy hammer,
Stopped by the elements, like a whaler, or
   A blundering novice in his new French grammar;
Good cause had he to doubt the chance of war,
   And as for Fortune—but I dare not damn her,
Because, were I to ponder to infinity,
The more I should believe in her divinity.

She rules the present, past, and all to be yet.
   She gives us luck in lotteries, love, and marriage;
I cannot say that she's done much for me yet;
   Not that I mean her bounties to disparage,
We've not yet closed accounts, and we shall see yet
   How much she'll make amends for past miscarriage.
Meantime the goddess I'll no more importune,
Unless to thank her when she's made my fortune.

To turn—and to return—the devil take it!
   This story slips for ever through my fingers,
Because, just as the stanza likes to make it,
   It needs must be, and so it rather lingers:
This form of verse began, I can't well break it,
   But must keep time and tune like public singers;
But if I once get through my present measure,
I'll take another when I'm next at leisure.

They went to the Ridotto ('tis a place
   To which I mean to go myself tomorrow,
Just to divert my thoughts a little space,
   Because I'm rather hippish, and may borrow
Some spirits, guessing at what kind of face
   May lurk beneath each mask; and as my sorrow
Slackens its pace sometimes, I'll make, or find,
Something shall leave it half an hour behind).

Now Laura moves along the joyous crowd,
   Smiles in her eyes, and simpers on her lips;
To some she whispers, others speaks aloud;
   To some she curtsies, and to some she dips;
Complains of warmth, and this complaint avowed,
   Her lover brings the lemonade, she sips;
She then surveys, condemns, but pities still
Her dearest friends for being dressed so ill.

One has false curls, another too much paint,
   A third—where did she buy that frightful turban?
A fourth's so pale she fears she's going to faint,
   A fifth's look's vulgar, dowdyish, and suburban,
A sixth's white silk has got a yellow taint,
   A seventh's thin muslin surely will be her bane.
And lo! an eighth appears—'I'll see no more!'
For fear, like Banquo's kings, they reach a score.

Meantime, while she was thus at others gazing,
   Others were levelling their looks at her;
She heard the men's half-whispered mode of praising,
   And, till 'twas done, determined not to stir;
The women only thought it quite amazing
   That, at her time of life, so many were
Admirers still—but 'Men are so debased,
Those brazen creatures always suit their taste.'

For my part, now, I ne'er could understand
   Why naughty women—but I won't discuss
A thing which is a scandal to the land,
   I only don't see why it should be thus;
And if I were but in a gown and band,
   Just to entitle me to make a fuss,
I'd preach on this till Wilberforce and Romilly
Should quote in their next speeches from my homily.

While Laura thus was seen, and seeing, smiling,
  Talking, she knew not why, and cared not what,
So that her female friends, with envy broiling,
  Beheld her airs and triumph, and all that;
And well-dressed males still kept before her filing,
  And passing bowed and mingled with her chat;
More than the rest one person seemed to stare
With pertinacity that's rather rare.

He was a Turk, the colour of mahogany;
  And Laura saw him, and at first was glad,
Because the Turks so much admire philogyny,
  Although their usage of their wives is sad;
'Tis said they use no better than a dog any
  Poor woman, whom they purchase like a pad;
They have a number, though they ne'er exhibit 'em,
Four wives by law, and concubines 'ad libitum'.

They lock them up, and veil, and guard them daily,
  They scarcely can behold their male relations,
So that their moments do not pass so gaily
  As is supposed the case with northern nations;
Confinement, too, must make them look quite palely;
  And as the Turks abhor long conversations,
Their days are either passed in doing nothing,
Or bathing, nursing, making love, and clothing.

They cannot read, and so don't lisp in criticism;
  Nor write, and so they don't affect the muse;
Were never caught in epigram or witticism,
  Have no romances, sermons, plays, reviews—
In harems learning soon would make a pretty schism,
  But luckily these beauties are no 'Blues';
No bustling Botherby have they to show 'em
'That charming passage in the last new poem'.

No solemn, antique gentleman of rhyme,
  Who having angled all his life for fame,
And getting but a nibble at a time,
  Still fussily keeps fishing on, the same
Small 'Triton of the minnows', the sublime
  Of mediocrity, the furious tame,
The echo's echo, usher of the school
Of female wits, boy bards—in short, a fool!

A stalking oracle of awful phrase,
   The approving *'Good!'* (by no means GOOD in law),
Humming like flies around the newest blaze,
   The bluest of bluebottles you e'er saw,
Teasing with blame, excruciating with praise,
   Gorging the little fame he gets all raw,
Translating tongues he knows not even by letter,
And sweating plays so middling, bad were better.

One hates an author that's *all author*, fellows
   In foolscap uniforms turned up with ink,
So very anxious, clever, fine, and jealous,
   One don't know what to say to them, or think,
Unless to puff them with a pair of bellows;
   Of coxcombry's worst coxcombs e'en the pink
Are preferable to these shreds of paper,
These unquenched snuffings of the midnight taper.

Of these same we see several, and of others,
   Men of the world, who know the world like men,
Scott, Rogers, Moore, and all the better brothers,
   Who think of something else besides the pen;
But for the children of the 'mighty mother's',
   The would-be wits, and can't-be gentlemen,
I leave them to their daily 'tea is ready',
Smug coterie, and literary lady.

The poor dear Mussulwomen whom I mention
   Have none of these instructive pleasant people,
And *one* would seem to them a new invention,
   Unknown as bells within a Turkish steeple;
I think 'twould almost be worth while to pension
   (Though best-sown projects very often reap ill)
A missionary author, just to preach
Our Christian usage of the parts of speech.

No chemistry for them unfolds her gases,
   No metaphysics are let loose in lectures,
No circulating library amasses
   Religious novels, moral tales, and strictures
Upon the living manners, as they pass us;
   No exhibition glares with annual pictures;
They stare not on the stars from out their attics,
Nor deal (thank God for that!) in mathematics.

Why I thank God for that is no great matter,
   I have my reasons, you no doubt suppose,
And as, perhaps, they would not highly flatter,
   I'll keep them for my life (to come) in prose;
I fear I have a little turn for satire,
   And yet methinks the older that one grows
Inclines us more to laugh than scold, though laughter
Leaves us so doubly serious shortly after.

Oh, mirth and innocence! Oh, milk and water!
   Ye happy mixtures of more happy days!
In these sad centuries of sin and slaughter,
   Abominable Man no more allays
His thirst with such pure beverage. No matter,
   I love you both, and both shall have my praise:
Oh, for old Saturn's reign of sugar candy!—
Meantime I drink to your return in brandy.

Our Laura's Turk still kept his eyes upon her,
   Less in the Mussulman than Christian way,
Which seems to say, 'Madam, I do you honour,
   And while I please to stare, you'll please to stay.'
Could staring win a woman, this had won her,
   But Laura could not thus be led astray;
She had stood fire too long and well, to boggle
Even at this stranger's most outlandish ogle.

The morning now was on the point of breaking,
   A turn of time at which I would advise
Ladies who have been dancing, or partaking
   In any other kind of exercise,
To make their preparations for forsaking
   The ballroom ere the sun begins to rise,
Because when once the lamps and candles fail,
His blushes make them look a little pale.

I've seen some balls and revels in my time,
   And stayed them over for some silly reason,
And then I looked (I hope it was no crime)
   To see what lady best stood out the season,
And though I've seen some thousands in their prime,
   Lovely and pleasing, and who still may please on,
I never saw but one (the stars withdrawn)
Whose bloom could after dancing dare the dawn.

The name of this Aurora I'll not mention,
    Although I might, for she was nought to me
More than that patent work of God's invention,
    A charming woman, whom we like to see;
But writing names would merit reprehension,
    Yet if you like to find out this fair *she*,
At the next London or Parisian ball
You still may mark her cheek out-blooming all.

Laura, who knew it would not do at all
    To meet the daylight after seven hours' sitting
Among three thousand people at a ball,
    To make her curtsy thought it right and fitting;
The Count was at her elbow with her shawl,
    And they the room were on the point of quitting,
When lo! those cursed gondoliers had got
Just in the very place where they *should not*.

In this they're like our coachmen, and the cause
    Is much the same—the crowd, and pulling, hauling,
With blasphemies enough to break their jaws,
    They make a never intermitted bawling.
At home, our Bow Street gemmen keep the laws,
    And here a sentry stands within your calling;
But for all that, there is a deal of swearing,
And nauseous words past mentioning of bearing.

The Count and Laura found their boat at last,
    And homeward floated o'er the silent tide,
Discussing all the dances gone and past;
    The dancers and their dresses, too, beside;
Some little scandals eke; but all aghast
    (As to their palace-stairs the rowers glide)
Sate Laura by the side of her Adorer,
When lo! the Mussulman was there before her.

'Sir,' said the Count, with brow exceeding grave,
    'Your unexpected presence here will make
It necessary for myself to crave
    Its import? But perhaps 'tis a mistake;
I hope it is so; and, at once to waive
    All compliment, I hope so for *your* sake;
You understand my meaning, or you *shall*.'
'Sir,' (quoth the Turk) ''tis no mistake at all:

GEORGE GORDON NOEL, LORD BYRON

'That lady is *my wife*!' Much wonder paints
  The lady's changing cheek, as well it might;
But where an Englishwoman sometimes faints,
  Italian females don't do so outright;
They only call a little on their saints,
  And then come to themselves, almost or quite;
Which saves much hartshorn, salts, and sprinkling faces,
And cutting stays, as usual in such cases.

She said—what could she say? Why, not a word:
  But the Count courteously invited in
The stranger, much appeased by what he heard:
  'Such things, perhaps, we'd best discuss within,'
Said he; 'Don't let us make ourselves absurd
  In public, by a scene, nor raise a din,
For then the chief and only satisfaction
Will be much quizzing on the whole transaction.'

They entered, and for coffee called—it came,
  A beverage for Turks and Christians both,
Although the way they make it's not the same.
  Now Laura, much recovered, or less loth
To speak, cries 'Beppo! what's your pagân name?
  Bless me! your beard is of amazing growth!
And how came you to keep away so long?
Are you not sensible 'twas very wrong?

'And are you *really, truly*, now a Turk?
  With any other women did you wive?
Is't true they use their fingers for a fork?
  Well, that's the prettiest shawl—as I'm alive!
You'll give it me? They say you eat no pork.
  And how so many years did you contrive
To—Bless me! did I ever? No, I never
Saw a man grown so yellow! How's your liver?

'Beppo! that beard of yours becomes you not:
  It shall be shaved before you're a day older:
Why do you wear it? Oh! I had forgot—
  Pray don't you think the weather here is colder?
How do I look? You shan't stir from this spot
  In that queer dress, for fear that some beholder
Should find you out, and make the story known.
How short your hair is! Lord! how grey it's grown!'

304

What answer Beppo made to these demands
   Is more than I know. He was cast away
About where Troy stood once, and nothing stands;
   Became a slave of course, and for his pay
Had bread and bastinadoes, till some bands
   Of pirates landing in a neighbouring bay,
He joined the rogues and prospered, and became
A renegado of indifferent fame.

But he grew rich, and with his riches grew so
   Keen the desire to see his home again,
He thought himself in duty bound to do so,
   And not be always thieving on the main;
Lonely he felt, at times, as Robin Crusoe,
   And so he hired a vessel come from Spain,
Bound for Corfu: she was a fine polacca,
Manned with twelve hands, and laden with tobacco.

Himself, and much (Heaven knows how gotten!) cash,
   He then embarked, with risk of life and limb,
And got clear off, although the attempt was rash;
   He said that *Providence* protected him—
For my part, I say nothing—lest we clash
   In our opinions: well, the ship was trim,
Set sail, and kept her reckoning fairly on,
Except three days of calm when off Cape Bonn.

They reached the island, he transferred his lading
   And self and livestock to another bottom,
And passed for a true Turkey-merchant, trading
   With goods of various names, but I've forgot 'em.
However, he got off by this evading,
   Or else the people would perhaps have shot him;
And thus at Venice landed to reclaim
His wife, religion, house, and Christian name.

His wife received, the patriarch re-baptized him
   (He made the church a present, by the way);
He then threw off the garments which disguised him,
   And borrowed the Count's smallclothes for a day:
His friends the more for his long absence prized him,
   Finding he'd wherewithal to make them gay,
With dinners, where he oft became the laugh of them,
For stories—but *I* don't believe the half of them.

Whate'er his youth had suffered, his old age
  With wealth and talking made him some amends;
Though Laura sometimes put him in a rage,
  I've heard the Count and he were always friends.
My pen is at the bottom of a page,
  Which being finished, here the story ends;
'Tis to be wished it had been sooner done,
But stories somehow lengthen when begun.

143   from *Don Juan*
                          (i)
                     Dedication

BOB Southey! You're a poet, poet laureate,
  And representative of all the race.
Although 'tis true that you turned out a Tory at
  Last, yours has lately been a common case.
And now my epic renegade, what are ye at
  With all the lakers, in and out of place?
A nest of tuneful persons, to my eye
Like 'four and twenty blackbirds in a pye,

'Which pye being opened they began to sing'
  (This old song and new simile holds good),
'A dainty dish to set before the King'
  Or Regent, who admires such kind of food.
And Coleridge too has lately taken wing,
  But like a hawk encumbered with his hood,
Explaining metaphysics to the nation.
I wish he would explain his explanation.

You, Bob, are rather insolent, you know,
  At being disappointed in your wish
To supersede all warblers here below,
  And be the only blackbird in the dish.
And then you overstrain yourself, or so,
  And tumble downward like the flying fish
Gasping on deck, because you soar too high, Bob,
And fall for lack of moisture quite a dry Bob.

143   pye] Southey's predecessor as Poet Laureate was H. J. Pye
dry Bob] slang for a 'dry' failure with a woman

And Wordsworth in a rather long *Excursion*
    (I think the quarto holds five hundred pages)
Has given a sample from the vasty version
    Of his new system to perplex the sages.
'Tis poetry, at least by his assertion,
    And may appear so when the Dog Star rages,
And he who understands it would be able
To add a story to the Tower of Babel.

You gentlemen, by dint of long seclusion
    From better company, have kept your own
At Keswick, and through still continued fusion
    Of one another's minds at last have grown
To deem, as a most logical conclusion,
    That poesy has wreaths for you alone.
There is a narrowness in such a notion,
Which makes me wish you'd change your lakes for ocean.

I would not imitate the petty thought,
    Nor coin my self-love to so base a vice,
For all the glory your conversion brought,
    Since gold alone should not have been its price.
You have your salary; was't for that you wrought?
    And Wordsworth has his place in the Excise.
You're shabby fellows—true—but poets still
And duly seated on the immortal hill.

Your bays may hide the baldness of your brows,
    Perhaps some virtuous blushes; let them go.
To you I envy neither fruit nor boughs,
    And for the fame you would engross below,
The field is universal and allows
    Scope to all such as feel the inherent glow.
Scott, Rogers, Campbell, Moore, and Crabbe will try
'Gainst you the question with posterity.

For me, who, wandering with pedestrian Muses,
    Contend not with you on the winged steed,
I wish your fate may yield ye, when she chooses,
    The fame you envy and the skill you need.
And recollect a poet nothing loses
    In giving to his brethren their full meed
Of merit, and complaint of present days
Is not the certain path to future praise.

He that reserves his laurels for posterity
   (Who does not often claim the bright reversion)
Has generally no great crop to spare it, he
   Being only injured by his own assertion.
And although here and there some glorious rarity
   Arise like Titan from the sea's immersion,
The major part of such appellants go
To—God knows where—for no one else can know.

If fallen in evil days on evil tongues,
   Milton appealed to the avenger, Time,
If Time, the avenger, execrates his wrongs
   And makes the word *Miltonic* mean *sublime*,
He deigned not to belie his soul in songs,
   Nor turn his very talent to a crime.
He did not loathe the sire to laud the son,
But closed the tyrant-hater he begun.

Think'st thou, could he, the blind old man, arise
   Like Samuel from the grave to freeze once more
The blood of monarchs with his prophecies,
   Or be alive again—again all hoar
With time and trials, and those helpless eyes
   And heartless daughters—worn and pale and poor,
Would he adore a sultan? He obey
The intellectual eunuch Castlereagh?

Cold-blooded, smooth-faced, placid miscreant!
   Dabbling its sleek young hands in Erin's gore,
And thus for wider carnage taught to pant,
   Transferred to gorge upon a sister shore,
The vulgarest tool that tyranny could want,
   With just enough of talent and no more,
To lengthen fetters by another fixed
And offer poison long already mixed.

An orator of such set trash of phrase,
   Ineffably, legitimately vile,
That even its grossest flatterers dare not praise,
   Nor foes—all nations—condescend to smile.
Not even a sprightly blunder's spark can blaze
   From that Ixion grindstone's ceaseless toil,
That turns and turns to give the world a notion
Of endless torments and perpetual motion.

A bungler even in its disgusting trade,
  And botching, patching, leaving still behind
Something of which its masters are afraid,
  States to be curbed and thoughts to be confined,
Conspiracy or congress to be made,
  Cobbling at manacles for all mankind,
A tinkering slave-maker, who mends old chains,
With God and man's abhorrence for its gains.

If we may judge of matter by the mind,
  Emasculated to the marrow, it
Hath but two objects, how to serve and bind,
  Deeming the chain it wears even men may fit,
Eutropius of its many masters, blind
  To worth as freedom, wisdom as to wit,
Fearless, because no feeling dwells in ice;
Its very courage stagnates to a vice.

Where shall I turn me not to view its bonds,
  For I will never feel them. Italy,
Thy late reviving Roman soul desponds
  Beneath the lie this state-thing breathed o'er thee.
Thy clanking chain and Erin's yet green wounds
  Have voices, tongues to cry aloud for me.
Europe has slaves, allies, kings, armies still,
And Southey lives to sing them very ill.

Meantime, Sir Laureate, I proceed to dedicate
  In honest simple verse this song to you.
And if in flattering strains I do not predicate,
  'Tis that I still retain my buff and blue;
My politics as yet are all to educate.
  Apostasy's so fashionable too,
To keep *one* creed's a task grown quite Herculean.
Is it not so, my Tory, ultra-Julian?

    Eutropius] Byzantine eunuch raised to the magistracy
        buff and blue] Whig colours in clothing
    ultra-Julian] more apostate than Julian the Apostate.

(ii)

Wordsworth

I know that what our neighbours call *longueurs*
   (We've not so good a word, but have the thing
In that complete perfection which ensures
   An epic from Bob Southey every spring)
Form not the true temptation which allures
   The reader; but 'twould not be hard to bring
Some fine examples of the *épopée*,
To prove its grand ingredient is ennui.

We learn from Horace, Homer sometimes sleeps;
   We feel without him, Wordsworth sometimes wakes,
To show with what complacency he creeps
   With his dear *Waggoners* around his lakes.
He wishes for 'a boat' to sail the deeps.
   Of ocean? No, of air. And then he makes
Another outcry for 'a little boat',
And drivels seas to set it well afloat.

If he must fain sweep o'er the ethereal plain,
   And Pegasus runs restive in his 'waggon',
Could he not beg the loan of Charles's Wain?
   Or pray Medea for a single dragon?
Or if, too classic for his vulgar brain,
   He feared his neck to venture such a nag on,
And he must needs mount nearer to the moon,
Could not the blockhead ask for a balloon?

'Pedlars' and 'boats' and 'waggons'! Oh ye shades
   Of Pope and Dryden, are we come to this?
That trash of such sort not alone evades
   Contempt, but from the bathos' vast abyss
Floats scum-like uppermost, and these Jack Cades
   Of sense and song above your graves may hiss—
The 'little boatman' and his 'Peter Bell'
Can sneer at him who drew 'Achitophel'!

Jack Cades] Jack Cade led the Kentish rising in 1450

(iii)
The Duke of Wellington

Oh Wellington! (Or 'Vilainton', for Fame
   Sounds the heroic syllables both ways.
France could not even conquer your great name,
   But punned it down to this facetious phrase—
Beating or beaten she will laugh the same.)
   You have obtained great pensions and much praise;
Glory like yours should any dare gainsay,
Humanity would rise, and thunder 'Nay!'

I don't think that you used Kinnaird quite well
   In Marinet's affair; in fact 'twas shabby
And like some other things won't do to tell
   Upon your tomb in Westminster's old abbey.
Upon the rest 'tis not worth while to dwell,
   Such tales being for the tea hours of some tabby,
But though your years as man tend fast to zero,
In fact your Grace is still but a young hero.

Though Britain owes (and pays you too) so much,
   Yet Europe doubtless owes you greatly more.
You have repaired Legitimacy's crutch,
   A prop not quite so certain as before.
The Spanish and the French, as well as Dutch,
   Have seen and felt how strongly you *restore*.
And Waterloo has made the world your debtor
(I wish your bards would sing it rather better).

You are 'the best of cut-throats'. Do not start;
   The phrase is Shakespeare's, and not misapplied.
War's a brain-spattering, windpipe-slitting art,
   Unless her cause by right be sanctified.
If you have acted *once* a generous part,
   The world, not the world's masters, will decide,
And I shall be delighted to learn who,
Save you and yours, have gained by Waterloo?

Kinnaird, Marinet] Lord Kinnaird fell out with Wellington over the arrest in
Paris in 1818 of Marinet, a French informer, Kinnaird thinking Marinet had
been given a safe conduct

I am no flatterer. You've supped full of flattery.
   They say you like it too; 'tis no great wonder:
He whose whole life has been assault and battery
   At last may get a little tired of thunder;
And swallowing eulogy much more than satire, he
   May like being praised for every lucky blunder,
Called saviour of the nations—not yet saved,
And Europe's liberator—still enslaved.

I've done. Now go and dine from off the plate
   Presented by the Prince of the Brazils,
And send the sentinel before your gate
   A slice or two from your luxurious meals:
He fought, but has not fed so well of late.
   Some hunger too they say the people feels.
There is no doubt that you deserve your ration,
But pray give back a little to the nation.

I don't mean to reflect; a man so great as
   You, my Lord Duke, is far above reflection.
The high Roman fashion too of Cincinnatus
   With modern history has but small connexion.
Though as an Irishman you love potatoes,
   You need not take them under your direction:
And half a million for your Sabine farm
Is rather dear! I'm sure I mean no harm.

Great men have always scorned great recompenses.
   Epaminondas saved his Thebes, and died,
Not leaving even his funeral expenses.
   George Washington had thanks, and nought beside,
Except the all-cloudless glory (which few men's is)
   To free his country. Pitt too had his pride
And as a high-souled minister of state is
Renowned for ruining Great Britain gratis.

Never had mortal man such opportunity,
   Except Napoleon, or abused it more.
You might have freed fallen Europe from the unity
   Of tyrants, and been blessed from shore to shore.
And *now*, what *is* your fame? Shall the Muse tune it ye?
   Now, that the rabble's first vain shouts are o'er?
Go, hear it in your famished country's cries!
Behold the world, and curse your victories!

As these new cantos touch on warlike feats,
  To you the unflattering Muse deigns to inscribe
Truths that you will not read in the gazettes,
  But which ('tis time to teach the hireling tribe
Who fatten on their country's gore and debts)
  Must be recited, and without a bribe.
You did great things, but not being great in mind
Have left undone the greatest—and mankind.

(iv)
Don Juan reaches the Capital of the Free

To our theme. The man who has stood on the Acropolis
  And looked down over Attica, or he
Who has sailed where picturesque Constantinople is,
  Or seen Timbuctoo, or hath taken tea
In small-eyed China's crockery-ware metropolis,
  Or sat amidst the bricks of Nineveh,
May not think much of London's first appearance—
But ask him what he thinks of it a year hence?

Don Juan had got out on Shooter's Hill,
  Sunset the time, the place the same declivity
Which looks along that vale of good and ill,
  Where London streets ferment in full activity;
While everything around was calm and still,
  Except the creak of wheels, which on their pivot he
Heard, and that bee-like, bubbling, busy hum
Of cities, that boil over with their scum.

I say, Don Juan, wrapt in contemplation,
  Walked on behind his carriage, o'er the summit,
And lost in wonder of so great a nation,
  Gave way to 't, since he could not overcome it.
'And here,' he cried, 'is Freedom's chosen station.
  Here peals the people's voice, nor can entomb it
Racks, prisons, inquisitions. Resurrection
Awaits it, each new meeting or election.

'Here are chaste wives, pure lives. Here people pay
  But what they please; and if that things be dear,
'Tis only that they love to throw away
  Their cash, to show how much they have a year.
Here laws are all inviolate; none lay
  Traps for the traveller; every highway's clear;
Here'—he was interrupted by a knife,
With 'Damn your eyes! your money or your life!'

These freeborn sounds proceeded from four pads
  In ambush laid, who had perceived him loiter
Behind his carriage; and, like handy lads,
  Had seized the lucky hour to reconnoitre,
In which the heedless gentleman who gads
  Upon the road, unless he prove a fighter,
May find himself, within that isle of riches,
Exposed to lose his life as well as breeches.

PERCY BYSSHE SHELLEY

1792–1822

144   from *Peter Bell, the Third*
                        (i)
                       Hell

HELL is a city much like London—
  A populous and a smoky city;
There are all sorts of people undone,
And there is little or no fun done;
  Small justice shown, and still less pity.

There is a Castles, and a Canning,
  A Cobbett, and a Castlereagh;
All sorts of caitiff corpses planning
All sorts of cozening for trepanning
  Corpses less corrupt than they.

There is a * * * , who has lost
   His wits, or sold them, none knows which;
He walks about a double ghost,
And though as thin as Fraud almost—
   Ever grows more grim and rich.

There is a Chancery Court; a King;
   A manufacturing mob; a set
Of thieves who by themselves are sent
Similar thieves to represent;
   An army; and a public debt.

Which last is a scheme of paper money,
   And means—being interpreted—
'Bees, keep your wax—give us the honey,
And we will plant, while skies are sunny,
   Flowers, which in winter serve instead.'

There is a great talk of revolution—
   And a great chance of despotism—
German soldiers—camps—confusion—
Tumults—lotteries—rage—delusion—
   Gin—suicide—and methodism;

Taxes too, on wine and bread,
   And meat, and beer, and tea, and cheese,
From which those patriots pure are fed,
Who gorge before they reel to bed
   The tenfold essence of all these.

There are mincing women, mewing,
   (Like cats, who *amant miserè*,)
Of their own virtue, and pursuing
Their gentler sisters to that ruin,
   Without which—what were chastity?

Lawyers—judges—old hobnobbers
   Are there—bailiffs—chancellors—
Bishops—great and little robbers—
Rhymesters—pamphleteers—stock-jobbers—
   Men of glory in the wars,—

Things whose trade is, over ladies
    To lean, and flirt, and stare, and simper,
Till all that is divine in woman
Grows cruel, courteous, smooth, inhuman,
    Crucified 'twixt a smile and whimper.

Thrusting, toiling, wailing, moiling,
    Frowning, preaching—such a riot!
Each with never-ceasing labour,
Whilst he thinks he cheats his neighbour,
    Cheating his own heart of quiet.

And all these meet at levees;
    Dinners convivial and political;
Suppers of epic poets; teas,
Where small talk dies in agonies;
    Breakfasts professional and critical;

Lunches and snacks so aldermanic
    That one would furnish forth ten dinners,
Where reigns a Cretan-tonguèd panic,
Lest news Russ, Dutch, or Alemannic
    Should make some losers, and some winners;

At conversazioni—balls—
    Conventicles—and drawing-rooms—
Courts of law—committees—calls
Of a morning—clubs—book-stalls—
    Churches—masquerades—and tombs.

And this is Hell—and in this smother
    All are damnable and damned;
Each one damning, damns the other;
They are damned by one another,
    By none other are they damned.

'Tis a lie to say, 'God damns!'
    Where was Heaven's Attorney–General
When they first gave out such flams?
Let there be an end of shams,
    They are mines of poisonous mineral.

Statesmen damn themselves to be
  Cursed; and lawyers damn their souls
To the auction of a fee;
Churchmen damn themselves to see
  God's sweet love in burning coals.

The rich are damned, beyond all cure,
  To taunt, and starve, and trample on
The weak and wretched; and the poor
Damn their broken hearts to endure
  Stripe on stripe, with groan on groan.

Sometimes the poor are damned indeed
  To take—not means for being blessed—
But Cobbett's snuff, revenge; that weed
From which the worms that it doth feed
  Squeeze less than they before possessed.

And some few, like we know who,
  Damned—but God alone knows why—
To believe their minds are given
To make this ugly Hell a Heaven;
  In which faith they live and die.

Thus, as in a town, plague-stricken,
  Each man be he sound or no
Must indifferently sicken;
As when day begins to thicken,
  None knows a pigeon from a crow—

So good and bad, sane and mad,
  The oppressor and the oppressed;
Those who weep to see what others
Smile to inflict upon their brothers;
  Lovers, haters, worst and best;

All are damned—they breathe an air,
  Thick, infected, joy-dispelling:
Each pursues what seems most fair,
Mining like moles, through mind, and there
Scoop palace-caverns vast, where Care
  In thronèd state is ever dwelling.

(ii)

Double Damnation

[*The Devil, having pursued Wordsworth's—or Peter Bell the Third's
—*Thanksgiving Ode *on the battle of Waterloo, in which he wrote
that Carnage was God's daughter, seeks at once to reward the poet.*]

   The Devil now knew his proper cue—
     Soon as he read the ode, he drove
To his friend Lord MacMurderchouse's,
A man of interest in both houses,
     And said: 'For money or for love,

   Pray find some cure or sinecure;
     To feed from the superfluous taxes
A friend of ours—a poet—fewer
Have fluttered tamer to the lure
     Than he.' His lordship stands and racks his

   Stupid brains, while one might count
     As many heads as he had boroughs—
At length replies; from his mean front,
Like one who rubs out an account,
     Smoothing away the unmeaning furrows:

   'It happens fortunately, dear Sir,
     I can. I hope I need require
No pledge from you that he will stir
In our affairs; like Oliver,
     That he'll be worthy of his hire.'

   These words exchanged, the news sent off
     To Peter, home the Devil hied—
Took to his bed; he had no cough,
No doctor, meat and drink enough,
     Yet that same night he died.

   The Devil's corpse was leaded down;
     His decent heirs enjoyed his pelf,
Mourning-coaches, many a one,
Followed his hearse along the town;
     Where was the Devil himself?

When Peter heard of his promotion,
   His eyes grew like two stars for bliss:
There was a bow of sleek devotion
Engendering in his back; each motion
   Seemed a Lord's shoe to kiss.

He hired a house, bought plate, and made
   A genteel drive up to his door,
With sifted gravel neatly laid—
As if defying all who said,
   Peter was ever poor.

But a disease soon struck into
   The very life and soul of Peter—
He walked about—slept—had the hue
Of health upon his cheeks—and few
   Dug better—none a heartier eater.

And yet a strange and horrid curse
   Clung upon Peter night and day;
Month after month the thing grew worse,
And deadlier than in this my verse
   I can find strength to say.

Peter was dull—he was at first
   Dull—oh, so dull—so very dull!
Whether he talked, wrote, or rehearsed—
Still with this dulness was he cursed—
   Dull—beyond all conception—dull.

No one could read his books—no mortal,
   But a few natural friends, would hear him;
The parson came not near his portal;
His state was like that of the immortal
   Described by Swift—no man could bear him.

His sister, wife, and children yawned,
   With a long, slow, and drear ennui,
All human patience far beyond;
Their hopes of Heaven each would have pawned,
   Anywhere else to be.

But in his verse, and in his prose,
    The essence of his dulness was
Concentrated and compressed so close,
'Twould have made Guatimozin doze
    On his red gridiron of brass.

A printer's boy, folding those pages,
    Fell slumbrously upon one side;
Like those famed Seven who slept three ages,
To wakeful frenzy's vigil-rages,
    As opiates, were the same applied.

Even the reviewers who were hired
    To do the work of his reviewing,
With adamantine nerves, grew tired;
Gaping and torpid they retired,
    To dream of what they should be doing.

And worse and worse, the drowsy curse
    Yawned in him, till it grew a pest—
A wide contagious atmosphere,
Creeping like cold through all things near;
    A power to infect and to infest.

His servant-maids and dogs grew dull;
    His kitten, late a sportive elf;
The weeds and lakes, so beautiful,
Of dim stupidity were full,
    All grew as dull as Peter's self.

The earth under his feet—the springs,
    Which lived within it a quick life,
The air, the winds of many wings,
That fan it with new murmurings,
    Were dead to their harmonious strife.

The birds and beasts within the wood,
    The insects, and each creeping thing,
Were now a silent multitude;
Love's work was left unwrought—no brood
    Near Peter's house took wing.

Guatimozin] Aztec emperor tortured and killed by Cortez

And every neighbouring cottager
  Stupidly yawned upon the other:
No jackass brayed; no little cur
Cocked up his ears; no man would stir
  To save a dying mother.

Yet all from that charmed district went
  But some half-idiot and half-knave,
Who rather than pay any rent,
Would live with marvellous content,
  Over his father's grave.

No bailiff dared within that space,
  For fear of the dull charm to enter;
A man would bear upon his face,
For fifteen months in any case,
  The yawn of such a venture.

Seven miles above—below—around—
  This pest of dulness holds its sway;
A ghastly life without a sound;
To Peter's soul the spell is bound—
  How should it ever pass away?

145   from *The Mask of Anarchy: Written
on the Occasion of the Massacre at Manchester*

As I lay asleep in Italy
There came a voice from over the Sea,
And with great power it forth led me
To walk in the visions of Poesy.

I met Murder on the way—
He had a mask like Castlereagh—
Very smooth he looked, yet grim;
Seven blood-hounds followed him:

All were fat; and well they might
Be in admirable plight,
For one by one, and two by two,
He tossed them human hearts to chew
Which from his wide cloak he drew.

Next came Fraud, and he had on,
Like Eldon, an ermined gown;
His big tears, for he wept well,
Turned to mill-stones as they fell.

And the little children, who
Round his feet played to and fro.
Thinking every tear a gem,
Had their brains knocked out by them.

Clothed with the Bible, as with light,
And the shadows of the night,
Like Sidmouth, next, Hypocrisy
On a crocodile rode by.

And many more Destructions played
In this ghastly masquerade,
All disguised, even to the eyes,
Like Bishops, lawyers, peers, or spies.

Last came Anarchy: he rode
On a white horse, splashed with blood;
He was pale even to the lips,
Like Death in the Apocalypse.

And he wore a kingly crown;
And in his grasp a sceptre shone;
On his brow this mark I saw—
'I AM GOD, AND KING, AND LAW!'

With a pace stately and fast,
Over English land he passed,
Trampling to a mire of blood
The adoring multitude.

And a mighty troop around,
With their trampling shook the ground,
Waving each a bloody sword,
For the service of their Lord.

And with glorious triumph, they
Rode through England proud and gay,
Drunk as with intoxication
Of the wine of desolation.

O'er fields and towns, from sea to sea,
Passed the Pageant swift and free,
Tearing up, and trampling down;
Till they came to London town.

And each dweller, panic-stricken,
Felt his heart with terror sicken
Hearing the tempestuous cry
Of the triumph of Anarchy.

For with pomp to meet him came,
Clothed in arms like blood and flame,
The hired murderers, who did sing
'Thou art God, and Law, and King.'

'We have waited, weak and lone
For thy coming, Mighty One!
Our purses are empty, our swords are cold,
Give us glory, and blood, and gold.'

Lawyers and priests, a motley crowd,
To the earth their pale brows bowed;
Like a bad prayer not over loud,
Whispering 'Thou art Law and God.'

Then all cried with one accord,
'Thou art King, and God, and Lord;
Anarchy, to thee we bow,
Be thy name made holy now!'

And Anarchy, the Skeleton,
Bowed and grinned to every one,
As well as if his education
Had cost ten millions to the nation.

For he knew the Palaces
Of our Kings were rightly his;
His the sceptre, crown, and globe,
And the gold-inwoven robe.

So he sent his slaves before
To seize upon the Bank and Tower,
And was proceeding with intent
To meet his pensioned Parliament.

THOMAS HOOD

1799–1845

146   *Our Village—by a Villager*

'Sweet Auburn, loveliest village of the plain'—*Goldsmith.*

OUR village, that 's to say not Miss Mitford's village, but our village
    of Bullock Smithy,
Is come into by an avenue of trees, three oak pollards, two elders,
    and a withy;
And in the middle, there's a green of about not exceeding an
    acre and a half;
It's common to all, and fed off by nineteen cows, six ponies, three
    horses, five asses, two foals, seven pigs, and a calf!
Besides a pond in the middle, as is held by a similar sort of common
    law lease,
And contains twenty ducks, six drakes, three ganders, two dead
    dogs, four drowned kittens, and twelve geese.
Of course the green's cropt very close, and does famous for
    bowling when the little village boys play at cricket;
Only some horse, or pig, or cow, or great jackass, is sure to come
    and stand right before the wicket.
There's fifty-five private houses, let alone barns and workshops,
    and pigstyes, and poultry huts, and such-like sheds;
With plenty of public-houses—two Foxes, one Green Man, three
    Bunch of Grapes, one Crown, and six King's Heads.
The Green Man is reckoned the best, as the only one that for love
    or money can raise
A postilion, a blue jacket, two deplorable lame white horses, and
    a ramshackled 'neat postchaise'.
There's one parish church for all the people, whatsoever may be
    their ranks in life or their degrees,
Except one very damp, small, dark, freezing cold, little
    Methodist chapel of ease;
And close by the churchyard there's a stonemason's yard, that
    when the time is seasonable
Will furnish with afflictions sore and marble urns and cherubims
    very low and reasonable.
There's a cage, comfortable enough; I've been in it with old Jack
    Jeffrey and Tom Pike;

For the Green Man next door will send you in ale, gin or anything else you like.

I can't speak of the stocks, as nothing remains of them but the
upright post;

But the pound is kept in repairs for the sake of Cob's horse, as is
always there almost.

There's a smithy of course, where that queer sort of a chap in his
way, Old Joe Bradley,

Perpetually hammers and stammers, for he stutters and shoes horses
very badly.

There's a shop of all sorts, that sells everything, kept by the widow
of Mr Task;

But when you go there it's ten to one she's out of every thing you
ask.

You'll know her house by the swarm of boys, like flies, about the
old sugary cask:

There are six empty houses, and not so well papered inside as out,

For billstickers won't beware, but sticks notices of sales and
election placards all about.

That's the Doctor's with a green door, where the garden pots in
the windows is seen;

A weakly monthly rose that don't blow, and a dead geranium, and
a tea-plant with five black leaves and one green.

As for hollyoaks at the cottage doors, and hone, ·ckles and
jasmines, you may go and whistle;

But the Tailor's front garden grows two cabbages, a dock, a
ha'porth of pennyroyal, two dandelions, and a thistle.

There are three small orchards—Mr Busby's the schoolmaster's
is the chief—

With two pear-trees that don't bear; one plum and an apple, that
every year is stripped by a thief.

There's another small day-school too, kept by the respectable Mrs
Gaby.

A select establishment, for six little boys and one big, and four
little girls and a baby;

There's a rectory, with pointed gables and strange odd chimneys
that never smokes,

For the rector don't live on his living like other Christian sort of
folks;

There's a barber's, once a week well filled with rough black-bearded,
shock-headed churls,

And a window with two feminine men's heads, and two masculine
ladies in false curls;

There's a butcher's, and a carpenter's, and a plumber's, and a
   small greengrocer's, and a baker,
But he won't bake on a Sunday, and there's a sexton that's a
   coal-merchant besides, and an undertaker;
And a toy-shop, but not a whole one, for a village can't compare
   with the London shops;
One window sells drums, dolls, kites, carts, bats, Clout's balls, and
   the other sells malt and hops.
And Mrs Brown, in domestic economy not to be a bit behind her
   betters,
Lets her house to a milliner, a watchmaker, a rat-catcher, a
   cobbler, lives in it herself, and it's the post-office for letters.
Now I've gone through all the village—ay, from end to end, save
   and except one more house,
But I haven't come to that—and I hope I never shall—and that's
   the Village Poor House!

THOMAS BABINGTON MACAULAY, LORD MACAULAY

1800–1859

147   *The Country Clergyman's Trip to Cambridge*
         An Election Ballad, 1827

> As I sat down to breakfast in state,
>   At my living of Tithing-cum-Boring,
> With Betty beside me to wait,
>   Came a rap that almost beat the door in.
> I laid down my basin of tea,
>   And Betty ceased spreading the toast.
> 'As sure as a gun, sir,' said she,
>   'That must be the knock of the post.'

A letter—and free—bring it here—
　　I have no correspondent who franks.
No! yes! can it be? Why, my dear,
　　'Tis our glorious, our Protestant Bankes.
'Dear sir, as I know you desire
　　That the Church should receive due protection,
I humbly presume to require
　　Your aid at the Cambridge election.

'It has lately been brought to my knowledge,
　　That the Ministers fully design
To suppress each cathedral and college,
　　And eject every learned divine.
To assist this detestable scheme
　　Three nuncios from Rome are come over;
They left Calais on Monday by steam,
　　And landed to dinner at Dover.

'An army of grim Cordeliers,
　　Well furnished with relics and vermin,
Will follow, Lord Westmoreland fears,
　　To effect what their chiefs may determine.
Lollards' bower, good authorities say,
　　Is again fitting up as a prison;
And a wood-merchant told me to-day
　　'Tis a wonder how faggots have risen.

'The finance scheme of Canning contains
　　A new Easter-offering tax;
And he means to devote all the gains
　　To a bounty on thumb-screws and racks.
Your living, so neat and compact—
　　Pray, don't let the news give you pain!—
Is promised, I know for a fact,
　　To an olive-faced padre from Spain.'

I read, and I felt my heart bleed,
　　Sore wounded with horror and pity;
So I flew, with all possible speed,
　　To our Protestant champion's committee.
True gentlemen, kind and well-bred!
　　No fleering! no distance! no scorn!
They asked after my wife, who is dead,
　　And my children who never were born.

327

They then, like high-principled Tories,
    Called our Sovereign unjust and unsteady,
And assailed him with scandalous stories,
    Till the coach for the voters was ready.
That coach might be well called a casket
    Of learning and brotherly love:
There were parsons in boot and in basket;
    There were parsons below and above.

There were Sneaker and Griper, a pair
    Who stick to Lord Mulesby like leeches;
A smug chaplain of plausible air,
    Who writes my Lord Goslingham's speeches;
Dr Buzz, who alone is a host,
    Who, with arguments weighty as lead,
Proves six times a week in the Post
    That flesh somehow differs from bread;

Dr Nimrod, whose orthodox toes
    Are seldom withdrawn from the stirrup;
Dr Humdrum, whose eloquence flows
    Like droppings of sweet poppy syrup;
Dr Rosygill puffing and fanning,
    And wiping away perspiration;
Dr Humbug, who proved Mr Canning
    The beast in St. John's Revelation.

A layman can scarce form a notion
    Of our wonderful talk on the road;
Of the learning, the wit, and devotion,
    Which almost each syllable showed:
Why divided allegiance agrees
    So ill with our free constitution;
How Catholics swear as they please,
    In hope of the priest's absolution;

How the Bishop of Norwich had bartered
    His faith for a legate's commission;
How Lyndhurst, afraid to be martyred,
    Had stooped to a base coalition;
How Papists are cased from compassion
    By bigotry stronger than steel;
How burning would soon come in fashion,
    And how very bad it must feel.

We were all so much touched and excited
   By a subject so direly sublime,
That the rules of politeness were slighted,
   And we all of us talked at a time;
And in tones, which each moment grew louder,
   Told how we should dress for the show,
And where we should fasten the powder,
   And if we should bellow or no.

Thus from subject to subject we ran,
   And the journey passed pleasantly o'er,
Till at last Dr Humdrum began;
   From that time I remember no more.
At Ware he commenced his prelection
   In the dullest of clerical drones:
And when next I regained recollection,
   We were rumbling o'er Trumpington stones.

148   *A Radical War Song*[1]

AWAKE, arise, the hour is come,
   For rows and revolutions;
There's no receipt like pike and drum
   For crazy constitutions.
Close, close the shop! Break, break the loom,
   Desert your hearths and furrows,
And throng in arms to seal the doom
   Of England's rotten boroughs.

We'll stretch that torturing Castlereagh
   On his own Dublin rack, sir;
We'll drown the King in eau de vie,
   The Laureate in his sack, sir,
Old Eldon and his sordid hag
   In molten gold we'll smother,
And stifle in his own green bag
   The Doctor and his brother.

[1] Written in 1820 after the trial and execution of the Cato Street conspirators.

---

148   The Doctor] nickname of Lord Sidmouth, who as the most repressive of Home Secretaries (against the Luddites, etc.) obtained the suspension of Habeas Corpus in 1817 by laying a 'green bag' of seditious papers before Parliament

In chains we'll hang in fair Guildhall
    The City's famed recorder,
And next on proud St. Stephen's fall,
    Though Wynn should squeak to order.
In vain our tyrants then shall try
    To 'scape our martial law, sir;
In vain the trembling Speaker cry
    That 'Strangers must withdraw,' sir.

Copley to hang offends no text;
    A rat is not a man, sir:
With schedules and with tax bills next
    We'll bury pious Van, sir.
The slaves who loved the Income Tax,
    We'll crush by scores, like mites, sir,
And him, the wretch who freed the blacks,
    And more enslaved the whites, sir.

The peer shall dangle from his gate,
    The bishop from his steeple,
Till all recanting, own, the State
    Means nothing but the People.
We'll fix the church's revenues
    On Apostolic basis,
One coat, one scrip, one pair of shoes
    Shall pay their strange grimaces.

We'll strap the bar's deluding train
    In their own darling halter,
And with his big church bible brain
    The parson at the altar.
Hail glorious hour, when fair Reform
    Shall bless our longing nation,
And Hunt receive commands to form
    A new administration.

Wynn] Charles Wynn M.P., friend of Southey, later Secretary for War.
Copley] John Copley, Solicitor-General, prosecuted Thistlewood
Van] Nicholas Vansittart, Chancellor of the Exchequer
Hunt] John Hunt, imprisoned, with his brother Leigh Hunt, for libelling the
Prince Regent

Carlile shall sit enthroned, where sat
Our Cranmer and our Secker;
And Watson show his snow-white hat
In England's rich Exchequer.
The breast of Thistlewood shall wear
Our Wellesley's star and sash, man;
And many a mausoleum fair
Shall rise to honest Cash, man.

Then, then beneath the nine-tailed cat
Shall they who used it writhe, sir;
And curates lean, and rectors fat,
Shall dig the ground they tithe, sir.
Down with your Bayleys, and your Bests,
Your Giffords, and your Gurneys:
We'll clear the island of the pests,
Which mortals name attorneys.

Down with your sheriffs, and your mayors,
Your registrars, and proctors,
We'll live without the lawyer's cares,
And die without the doctor's.
No discontented fair shall pout
To see her spouse so stupid;
We'll tread the torch of Hymen out,
And live content with Cupid.

Then, when the high-born and the great
Are humbled to our level,
On all the wealth of Church and State,
Like aldermen, we'll revel.
We'll live when hushed the battle's din,
In smoking and in cards, sir,
In drinking unexcised gin,
And wooing fair poissardes, sir.

Carlile] Richard Carlile, republican and freethinker
Watson] James Watson, tried for treason in 1817
Thistlewood] Arthur Thistlewood, leader of the Cato Street conspiracy, hanged 1820
Bayleys, Bests, Giffords, Gurneys] John Bayley, judge; W. D. Best, Attorney General;
Robert Gifford, one of the prosecutors in the Cato Street trial, and Attorney General;
Sir John Gurney, one of the prosecuting lawyers in the Cato Street Conspiracy trial
poissardes] the *poissardes* were the rabid market women round the guillotine in Paris

WINTHROP MACKWORTH PRAED

1802–1839

149   *Stanzas to the Speaker Asleep*

SLEEP, Mr Speaker! it's surely fair,
If you don't in your bed, that you should in your chair;
Longer and longer still they grow,
Tory and Radical, Aye and No;
Talking by night, and talking by day;
Sleep, Mr Speaker—sleep, sleep while you may!

Sleep, Mr Speaker! slumber lies
Light and brief on a Speaker's eyes;
Fielden or Finn, in a minute or two,
Some disorderly thing will do;
Riot will chase repose away:
Sleep, Mr Speaker—sleep, sleep while you may!

Sleep, Mr Speaker! Cobbett will soon
Move to abolish the sun and moon;
Hume, no doubt, will be taking the sense
Of the House on a saving of thirteen-pence;
Grattan will growl, or Baldwin bray:
Sleep, Mr Speaker—sleep, sleep while you may!

Sleep, Mr Speaker! dream of the time
When loyalty was not quite a crime;
When Grant was a pupil in Canning's school;
When Palmerston fancied Wood a fool:
Lord! how principles pass away!—
Sleep, Mr Speaker—sleep, sleep while you may!

Sleep, Mr Speaker! sweet to men
Is the sleep that comes but now and then;
Sweet to the sorrowful, sweet to the ill,
Sweet to the children that work in a mill;
You have more need of sleep than they:
Sleep, Mr Speaker—sleep, sleep while you may!

150   from *The Chaunt of the Brazen Head*

Tory and Whig

I THINK the thing you call Renown,
    The unsubstantial vapour
For which the soldier burns a town,
    The sonneteer a taper,
Is like the mist which, as he flies,
    The horseman leaves behind him;
He cannot mark its wreaths arise,
    Or if he does they blind him.

I think one nod of Mistress Chance
    Makes creditors of debtors,
And shifts the funeral for the dance,
    The sceptre for the fetters:
I think that Fortune's favoured guest
    May live to gnaw the platters,
And he that wears the purple vest
    May wear the rags and tatters.

I think the Tories love to buy
    'Your Lordship's and 'your Grace's,
By loathing common honesty,
    And lauding commonplaces:
I think that some are very wise,
    And some are very funny,
And some grow rich by telling lies.
    And some by telling money.

I think the Whigs are wicked knaves—
    (And very like the Tories)—
Who doubt that Britain rules the waves,
    And ask the price of glories:
I think that many fret and fume
    At what their friends are planning,
And Mr Hume hates Mr Brougham
    As much as Mr Canning.

I think that friars and their hoods,
   Their doctrines and their maggots,
Have lighted up too many feuds,
   And far too many faggots:
I think, while zealots fast and frown,
   And fight for two or seven,
That there are fifty roads to Town,
   And rather more to Heaven.

151   *Royal Education*[1]

A NURSERY SONG

I AM a babe of Royalty;
   Queen CHARLOTTE was my grannam;
And Parliament has voted me
   Six thousand pounds per annum,
To teach me how to read and write,
   To teach me elocution,
To teach me how to feast and fight
   For the King and Constitution,
      As a well-taught Prince should do,
   Who is taught by contribution.

I'll have a doll of porphyry,
   With diamonds in her curls,
And a rocking-horse of ivory,
   And a skipping-rope of pearls;
I'll have a painted paper kite,
   With banker's bills for wings,
And a golden fiddle to play at night,
   With silver wire for strings,
      As a well-taught Prince should have,
   Who is sprung from the German Kings.

---

[1] The Duke of Cumberland, afterwards King of Hanover, having been voted £6,000 per annum, in 1826, for the education of his son

My Woman of the Bedchamber
  Shall dress in the finest silk;
And a Nobleman of Hanover
  Shall boil my bread and milk;
My breeches shall be of cloth of gold,
  My nightcap of Mechlin lace;
And Cologne water, hot and cold,
  Shall be ready to wash my face,
    As a well-taught Prince should wash,
    Who is come of a royal race.

And when my coach and six shall jog,
  With horns, hussars, and banners,
To some gaunt German pedagogue,
  Who teaches Greek and manners,
How very ready I shall be
  To show that I'm fit for ruling,
By gaming and by gallantry,
  And other kinds of fooling,
    Which a well-taught Prince should learn,
    Who costs so much in schooling.

I'll learn of Uncle GEORGE to make
  A sword knot, and a bow,
And I'll learn of Uncle YORK to take
  The long odds, and a vow;
And Uncle CLARENCE shall supply
  The science of imprecation,
And you, my own papa shall try,
  To teach me fabrication,
    Which a well-taught Prince should study,
    Whose tutors are paid by the nation.

I'll learn from PEEL his lunacy
  About the Priests and Popes,
From ***, to live in infamy,
  From CANNING, to talk in tropes;
From BLOMFIELD to discern new lights,
  To darken the old from SCOTT,
From LIVERPOOL, the chartered rights
  Which an Englishman—has not,
    As a well-taught Prince should know,
    Who is born for a Kingly lot.

While Education, day by day,
  My native wit enlarges,
Oh, shall I not at last repay
  The Country's heavy charges?
As wise as any other GUELPH,
  As useful, and as dear,
Oh, shall I not procure myself
  A People's scorn and fear?
    Which a well-taught Prince should earn,
With six thousand pounds a year.

WILLIAM MAKEPEACE THACKERAY
1811–1863

152   *The Speculators*

THE night was stormy and dark,   The town was shut up in
sleep: Only those were abroad who were out on a lark,   Or those
who'd no beds to keep.

I passed through the lonely street,   The wind did sing and
blow;   I could hear the policeman's feet   Clapping to and fro.

There stood a potato-man   In the midst of all the wet;   He
stood with his 'tato-can   In the lonely Haymarket.

Two gents of dismal mien,   And dank and greasy rags,   Came
out of a shop for gin,   Swaggering over the flags:

Swaggering over the stones,   These shabby bucks did walk;
And I went and followed those seedy ones,   And listened to their talk.

Was I sober or awake?   Could I believe my ears?   Those
dismal beggars spake   Of nothing but railroad shares.

I wondered more and more: Says one—'Good friend of mine,
How many shares have you wrote for?   In the Diddlesex Junction
line?'

'I wrote for twenty,' says Jim,   'But they wouldn't give
me one;'   His comrade straight rebuked him   For the folly he
had done;

'O Jim, you are unawares   Of the ways of this bad town;
I always write for five hundred shares,   And *then* they put me
down.'

'And yet you got no shares,'   Says Jim, 'for all your
boast;   'I *would* have wrote,' says Jack, 'but where   Was
the penny to pay the post?'

'I lost, for I couldn't pay   That first instalment up;   But
here's taters smoking hot—I say   Let's stop my boy and sup.'

And at this simple feast   The while they did regale, I drew
each ragged capitalist   Down on my left thumb-nail.

Their talk did me perplex,   All night I tumbled and tost,
And thought of railroad specs.,   And how money was won and lost.

'Bless railroads everywhere,'   I said, 'and the world's
advance;   Bless every railroad share   In Italy, Ireland, France;
For never a beggar need now despair,   And every rogue has a
chance.'

153 *Damages, Two Hundred Pounds*

SPECIAL Jurymen of England! who admire your country's laws,
And proclaim a British Jury worthy of the realm's applause;
Gaily compliment each other at the issue of a cause
Which was tried at Guildford 'sizes, this day week as ever was.

Unto that august tribunal comes a gentleman in grief,
(Special was the British Jury, and the Judge, the Baron Chief),
Comes a British man and husband—asking of the law relief,
For his wife was stolen from him—he'd have vengeance on the thief.

Yes, his wife, the blessed treasure with the which his life was
  crowned,
Wickedly was ravished from him by a hypocrite profound.

And he comes before twelve Britons, men for sense and truth
   renowned,
To award him for his damage, twenty hundred sterling pound.

He by counsel and attorney there at Guildford does appear,
Asking damage of the villain who seduced his lady dear:
But I can't help asking, though the lady's guilt was all too clear,
And though guilty the defendant, wasn't the plaintiff rather queer?

First the lady's mother spoke, and said she'd seen her daughter cry
But a fortnight after marriage: early times for piping eye.
Six months after, things were worse, and the piping eye was black,
And this gallant British husband caned his wife upon the back.

Three months after they were married, husband pushed her to the
   door,
Told her to be off and leave him, for he wanted her no more;
As she would not go, why *he* went: thrice he left his lady dear,
Left her, too, without a penny, for more than a quarter of a year.

Mrs Frances Duncan knew the parties very well indeed,
She had seen him pull his lady's nose and make her lip to bleed;
If he chanced to sit at home not a single word he said;
Once she saw him throw the cover of a dish at his lady's head.

Sarah Green, another witness, clear did to the Jury note
How she saw this honest fellow seize his lady by the throat,
How he cursed her and abused her, beating her into a fit,
Till the pitying next-door neighbours crossed the wall and
   witnessed it.

Next door to this injured Briton Mr Owers, a butcher, dwelt;
Mrs Owers's foolish heart towards this erring dame did melt;
(Not that she had erred as yet, crime was not developed in her)
But being left without a penny, Mrs Owers supplied her dinner—
God be merciful to Mrs Owers, who was merciful to this sinner!

Caroline Naylor was their servant, said they led a wretched life,
Saw this most distinguished Briton fling a teacup at his wife;
He went out to balls and pleasures, and never once, in ten months'
   space,
Sate with his wife, or spoke her kindly. This was the defendant's
   case.

Pollock, C. B., charged the Jury; said the woman's guilt was clear:
That was not the point, however, which the Jury came to hear
But the damage to determine which, as it should true appear,
This most tender-hearted husband, who so used his lady dear,

Beat her, kicked her, caned her, cursed her, left her starving, year
    by year,
Flung her from him, parted from her, wrung her neck, and boxed
    her ear—
What the reasonable damage this afflicted man could claim,
By the loss of the affections of this guilty graceless dame?

Then the honest British Twelve, to each other turning round,
Laid their clever heads together with a wisdom most profound:
And towards his Lordship looking, spoke the foreman wise and
    sound;
'My Lord, we find for this here plaintiff damages two hundred
    pound.'

So, God bless the Special Jury! pride and joy of English ground,
And the happy land of England, where true justice does abound!
British Jurymen and husbands; let us hail this verdict proper;
If a British wife offends you, Britons, you've a right to whop her.

Though you promised to protect her, though you promised to
    defend her,
You are welcome to neglect her: to the devil you may send her:
You may strike her, curse, abuse her; so declares our law
    renowned;
And if after this you lose her—why you're paid two hundred
    pound.

CHARLES DICKENS

1812–1870

154   *The Fine Old English Gentleman*
New Version
to be said or sung at all Conservative Dinners

I'LL sing you a new ballad, and I'll warrant it first-rate,
Of the days of that old gentleman who had that old estate;
When they spent the public money at a bountiful old rate
On ev'ry mistress, pimp, and scamp, at ev'ry noble gate,
      In the fine old English Tory times;
      Soon may they come again!

The good old laws were garnished well with gibbets, whips, and chains,
With fine old English penalties, and fine old English pains,
With rebel heads, and seas of blood once hot in rebel veins;
For all these things were requisite to guard the rich old gains
      Of the fine old English Tory times;
      Soon may they come again!

This brave old code, like Argus, had a hundred watchful eyes,
And ev'ry English peasant had his good old English spies,
To tempt his starving discontent with fine old English lies,
Then call the good old Yeomanry to stop his peevish cries,
      In the fine old English Tory times;
      Soon may they come again!

The good old times for cutting throats that cried out in their need,
The good old times for hunting men who held their fathers' creed,
The good old times when William Pitt, as all good men agreed,
Came down direct from Paradise at more than railroad speed....
      Oh the fine old English Tory times;
      When will they come again!

In those rare days, the press was seldom known to snarl or bark,
But sweetly sang of men in pow'r, like any tuneful lark;
Grave judges, too, to all their evil deeds were in the dark;
And not a man in twenty score knew how to make his mark.
      Oh the fine old English Tory times;
      Soon may they come again!

Those were the days for taxes, and for war's infernal din;
For scarcity of bread, that fine old dowagers might win;
For shutting men of letters up, through iron bars to grin,
Because they didn't think the Prince was altogether thin,
      In the fine old English Tory times;
      Soon may they come again!

But Tolerance, though slow in flight, is strong-winged in the main;
That night must come on these fine days, in course of time was plain;
The pure old spirit struggled, but its struggles were in vain;
A nation's grip was on it, and it died in choking pain,
      With the fine old English Tory days,
      All of the olden time.

The bright old day now dawns again; the cry runs through the land,
In England there shall be dear bread—in Ireland, sword and brand;
And poverty, and ignorance, shall swell the rich and grand,
So, rally round the rulers with the gentle iron hand,
      Of the fine old English Tory days;
      Hail to the coming time!

JAMES RUSSELL LOWELL
1819–1891

155   from *A Fable for Critics*

[*Apollo speaks*]

THERE are truths you Americans need to be told,
And it never'll refute them to swagger and scold;
John Bull, looking o'er the Atlantic, in choler
At your aptness for trade, says you worship the dollar;
But to scorn such eye-dollar-try's what very few do,
And John goes to that church as often as you do.
No matter what John says, don't try to outcrow him,
'Tis enough to go quietly on and outgrow him;
Like most fathers, Bull hates to see Number One
Displacing himself in the mind of his son,
And detests the same faults in himself he'd neglected
When he sees them again in his child's glass reflected;
To love one another you're too like by half;
If he is a bull, you're a pretty stout calf,
And tear your own pasture from naught but to show
What a nice pair of horns you're beginning to grow.

There are one or two things I should just like to hint,
For you don't often get the truth told you in print;
The most of you (this is what strikes all beholders)
Have a mental and physical stoop in the shoulders;
Though you ought to be free as the winds and the waves,
You've the gait and the manners of runaway slaves;
Though you brag of your New World, you don't half believe in it;
And as much of the Old as is possible weave in it;
Your goddess of freedom, a tight, buxom girl,
With lips like a cherry and teeth like a pearl,
With eyes bold as Herë's, and hair floating free,
And full of the sun as the spray of the sea,
Who can sing at a husking or romp at a shearing,
Who can trip through the forests alone without fearing,
Who can drive home the cows with a song through the grass,
Keeps glancing aside into Europe's cracked glass,
Hides her red hands in gloves, pinches up her lithe waist,

And makes herself wretched with transmarine taste;
She loses her fresh country charm when she takes
Any mirror except her own rivers and lakes.

  You steal Englishmen's books and think Englishmen's thought,
With their salt on her tail your wild eagle is caught;
Your literature suits its each whisper and motion
To what will be thought of it over the ocean;
The cast clothes of Europe your statesmanship tries
And mumbles again the old blarneys and lies;—
Forget Europe wholly, your veins throb with blood,
To which the dull current in hers is but mud:
Let her sneer, let her say your experiment fails,
In her voice there's a tremble e'en now while she rails,
And your shore will soon be in the nature of things
Covered thick with gilt drift-wood of castaway kings,
Where alone, as it were in a Longfellow's Waif,
Her fugitive pieces will find themselves safe.

ARTHUR HUGH CLOUGH
1819–1861

156   from *Amours de Voyage*

(i)
Blessed Empire of Purse and Policeman

WHEN God makes a great Man he intends all others to crush him:
Pharaoh indeed, it is true, didn't put down Moses, but then that
Happened in barbarous times ere Polity rose to perfection
Ere the World had known bankers, and funds, and representation.
Rise up therefore ye Kings, and ye, ye Presidents! bring forth
Bayonet, mortar and bomb, and that patent tool the soldier!
Murder and mangle and waste and establish order. But meantime
Honour to lofty Speech and the Voice of the godlike spirit;
Yea—*though* journals write and ministers make explanations,
Spite of the able Débats, and the Eloquent Odillon-Barrot,
Honour yet to the Tongue, and the Pen of the Ready Writer,
Honour to speech and great honour to thee, thou noble Mazzini!—
Rise up therefore ye Kings and ye, ye Presidents—Ah, but
What is the use of all this? let me sing the song of the shopman

343

And my last word be like his: let me shout, with the chorus of journals,
O happy Englishmen we! that so truly can quote from Lucretius
Suave mari magno—how pleasant indeed in a tempest
Safe from the window to watch and behold the great trouble of others.
O blessed government ours, blessed Empire of Purse and Policeman,
Fortunate islands of Order, Utopia of—breeches-pockets,
O happy England, and oh great glory of self-laudation.

(ii)
Dulce it is, and Decorum, no doubt

[*From Rome, in the summer of 1849, when a French army approached
to restore the Pope to temporal power and destroy the young Roman
Republic, Claude, protagonist of* Amours de Voyage, *continues his corres-
pondence with his friend Eustace in London, in these four letters*]

I

What do the people say, and what does the government do?—you
Ask, and I know not at all. Yet fortune will favour your hopes; and
I, who avoided it all, am fated, it seems, to describe it.
I, who nor meddle nor make in politics—I who sincerely
Put not my trust in leagues nor any suffrage by ballot,
Never predicted Parisian millenniums, never beheld a
New Jerusalem coming down dressed like a bride out of heaven
Right on the Place de la Concorde—I, nevertheless, let me say it,
Could in my soul of souls, this day, with the Gaul at the gates, shed
One true tear for thee, thou poor little Roman Republic!
What, with the German restored, with Sicily safe to the Bourbon,
Not leave one poor corner for native Italian exertion?
France, it is foully done! and you, poor foolish England—
You, who a twelvemonth ago said nations must choose for themselves,
     you
Could not, of course, interfere—you, now, when a nation has chosen—
Pardon this folly! *The Times* will, of course, have announced the
     occasion,
Told you the news of today; and although it was slightly in error
When it proclaimed as a fact the Apollo was sold to a Yankee,
You may believe when it tells you the French are at Civita Vecchia.

II

Dulce it is, and *decorum*, no doubt, for the country to fall—to
Offer one's blood an oblation to Freedom, and die for the Cause; yet
Still, individual culture is also something, and no man
Finds quite distinct the assurance that he of all others is called on,
Or would be justified, even, in taking away from the world that
Precious creature, himself. Nature sent him here to abide here,
Else why sent him at all? Nature wants him still, it is likely.
On the whole, we are meant to look after ourselves; it is certain
Each has to eat for himself, digest for himself, and in general
Care for his own dear life, and see to his own preservation;
Nature's intentions, in most things uncertain, in this are decisive;
Which, on the whole, I conjecture the Romans will follow, and I shall.
    So we cling to our rocks like limpets; Ocean may bluster,
Over and under and round us; we open our shells to imbibe our
Nourishment, close them again, and are safe, fulfilling the purpose
Nature intended—a wise one, of course, and a noble, we doubt not.
Sweet it may be and decorous, perhaps, for the country to die; but,
On the whole, we conclude the Romans won't do it, and I shan't.

III

Will they fight? They say so. And will the French? I can hardly,
Hardly think so; and yet—He is come, they say, to Palo,
He is passed from Monterone, at Santa Severa
He hath laid up his guns. But the Virgin, the Daughter of Roma,
She hath despised thee and laughed thee to scorn—the Daughter of
    Tiber,
She hath shaken her head and built barricades against thee!
Will they fight! I believe it. Alas! 'tis ephemeral folly,
Vain and ephemeral folly, of course, compared with pictures,
Statues, and antique gems!—Indeed: and yet indeed too,
Yet, methought, in broad day did I dream—tell it not in St. James's,
Whisper it not in thy courts, O Christ Church!—yet did I, waking,
Dream of a cadence that sings, *Si tombent nos jeunes héros, la
Terre en produit de nouveaux contre vous tous prêts à se battre;*
Dreamt of great indignations and angers transcendental,
Dreamt of a sword at my side and a battle-horse underneath me.

IV

Now supposing the French or the Neapolitan soldier
Should by some evil chance come exploring the Maison Serny
(Where the family English are all to assemble for safety),
Am I prepared to lay down my life for the British female?
Really, who knows? One has bowed and talked, till, little by little,
All the natural heat has escaped of the chivalrous spirit.
Oh, one conformed, of course; but one doesn't die for good manners,
Stab or shoot, or be shot, by way of a graceful attention.
No, if it should be at all, it should be on the barricades there;
Should I incarnadine ever this inky pacifical finger,
Sooner far should it be for this vapour of Italy's freedom,
Sooner far by the side of the d——d and dirty plebeians.
Ah, for a child in the street I could strike; for the full-blown lady—
Somehow, Eustace, alas! I have not felt the vocation.
Yet these people of course will expect, as of course, my protection,
Vernon in radiant arms stand forth for the lovely Georgina,
And to appear, I suppose, were but common civility. Yes, and
Truly I do not desire they should either be killed or offended.
Oh, and of course you will say, 'When the time comes, you will be
      ready.'
Ah, but before it comes, am I to presume it will be so?
What I cannot feel now, am I to suppose that I shall feel?
Am I not free to attend for the ripe and indubious instinct?
Am I forbidden to wait for the clear and lawful perception?
Is it the calling of man to surrender his knowledge and insight
For the mere venture of what may, perhaps, be the virtuous action?
Must we, walking our earth, discerning a little, and hoping
Some plain visible task shall yet for our hands be assigned us,—
Must we abandon the future for fear of omitting the present,
Quit our own fireside hopes at the alien call of a neighbour,
To the mere possible shadow of Deity offer the victim?
And is all this, my friend, but a weak and ignoble refining,
Wholly unworthy the head or the heart of Your Own Correspondent?

from *Spectator ab Extra*

Le Diner

COME along, 'tis the time, ten or more minutes past,
And he who came first had to wait for the last;
The oysters ere this had been in and been out;
Whilst I have been sitting and thinking about
　　How pleasant it is to have money, heigh-ho!
　　How pleasant it is to have money.

A clear soup with eggs; *voilà tout*; of the fish
The *filets de sole* are a moderate dish
À la Orly, but you're for red mullet, you say:
By the gods of good fare, who can question today
　　How pleasant it is to have money, heigh-ho!
　　How pleasant it is to have money.

After oysters, sauterne; then sherry; champagne;
Ere one bottles goes, comes another again;
Fly up, thou bold cork, to the ceiling above,
And tell to our ears in the sound that they love
　　How pleasant it is to have money, heigh-ho!
　　How pleasant it is to have money.

I've the simplest of palates; absurd it may be,
But I almost could dine on a *poulet-au-riz*,
Fish and soup and omelette and that—but the deuce—
There were to be woodcocks, and not *Charlotte Russe*!
　　So pleasant it is to have money, heigh-ho!
　　So pleasant it is to have money.

Your chablis is acid, away with the hock,
Give me the pure juice of the purple médoc:
St. Péray is exquisite; but, if you please,
Some burgundy just before tasting the cheese.
　　So pleasant it is to have money, heigh-ho!
　　So pleasant it is to have money.

As for that, pass the bottle, and d——n the expense,
I've seen it observed by a writer of sense,
That the labouring classes could scarce live a day,
If people like us didn't eat, drink, and pay.
   So useful it is to have money, heigh-ho!
   So useful it is to have money.

One ought to be grateful, I quite apprehend,
Having dinners and suppers and plenty to spend,
And so suppose now, while the things go away,
By way of a grace we all stand up and say
   How pleasant it is to have money, heigh-ho!
   How pleasant it is to have money.

158   *The Latest Decalogue*

THOU shalt have one God only; who
Would be at the expense of two?
No graven images may be
Worshipped, except the currency:
Swear not at all; for for thy curse
Thine enemy is none the worse:
At church on Sunday to attend
Will serve to keep the world thy friend:
Honour thy parents; that is, all
From whom advancement may befall:
Thou shalt not kill; but needst not strive
Officiously to keep alive:
Do not adultery commit;
Advantage rarely comes of it:
Thou shalt not steal; an empty feat,
When it's so lucrative to cheat:
Bear not false witness; let the lie
Have time on its own wings to fly:
Thou shalt not covet; but tradition
Approves all forms of competition.

The sum of all is, thou shalt love,
If any body, God above:
At any rate shall never labour
More than thyself to love thy neighbour.

CHARLES LUTWIDGE DODGSON
(LEWIS CARROLL)
1832–1898

Poeta Fit, non Nascitur

'How shall I be a poet?
  How shall I write in rhyme:
You told me once "the very wish
  Partook of the sublime."
Then tell me how! Don't put me off
  With your "another time"!'

The old man smiled to see him,
  To hear his sudden sally;
He liked the lad to speak his mind
  Enthusiastically;
And thought 'There's no hum-drum in him,
  Nor any shilly-shally.'

'And would you be a poet
  Before you've been to school?
Ah, well! I hardly thought you
  So absolute a fool.
First learn to be spasmodic—
  A very simple rule.

'For first you write a sentence,
  And then you chop it small;
Then mix the bits, and sort them out
  Just as they chance to fall:
The order of the phrases makes
  No difference at all.

'Then, if you'd be impressive,
  Remember what I say,
That abstract qualities begin
  With capitals alway:
The True, the Good, the Beautiful—
  Those are the things that pay!

'Next, when you are describing
　A shape, or sound, or tint;
Don't state the matter plainly,
　But put it in a hint;
And learn to look at all things
　With a sort of mental squint.'

'For instance, if I wished, Sir,
　Of mutton-pies to tell,
Should I say "dreams of fleecy flocks
Pent in a wheaten cell"?'
'Why, yes,' the old man said: 'that phrase
Would answer very well.

'Then fourthly, there are epithets
　That suit with any word—
As well as Harvey's Reading Sauce
　With fish, or flesh, or bird—
Of these, "wild", "lonely", "weary", "strange",
　Are much to be preferred.'

'And will it do, O will it do
　To take them in a lump—
As "the wild man went his weary way
　To a strange and lonely pump"?'
'Nay, Nay! You must not hastily
　To such conclusions jump.

'Such epithets, like pepper,
　Give zest to what you write;
And, if you strew then sparely,
　They whet the appetite:
But if you lay them on too thick,
　You spoil the matter quite!

'Last, as to the arrangement:
　Your reader, you should show him.
Must take what information he
　Can get, and look for no im-
mature disclosure of the drift
　And purpose of your poem.

'Therefore, to test his patience—
  How much he can endure—
Mention no places, names, or dates,
  And evermore be sure
Throughout the poem to be found
  Consistently obscure.

'First fix upon the limit
  To which it shall extend:
Then fill it up with "Padding"
  (Beg some of any friend):
Your great SENSATION–STANZA
  You place towards the end.'

'And what is a Sensation,
  Grandfather, tell me pray?
I think I never heard the word
  So used before today:
Be kind enough to mention one
  "Exempli gratiâ."'

And the old man, looking sadly
  Across the garden-lawn,
Where here and there a dew-drop
  Yet glittered in the dawn,
Said 'Go to the Adelphi,
  And see the "Colleen Bawn".

'The word is due to Boucicault—
  The theory is his,
Where Life becomes a Spasm,
  And History a Whiz:
If that is not Sensation,
  I don't know what it is.

'Now try your hand, ere Fancy
  Have lost its present glow—'
'And then,' his grandson added,
  'We'll publish it, you know:
Green cloth—gold-lettered at the back—
  In duodecimo!'

Then proudly smiled that old man
  To see the eager lad
Rush madly for his pen and ink
  And for his blotting-pad—
But, when he thought of *publishing*,
  His face grew stern and sad.

SAMUEL BUTLER

1835–1902

160   *The Righteous Man*

THE righteous man will rob none but the defenceless,
Whatsoever can reckon with him he will neither plunder nor kill;
He will steal an egg from a hen or a lamb from an ewe,
For his sheep and his hens cannot reckon with him hereafter—
They live not in any odour of defencefulness:
Therefore right is with the righteous man, and he taketh advantage
      righteously,
Praising God and plundering.

The righteous man will enslave his horse and his dog,
Making them serve him for their bare keep and for nothing further,
Shooting them, selling them for vivisection when they can no longer
      profit him,
Backbiting them and beating them if they fail to please him;
For his horse and his dog can bring no action for damages,
Wherefore, then, should he not enslave them, shoot them, sell them
      for vivisection?

But the righteous man will not plunder the defenceful—
Not if he be alone and unarmed—for his conscience will smite him;
He will not rob a she-bear of her cubs, nor an eagle of her eaglets—
Unless he have a rifle to purge him from the fear of sin:
Then may he shoot rejoicing in innocency—from ambush or a safe
      distance;
Or he will beguile them, lay poison for them, keep no faith with them;
For what faith is there with that which cannot reckon hereafter,
Neither by itself, nor by another, nor by any residuum of ill
      consequences?
Surely, where weakness is utter, honour ceaseth.

Nay, I will do what is right in the eyes of him who can harm me,
And not in those of him who cannot call me to account.
Therefore yield me up thy pretty wings, O humming-bird!
Sing for me in a prison, O lark!
Pay me thy rent, O widow! for it is mine.
Where there is reckoning there is sin,
And where there is no reckoning sin is not.

161   *A Psalm of Montreal*

STOWED away in a Montreal lumber room
The Discobolus standeth and turneth his face to the wall;
Dusty, cobweb-covered, maimed and set at naught,
Beauty crieth in an attic and no man regardeth:
                              O God! O Montreal!

Beautiful by night and day, beautiful in summer and winter,
Whole or maimed, always and alike beautiful—
He preacheth gospel of grace to the skins of owls
And to one who seasoneth the skins of Canadian owls:
                              O God! O Montreal!

When I saw him I was wroth and I said, 'O Discobolus!
Beautiful Discobolus, a Prince both among gods and men!
What doest thou here, how camest thou hither, Discobolus,
Preaching gospel in vain to the skins of owls?'
                              O God! O Montreal!

And I turned to the man of skins and said unto him, 'O thou man of
        skins,
Wherefore has thou done thus to shame the beauty of the Discobolus?'
But the Lord had hardened the heart of the man of skins
And he answered, 'My brother-in-law is haberdasher to Mr Spurgeon.'
                              O God! O Montreal!

'The Discobolus is put here because he is vulgar—
He has neither vest nor pants with which to cover his limbs;
I, Sir, am a person of more respectable connections—
My brother-in-law is haberdasher to Mr Spurgeon.'
                              O God! O Montreal!

Then I said, 'O brother-in-law to Mr Spurgeon's haberdasher,
Who seasonest also the skins of Canadian owls,
Thou callest trousers "pants", whereas I call them "trousers",
Therefore thou art in hell-fire and may the Lord pity thee!'
                              O God! O Montreal!

'Preferrest thou the gospel of Montreal to the gospel of Hellas,
The gospel of thy connection with Mr Spurgeon's haberdashery to the
    gospel of the Discobolus?'
Yet none the less blasphemed he beauty saying, 'The Discobolus hath
    no gospel,
But my brother-in-law is haberdasher to Mr Spurgeon.'
                              O God! O Montreal!

SIR W. S. GILBERT
1836–1911

162   *Anglicized Utopia*

SOCIETY has quite forsaken all her wicked courses,
Which empties our police courts, and abolishes divorces.
          (Divorce is nearly obsolete in England.)
No tolerance we show to undeserving rank and splendour;
For the higher his position is, the greater the offender.
          (That's a maxim that is prevalent in England.)
No Peeress at our Drawing-Room before the Presence passes
Who wouldn't be accepted by the lower-middle classes;
Each shady dame, whatever be her rank, is bowed out neatly.
In short, this happy country has been Anglicized completely!
          It really is surprising
          What a thorough Anglicizing
We've brought about—Utopia's quite another land;
          In her enterprising movements,
          She is England—with improvements,
Which we dutifully offer to our mother-land!

Our city we have beautified—we've done it willy-nilly—
And all that isn't Belgrave Square is Strand and Piccadilly.
(They haven't any slummeries in England.)
We have solved the labour question with discrimination polished,
So poverty is obsolete and hunger is abolished—
(They are going to abolish it in England.)
The Chamberlain our native stage has purged, beyond a question,
Of 'risky' situation and indelicate suggestion;
No piece is tolerated if it's costumed indiscreetly—
In short, this happy country has been Anglicized completely!
  It really is surprising
  What a thorough Anglicizing
We've brought about—Utopia's quite another land;
  In her enterprising movements,
  She is England—with improvements,
Which we dutifully offer to our mother-land!

Our Peerage we've remodelled on an intellectual basis,
Which certainly is rough on our hereditary races—
(They are going to remodel it in England.)
The Brewers and the Cotton Lords no longer seek admission,
And Literary Merit meets with proper recognition—
(As Literary Merit does in England!)
Who knows but we may count among our intellectual chickens
Like them an Earl of Thackeray and p'raps a Duke of Dickens—
Lord Fildes and Viscount Millais (when they come) we'll welcome
  sweetly—
And then, this happy country will be Anglicized completely!
  It really is surprising
  What a thorough Anglicizing
We've brought about—Utopia's quite another land;
  In her enterprising movements,
  She is England—with improvements,
Which we dutifully offer to our mother-land!

A. E. HOUSMAN
1859–1936

163   *'Some can Gaze, and not be Sick'*

SOME can gaze and not be sick,
But I could never learn the trick.
There's this to say for blood and breath,
They give a man a taste for death.

164   *'The Laws of God, the Laws of Man'*

THE laws of God, the laws of man,
He may keep that will and can;
Not I: let God and man decree
Laws for themselves and not for me;
And if my ways are not as theirs
Let them mind their own affairs.
Their deeds I judge and much condemn,
Yet when did I make laws for them?
Please yourselves, say I, and they
Need only look the other way.
But no, they will not;they must still
Wrest their neighbour to their will,
And make me dance as they desire
With jail and gallows and hell-fire.
And how am I to face the odds
Of man's bedevilment and God's?
I, a stranger and afraid
In a world I never made.
They will be master, right or wrong;
Though both are foolish, both are strong.
And since, my soul, we cannot fly
To Saturn nor to Mercury,
Keep we must, if keep we can,
These foreign laws of God and man.

RUDYARD KIPLING
1865–1936

165   *The Gods of the Copybook Headings*
1919

As I pass through my incarnations in every age and race,
I make my proper prostrations to the Gods of the Market-Place.
Peering through reverent fingers I watch them flourish and fall,
And the Gods of the Copybook Headings, I notice, outlast them all.

We were living in trees when they met us. They showed us each in turn
That Water would certainly wet us, as Fire would certainly burn:
But we found them lacking in Uplift, Vision and Breadth of Mind,
So we left them to teach the Gorillas while we followed the March of
    Mankind.

We moved as the Spirit listed. *They* never altered their pace,
Being neither cloud nor wind-borne like the Gods of the Market-Place;
But they always caught up with our progress, and presently word
    would come
That a tribe had been wiped off its icefield, or the lights had gone out
    in Rome.

With the Hopes that our World is built on they were utterly out of
    touch,
They denied that the Moon was Stilton; they denied she was even
    Dutch.
They denied that Wishes were Horses; they denied that a Pig had
    Wings.
So we worshipped the Gods of the Market Who promised these
    beautiful things.

When the Cambrian measures were forming, They promised perpetual
    peace.
They swore, if we gave them our weapons, that the wars of the tribes
    would cease.
But when we disarmed They sold us and delivered us bound to our foe,
And the Gods of the Copybook Headings said: '*Stick to the Devil you
    know.*'

On the first Feminian Sandstones we were promised the Fuller Life
(Which started by loving our neighbour and ended by loving his wife)
Till our women had no more children and the men lost reason and faith,
And the Gods of the Copybook Headings said '*The Wages of Sin is
Death.*'

In the Carboniferous Epoch we were promised abundance for all,
By robbing selected Peter to pay for collective Paul;
But, though we had plenty of money, there was nothing our money
could buy,
And the Gods of the Copybook Headings said: '*If you don't work you
die.*'

Then the Gods of the Market tumbled, and their smooth-tongued
wizards withdrew,
And the hearts of the meanest were humbled and began to believe it
was true
That All is not Gold that Glitters, and Two and Two make Four—
And the Gods of the Copybook Headings limped up to explain it once
more.

* * * * *

As it will be in the future, it was at the birth of Man—
There are only four things certain since Social Progress began:—
That the Dog returns to his Vomit and the Sow returns to her Mire,
And the burnt Fool's bandaged finger goes wabbling back to the Fire;

And that after this is accomplished, and the brave new world begins
When all men are paid for existing and no man must pay for his sins,
As surely as Water will wet us, as sure as Fire will burn,
The Gods of the Copybook Headings with terror and slaughter return!

166   *The Hyænas*

AFTER the burial-parties leave
    And the baffled kites have fled;
The wise hyænas come out at eve
    To take account of our dead.

How he died and why he died
    Troubles them not a whit.
They snout the bushes and stones aside
    And dig till they come to it.

They are only resolute they shall eat
That they and their mates may thrive,
And they know that the dead are safer meat
Than the weakest thing alive.

(For a goat may butt, and a worm may sting,
And a child will sometimes stand;
But a poor dead soldier of the King
Can never lift a hand.)

They whoop and halloo and scatter the dirt
Until their tushes white
Take good hold in the army shirt,
And tug the corpse to light,

And the pitiful face is shewn again
For an instant ere they close;
But it is not discovered to living men—
Only to God and to those

Who, being soulless, are free from shame,
Whatever meat they may find.
Nor do they defile the dead man's name—
That is reserved for his kind.

167   *The Old Men*
                    1922

THIS is our lot if we live so long and labour unto the end—
That we outlive the impatient years and the much too patient friend:
And because we know we have breath in our mouth and think we have
       thoughts in our head,
We shall assume that we are alive, whereas we are really dead.

We shall not acknowledge that old stars fade or brighter planets arise
(That the sere bush buds or the desert blooms or the ancient well-head
      dries),
Or any new compass wherewith new men adventure 'neath new skies.

We shall lift up the ropes that constrained our youth, to bind on our
　　children's hands;
We shall call to the water below the bridges to return and replenish
　　our lands;
We shall harness horses (Death's own pale horses) and scholarly plough
　　the sands.

We shall lie down in the eye of the sun for lack of a light on our way—
We shall rise up when the day is done and chirrup, 'Behold, it is day!'
We shall abide till the battle is won ere we amble into the fray.

We shall peck out and discuss and dissect, and avert and extrude to
　　our mind,
The flaccid tissues of long-dead issues offensive to God and mankind—
(Precisely like vultures over an ox that the Army has left behind).

We shall make walk preposterous ghosts of the glories we once
　　created—
Immodestly smearing from muddled palettes amazing pigments mis-
　　mated—
And our friends will weep when we ask them with boasts if our natural
　　force be abated.

The Lamp of our Youth will be utterly out, but we shall subsist on
　　the smell of it;
And whatever we do, we shall fold our hands and suck our gums and
　　think well of it.
Yes, we shall be perfectly pleased with our work, and that is the
　　Perfectest Hell of it!

This is our lot if we live so long and listen to those who love us—
That we are shunned by the people about and shamed by the Powers above
　　us.
Wherefore be free of your harness betimes; but, being free, be assured,
That he who hath not endured to the death, from his birth he hath never
　　endured!

EDGAR LEE MASTERS
1869–1950

168   *Judge Somers*

How does it happen, tell me,
That I who was most erudite of lawyers,
Who knew Blackstone and Coke
Almost by heart, who made the greatest speech
The court-house ever heard, and wrote
A brief that won the praise of Justice Breese—
How does it happen, tell me,
That I lie here unmarked, forgotten,
While Chase Henry, the town drunkard,
Has a marble block, topped by an urn,
Wherein Nature, in a mood ironical,
Has sown a flowering weed?

169   *Carl Hamblin*

The press of the Spoon River *Clarion* was wrecked,
And I was tarred and feathered,
For publishing this on the day the Anarchists were hanged in Chicago:
'I saw a beautiful woman with bandaged eyes
Standing on the steps of a marble temple.
Great multitudes passed in front of her,
Lifting their faces to her imploringly.
In her left hand she held a sword.
She was brandishing the sword,
Sometimes striking a child, again a laborer,
Again a slinking woman, again a lunatic.
In her right hand she held a scale;
Into the scale pieces of gold were tossed
By those who dodged the strokes of the sword.
A man in a black gown read from a manuscript:
"She is no respecter of persons."
Then a youth wearing a red cap
Leaped to her side and snatched away the bandage.

And lo, the lashes had been eaten away
From the oozy eye-lids;
The eye-balls were seared with a milky mucus;
The madness of a dying soul
Was written on her face—
But the multitude saw why she wore the bandage.'

170   *Editor Whedon*

To be able to see every side of every question;
To be on every side, to be everything, to be nothing long;
To pervert truth, to ride it for a purpose,
To use great feelings and passions of the human family
For base designs, for cunning ends,
To wear a mask like the Greek actors—
Your eight-page paper—behind which you huddle,
Bawling through the megaphone of big type:
'This is I, the giant.'
Thereby also living the life of a sneak-thief,
Poisoned with the anonymous words
Of your clandestine soul.
To scratch dirt over scandal for money,
And exhume it to the winds for revenge,
Or to sell papers,
Crushing reputations, or bodies, if need be,
To win at any cost, save your own life.
To glory in demoniac power, ditching civilization,
As a paranoiac boy puts a log on the track
And derails the express train.
To be an editor, as I was.
Then to lie here close by the river over the place
Where the sewage flows from the village,
And the empty cans and garbage are dumped,
And abortions are hidden.

EDWIN ARLINGTON ROBINSON
1869–1935

Miniver Cheevy

MINIVER Cheevy, child of scorn,
  Grew lean while he assailed the seasons;
He wept that he was ever born,
  And he had reasons.

Miniver loved the days of old
  When swords were bright and steeds were prancing;
The vision of a warrior bold
  Would set him dancing.

Miniver sighed for what was not,
  And dreamed, and rested from his labors;
He dreamed of Thebes and Camelot,
  And Priam's neighbors.

Miniver mourned the ripe renown
  That made so many a name so fragrant;
He mourned Romance, now on the town,
  And Art, a vagrant.

Miniver loved the Medici,
  Albeit he had never seen one;
He would have sinned incessantly
  Could he have been one.

Miniver cursed the commonplace
  And eyed a khaki suit with loathing;
He missed the medieval grace
  Of iron clothing.

Miniver scorned the gold he sought,
  But sore annoyed was he without it;
Miniver thought, and thought, and thought,
  And thought about it.

Miniver Cheevy, born too late,
  Scratched his head and kept on thinking;
Miniver coughed, and called it fate,
  And kept on drinking.

HILAIRE BELLOC
1870–1953

172   *The Justice of the Peace*

DISTINGUISH carefully between these two,
  This thing is yours, that other thing is mine.
You have a shirt, a brimless hat, a shoe
  And half a coat. I am the Lord benign
Of fifty hundred acres of fat land
To which I have a right. You understand?

I have a right because I have, because,
  Because I have—because I have a right.
Now be quite calm and good, obey the laws,
  Remember your low station, do not fight
Against the goad, you know, it pricks
Whenever the uncleanly demos kicks.

I do not envy you your hat, your shoe.
  Why should you envy me my small estate?
It's fearfully illogical in you
  To fight with economic force and fate.
Moreover, I have got the upper hand,
And mean to keep it. Do you understand?

173   *Lord Lundy*

*who was too freely moved to tears, and thereby
ruined his political career*

LORD Lundy from his earliest years
Was far too freely moved to Tears.
For instance, if his Mother said,
'Lundy! It's time to go to Bed!'
He bellowed like a Little Turk.
Or if his father, Lord Dunquerque,
Said, 'Hi!' in a Commanding Tone,
'Hi, Lundy! Leave the Cat alone!'
Lord Lundy, letting go its tail,
Would raise so terrible a wail
As moved his Grandpapa the Duke
To utter the severe rebuke:
'When I, Sir! was a little Boy,
An Animal was not a Toy!'

His father's Elder Sister, who
Was married to a Parvenoo,
Confided to Her Husband, 'Drat!
The Miserable, Peevish Brat!
Why don't they drown the Little Beast?'
Suggestions which, to say the least,
Are not what we expect to hear
From Daughters of an English Peer.
His grandmamma, His Mother's Mother,
Who had some dignity or other,
The Garter, or no matter what,
I can't remember all the Lot!
Said, 'Oh! that I were Brisk and Spry
To give him that for which to cry!'
(An empty wish, alas! for she
Was Blind and nearly ninety-three).

The Dear old Butler thought—but there!
I really neither know nor care

Lord Lundy] Earl Beauchamp, appointed Governor of New South Wales in
1889 at the age of twenty-seven

For what the Dear Old Butler thought!
In my opinion, Butlers ought
To know their place, and not to play
The Old Retainer night and day.
I'm getting tired and so are you,
Let's cut the Poem into two!

LORD LUNDY

(Second Canto)

It happened to Lord Lundy then,
As happens to so many men:
Towards the age of twenty-six,
They shoved him into politics;
In which profession he commanded
The income that his rank demanded
In turn as Secretary for
India, the Colonies, and War.
But very soon his friends began
To doubt if he were quite the man:
Thus, if a member rose to say
(As members do from day to day),
'Arising out of that reply . . . !'
Lord Lundy would begin to cry.
A Hint at harmless little jobs
Would shake him with convulsive sobs.

While as for Revelations, these
Would simply bring him to his knees,
And leave him whimpering like a child.
It drove his Colleagues raving wild!
They let him sink from Post to Post,
From fifteen hundred at the most
To eight, and barely six—and then
To be Curator of Big Ben! . . .
And finally there came a Threat
To oust him from the Cabinet!

The Duke—his aged grand-sire—bore
The shame till he could bear no more.

He rallied his declining powers,
Summoned the youth to Brackley Towers,
And bitterly addressed him thus—
'Sir! you have disappointed us!
We had intended you to be
The next Prime Minister but three:
The stocks were sold; the Press was squared;
The Middle Class was quite prepared.
But as it is! . . . My language fails!
Go out and govern New South Wales!'
*   *   *
The Aged Patriot groaned and died:
And gracious! how Lord Lundy cried!

174   *On a General Election*

THE accursèd power which stands on Privilege
(And goes with Women, and Champagne and Bridge)
Broke—and Democracy resumed her reign:
(Which goes with Bridge, and Women and Champagne).

175   *Epitaph on the Favourite*
                Dog of a Politician

HERE lies a Dog: may every Dog that dies
Lie in security—as this Dog lies.

176   *Epitaph on the Politician himself*

HERE richly, with ridiculous display,
The Politician's corpse was laid away.
While all of his acquaintance sneered and slanged
I wept: for I had hoped to see him hanged.

177   *Another on the Same*

THIS, the last ornament among the peers,
Bribed, bullied, swindled and blackmailed for years:
But Death's what even Politicians fail
To bribe or swindle, bully or blackmail.

178   *Lines to a Don*

REMOTE and ineffectual Don
That dared attack my Chesterton,
With that poor weapon, half-impelled,
Unlearnt, unsteady, hardly held,
Unworthy for a tilt with men –
Your quavering and corroded pen;
Don poor at Bed and worse at Table,
Don pinched, Don starved, Don miserable;
Don stuttering, Don with roving eyes,
Don nervous, Don of crudities;
Don clerical, Don ordinary,
Don self-absorbed and solitary;
Don here-and-there, Don epileptic;
Don puffed and empty, Don dyspeptic;
Don middle-class, Don sycophantic,
Don dull, Don brutish, Don pedantic;
Don hypocritical, Don bad,
Don furtive, Don three-quarters mad;
Don (since a man must make an end),
Don that shall never be my friend.
          *   *   *
Don different from those regal Dons!
With hearts of gold and lungs of bronze,
Who shout and bang and roar and brawl
The Absolute across the hall,
Or sail in amply billowing gown
Enormous through the Sacred Town,
Bearing from College to their homes
Deep cargoes of gigantic tomes;
Dons admirable! Dons of Might!
Uprising on my inward sight
Compact of ancient tales, and port

And sleep—and learning of a sort.
Dons English, worthy of the land;
Dons rooted; Dons that understand.
Good Dons perpetual that remain
A landmark, walling in the plain—
The horizon of my memories—
Like large and comfortable trees.

*   *   *

Don very much apart from these,
Thou scapegoat Don, thou Don devoted,
Don to thine own damnation quoted,
Perplexed to find thy trivial name
Reared in my verse to lasting shame.
Don dreadful, rasping Don and wearing,
Repulsive Don – Don past all bearing.
Don of the cold and doubtful breath,
Don despicable, Don of death;
Don nasty, skimpy, silent, level;
Don evil; Don that serves the devil.
Don ugly – that makes fifty lines.
There is a Canon which confines
A Rhymed Octosyllabic Curse
If written in Iambic Verse
To fifty lines. I never cut;
I far prefer to end it—but
Believe me I shall soon return.
My fires are banked, but still they burn
To write some more about the Don
That dared attack my Chesterton.

179   *To Dives*

DIVES, when you and I go down to Hell,
Where scribblers end and millionaires as well,
We shall be carrying on our separate backs
Two very large but very different packs;
And as you stagger under yours, my friend,
Down the dull shore where all our journeys end,
And go before me (as your rank demands)
Towards the infinite flat underlands,
And that dear river of forgetfulness—
Charon, a man of exquisite address

(For, as your wife's progenitors could tell,
They're very strict on etiquette in Hell),
Will, since you are a lord, observe, 'My lord,
We cannot take these weighty things aboard!'
Then down they go, my wretched Dives, down
The fifteen sorts of boots you kept for town;
The hat to meet the Devil in; the plain
But costly ties; the cases of champagne;
The solid watch, and seal, and chain, and charm;
The working model of a Burning Farm
(To give the little Belials); all the three
Biscuits for Cerberus; the guarantee
From Lambeth that the Rich can never burn,
And even promising a safe return;
The admirable overcoat, designed
To cross Cocytus—very warmly lined:
Sweet Dives, you will leave them all behind
And enter Hell as tattered and as bare
As was your father when he took the air
Behind a barrow-load in Leicester Square.
Then turned to me, and noting one that brings
With careless step a mist of shadowy things:
Laughter and memories, and a few regrets,
Some honour, and a quantity of debts,
A doubt or two of sorts, a trust in God,
And (what will seem to you extremely odd)
His father's granfer's father's father's name,
Unspoilt, untitled, even spelt the same;
Charon, who twenty thousand times before
Has ferried Poets to the ulterior shore,
Will estimate the weight I bear, and cry—
'Comrade!' (He has himself been known to try
His hand at Latin and Italian verse,
Much in the style of Virgil—only worse)
'We let such vain imaginaries pass!'
Then tell me, Dives, which will look the ass—
You, or myself? Or Charon? Who can tell?
They order things so damnably in Hell.

STEPHEN CRANE
1871–1900

180   *'A Man said to the Universe'*

A MAN said to the universe:
'Sir, I exist!'
'However,' replied the universe,
'The fact has not created in me
A sense of obligation.'

SIR MAX BEERBOHM
1872–1956

181   *Ballade Tragique à Double Refrain*

SCENE: A Room in Windsor Castle   TIME: The Present
Enter a Lady-in-Waiting and a Lord-in-Waiting

SHE: Slow pass the hours—ah, passing slow!
                My doom is worse than anything
           Conceived by Edgar Allan Poe:
                The Queen is duller than the King.

HE: Lady, your mind is wandering;
           You babble what you do not mean.
                Remember, to your heartening,
           The King is duller than the Queen.

SHE: No, most emphatically No!
                To one firm-rooted fact I cling
           In my now chronic vertigo:
                The Queen is duller than the King.

HE: Lady, you lie. Last evening
           I found him with a Rural Dean,
                Talking of district-visiting ...
           The King is duller than the Queen.

SHE: At any rate he doesn't sew!
            You don't see *him* embellishing
            Yard after yard of calico ...
            The Queen is duller than the King.
            Oh to have been an underling
            To (say) the Empress Josephine!

HE: Enough of your self-pitying!
            The King is duller than the Queen.

SHE (*firmly*): The Queen is duller than the King.

HE: Death then for you shall have no sting.
            [*Stabs her and, as she falls dead, produces phial
            from breast-pocket of coat.*]

            Nevertheless, sweet friend Strychnine,
            [*Drinks.*]

            The King—is—duller than—the Queen.

            [*Dies in terrible agony.*]

182   *A Luncheon*[1]

            LIFT latch, step in, be welcome, Sir,
            Albeit to see you I'm unglad
            And your face is fraught with a deathly shyness
            Bleaching what pink it may have had.
            Come in, come in, Your Royal Highness.

            Beautiful weather?—Sir, that's true,
            Though the farmers are casting rueful looks
            At tilth's and pasture's dearth of spryness.—
            Yes, Sir, I've written several books.—
            A little more chicken, Your Royal Highness?

            Lift latch, step out, your car is there,
            To bear you hence from this antient vale.
            We are both of us aged by our strange brief nighness,
            But each of us lives to tell the tale.
            Farewell, farewell, Your Royal Highness.

[1] Thomas Hardy entertains the Prince of Wales to lunch at Max Gate, 20 July 1923.

G. K. CHESTERTON
1874–1936

from *Songs of Education*

(i)

History.

Form 991785, Sub-Section D

THE Roman threw us a road, a road,
And sighed and strolled away:
The Saxon gave us a raid, a raid,
A raid that came to stay;
The Dane went west, but the Dane confessed
That he went a bit too far;
And we all became, by another name,
The Imperial race we are.

Chorus
The Imperial race, the inscrutable race,
The invincible race we are.

Though Sussex hills are bare, are bare,
And Sussex weald is wide,
From Chichester to Chester
Men saw the Norman ride;
He threw his sword in the air and sang
To a sort of a light guitar;
It was all the same, for we all became
The identical nobs we are.

Chorus
The identical nobs, individual nobs
Unmistakable nobs we are.

The people lived on the land, the land,
They pottered about and prayed;
They built a cathedral here and there
Or went on a small crusade:
Till the bones of Becket were bundled out
For the fun of a fat White Czar,
And we all became, in spoil and flame,
The intelligent lot we are.

Chorus
The intelligent lot, the intuitive lot,
The infallible lot we are.

O Warwick woods are green, are green,
But Warwick trees can fall:
And Birmingham grew so big, so big,
And Stratford stayed so small.
Till the hooter howled to the morning lark
That sang to the morning star;
And we all became, in freedom's name,
The fortunate chaps we are.

Chorus
The fortunate chaps, felicitous chaps,
The fairy-like chaps we are.

The people they left the land, the land,
But they went on working hard;
And the village green that had got mislaid
Turned up in the squire's back-yard:
But twenty men of us all got work
On a bit of his motor car;
And we all became, with the world's acclaim,
The marvellous mugs we are:

Chorus
The marvellous mugs, miraculous mugs,
The mystical mugs we are.

(ii)
Geography.
Form 17955301, Sub-Section Z

The earth is a place on which England is found,
And you find it however you twirl the globe round;
For the spots are all red and the rest is all grey,
And that is the meaning of Empire Day.

Gibraltar's a rock that you see very plain,
And attached to its base is the district of Spain.
And the island of Malta is marked further on,
Where some natives were known as the Knights of St. John.
Then Cyprus, and east to the Suez Canal,
That was conquered by Dizzy and Rothschild his pal
With the Sword of the Lord in the old English way;
And that is the meaning of Empire Day.

Our principal imports come far as Cape Horn;
For necessities, cocoa; for luxuries, corn;
Thus Brahmins are born for the rice-field, and thus,
The Gods made the Greeks to grow currants for us;
Of earth's other tributes are plenty to choose,
Tobacco and petrol and Jazzing and Jews:
The Jazzing will pass but the Jews they will stay;
And that is the meaning of Empire Day.

Our principal exports, all labelled and packed,
At the ends of the earth are delivered intact:
Our soap or our salmon can travel in tins
Between the two poles and as like as two pins;
So that Lancashire merchants whenever they like
Can water the beer of a man in Klondike
Or poison the meat of a man in Bombay;
And that is the meaning of Empire Day.

The day of St. George is a musty affair
Which Russians and Greeks are permitted to share;
The day of Trafalgar is Spanish in name
And the Spaniards refuse to pronounce it the same;
But the day of the Empire from Canada came
With Morden and Borden and Beaverbrook's fame
And saintly seraphical souls such as they:
And that is the meaning of Empire Day.

184   *Antichrist, or the Reunion of*
         Christendom: An Ode

'A Bill which has shocked the conscience of every Christian community
in Europe'—*Mr F. E. Smith, on the Welsh Disestablishment Bill*

ARE they clinging to their crosses,
          F. E. Smith,
Where the Breton boat-fleet tosses,
          Are they, Smith?
Do they, fasting, trembling, bleeding,
          Wait the news from this our city?
Groaning 'That's the Second Reading!'
          Hissing 'There is still Committee!'
If the voice of Cecil falters,
          If McKenna's point has pith,
Do they tremble for their altars?
          Do they, Smith?

Russian peasants round their pope
          Huddled, Smith,
Hear about it all, I hope,
          Don't they, Smith?
In the mountain hamlets clothing
          Peaks beyond Caucasian pales,
Where Establishment means nothing
          And they never heard of Wales,
Do they read it all in Hansard
          With a crib to read it with—
'Welsh Tithes: Dr Clifford Answered.'
          Really, Smith?

In the lands where Christians were,
         F. E. Smith,
In the little lands laid bare,
         Smith, O Smith!
Where the Turkish bands are busy,
      And the Tory name is blessed
Since they hailed the Cross of Dizzy
      On the banners from the West!
Men don't think it half so hard if
      Islam burns their kin and kith,
Since a curate lives in Cardiff
         Saved by Smith.

It would greatly, I must own,
         Soothe me, Smith!
If you left this theme alone,
         Holy Smith!
For your legal cause or civil
      You fight well and get your fee;
For your God or dream or devil
      You will answer, not to me.
Talk about the pews and steeples
      And the Cash that goes therewith!
But the souls of Christian peoples ...
         Chuck it, Smith!

WYNDHAM LEWIS
1884–1957

185   from *If So the Man You Are*

(i)
The Man I Am

I

I'M no He-man you know, I'm not a He.
I'm not a chesty fellow that says *Gee*!
I'm not you know a guy that lives on pep.
I'm not a red-blood person who snaps *Yep*!

You know I've never hunted ovibos,
Nor caribou. I'd make a rotten boss
For any 'outfit'. Oh you know I'm not
Clever with Winchester or cooking-pot.
A Tempyo statuette perhaps, the Monk Ganjin,
Perhaps a patina laid very thin,
An affair of Han or Tang, lacquered Mitsuda,
Or the brackets of a japanese pagoda—
Those things are in my line. I am very sure
I should never make a Nansen or Maclure.
Forgive my frankness girls! I'm not quite yet
So destitute of manners to forget
What to sex-urge is due, film-etiquette,
What to the Garbo, what to Crawford's curls.
I'm sorry if I've been too brutal girls!

2

I'm not the man that lifts the broad black hat.
I'm not the man's a *preux*, clichéed for chat.
I'm not the man that's sensitive to sex.
I'm not the fair Novello of the Waacs.
I'm not at breaking wind behind a hand
Too good. I'm not when hot the man that fanned
His cheek with a mouchoir. I'm not that kind.
I'm not a sot, but water leaves me blind,
I'm not too careful with a drop of Scotch,
I'm not particular about a blotch.
I'm not alert to spy out a blackhead,
I'm not the man that minds a dirty bed.
I'm not the man to ban a friend because
He breasts the brine in lousy bathing-drawers.
I'm not the guy to balk at a low smell,
I'm not the man to insist on asphodel.
This sounds like a He-fellow don't you think?
It sounds like that. I belch, I bawl, I drink.

3

The man I am to live and to let live.
The man I am to forget and to forgive.

Maclure] William Maclure, who began his vast geological survey of the U.S.A.
in 1807

The man I am to turn upon my heel
If neighbours crude hostility reveal.
The man I am to stand a world of pain.
The man I am to turn my back on gain.
The man I am somewhat to overdo
The man's part—to be simple, and brave and true.
The man I am to twist my coat about
A beggar in a cold wind. Clout for clout,
I am the man to part with more than most—
I am the perfect guest, the perfect host.
The man I am (don't take this for a boast)
To tread too softly, maybe, if I see
A dream's upon my neighbour's harsh tapis.
The man I am to exact what is due to men,
The man to exact it only with the pen—
The man I am to let the machete rust,
The man I am to cry—Dust to the dust!
'The Word commands our Flesh to Dust'—that's me!
I am the man to shun Hamlet's soliloquy.

(ii)
Cat Conscious

Am I too dangerous, that no man can let
This 'wild beast' out, but keep it as a pet?
Must I on charity be so sustained,
And never be unwittingly unchained?
Must I be given *nothing*, lest I take
Too much from the world's *trop-plein*? Fake after fake,
Encouraged, must usurp the place is mine?
And yet had I demanded a gold-mine,
Or aimed to be dictator of the West,
I could not be regarded as a pest
More than I am by asphalt-inkslinger
Alike, and in-the-manger monied cur—
Nor more askance if my pen were a sword
Excalibur, itching to strike abroad!
What is it that men fear beyond everything?
Obviously an open person. Bring
One of us 'truthful ones' too near, their nests
Would be unfeathered. Experience invests

Us with such terrors, us whose tongues are clean,
It is rarely in the high-places we are seen.
If such as I were made too famous, oh
What would he not be doing here below!
Hence very aged men—else ruffians tried—
Are puffed and boosted, flattered and glorified.
The Shaws of this world, they are *safe*, that's it!
In the toothless head there's no danger for the bit.
So there you have (in this political age)
The secret of the dishonour of the sage—
The one that's young enough to have some teeth,
The one that's suspected honest underneath.

*

The man I am to blow the bloody gaff
If I were given platforms? The riff-raff
May be handed all the trumpets that you will.
Not so the golden-tongued. The window-sill
Is all the pulpit they can hope to get,
Of a slum-garret, sung by Mistinguette,
Too high up to be heard, too poor to attract
Anyone to their so-called 'scurrilous' tract.
What wind an honest mind advances? Look
No wind of sickle and hammer, of bell and book,
No wind of any party, or blowing out
Of any mountain hemming us about
Of 'High Finance', or the foothills of same.
The man I am who does *not* play the game!
Of those incalculable ones I am
Not to be trusted with free-speech to damn,
To be given enough rope—just enough to hang.
To be hobbled in a dry field. As the bird sang
Who punctured poor Cock Robin, by some sparrow
Condemned to be shot at with toy bow and arrow.
You will now see how it stands with all of those
Who strong propensities for truth disclose.
It's no use buddy—you are for it boy
If not from head to foot a pure alloy!
If so the man you are that lets the cat
Out of the bag, you're a marked fellow and that's flat.

*

If so the man you are to let the cat
Outside, expect your beer a little flat!
If so the man you are to keep it in
Always, then never worry. You will win!
Should things go slow at first, they're watching you—
To see if you're cat-conscious! If you say boo
To goose or serpent. But keep pussy down,
And out of sight, the finest house in town
Is yours for the asking and you'll be a knight
If you want to be—if the *cat* is out of sight!
They *must* see where the bloody cat will jump
All said and done. If with a scandalous bump
Or deftly on all fours. *You* are the cat
You see, in that connection—a puss to pat
Or to garrot. I'm positive you're that—
I mean the former. If you're up to scratch
No one on you will be a mouldy patch.—
If so the man you are to let the puss
Out of the knapsack, you're a simple goose.
You must know who your enemy is my god
By this time, or you're a very brainless sod!

*

If so the man you are to pick up sticks
Then why expect to have a house of bricks?
Merchant of fag-ends, if that's what you are,
Why should they give you a full-sized cigar?
If so the man you are commissionaire
Stock-still to stand for a pittance, why that's fair,
If so the man you are! I can't see why
Whacked from your hobo-holding you need cry.
Balata or gold, if so the man you are
The optimist-prospector, spit on your star:
Who would hand out a hoot if such a man
Had fits of grief? I don't see how *I* can.
If so the man you be to set your cap
At Croesus' crooked daughters you're a low chap.
For you may marry gold, or ships or rubber
Only if you're a proper money-grubber,
If so the man you be—I'm betting boy
You're not that cold, well-turned, steel-hammered toy.
If so the man you were, upon my lice,
I'd not give you this spate of good advice!—

Since so the man you are to turn your back
Upon the baton, so I think, in your knapsack.

*

If so the man you are commissionaire,
If so the man *marchand de mégots* there,
If so the man you are, *oh merd alors!*
If so the man to bang each taxi-door,
If so the man bemedalled, a 'man's-man' too,
If so the man you are to *all* men true,
If so you are the servant-man, why then,
If so the man (a scarecrow among men)
If such the man you are, these words we waste,
If so the man by nature's hand disgraced.
If so the man you be for the back-seat,
If so the man out of the hand to eat,
A fetch-and-carry fellow to salute,
If so the man that's just above the brute.
If so the man like the majority of men,
If so the man that's envious of the pen,
If so the man you are of the other cheek,
If so the man that's venomous and sleek,
If so the man that's Everyman, these words,
If so a man, we throw to the dicky-birds!

(iii)
A Few Enemy Thrusts

You now solicit a few Enemy thrusts
At the stock poets' thickly bay-leaved busts.
Ranged in that portrait-place, of marble and clay,
August with the as-yet unwithered bay.
I seem to note a roman profile bland,
I hear the drone from out the cactus-land:
That must be the poet of the Hollow Men:
The lips seem bursting with a deep Amen.
I espy Ezra, bearded like the Kaiser,
And wistful Earp, like a mediaeval sizar,
The learned beneficiary of provisions,
Gone to the buttery to lubricate his visions.
And there's Roy Campbell, stiff-chested and slim,
Posed for veronicas before wild terrapim.

Moore, the sturgeon of the Hampstead Hill,
Nations of Greeks and Hebrews drives at will
Across a gothic landscape: and James Joyce
For the third time his thirteen poems deploys.
Read broods above old battles. Sacheverell
Odd bloated ghosts compelling to retell
Their famous victories. The greater Yeats,
Turning his back on Ossian, relates
The blasts of more contemporary fates.
And Richard Aldington, equipped to sing
The beauties of an impossible greek spring.
Graves, Osbert, and Sassoon, and many others,
Brothers-in-arms and pen-aborted brothers:
And Auden (most recent bust) with playground whistle:
MacDiarmid beneath a rampant thistle.—
As it's my role to provide the personal chord,
These names I hope some slight kick will afford.
We are not very rich in laurelled heads—
We are a little age, where the blind pygmy treads
In hypnotized crusades against all splendour,
Perverts male prowess to the middle gender.
We are a critic-company, what's more.
The Ronin, the Wave-Men, camp in the ruined door.

D. H. LAWRENCE
1885–1930

186   *How Beastly the Bourgeois Is—*

How beastly the bourgeois is
especially the male of the species—

Presentable eminently presentable—
shall I make you a present of him?

Isn't he handsome? isn't he healthy? Isn't he a fine specimen?
doesn't he look the fresh clean englishman, outside?

185   Ronin] samurai on their own without a master

Isn't it god's own image? tramping his thirty miles a day
after partridges, or a little rubber ball?
wouldn't you like to be like that, well off, and quite the thing?

Oh, but wait!
Let him meet a new emotion, let him be faced with another man's
    need,
let him come home to a bit of moral difficulty, let life face him with
    a new demand on his understanding
and then watch him go soggy, like a wet meringue.
Watch him turn into a mess, either a fool or a bully.
Just watch the display of him, confronted with a new demand on his
    intelligence,
a new life-demand.

How beastly the bourgeois is
especially the male of the species—

Nicely groomed like a mushroom
standing there so sleek and erect and eyeable—
and like a fungus, living on the remains of bygone life
sucking his life out of the dead leaves of greater life than his own.

And even so, he's stale, he's been there too long.
Touch him, and you'll find he's all gone inside
just like an old mushroom, all wormy inside, and hollow
under a smooth skin and an upright appearance.

Full of seething, wormy, hollow feelings
rather nasty—
How beastly the bourgeois is!

Standing in their thousands, these appearances, in damp England
what a pity they can't all be kicked over
like sickening toadstools, and left to melt back, swiftly
into the soil of England.

187   *When Wilt Thou Teach the People—?*

WHEN wilt thou teach the people,
God of justice, to save themselves—?
They have been saved so often
and sold.

O God of justice, send no more saviours
of the people!

When a saviour has saved a people
they find he has sold them to his father.
They say: We are saved, but we are starving.
He says: The sooner will you eat imaginary cake in the mansions
    of my father.
They say: Can't we have a loaf of common bread?
He says: No, you must go to heaven, and eat the most marvellous
    cake.—

Or Napoleon says: Since I have saved you from the ci-devants,
you are my property, be prepared to die for me, and to work for me.—

Or later republicans say: You are saved,
therefore you are our savings, our capital
with which we shall do big business.—

Or Lenin says: You are saved, but you are saved wholesale.
You are no longer men, that is bourgeois;
you are items in the soviet state,
and each item will get its ration,
but it is the soviet state alone which counts
the items are of small importance,
the state having saved them all.—

And so it goes on, with the saving of the people.
God of justice, when wilt thou teach them to save themselves?

EZRA POUND
1885–1972

188   *Reflection and Advice*

O SMOOTH flatterers, go over sea,
        Go to my country,
Tell her she is 'Mighty among the nations'.
        Do it rhetorically!

Say there are no oppressions,
Say it is a time of peace,
Say that labor is pleasant,
Say there are no oppressions,
Speak of the American virtues,
        And you will not lack your reward.

Say that the keepers of shops pay a fair wage to the women,
Say that all men are honest and desirous of good above all things,
        You will not lack your reward.

Say that I am a traitor and a cynic,
Say that the art is well served by the ignorant pretenders,
        You will not lack your reward.

Praise them that are praised by the many:
        You will not lack your reward.

Call this a time of peace,
Speak well of amateur harlots,
Speak well of disguised procurers,
Speak well of shop-walkers,
Speak well of employers of women,
Speak well of exploiters,
Speak well of the men in control,
Speak well of popular preachers:
        You will not lack your reward.

Speak of the open-mindedness of scholars:
>You will not lack your reward.

Say that you love your fellow men,
O most magnanimous liar:
>You will not lack your reward.

189   from *L'Homme Moyen Sensuel*

(i)

'TIS of my country that I would endite,
In hope to set some misconceptions right.
My country? I love it well, and those good fellows
Who, since their wit's unknown, escape the gallows.
But you stuffed coats who're neither tepid nor distinctly boreal,
Pimping, conceited, placid, editorial,
Could I but speak as 'twere in the 'Restoration'
I would articulate your perdamnation.
This year perforce I must with circumspection—
For Mencken states somewhere, in this connection:
'It is a moral nation we infest.'
Despite such reins and checks I'll do my best,
An art! You all respect the arts, from that infant tick
Who's now the editor of *The Atlantic*,
From Comstock's self, down to the meanest resident,
Till up again, right up, we reach the president,
Who shows his taste in his ambassadors:
A novelist, a publisher, to pay old scores,
A novelist, a publisher and a preacher,
That's sent to Holland, a most particular feature,
Henry Van Dyke, who thinks to charm the Muse you pack her in
A sort of stinking deliquescent saccharine.
The constitution of our land, O Socrates,
Was made to incubate such mediocrities,

189   Comstock] Anthony Comstock, American campaigner against obscene literature
Henry Van Dyke] Princeton professor and sentimental essayist (1852–1933)

These and a state in books that's grown perennial
And antedates the Philadelphia centennial.
Still I'd respect you more if you could bury
Mabie, and Lyman Abbot and George Woodberry,
For minds so wholly founded upon quotations
Are not the best of pulse for infant nations.
Dulness herself, that abject spirit, chortles
To see your forty self-baptized immortals,
And holds her sides where swelling laughter cracks 'em
Before the 'Ars Poetica' of Hiram Maxim.

(ii)

Alas, eheu, one question that sorely vexes
The serious social folk is 'just what sex is'.
Though it will, of course, pass off with social science
In which their mentors place such wide reliance ...
De Gourmont says that fifty grunts are all that will be prized,
Of language, by men wholly socialized,
With signs as many, that shall represent 'em
When thoroughly socialized printers want to print 'em.
'As free of mobs as kings'? I'd have men free of that invidious,
Lurking, serpentine, amphibious and insidious
Power that compels 'em
To be so much alike that every dog that smells 'em,
Thinks one identity is
Smeared o'er the lot in equal quantities.
Still we look toward the day when man, with unction,
Will long only to be a *social function*,
And even Zeus' wild lightning fear to strike
Lest it should fail to treat all men alike.
And I can hear an old man saying: 'Oh, the rub!
I see them sitting in the Harvard Club,
And rate 'em up at just so much per head,
Till I have viewed straw hats and their habitual clothing
All the same style, same cut, with perfect loathing.'

Mabie] Hamilton Wright Mabie (1845–1916), New York editor and critic of
backward-looking views
Lyman Abbot] U.S. cleric and pietistic editor (1855–1950)
George Woodberry] U.S. poet and reactionary critic
Hiram Maxim] inventor of the Maxim gun

SIEGFRIED SASSOON
1886–1967

190   *Lamentations*

I FOUND him in the guard-room at the Base.
From the blind darkness I had heard his crying
And blundered in. With puzzled, patient face
A sergeant watched him; it was no good trying
To stop it; for he howled and beat his chest.
And, all because his brother had gone west,
Raved at the bleeding war; his rampant grief
Moaned, shouted, sobbed, and choked, while he was kneeling
Half-naked on the floor. In my belief
Such men have lost all patriotic feeling.

191   *'They'*

THE Bishop tells us: 'When the boys come back
They will not be the same; for they'll have fought
In a just cause: they lead the last attack
On Anti-Christ; their comrades' blood has bought
New right to breed an honourable race,
They have challenged Death and dared him face to face.'

'We're none of us the same!' the boys reply.
'For George lost both his legs; and Bill's stone blind;
Poor Jim's shot through the lungs and like to die;
And Bert's gone syphilitic: you'll not find
A chap who's served that hasn't found *some* change.'
And the Bishop said: 'The ways of God are strange!'

JOHN CROWE RANSOM
1888–1974

Philomela

PROCNE, Philomela, and Itylus,
Your names are liquid, your improbable tale
Is recited in the classic numbers of the nightingale,
Ah, but our numbers are not felicitous,
It goes not liquidly for us.

Perched on a Roman ilex, and duly apostrophized,
The nightingale descanted unto Ovid;
She has even appeared to the Teutons, the swilled and gravid;
At Fontainebleau it may be the bird was gallicized;
Never was she baptized.

To England came Philomela with her pain,
Fleeing the hawk her husband; querulous ghost,
She wanders when he sits heavy on his roost,
Utters herself in the original again,
The untranslatable refrain.

Not to these shores she came! this other Thrace,
Environ barbarous to the royal Attic;
How could her delicate dirge run democratic,
Delivered in a cloudless boundless public place
To an inordinate race?

I pernoctated with the Oxford students once,
And in the quadrangles, in the cloisters, on the Cher,
Precociously knocked at antique doors ajar,
Fatuously touched the hems of the hierophants,
Sick of my dissonance.

I went out to Bagley Wood, I climbed the hill;
Even the moon had slanted off in a twinkling,
I heard the sepulchral owl and a few bells tinkling,
There was no more villainous day to unfulfil,
The diuturnity was still.

these shores] i.e. the United States

Out of the darkness where Philomela sat,
Her fairy numbers issued. What then ailed me?
My ears are called capacious but they failed me,
Her classics registered a little flat!
I rose, and venomously spat.

Philomela, Philomela, lover of song,
I am in despair if we may make us worthy,
A bantering breed sophistical and swarthy;
Unto more beautiful, persistently more young,
Thy fabulous provinces belong.

ROBERT NICHOLS
1893–1944

193   from *Fisbo*

TALKING of Ezra Pound and long-dead pantos,
How like the old clown's sausages are his cantos!—
Yard after yard of unlikeable comestible,
Chockful of bran and highly indigestible.
However, we near the last sausage in the rope
And, seeing it in sight, begin to hope,
Certain of one thing, now the worst is passed
The last must be the best because the last.

E. E. CUMMINGS
1894–1962

194   *'in heavenly realms of hellas dwelt'*

in heavenly realms of hellas dwelt
two very different sons of zeus:
one,handsome strong and born to dare
—a fighter to his eyelashes—
the other,cunning ugly lame;
but as you'll shortly comprehend
a marvellous artificer

E. E. CUMMINGS

now Ugly was the husband of
(as happens every now and then
upon a merely human plane)
someone completely beautiful;
and Beautiful,who(truth to sing)
could never quite tell right from wrong,
took brother Fearless by the eyes
and did the deed of joy with him

then Cunning forged a web so subtle
air is comparatively crude;
an indestructible occult
supersnare of resistless metal:
and(stealing toward the blissful pair)
skilfully wafted over themselves this implacable unthing

next,our illustrious scientist
petitions the celestial host
to scrutinize his handiwork:
they(summoned by that savage yell
from shining realms of regions dark)
laugh long at Beautiful and Brave
—wildly who rage,vainly who strive;
and being finally released
flee one another like the pest

thus did immortal jealousy
quell divine generosity,
thus reason vanquished instinct and
matter became the slave of mind;
thus virtue triumphed over vice
and beauty bowed to ugliness
and logic thwarted life:and thus—
but look around you,friends and foes

my tragic tale concludes herewith:
soldier,beware of mrs smith

195   *'i sing of Olaf glad and big'*

i sing of Olaf glad and big
whose warmest heart recoiled at war:
a conscientious object-or

his wellbelovéd colonel (trig
westpointer most succinctly bred)
took erring Olaf soon in hand;
but—though an host of overjoyed
noncoms (first knocking on the head
him) do through icy waters roll
that helplessness which others stroke
with brushes recently employed
anent this muddy toiletbowl,
while kindred intellects evoke
allegiance per blunt instruments—
Olaf (being to all intents
a corpse and wanting any rag
upon what God unto him gave)
responds, without getting annoyed
'I- will not kiss your f.ing flag'

straightway the silver bird looked grave
(departing hurriedly to shave)

but—though all kinds of officers
(a yearning nation's blueeyed pride)
their passive prey did kick and curse
until for wear their clarion
voices and boots were much the worse,
and egged the firstclassprivates on
his rectum wickedly to tease
by means of skilfully applied
bayonets roasted hot with heat—
Olaf (upon what were once knees)
does almost ceaselessly repeat
'there is some s. I will not eat'

our president, being of which
assertions duly notified
threw the yellowsonofabitch
into a dungeon, where he died

Christ (of His mercy infinite)
i pray to see; and Olaf, too

preponderatingly because
unless statistics lie he was
more brave than me: more blond than you.

ROBERT GRAVES
1895–

196   *Queen Mother to New Queen*

ALTHOUGH only a fool would mock
The secondary joys of wedlock
(Which need no recapitulation),
The primary's the purer gold,
Even in our exalted station,
For all but saint or hoary cuckold.

Therefore, if ever the King's eyes
Turn at odd hours to your sleek thighs,
Make no delay or circumvention
But do as you should do, though strict
To guide back his bemused attention
Towards privy purse or royal edict,

And stricter yet to leave no stain
On the proud memory of his reign—
You'll act the wronged wife, if you love us.
Let them not whisper, even in sport:
'His Majesty's turned parsimonious
And keeps no whore now but his Consort.'

197 *Tilth*

('Robert Graves, the British veteran, is no longer in the poetic swim. He still resorts to traditional metres and rhyme, and to such out-dated words as *tilth*; withholding his 100% approbation also from contemporary poems that favour sexual freedom.'

From a New York critical weekly)

GONE are the drab monosyllabic days
When 'agricultural labour' still was *tilth*;
And '100% approbation', *praise*;
And 'pornographic modernism', *filth*—
Yet still I stand by *tilth* and *filth* and *praise*.

198 *The Laureate*

LIKE a lizard in the sun, though not scuttling
When men approach, this wretch, this thing of rage,
Scowls and sits rhyming in his horny age.

His time and truth he has not bridged to ours,
But shrivelled by long heliotropic idling
He croaks at us his out-of-date humours.

Once long ago here was a poet; who died.
See how remorse twitching his mouth proclaims
It was no natural death, but suicide.

Arrogant, lean, unvenerable, he
Still turns for comfort to the western flames
That glitter a cold span above the sea.

199 *1805*

AT Viscount Nelson's lavish funeral,
    While the mob milled and yelled about St. Paul's,
A General chatted with an Admiral:

'One of your Colleagues, Sir, remarked today
    That Nelson's *exit*, though to be lamented,
Falls not inopportunely, in its way.'

'He was a thorn in our flesh,' came the reply—
  'The most bird-witted, unaccountable,
Odd little runt that ever I did spy.

'One arm, one peeper, vain as Pretty Poll,
  A meddler, too, in foreign politics
And gave his heart in pawn to a plain moll.

'He would dare lecture us Sea Lords, and then
  Would treat his ratings as though men of honour
And play at leap-frog with his midshipmen!

'We tried to box him down, but up he popped,
  And when he'd banged Napoleon at the Nile
Became too much the hero to be dropped.

'You've heard that Copenhagen "blind eye" story?
  We'd tied him to Nurse Parker's apron-strings—
By G—d, he snipped them through and snatched the glory!'

'Yet,' cried the General, 'six-and-twenty sail
  Captured or sunk by him off Tráfalgár—
That writes a handsome *finis* to the tale.'

'Handsome enough. The seas are England's now.
  That fellow's foibles need no longer plague us.
He died most creditably, I'll allow.'

'And, Sir, the secret of his victories?'
  'By his unServicelike, familiar ways, Sir,
He made the whole Fleet love him, damn his eyes!'

EDGELL RICKWORD
1898–

200   *The Handmaid of Religion*

*'The writers of books, the painters of pictures, the actors for the stage
or on the screen, the women by the fashion of their dress, who render
self-control more difficult for the average normal man or woman ...
are doing moral evil.'*

              THE CARDINAL ARCHBISHOP OF WESTMINSTER.

*'I am, as is perhaps well known, a Protestant. But I am quite sure that
these words will be concurred in by the heads of my own Church and by
the heads of the great Nonconformist Churches.'*

              THE HOME SECRETARY, VISCOUNT BRENTFORD.

DEAR Queenie, though it breaks my heart,
I fear that you and I must part,
in case we sink too deep in sin,
I for my verse, you for your skin—
I mean the double envelope
that rouses, and confirms, our hope—
you sack, whose rose-leaf wrappings hide
what harsh Tertullian specified!
Here lies the parting of our ways,
and once again the woman pays:
the vows of Art I can abjure
and save my soul in shoddy rhyme,
but, stripped, your beauty would endure,
no less a sin, in fact a crime.
One article your harsher code
admits, to save you actual flaying—
to choose some unbecoming mode,
but that, I fear, is past obeying.

Poor girl, but such is moral law,
expounded without any flaw;
and to your harm I must confess
you have an artist's touch in dress:

397

for in the squalor of the crowd,
dull replicas, or grossly loud,
when you pass by, men's average eyes
gleam with a spark I recognize.
They glimpse a moment other lives,
including, doubtless, other wives,
and with this dim idea of beauty
return disturbed to home and duty,
where but for you the docile soul
might rot in perfect self-control.

I have a much more complex task,
and seven sins I must unmask,
lurking disguised in every line
to snatch my reader's soul and mine;
for, though our moralists annex
all blame to the one sin of sex,
Churchmen, when manners were more genial,
found fleshly lapses almost venial;
at least when measured side by side
with sins of spiritual pride;
but now it's safer to blaspheme
than to revive a classic theme.

Even Jix, that stalwart in theology,
reduces history to pornology,
with one stroke of a master-mind
leaves Gibbon limping far behind,
and reconstructs the fall of Rome
from recent goings-on at home.
Neither barbarians nor malaria
destroyed Rome's grip on her vast area,
but naughty novels sold in shops
unhindered by censorious cops.[1]

Since perfect form is what inspires
Mind with unquenchable desires,

[1] 'I suppose nothing contributed more to the degradation of the Roman Empire than the stream of pernicious literature which flowed like an open sewer through that great city.'   VISCOUNT BRENTFORD

Jix] nickname of Lord Brentford (Sir William Joynson-Hicks), Home Secretary

and in the Dionysian rage
Flesh strides an ampler, braver stage,
the arts, perhaps, are more obscene
than Jix or Bourne can even mean,
whose dicta echo one another's
like any spiritual brothers'.[1]
But as we both must earn our bread,
and such as they are still our head,
my Queenie, let us now conform,
and so ride out the impending storm;
for who would risk their job, and hell,
for dressing, or for writing, well?

Since Beauty's famous 'single hair'
seems planned a comprehensive snare,
(Wise Providence! Perverted Man!)
we will be sluttish as we can.
I will compete with tedious Quarles
whilst you subdue the infants' squalls
and in our bed, only at need,
we will such normal monsters breed—
their tendency to misbehaving
purged of all aesthetic craving—
as must, for this wise Prelate's part,
be supreme arbiters of Art.

---

[1] 'There are other matters in life of greater importance than the free development of a particular form of Art.'   THE VISCOUNT.
'No silly prating ... that the claims of Art must be satisfied.'   THE CARDINAL.

201 *The Contemporary Muse*
After reading an Anthology of the
work of about three hundred
living poets

'WHAT thing did I love that walks the street
on limping, foul, and garish-leathered feet?
A simpering, baby-faced suburban trull
come up to Town to find the fools more dull
than in her native Wimbledon, and bent
on turning an honest pound to pay her rent.
And I, damned wretch, once glamoured by her smile,
trailed her sad buttocks nearly half a mile;
her drained and sodden flesh where Browning heaved
spasmodic vows which impotence believed;
and Tennyson laboured all a summer's day
crowning a snotty brat Queen o' the May;
but that was in her middle prime, and now
she's milked of favours easily as a cow,
whilst through a turnstile all her lovers wend,
checked by tired critics at the further end.

Shall I go through the list from A to Z,
or shall we, sweetheart, take a trip to bed?'
'Why stir the wasps that rim Fame's luscious pot?
Love costs us nothing, satire costs a lot!'

ERNEST HEMINGWAY
1899–1961

202 *The Earnest Liberal's Lament*

I KNOW monks masturbate at night
That pet cats screw
That some girls bite
And yet
What can I do
To set things right?

YVOR WINTERS

1900–1968

203   *A Fragment*

I CANNOT find my way to Nazareth.
I have had enough of this. Thy will is death,
And this unholy quiet is thy peace.
Thy will be done; and let discussion cease.

ROY CAMPBELL

1901–1957

204   *A Veld Eclogue: The Pioneers*

ON the bare veld where nothing ever grows
Save beards and nails and blisters on the nose,
Johnny and Piet, two simple shepherds, lay
Watching their flock grow thinner every day—
Their one joint Nanny-goat, poor trustful thing,
That by the fence had waited since last spring
Lest any of the stakes that there were stuck
Should sprout a withered leaf for her to suck.
Rough was the labour of those hardy swains,
Sometimes they lay and waited for the rains,
Sometimes with busy twigs they switched the flies
Or paused to damn a passing nigger's eyes:
Sometimes, as now, they peeled them off their hose
And hacked the jiggers from their gnarly toes.
At times they lay and watched their blisters heal,
At others, sweated forth a scanty meal
Prone on their backs between their Nanny's shins—
After the manner of the Roman twins.
What wonder then, at such a flurry kept,
That sometimes—oftenest of all—they slept?

204   *The explanatory notes to this poem are Roy Campbell's own*
            jiggers] subcutaneous parasites

Yet for all that their simple hearts were gay,
And often would they trill the rustic lay,
For though the times were hard they could not bilk
Their brains of nonsense or their guts of milk;
And loud upon the hills with merry clang
The grand old saga of 'Ferreira' rang,
Till the baboons upon the topmost krans
Would leap for joy, career into a dance,
And all their Simian dignity forgot
Would hold a sort of Nagmaal on the spot,
Or, if to such comparisons we stoop—
A special rally of the Empire Group.
Think not that I on racial questions touch,
For one was Durban-born, the other Dutch.
I draw no line between them: for the two
Despise each other, and with reason too!
But, in this case, they both forgave the sin,
Each loved the other as a very twin—
One touch of tar-brush makes the whole world kin.
That they were true-bred children of the veld
It could as easily be seen as smelt,
For clumsier horsemen never sat astride,
Worse shots about their hunting never lied—
Though Piet once laid a lioness out straight,
I must confess—through aiming at its mate;
And Johnny, though he stalked extremely well,
Even against the wind the game could smell:
Even a pole-cat wheezing with catarrh
Could have perceived his presence from afar.
One knew them at a glance for Pioneers
Though Piet, but two years since, had washed his ears:
Their musty jackets and moth-eaten hair
Showed them for children of the Open Air;
Besides red tufts, there shone upon their faces
That 'nameless something' which Bolitho traces
To gazing out across the 'open spaces',
As if the sharpest Taakhaar that he knows
Can see an inch beyond his own red nose,

Ferreira] a smutty folk-song in Afrikaans
Nagmaal] a reunion of South African peasants and their families for purposes of social
festivity, commerce and religious debauchery
Empire Group] a society whose meetings are mentally and morally analogous to the
above

As if the meanest cockney in existence
Can't see the sky at a far greater distance
With sun and moon and stars to blink his eyes on
Much farther off than any fenced horizon,
And Sirius and Aldebaran, forsooth,
As far away as he is from the truth.
But 'nameless somethings' and 'unbounded spaces'
Are still the heritage of 'younger races'—
At least our novelists will have it so,
And, reader, who are we to tell them, 'No!'
We, who have never heard the 'call', or felt
The witching whatdyecallum of the veld?
As for that 'nameless something', it was there
Plain as the grime upon their ragged hair—
Bolitho calls it an 'inspired alertness'
And so it seemed (in spite of their inertness)—
A worried look, as if they half-expected
Something to happen, or half-recollected
Anything having happened there at all
Since old Oom Jaapie's heifer calved last fall.
As for the 'boundless spaces'—wild and free
They stretched around as far as eye could see,
Which, though not very far, was yet enough
To show a tree, four houses, and a bluff.
Geographers, who say the world's a sphere,
Are either ignorant, or mazed with beer,
Or liars—or have never read two pages
Of any of our novelists or sages
Who tell us plainly that the world's more wide
On the colonial than the other side,
That states and kingdoms are less vast and grand
Than ranches, farms and mealie-planted land,
And that wherever on the world's bald head
A province or protectorate is spread
The place straightway to vast proportions jumps
As with the goitre or a dose of mumps—
So that in shape our cosmos should compare

Bolitho] Hector, not William. Prolific and popular interpreter of the 'New Earth', the 'Open Spaces', etc., to which he even relates the present writer's poems. Accounting for the mental and physical 'superiority' of the Colonial to the European, Bolitho writes—'"It's the distance that does it," said my millionaire, looking at me with his rather fine head chiselled on a background of cream madonna-lilies, "it's the distance that does it."'

Less with an apple than a warty pear.
For all our scenery's in grander style
And there are far more furlongs to the mile
In Africa than Europe—though, no doubt
None but colonials have found this out.
For though our Drakenberg's most lofty scalps
Would scarcely reach the waist-line of the Alps,
Though Winterberg, beside the Pyrenees,
Would scarcely reach on tip-toe to their knees,
Nobody can deny that our hills rise
Far more majestically – for their size!
I mean that there is something grander, yes,
About the veld, than I can well express,
Something more vast—perhaps I don't mean that—
Something more round, and square, and steep, and flat—
No, well perhaps it's not quite that I mean
But something, rather, half-way in between,
Something more 'nameless'—That's the very word!
Something that can't be felt, or seen, or heard,
Or even thought—a kind of mental mist
That doesn't either matter or exist
But without which it would go very hard
With many a local novelist and bard—
Being the only trick they've ever done,
To bring in local colour where there's none;
And if I introduce the system too,
Blame only the traditions I pursue.
We left our shepherds in their open spaces
Sunning the 'nameless somethings' on their faces,
And also (but that's neither here nor there)
Scratching the 'nameless somethings' in their hair.
And there I'll leave them to complete my rhyme
In conversation learned and sublime:

PIET

That you're a poet, Johnny, you declare
Both in your verses and your length of hair,

And sure, why not? we've prophets in the land
Fit with the best of Israel's line to stand—
For Balaam's donkey only made him curse
But Totius' Ox inspired him into verse,
And I have often thought some work of note
Could well be written round our faithful goat;
The heroes of Thermopylae were writers
And sculptors too—in spite of being fighters—
The heroes of Bull-hoek and Bondleswaart
Should not be backward in the field of art.
Come—the Jew's-harp!—I'll thrum it while you sing,
Arise, and soar on music's golden wing!

JOHNNY

A simple goat was in her owners blest,
They milked her twice a day, then let her rest:
No wrangling rose between them—all was fair—
Which owned the head, or tail, they did not care:
Think not that I on racial questions touch
For one was British and the other Dutch.

So Johnny sang. His song was brief and true—
Had Creswell, Smuts or Hertzog half his nous,
There would be far more goats on the Karroo
And far less in the Senate and the House.

Totius] *nom de plume* of a popular Afrikaans bard. His masterpiece, *Die Os* (The Ox), is highly praised by Dr Hermann, the Cape Town Bergson, on account of the poet's having identified his mind and soul so completely with that of his subject. See *The Wayzgoose* (first page, with footnote).

> 'A clime so prosperous both to men and kine
> That which were which a sage could scarce define.'

Bull-hoek (pron. *hook*) and Bondleswaart] (i) shooting raid on unarmed religious sect; (ii) bombing raid, by air, on a village which complained at a dog-tax.

205   *A Good Resolution*

ENOUGH of those who study the oblique,
Inverted archæologists, who seek
The New, as if it were some quaint antique—

Nomads of Time, and pungent with its must,
Who took the latest crinolines on trust
As wigwams for their vagrant wanderlust;

Of jargons that a fuddled Celt will mix
By the blue light of methylated wicks,
Fishing dead words like kippers from the Styx;

Sham Brownings, too, who'll cloud a shallow stream,
Or in a haystack hide a needle theme
Till platitudes like propositions seem—

With *pontes asinorum* bridging ditches
That, fully-armed, without the aid of witches,
Old knights could hurdle in their cast-iron breeches.

Hide poverty beneath a chequered shirt
And trust from common eyesight to divert
The jagged ribs that corrugate the dirt.

I will go stark: and let my meanings show
Clear as a milk-white feather in a crow
Or a black stallion on a field of snow.

206   *Georgian Spring*

WHO does not love the spring deserves no lovers—
For peaches bloom in Georgia in the spring,
New quarterlies resume their yellow covers,
Anthologies on every bookshelf sing.
The publishers put on their best apparel
To sell the public everything it wants—
A thousand meek soprano voices carol
The loves of homosexuals or plants.
Now let the Old Cow perish, for the tune

Would turn the fatted calf to bully beef:
We know, we know, that 'silver is the Moon',
That 'skies are blue' was always our belief:
That 'grass is green' there can be no denying,
That titled whores in love can be forgot—
All who have heard poor Georgiana sighing
Would think it more surprising were they not:
As for the streams, why, any carp or tench
Could tell you that they 'sparkle on their way'.
Now for the millionth time the 'country wench'
Has lost her reputation 'in the hay'.
But still the air is full of happy voices,
All bloody: but no matter, let them sing!
For who would frown when all the world rejoices,
And who would contradict when, in the spring,
The English Muse her annual theme rehearses
To tell us birds are singing in the sky?
Only the poet slams the door and curses,
And all the little sparrows wonder why!

207   from *The Wayzgoose*

ATTEND my fable if your ears be clean,
In fair Banana Land we lay our scene—
South Africa, renowned both far and wide—
For politics and little else beside:
Where, having torn the land with shot and shell,
Our sturdy pioneers as farmers dwell,
And, 'twixt the hours of strenuous sleep, relax
To shear the fleeces or to fleece the blacks:
Where every year a fruitful increase bears
Of pumpkins, cattle, sheep, and millionaires—
A clime so prosperous both to men and kine
That which were which a sage could scarce define;
Where fat white sheep upon the mountains bleat
And fatter politicians in the street;
Where lemons hang like yellow moons ashine
And grapes the size of apples load the vine;
Where apples to the weight of pumpkins go
And donkeys to the height of statesmen grow,
Where trouts the size of salmon throng the creeks
And worms the size of magistrates—the beaks;

Where the precocious tadpole, from his bog,
Becomes a journalist ere half a frog;
Where every shrimp his proud career may carve
And only brain and muscle have to starve.
The 'garden colony' they call our land,
And surely for a garden it was planned:
What apter phrase with such a place could cope
Where vegetation has so fine a scope,
Where *weeds* in such variety are found
And all the rarest *parasites* abound,
Where pumpkins to professors are promoted
And turnips into Parliament are voted?
Where else do men by vegetating vie
And run to seed so long before they die?
In Eden long ere colonies took root
Knowledge was first delivered from a Fruit,
All Sciences from one poor Tree begin
And have a vegetable origin,
And to this day, as I have often seen,
It is accounted learned to be *green*.
What wonder then if fruits should still be found
Purveying wisdom to the world around.
What wonder if, assuming portly airs,
Beetroots should sit in editorial chairs,
Or any cabbage win the critics' praise
Who wears his own green leaves instead of bays!
What wonder then if, as the ages pass,
Our universities, with domes of glass,
Should to a higher charter prove their claims
And be exalted to tomato-frames,
Whose crystal roofs should hatch with genial ray
A hundred mushroom poets every day;
Where Brussels scientists should hourly sprout
And little shrubs as sages burgeon out;
Where odes from beds of guano should be sprung
And new philosophies from horses' dung?
Wisdom in stones some reverend poet found,
But here it is as common as the ground—
Behold our Vegetable Athens rise
Where all the *acres* in the Land are *wise*!

STEVIE SMITH

1902–1971

Lord Barrenstock

LORD Barrenstock and Epicene,
What's it to me that you have been
In your pursuit of interdicted joys
Seducer of a hundred little boys?

Your sins are red about your head
And many people wish you dead.

You trod the widow in the mire
Wronged the son, deceived the sire.

You put a fence about the land
And made the people's cattle graze on sand.

Ratted from many a pool and forced amalgamation
And dealt in shares which never had a stock exchange quotation.

Non flocci facio, I do not care
For wrongs you made the other fellow bear:
'Tis not for these unsocial acts not these
I wet my pen. I would not have you tease,
With a repentance smug and overdue
For all the things you still desire to do,
The ears of an outraged divinity:
But oh your tie is crooked and I see
Too plain you had an éclair for your tea.

It is this nonchalance about your person—
That is the root of my profound aversion.

You are too fat. In spite of stays
Your shape is painful to the polished gaze;

Your uncombed hair grows thin and daily thinner,
In fact you're far too ugly to be such a sinner.

Lord Barrenstock and Epicene, consider all that you have done
Lord Epicene and Barrenstock, yet not two Lords but one,
I think you are an object not of fear but pity
Be good, my Lord, since you cannot be pretty.

PHYLLIS McGINLEY

1905–

209   *Office Party*

THIS holy night in open forum
   Miss McIntosh, who handles Files,
Has lost one shoe and her decorum.
   Stately, the frozen chairman smiles

On Media, desperately vocal.
   Credit, though they have lost their hopes
Of edging toward an early Local,
   Finger their bonus envelopes.

The glassy boys, the bursting girls
   Of Copy, start a Conga clatter
To a swung carol. Limply curls
   The final sandwich on the platter

Till hark! a herald Messenger
   (Room 414) lifts loudly up
His quavering tenor. Salesmen stir
   Libation for his Lily cup.

'Noel,' he pipes, 'Noel, Noel.'
   Some wag beats tempo with a ruler.
And the plump blonde from Personnel
   Is sick behind the water cooler.

210   *How to Start a War*

SAID Zwingli to Muntzer,
'I'll have to be blunt, sir.
I don't like your version
Of Total Immersion.
And since God's on my side
And I'm on the dry side,
You'd better swing ovah
To me and Jehovah.'

Cried Muntzer, 'It's schism,
Is Infant Baptism!
Since I've had a sign, sir,
That God's will is mine, sir,
Let all men agree
With Jehovah and me,
Or go to Hell, singly,'
Said Muntzer to Zwingli,

As each drew his sword
On the side of the Lord.

211   *The Day After Sunday*

ALWAYS on Mondays, God's in the morning papers,
    His Name is a headline, His Works are rumored abroad.
Having been praised by men who are movers and shapers,
    From prominent Sunday pulpits, newsworthy is God.

On page 27, just opposite Fashion Trends,
    One reads at a glance how He scolded the Baptists a little,
Was firm with the Catholics, practical with the Friends,
    To Unitarians pleasantly noncommittal.

In print are His numerous aspects, too: God smiling,
    God vexed, God thunderous, God whose mansions are pearl,
Political God, God frugal, God reconciling
    Himself with science, God guiding the Camp Fire Girl.

Always on Monday morning the press reports
   God as revealed to His vicars in various guises—
Benevolent, stormy, patient, or out of sorts.
   God knows which God is the God God recognizes.

212   from *Spectator's Guide to Contemporary Art*

(i)

On the Farther Wall, Marc Chagall

ONE eye without a head to wear it
Sits on the pathway, and a chicken,
Pursued perhaps by astral ferret,
Flees, while the plot begins to thicken.
Two lovers kiss. Their hair is kelp.
Nor are the titles any help.

(ii)

Squeeze Play

Jackson Pollock had a quaint
Way of saying to his sibyl,
'Shall I dribble?
Should I paint?'
And with never an instant's quibble,
Sibyl always answered,
'Dribble.'

213   *Speaking of Television:*
            Robin Hood

ZOUNDS, gramercy, and rootity-toot!
Here comes the man in the green flannel suit.

214   *Daniel at Breakfast*

HIS paper propped against the electric toaster
   (Nicely adjusted to his morning use),
Daniel at breakfast studies world disaster
   And sips his orange juice.

The words dismay him. Headlines shrilly chatter
  Of famine, storm, death, pestilence, decay.
Daniel is gloomy, reaching for the butter.
  He shudders at the way

War stalks the planet still, and men know hunger,
  Go shelterless, betrayed, may perish soon.
The coffee's weak again. In sudden anger
  Daniel throws down his spoon

And broods a moment on the kitchen faucet
  The plumber mended, but has mended ill;
Recalls tomorrow means a dental visit,
  Laments the grocery bill.

Then, having shifted from his human shoulder
  The universal woe, he drains his cup,
Rebukes the weather (surely turning colder),
  Crumples his napkin up
And, kissing his wife abruptly at the door,
Stamps fiercely off to catch the 8:04.

SIR JOHN BETJEMAN

1906–

215   *How to Get On in Society*

PHONE for the fish-knives, Norman
  As Cook is a little unnerved;
You kiddies have crumpled the serviettes
  And I must have things daintily served.

Are the requisites all in the toilet?
  The frills round the cutlets can wait
Till the girl has replenished the cruets
  And switched on the logs in the grate.

413

It's ever so close in the lounge dear,
   But the vestibule's comfy for tea
And Howard is out riding on horseback
   So do come and take some with me.

Now here is a fork for your pastries
   And do use the couch for your feet;
I know that I wanted to ask you—
   Is trifle sufficient for sweet?

Milk and then just as it comes dear?
   I'm afraid the preserve's full of stones;
Beg pardon, I'm soiling the doileys
   With afternoon tea-cakes and scones.

216   *Huxley Hall*

In the Garden City Café with its murals on the wall
Before a talk on 'Sex and Civics' I meditated on the Fall.

Deep depression settled on me under that electric glare
While outside the lightsome poplars flanked the rose-beds in the
    square.

While outside the carefree children sported in the summer haze
And released their inhibitions in a hundred different ways.

She who eats her greasy crumpets snugly in the inglenook
Of some birch-enshrouded homestead, dropping butter on her book

Can she know the deep depression of this bright, hygienic hell?
And her husband, stout free-thinker, can he share in it as well?

Not the folk-museum's charting of man's Progress out of slime
Can release me from the painful seeming accident of Time.

Barry smashes Shirley's dolly, Shirley's eyes are crossed with hate,
Comrades plot a Comrade's downfall 'in the interests of the State'.

Not my vegetarian dinner, not my lime-juice minus gin,
Quite can drown a faint conviction that we may be born in Sin.

217   *In Westminster Abbey*

LET me take this other glove off
   As the *vox humana* swells,
And the beauteous fields of Eden
   Bask beneath the Abbey's bells.
Here, where England's statesmen lie,
Listen to a lady's cry.

Gracious Lord, oh bomb the Germans.
   Spare their women for Thy Sake,
And if that is not too easy
   We will pardon Thy Mistake.
But, gracious Lord, whate'er shall be,
Don't let anyone bomb me.

Keep our Empire undismembered
   Guide our Forces by Thy Hand,
Gallant blacks from far Jamaica,
   Honduras and Togoland;
Protect them Lord in all their fights,
And, even more, protect the whites.

Think of what our Nation stands for,
   Books from Boots' and country lanes,
Free speech, free passes, class distinction,
   Democracy and proper drains.
Lord, put beneath Thy special care
One-eighty-nine Cadogan Square.

Although dear Lord I am a sinner,
   I have done no major crime;
Now I'll come to Evening Service
   Whensoever I have the time.
So, Lord, reserve for me a crown,
And do not let my shares go down.

I will labour for Thy Kingdom,
  Help our lads to win the war.
Send white feathers to the cowards
  Join the Women's Army Corps,
Then wash the Steps around Thy Throne
In the Eternal Safety Zone.

Now I feel a little better,
  What a treat to hear Thy Word,
Where the bones of leading statesmen,
  Have so often been interr'd.
And now, dear Lord, I cannot wait
Because I have a luncheon date.

W. H. AUDEN

1907–1973

218   from *A Happy New Year*

A Field of Folk

[*The English converge on a field of folk, a Scotch moorland, in bleak
December, and are described in stanzas which afford 'blurring images of
the dingy difficult life of our generation'.*]

(i)

IN corduroy trousers and seedy black coats
  A dozen performers had managed to come
With red flannel mufflers pinned at their throats,
  Five cornets, three trombones, an harmonium
  A harp, an accordion and a great big drum.
The choir who followed on ladies' bikes
Were singing a hymn by John Bacchus Dykes.

But just as their drawn-out Amen ceased
  Came a second-hand Thorneycroft lorry bringing
Four saxophone boys to play up the East:
  'Rhythm. Spring. Waggle that thing
  Do Do De O' they were singing.
Each wore tails, had a mascot cat,
And perched on each head was a celluloid hat.

And now at last the main bodies came
  Glancing at each other in suspicious fear.
When eyes met they darted sideways in shame
  Or braved it out in an awkward stare.
The equipment was curious they had found to wear,
Silk stockings, cigar boxes, covers of sumps,
Newspapers, ham-frills, and bicycle-pumps.

So many bodies looking ashamed,
  So many eyes which expected worse,
So many legs too lanky or lamed,
  So many mouths like a missioner's purse,
  So many cases which needed a nurse,
So many dreading the Arm of the Law
Were never seen in one place before.

So much stammering over easy words,
  So much laughter spasmodic and queer,
So much speech that resembled a bird's,
  So much drawling concealing a fear,
  So much effort to sound sincere,
So much talk which was aimed at the floor
Was never heard in one place before.

(ii)
Doctors attended behind each chair,
  Behind the men was Sir Thomas Horder,
Behind the women Dr Norman Haire;
  Maisie Gay and Sir Harry Lauder
  Were told off to keep the ranks in order;
Ramsay MacDonald was rubbing his seat:
At last he'd been invited to a Leicestershire Meet.

Thomas was only demanding fair play,
  Baldwin was wiping his nose on his pipe;
Snowden was for making the landlord pay;
  Limping but keeping a stiff upper lip
  Churchill was speaking of a battleship;
It was some little time before I had guessed
He wasn't describing a woman's breast.

(iii)

A colonel from Cheltenham stopped everyone
    To tell them the lost Ten Tribes were there.
The Dolmetsch family, father and son
    Who had driven in a brake from Haslemere,
    Were giving a concert, but no one could hear.
Lord Baden-Powell with a piece of string
Was proving that reef-knots honour the King.

(iv)

On a lorry the centre of a gaping crowd
    A man was eating a hedgehog whole;
Presently he rose and said very loud
    'The colon we know is the seat of the soul;
    Keep the colon clean by conscious control.'
In the middle distance a titled whore
Was distributing trusses to the ruptured poor.

(v)

A cry went through me like a stab of a knife
    And the flex of the telephone gave with a snap,
'Life. Life. Eternal Life.'
    Striking out wildly like a beast in a trap
    A youth charged head down; under his cap
A trickle of blood from a bullet smear showed
As he zig-zagged shrieking down the road.

Orders were shouted, a hubbub arose:
    'Look out. A deserter. We want that man.
Gup Vexer, Bramble, Verse out of Prose!'
    Waving rattles the healers ran.
    Dr Ernest Jones was well in the van,
And panting and pounding after the rest
My old headmaster in a little pink vest.

Comments were uttered from every direction.
    'There goes the result of a banker's ramp.'
'He only wants a regular sexual connection.'
    'In Germany they'd send him to a summer camp.'
    'The cure for all this is a sunlight lamp.'
'In Russia such cases are unknown now for years,
In Russia they've got some ripping new rears.'

219

The Unknown Citizen
(To JS 07/378
This Marble Monument
Is Erected by the State)

HE was found by the Bureau of Statistics to be
One against whom there was no official complaint,
And all the reports on his conduct agree
That, in the modern sense of an old-fashioned word, he was a saint,
For in everything he did he served the Greater Community.
Except for the War till the day he retired
He worked in a factory and never got fired,
But satisfied his employers, Fudge Motors Inc.
Yet he wasn't a scab or odd in his views,
For his Union reports that he paid his dues,
(Our report on his Union shows it was sound)
And our Social Psychology workers found
That he was popular with his mates and liked a drink.
The Press are convinced that he bought a paper every day
And that his reactions to advertisements were normal in every way.
Policies taken out in his name prove that he was fully insured,
And his Health-card shows he was once in hospital but left it cured.
Both Producers Research and High-Grade Living declare
He was fully sensible to the advantages of the Instalment Plan
And had everything necessary to the Modern Man,
A phonograph, a radio, a car and a frigidaire.
Our researchers into Public Opinion are content
That he held the proper opinions for the time of year;
When there was peace, he was for peace; when there was war, he went.
He was married and added five children to the population,
Which our Eugenist says was the right number for a parent of his
        generation,
And our teachers report that he never interfered with their education.
Was he free? Was he happy? The question is absurd:
Had anything been wrong, we should certainly have heard.

from *Letter to Lord Byron*

(i)

YOU lived and moved among the best society
And so could introduce your hero to it
Without the slightest tremor of anxiety;
   Because he was your hero and you knew it,
   He'd know instinctively what's done, and do it.
He'd find our day more difficult than yours
For Industry has mixed the social drawers.

We've grown, you see, a lot more democratic,
   And Fortune's ladder is for all to climb;
Carnegie on this point was most emphatic.
   A humble grandfather is not a crime,
   At least, if father made enough in time!
Today, thank God, we've got no snobbish feeling
Against the more efficient modes of stealing.

The porter at the Carlton is my brother,
   He'll wish me a good evening if I pay,
For tips and men are equal to each other.
   I'm sure that *Vogue* would be the first to say
   Que le Beau Monde is socialist today;
And many a bandit, not so gently born
Kills vermin every winter with the Quorn.

Adventurers, though, must take things as they find them
   And look for pickings where the pickings are.
The drives of love and hunger are behind them,
   They can't afford to be particular:
   And those who like good cooking and a car,
A certain kind of costume or a face,
Must seek them in a certain kind of place.

Don Juan was a mixer and no doubt
   Would find this century as good as any
For getting hostesses to ask him out,
   And mistresses that need not cost a penny.
   Indeed our ways to waste time are so many,
Thanks to technology, a list of these
Would take a longer book than *Ulysses*.

Yes, in the smart set he would know his way
  By second nature with no tips from me.
Tennis and Golf have come in since your day;
  But those who are as good at games as he
  Acquire the back-hand quite instinctively,
Take to the steel-shaft and hole out in one,
Master the books of Ely Culbertson.

I see his face in every magazine.
  'Don Juan at lunch with one of Cochran's ladies.'
'Don Juan with his red setter May MacQueen.'
  'Don Juan, who's just been wintering in Cadiz,
  Caught at the wheel of his maroon Mercedes.'
'Don Juan at Croydon Aerodrome.' 'Don Juan
Snapped in the paddock with the Agha Khan.'

But if in highbrow circles he would sally
  It's just as well to warn him there's no stain on
Picasso, all-in-wrestling, or the Ballet.
  Sibelius is the man. To get a pain on
  Listening to Elgar is a sine qua non.
A second-hand acquaintance of Pareto's
Ranks higher than an intimate of Plato's.

The vogue for Black Mass and the cult of devils
  Has sunk. The Good, the Beautiful, the True
Still fluctuate about the lower levels.
  Joyces are firm and there there's nothing new.
  Eliots have hardened just a point or two.
Hopkins are brisk, thanks to some recent boosts.
There's been some further weakening in Prousts.

I'm saying this to tell you who's the rage,
  And not to loose a sneer from my interior.
Because there's snobbery in every age,
  Because some names are loved by the superior,
  It does not follow they're the least inferior:
For all I know the Beatific Vision's
On view at all Surrealist Exhibitions.

(ii)

England, my England—you have been my tutrix—
The Mater, on occasions, of the free,
Or, if you'd rather, Dura Virum Nutrix,
    Whatever happens I am born of Thee;
    And Englishmen, all foreigners agree,
Taking them by and large, and as a nation,
All suffer from an Oedipus fixation.

With all thy faults, of course we love thee still;
    We'd better for we have to live with you,
From Rhondda Valley or from Bredon Hill,
    From Rotherhithe, or Regent Street, or Kew
    We look you up and down and whistle 'Phew!
Mother looks odd today dressed up in peers,
Slums, aspidistras, shooting-sticks, and queers.'

Cheer up! There're several singing birds that sing.
    There's six feet six of Spender for a start;
Eliot has really stretched his eagle's wing,
    And Yeats has helped himself to Parnell's heart;
    This book has samples of MacNeice's art;
There's Wyndham Lewis fuming out of sight,
That lonely old volcano of the Right.

I'm marking time because I cannot guess
    The proper place to which to send this letter,
c/o Saint Peter or The Infernal Press?
    I'll try the Press. World-culture is its debtor;
    It has a list that Faber's couldn't better.
For Heaven gets all the lookers for her pains,
But Hell, I think, gets nearly all the brains.

The congregation up there in the former
    Are those whose early upbringing was right,
Who never suffered from a childish trauma;
    As babies they were Truby King's delight;
    They're happy, lovely, but not overbright.
For no one thinks unless a complex makes him,
Or till financial ruin overtakes him.

Complex or Poverty; in short The Trap.
　Some set to work to understand the spring;
Others sham dead, pretend to take a nap;
　'It is a motor-boat', the madmen sing;
　The artist's action is the queerest thing:
He seems to like it, couldn't do without it,
And only wants to tell us all about it.

While Rome is burning or he's out of sorts
　'Causons, causons, mon bon,' he's apt to say,
'What does it matter while I have these thoughts?'
　Or so I've heard, but Freud's not quite O.K.
　No artist works a twenty-four-hour day.
In bed, asleep or dead, it's hard to tell
The highbrow from l'homme moyen sensuel.

'Es neigen die Weisen zu Schönem sich.'
　Your lordship's brow that never wore a hat
Should thank your lordship's foot that did the trick.
　Your mother in a temper cried, 'Lame Brat!'
　Posterity should thank her much for that.
Had she been sweet she surely would have taken
Juan away and saved your moral bacon.

The match of Hell and Heaven was a nice
　Idea of Blake's, but won't take place, alas.
You can choose either, but you can't choose twice;
　You can't, at least in this world, change your class;
　Neither is alpha plus though both will pass:
And don't imagine you can write like Dante,
Dive like your nephew, crochet like your auntie.

The Great Utopia, free of all complexes,
　The Withered State is, at the moment, such
A dream as that of being both the sexes.
　I like Wolf's *Goethe-Lieder* very much,
　But doubt if *Ganymede's* appeal will touch
—That marvellous cry with its ascending phrases—
Capitalism in its later phases.

Are Poets saved? Well, let's suppose they are,
    And take a peep. I don't see any books.
Shakespeare is lounging grandly at the bar,
    Milton is dozing, judging by his looks,
    Shelley is playing poker with two crooks,
Blake's adding pince-nez to an ad. for Players,
Chaucer is buried in the latest Sayers.

Lord Alfred rags with Arthur on the floor,
    Housman, all scholarship forgot at last,
Sips up the stolen waters through a straw,
    Browning's complaining that Keats bowls too fast,
    And you have been composing as they passed
A clerihew on Wordsworth and his tie,
A rather dirty limerick on Pye.

I hope this reaches you in your abode,
    This letter that's already far too long,
Just like the Prelude or the Great North Road;
    But here I end my conversational song.
    I hope you don't think mail from strangers wrong.
As to its length, I tell myself you'll need it,
You've all eternity in which to read it.

LOUIS MACNEICE
1907–1963

221   *The Truisms*

HIS father gave him a box of truisms
Shaped like a coffin, then his father died;
The truisms remained on the mantelpiece
As wooden as the playbox they had been packed in
Or that other his father skulked inside.

Then he left home, left the truisms behind him
Still on the mantelpiece, met love, met war,
Sordor, disappointment, defeat, betrayal,
Till through disbeliefs he arrived at a house
He could not remember seeing before,

And he walked straight in; it was where he had come from
And something told him the way to behave.
He raised his hand and blessed his home;
The truisms flew and perched on his shoulders
And a tall tree sprouted from his father's grave.

222 · *Bagpipe Music*

IT'S no go the merrygoround, it's no go the rickshaw,
All we want is a limousine and a ticket for the peepshow.
Their knickers are made of crêpe-de-chine, their shoes are made of
    python,
Their halls are lined with tiger rugs and their walls with heads of bison.

John MacDonald found a corpse, put it under the sofa,
Waited till it came to life and hit it with a poker,
Sold its eyes for souvenirs, sold its blood for whisky,
Kept its bones for dumb-bells to use when he was fifty.

It's no go the Yogi-Man, it's no go Blavatsky,
All we want is a bank balance and a bit of skirt in a taxi.

Annie MacDougall went to milk, caught her foot in the heather,
Woke to hear a dance record playing of Old Vienna.
It's no go your maidenheads, it's no go your culture,
All we want is a Dunlop tyre and the devil mend the puncture.

The Laird o'Phelps spent Hogmanay declaring he was sober,
Counted his feet to prove the fact and found he had one foot over.
Mrs Carmichael had her fifth, looked at the job with repulsion,
Said to the midwife 'Take it away; I'm through with over-production'.

It's no go the gossip column, it's no go the ceilidh,
All we want is a mother's help and a sugar-stick for the baby.

Willie Murray cut his thumb, couldn't count the damage,
Took the hide of an Ayrshire cow and used it for a bandage.
His brother caught three hundred cran when the seas were lavish,
Threw the bleeders back in the sea and went upon the parish.

It's no go the Herring Board, it's no go the Bible,
All we want is a packet of fags when our hands are idle.

It's no go the picture palace, it's no go the stadium,
It's no go the country cot with a pot of pink geraniums,
It's no go the Government grants, it's no go the elections,
Sit on your arse for fifty years and hang your hat on a pension.

It's no go my honey love, it's no go my poppet;
Work your hands from day to day, the winds will blow the profit.
The glass is falling hour by hour, the glass will fall for ever,
But if you break the bloody glass you won't hold up the weather.

GAVIN EWART

1916–

223   *Xmas for the Boys*

A CLOCKWORK skating Wordsworth on the ice,
An automatic sermonizing Donne,
A brawling Marlowe shaking out the dice,
A male but metaphysical Thom Gunn.
Get them all now—the latest greatest set
Of all the Poets, dry to sopping wet.

A mad, ferocious, disappointed Swift
Being beaten by a servant in the dark.
Eliot going up to Heaven in a lift,
Shelley going overboard, just for a lark.
Although the tempo and the talent varies
Now is the time to order the whole series.

An electronic Milton, blind as a bat,
A blood-spitting consumptive Keats,
Tennyson calmly raising a tall hat,
Swinburne being whipped in certain dark back streets.
All working models, correct from head to toe—
But Shakespeare's extra, as you ought to know.

D. J. ENRIGHT

1920–

Since Then

So many new crimes since then!—

    simple simony
    manducation of corpses
    infringement of copyright
    offences against the sumptuary laws
    postlapsarian undress
    violation of the Hay-Pauncefote Treaty
    extinction of the dodo
    champerty and malversation
    travelling by public transport without a ticket
    hypergamy and other unnatural practices
    courting in bed
    free verse
    wilful longevity
    dumb insolence
    bootlegging and hijacking
    jackbooting and highlegging
    arsenic and old lace
    robbing a hen-roost
    leaving unattended bombs in unauthorized places
    high dudgeon
    the cod war
    massacre of innocents
    bed-wetting
    escapism
    transporting Bibles without a licence

But so many new punishments, too!—

    blinding with science
    death by haranguing
    licking of envelopes
    palpation of the obvious
    invasion of the privacies

fistula in ano
hard labour down the minds
solitary conjunction
mortification of the self-esteem
the Plastic Maiden
hat-rack and trouser-press
the death of a thousand budgerigars
spontaneous combustion
self-employment
retooling of the economy
jacks in orifice
boredom of the genitals
trampling by white elephants
deprivation of forgetfulness
loss of pen-finger
severance pay
strap-hanging
early closing
sequestration of the funny-bone
mortgage and deadlock

'Fair do's,' murmured the old Adam, 'I am well pleased.'
He had come a long way since he named the animals.

225   *Apocalypse*

'After the New Apocalypse, very few members were still in possession of their instruments. Hardly a musician could call a decent suit his own. Yet, by the early summer
of 1945, strains of sweet music floated on the air again. While the town still reeked
of smoke, charred buildings and the stench of corpses, the Philharmonic Orchestra
bestowed the everlasting and imperishable joy which music never fails to give.'
                        (*From* 'The Muses on the Banks of the Spree',
                                      a German tourist brochure)

I T soothes the savage doubts.
One Bach outweighs ten Belsens. If 200,000 people
Were remaindered at Hiroshima, the sales of So-and-So's
New novel reached a higher figure in as short a time.
So, imperishable paintings reappeared;
Texts were reprinted;
Public buildings reconstructed;
Human beings reproduced.

After the Newer Apocalypse, very few members
Were still in possession of their instruments
(Very few were still in possession of their members),
And their suits were chiefly indecent.
Yet, while the town still reeked of smoke etc.,
The Philharmonic Trio bestowed etc.

A civilization vindicated,
A race with three legs still to stand on!
True, the violin was later silenced by leukaemia,
And the pianoforte crumbled softly into dust.
But the flute was left. And one is enough.
All, in a sense, goes on. All is in order.

And the ten-tongued mammoth larks,
The forty-foot crickets and the elephantine frogs
Decided that the little chap was harmless,
At least he made no noise, on the banks of whatever river it used to be.

One day, a reed-warbler stepped on him by accident.
However, all, in a sense, goes on. Still the everlasting and imperishable
    joy
Which music never fails to give is being given.

PHILIP LARKIN

1922–

226   *Fiction and the Reading Public*

GIVE me a thrill, says the reader,
Give me a kick;
I don't care how you succeed, or
What subject you pick.
Choose something you know all about
That'll sound like real life:
Your childhood, your Dad pegging out,
How you sleep with your wife.

But that's not sufficient, unless
You make me feel good—
Whatever you're 'trying to express'
Let it be understood
That 'somehow' God plaits up the threads,
Makes 'all for the best',
That we may lie quiet in our beds
And not be 'depressed'.

For I call the tune in this racket:
I pay your screw,
Write reviews and the bull on the jacket—
So stop looking blue
And start serving up your sensations
Before it's too late;
Just please me for two generations—
You'll be 'truly great'.

KINGSLEY AMIS

1922–

227   *The Last War*

THE first country to die was normal in the evening,
Ate a good but plain dinner, chatted with some friends
Over a glass, and went to bed soon after ten;
And in the morning was found disfigured and dead.
        That was a lucky one.

At breakfast the others heard about it, and kept
Their eyes on their plates. Who was guilty? No one knew,
But by lunch-time three more would never eat again.
The rest appealed for frankness, quietly cocked their guns,
        Declared 'This can't go on.'

They were right. Only the strongest turned up for tea:
The old ones with the big estates hadn't survived
The slobbering blindfold violence of the afternoon.
One killer or many? Was it a gang, or all-against-all?
        Somebody must have known.

But each of them sat there watching the others, until
Night came and found them anxious to get it over.
Then the lights went out. A few might have lived, even then;
Innocent, they thought (at first) it still mattered what
  You had or hadn't done.

They were wrong. One had been lenient with his servants;
Another ran an island brothel, but rarely left it;
The third owned a museum, the fourth a remarkable gun;
The name of a fifth was quite unknown, but in the end
  What was the difference? None.

Homicide, pacifist, crusader, cynic, gentile, jew
Staggered about moaning, shooting into the dark.
Next day, to tidy up as usual, the sun came in
When they and their ammunition were all used up,
  And found himself alone.

Upset, he looked them over, to separate, if he could,
The assassins from the victims, but every face
Had taken on the flat anonymity of pain;
And soon they'll all smell alike, he thought, and felt sick,
  And went to bed at noon.

ADRIAN MITCHELL

1932–

228   *Fifteen Million Plastic Bags*

   I WAS walking in a government warehouse
   Where the daylight never goes
   I saw fifteen million plastic bags
   Hanging in a thousand rows.

   Five million bags were six feet long
   Five million bags were five foot five
   Five million were stamped with Mickey Mouse
   And they came in a smaller size.

Were they for guns or uniforms
Or a dirty kind of party game?
Then I saw each bag had a number
And every bag bore a name.

And five million bags were six feet long
Five million were five foot five
Five million were stamped with Mickey Mouse
And they came in a smaller size

So I've taken my bag from the hanger
And I've pulled it over my head
And I'll wait for the priest to zip it
So the radiation won't spread

Now five million bags are six feet long
Five million are five foot five
Five million are stamped with Mickey Mouse
And they come in a smaller size.

229   *Quite Apart from the Holy Ghost*

I REMEMBER God as an eccentric millionaire,
Locked in his workshop, beard a cloud of foggy-coloured hair,
Making the stones all different, each flower and disease,
Putting the Laps in Lapland, making China for the Chinese,
Laying down the Lake of Lucerne as smooth as blue-grey lino,
Wearily inventing the appendix and the rhino,
Making the fine fur for the mink, fine women for the fur,
Man's brain a gun, his heart a bomb, his conscience—a blur.

Christ I can see much better from here,
And Christ upon the Cross is clear.
Jesus is stretched like the skin of a kite
Over the Cross, he seems in flight
Sometimes. At times it seems more true
That he is meat nailed up alive and pain all through.
But it's hard to see Christ for priests. That happens when
A poet engenders generations of advertising men.

JOHN FULLER

1937–

230   *God Bless America*

WHEN they confess that they have lost the penial bone and outer space
   is
Once again a numinous void, when they're kept out of Other Places,
And Dr Fieser falls asleep at last and dreams of unburnt faces,
When gold medals are won by the ton for forgetting about the different
   races,
                       God Bless America.

When in the Latin shanties the scented priesthood suffers metem-
   psychosis
And with an organ entry *tutti copula* the dollar uncrosses
Itself and abdicates, when the Pax Americana cuts its losses
And a Pinkville memorial's built in furious shame by Saigon's puppet
   bosses,
                       God Bless America.

When they can be happy without noise, without knowing where on
   earth they've been,
When they cease to be intellectual tourists and stop wanting to be clean,
When they send their children to bed at the proper time and say just
   what they mean,
And no longer trust the Quarterly Symposium and the Vicarious
   Screen,
                       God Bless America.

When they feel thoroughly desolated by the short-lived Christ they
   pray to,
When they weep over their plunder of Europe stone by stone, releasing
   Plato
And other Freshman Great Books, when they switch off their Hoover
   and unplug Nato,
Pulling the chain on the CIA and awarding *Time* a rotten potato,
                       God Bless America.

When qua-birds, quickhatches and quinnets agree at last to admit the
    quail,
When Captain Queeg is seen descending from the bridge as small
    and pale
As everyone else, and is helped with sympathetic murmurs to the rail,
When the few true defenders of love and justice survive to tell the tale,
                  Then, perhaps then, God Bless America.

JAMES FENTON 1949–
and JOHN FULLER 1937–

231   *Poem against Catholics*

THE boring executors approach their locks,
Fumbling with keys and more than half-way dense:
Sylvia Plath is given to C. B. Cox,
Lawrence to Leavis, Pope to Joseph Spence,
Pound to *Agenda*, Eliot to his wife,
Hopkins to Bridges and Kafka to Max Brod—
But Jesus gave the *Church* eternal life!
God we hate Catholics and their Catholic God.

It isn't that we'd rather someone who
Instead of singing simply *says* you it.
The whole palaver simply isn't *true*.
We'd not *prefer* a Quaker to a Jesuit.
But in the Proselytising Handicap
The odds are even where they ride roughshod
And drive their spurs into the suffering map.
God we hate Catholics and their Catholic God.

Graham Greene finds them everywhere he travels
With submachineguns underneath their cassocks.
You can be certain, as the plot unravels,
They're smuggling opium in knee-worn hassocks.
Police-chiefs quote Pascal. Priests hit the bottle.
Strong men repent in Nishni-Novgorod.
The whole *galère* one could with pleasure throttle.
God we hate Catholics and their Catholic God.

The object of their worship makes us *cross*,
Since their employment of it is so gainful.
They sold it off like bits of candy-floss.
(Surely the Romans meant it to be painful?)
Their tortured idols are so psychedelic
With gold and lapis artwork *à la mode*,
And nearly every thumbscrew is a relic.
God we hate Catholics and their Catholic goad.

They call their horrid children after saints
And educate them by such dubious means
They eagerly succumb to strange complaints
Or turn psychotic in their early teens.
'Ursula worries me,' exclaims her mother.
'Her manner recently has been so odd.
I've *told* her she must *not* cremate her brother.'
God we hate Catholics and their Catholic God.

See in the summerhouse where Father Flynn
Fingers his rosary and sets to work
Explaining why the church holds it a sin:
'You mustn't ever hold it. That's called jerk-
ing off. Six *mea culpas*, Benedict.'
He's coaching him for Ampleforth, poor sod.
He'll get some education, we predict.
God we hate Catholics and their Catholic God.

'Not now,' cries Mrs Macnamara, '*later!*'
When leapt on by her husband (what a beast).
'It says so on my Catholic calculator.
It also says so on my Catholic priest.'
She'd do much better with a mortal coil
To spoil the child and spare the husband's rod.
Why don't they put a bill through in the Dáil?
God we hate Catholics and their Catholic God.

Their sheer resourcefulness one can't disparage.
External Combustion was their own invention,
So (indisputably) divorceless marriage
Which like a sardine key creates some tension.
But *only once*. What mortal supermen!
Or else what Paul said must have been a cod
Since those who marry twice must burn again.
God we hate Catholics and their Catholic God.

Rich English Catholics, busy doing good work
For filthy mission schools in fascist states.
Oily confessors crawling from the woodwork
With first-class tickets to the pearly gates.
How nice that Lady Priesthole looks so well.
She's left her housemaid's knee behind in Lourdes.
But where's the housemaid? God alone can tell.
God we hate Catholics and their Catholic Gourdes.

High Anglo-Catholics are beneath contempt—
All intellectual and moral wrecks.
They love the frills but hold themselves exempt
From self-denial in the line of sex.
As press-ups are to health-fiends, genuflection
Is to the average Anglo-Catholic Prod.
What a good way to nourish one's erection.
God we hate Catholics and their Catholic God.

When Sister Flanagan from Houston Texas
Edited Baron Corvo for her Master's,
She changed the pronouns to reverse the sexes
As frills on chesterfields concealed their castors.
The text was passed unnoticed by the Syndics
And causes some confusion in the Bod.
Wait till she gets the Bible on the Index!
God we hate Catholics and their Catholic God.

A rugby-playing Catholic novelist,
Piers Paul Read, was lucky to be chosen
(Out of, we gather, a distinguished list)
To write about a new idea in frozen
Foods: when a rugby team crashed near Peru
On slopes the human toe had never trod
They ate each other. What a thing to do!
God—they ate Catholics and their Catholic God!

CLIVE JAMES

1939–

232   from *To Pete Atkin: A Letter from Paris*

THE weather's cleared. We're filming at *Versailles*,
Palatial residence of Sun-King *Louis*,
Where everything is landscaped save the sky
And even that seems strangely free of *pluie*
For this one day at least. I find that I
Am sneakily inclined to murmur 'phooey'
When faced with all this Classical Giganticism:
In fact it almost makes me like Romanticism.

Proportion, yes: the joint's got that to burn.
Sa regularity of window arch,
Ses ranks of cornucopia and urn.
Those balustrades like soldiers on the march!
Those gardens, haunt of robot coot and hern!
The whole confection fairly reeks of starch:
A dude-ranch frozen with neurotic tension,
It chills the very notion of Dissension.

And that was what *le Roi Soleil* was after,
Without a doubt. His Absolutist frown
Is there in every pediment and rafter,
A stare of disapproval beating down
Propensities to any form of laughter
Beyond the courtly Hollow kind. The Crown
Made sure to keep this 4-star barracks filled
With dupes who thought they danced but really drilled.

Grim-jawed Solemnity may have its worth
But Geniality is just as serious
And *gravitas* is half-dead without Mirth.
I don't mean one should roll around delirious
But Art must take the air, not hug the earth—
Authoritative needn't mean Imperious.
To preach cold concepts like the Golden Section
Is over-mightily to seek Perfection.

We should be glad, then, that we work in Rock
Whose mark for ordered Symmetry is Zero.
Its *cognoscenti*, talking total cock
Concerning slack-mouthed bitch or dildoed hero,
Combine the thickness of a Mental Block
With all the musicality of *Nero*:
And yet despite their I.Q.'s in two figures
They've sussed out where the only decent gig is.

In liking Anti-Intellectualism
They're wrong, but right to value simple Verve.
A long way gone in pale Eclecticism,
Like all those nostrums that no longer serve
(*Vedanta, Joan the Wad, Collectivism*)
The Classical Succession's lost its nerve—
Or else it shrieks an *avant-gardiste* foolery
That makes the average Rock Song shine like joolery.

But here the shine's gone off a hard half-day:
We're wrapping up with no shots left to do.
Inside a camera-car I'm borne away
Along a six-lane speedway to *St Cloud*,
Where signboards set to lead non-Frogs astray
Now send us back *Versailles*-wards. Sacray bloo.
Our pub will keep a meal, though ... Bloody Hell!
No food: we have to work *tonight* as well.

* * *

Throughout the evening's shooting in *Pigalle*
I marvel, as the red lights glow infernally,
That they can pull down places like *Les Halles*
When (rain or shine, nocturnally, diurnally,
Uncaring if you snigger, sneer or snarl)
Grim tat and tit dance cheek by jowl eternally
In *this* dump. What a drag! But it's survival
Is no surprise if *Taste*'s its only rival.

Alone at last, I'm much too tired to sleep
(A hemistitch from *Lorenz Hart*. You tumbled?)
The drapes down-soft, the wall-to-wall knee-deep,
My hotel bedroom ought to leave me humbled.
By rights I should conk out without a peep,
But can't. The boys who did the *décor* fumbled:
It's just too scrumptious to be borne, too peachy.
They've ladled on an acre too much chi-chi.

CLIVE JAMES

The *Gauche* and not the *Droite*'s the *Rive* for me.
To kip beneath plush quilts is not the same
As gazing *sur les toits* of that Paree
They fly behind the garret window-frame,
Heraldic as France Ancient's *fleur-de-lys*,
To charm you through Act I of *La Bohème*—
Unless I've got *Parnasse* mixed up with *Martre*.
(You know I *still* can't tell those *Monts* apartre?)

So much for *Taste*, then, and the same goes double
For those more recent phantoms, such as *Youth*.
As clear and brilliant as the tiny bubble
That canopies a baby's first front tooth,
There swells through time of sloth and troughs of trouble
The Artist's one eternal, guiding Truth—
Ars longa, vita brevis. Is that *Horace?*
It could be someone weird, like *William Morris.*

* * *

I'm writing half-way up the *Eiffel Tower*
While knocking back a rich *café au lait.*
We've been at work this high about an hour
And here my part will end, at Noon today.
It gives a heady, *Zeus*-like sense of power
To watch, from *au-dessus de la mêlée*,
The myriad formiculant mere mortals
Who circumvest this crazy structure's portals.

Much earlier, and lovely in the Dawn,
The gardens of the *Louvre* were full of mist.
The *Tuileries* lay like a smoking lawn
As I, my trusty notebook in my fist,
Saw *Paris* come unfolded like a fawn
And glitter like a powdered amethyst—
Whereat I felt, involved in her fragility,
A thumping streak of Tough Bitch durability.

We're all aware of how the Continuity
Of Western Culture's frazzled to a thread.
It doesn't take a soothsayer's acuity
To see the whole shebang might wind up dead.
One's sorely tempted to, in perpetuity,
Give up the struggle and go back to bed:
And yet TRADITION, though we can't renew it,
Demands we add our Certain Something to it

439

No matter what. I leave from *Charles de Gaulle*
At *Roissy* this p.m. S-F HQ!
The planes feed in a cluster, like shoal
Of mutant carp stuck nose to nose with glue
Around a doughnut in whose abstract hole
Aphasic humans escalating through
Translucent pipelines linking zones to domes
Seem pastel genes in giant chromosomes.

And that's the Future, baby. Like the Past
It's flowing, but unlike it it flows faster.
Ici Paris, below me. Will it last?
A heap of ageing bricks and wood and plaster—
Bombe glacée with one atomic blast.
A single finger's tremble from disaster.
But then, who isn't? So what else is new?
See you in *London*: there's a lot to do.

ACKNOWLEDGEMENTS

THE editor and publishers wish to thank the following for their permission to reproduce copyright poems:

Kingsley Amis: Extract from 'The Last War'. Reprinted by permission of Jonathan Clowes on behalf of the author.

W. H. Auden: 'The Unknown Citizen' (Copyright 1940 and renewed 1968 by Wystan Hugh Auden) from *Collected Poems*. Extracts from 'A Happy New Year' and 'Letter to Lord Byron' (Copyright 1937 by Wystan Hugh Auden) from *The English Auden: Poems, Essays and Dramatic Writings* (Copyright © 1977 by E. M. William Meredith and Monroe E. Spears). Reprinted by permission of Faber & Faber Ltd, and Random House Inc.

Sir Max Beerbohm: From *Max in Verse: Rhymes and Parodies*, ed. J. G. Riewald (Copyright © by J. G. Riewald). Reprinted by permission of William Heinemann Ltd and The Stephen Greene Press.

Hilaire Belloc: From *Sonnets and Verse* (Gerald Duckworth & Co. Ltd). Reprinted by permission of A. D. Peters & Co. Ltd.

Sir John Betjeman: From *Collected Poems*. Reprinted by permission of John Murray (Publishers) Ltd and Houghton Mifflin Company.

Roy Campbell: 'A Veld Eclogue' and 'Georgian Spring' from *Adamastor* (Faber & Faber Ltd). Reprinted by permission of Curtis Brown Ltd on behalf of the Estate of Roy Campbell. Extract from 'A Good Resolution' from 'Mithraic Emblems' in *Collected Poems*. Reprinted by permission of The Bodley Head and Regnery Gateway Inc. Extract from *The Wayzgoose*. Reprinted by permission of Jonathan Cape Ltd and the Executors of the Roy Campbell Estate.

G. K. Chesterton: From *The Collected Poems of G. K. Chesterton* (Methuen & Co. Ltd) (Copyright 1932 by Dodd, Mead & Company, Inc., and renewed 1959 by Oliver Chesterton). Reprinted by permission of A. P. Watt & Son on behalf of the Estate of the late G. K. Chesterton, and Dodd, Mead and Co. Inc.

E. E. Cummings: 'in heavenly realms of hellas dwelt' (© 1963 by Marion Morehouse Cummings) from *Complete Poems 1913–1962*. Reprinted by permission of Granada Publishing Ltd, and Harcourt Brace Jovanovich, Inc. 'i sing of Olaf' (Copyright © 1931 and renewed in 1959 by E. E. Cummings) from *Complete Poems 1913–1962* and also from *Viva*. Reprinted by permission of Granada Publishing Ltd, and Liveright Publishing Corporation.

D. J. Enright: 'Since Then' from *Sad Ires*, 'Apocalypse' from *Addictions* (both Chatto and Windus Ltd). Reprinted by permission of Bolt & Watson Ltd.

Gavin Ewart: From *The Deceptive Grin of the Gravel Porters* (London Magazine Editions). Reprinted by permission of the author.

441

ACKNOWLEDGEMENTS

James Fenton and John Fuller: First appeared in *The New Review*. Reprinted by permission of the authors.

John Fuller: From *Cannibals and Missionaries*. Reprinted by permission of Martin Secker & Warburg Ltd.

Robert Graves: From *Collected Poems* (Cassell & Co. Ltd). Reprinted by permission of A. P. Watt & Son on behalf of Mr Robert Graves.

Ernest Hemingway: 'The Earnest Liberal's Lament' from *88 Poems* (© 1979 by The Ernest Hemingway Foundation and Nicholas Gerogiannis). Reprinted by permission of Harcourt Brace Jovanovich, Inc.

A. E. Housman: 'The laws of God, the laws of man' from *The Collected Poems of A. E. Housman* (Copyright 1922 by Holt, Rinehart and Winston, Copyright 1950 by Barclays Bank Ltd). Reprinted by permission of Holt, Rinehart and Winston. 'Some can gaze and not be sick' from *My Brother, A. E. Housman* by Laurence Housman (Copyright 1937, 1938 by Laurence Housman). Reprinted by permission of Charles Scribner's Sons. The poems are also reprinted from *Collected Poems* by permission of The Society of Authors as the literary representatives of the Estate of A. E. Housman, and Jonathan Cape Ltd as publishers.

Clive James: From *Fan Mail* (Faber & Faber Ltd). Reprinted by permission of A. D. Peters & Co. Ltd.

Rudyard Kipling: From *The Definitive Edition of Rudyard Kipling's Verse*. Reprinted by permission of A. P. Watt & Son Ltd, on behalf of The National Trust, Macmillan, London and Basingstoke, and Doubleday & Co. Inc., and also by permission of The Executors of the Estate of Mrs George Bambridge.

Philip Larkin: First appeared in *Essays in Criticism*. Reprinted by permission of the author.

D. H. Lawrence: From *The Complete Poems of D. H. Lawrence* (William Heinemann Ltd), (Copyright 1971 by Angelo Ravagli and C. M. Weekley). Reprinted by permission of Laurence Pollinger Ltd, Viking Penguin Inc., and the Executors of the Estate of the late Mrs Frieda Lawrence Ravagli.

D. B. Wyndham Lewis: From *One Way Song* (Faber & Faber Ltd). Reprinted by permission of A. D. Peters & Co. Ltd.

Phyllis McGinley: 'The Day After Sunday', and 'Daniel at Breakfast' from *The Love Letters of Phyllis McGinley*. (Copyright 1951, 1952, 1953, 1954 by Phyllis McGinley). 'Office Party', 'How to Start a War', 'On the Farther Wall, Marc Chagall', 'Squeeze Play' and 'Speaking of Television: Robin Hood' from *Times Three*. (Copyright © 1932–1960 by Phyllis McGinley). Reprinted by permission of Martin Secker & Warburg Ltd, and Viking Penguin Inc.

Louis MacNeice: From *Collected Poems* (Faber & Faber Ltd). Reprinted by permission of David Higham Associates Ltd.

Edward Lee Masters: From *Spoon River Anthology* (Macmillan Inc.). Reprinted by permission of Mrs E. L. Masters.

Adrian Mitchell: From *Poems*. Reprinted by permission of Jonathan Cape Ltd.

Robert Nichols: From *Fisbo* (Heinemann). Reprinted by permission of Hope Leresche & Sayle.

442

ACKNOWLEDGEMENTS

Ezra Pound: 'Reflection and Advice' from *Collected Early Poems of Ezra Pound*. (Copyright © 1976 by the Trustees of the Ezra Pound Literary Property Trust. All rights reserved.) Extracts from 'L'Homme Moyen Sensuel' from *Personae* (Copyright 1926 by Ezra Pound). Reprinted by permission of New Directions Inc. These poems are also reprinted from *Collected Shorter Poems* by permission of Faber & Faber Ltd.

John Crowe Ransom: 'Philomela' (Copyright 1924 by Alfred A. Knopf, Inc. Copyright 1952, by John Crowe Ransom). From *Selected Poems* (Eyre Methuen Ltd). Reprinted by permission of Laurence Pollinger Ltd., and Alfred Knopf, Inc.

Edgell Rickword: From *Behind the Eyes: Collected Poems*. Reprinted by permission of Carcanet New Press Ltd.

Edwin Arlington Robinson: From *The Town Down the River* (Copyright 1910 by Charles Scribner's Sons, renewal copyright 1938 Ruth Nivison). Reprinted by permission of Charles Scribner's Sons.

Siegfried Sassoon: From *Collected Poems* (Faber & Faber Ltd) (Copyright 1918, 1920 by E. P. Dutton & Co., Copyright 1936, 1946, 1947, 1948 by Siegfried Sassoon). Reprinted by permission of G. T. Sassoon, and Viking Penguin Inc.

Stevie Smith: From *The Collected Poems of Stevie Smith* (Allen Lane). Reprinted by permission of James MacGibbon as executor.

Yvor Winters: From *Collected Poems*. Reprinted by permission of Carcanet Press Ltd.

While every effort has been made to secure permission, we may have failed in a few cases to trace the copyright holder. We apologize for any apparent negligence.

NOTES AND REFERENCES

No references in the Notes are given to poems by authors whose collected poems are easily available. For details of poems still in copyright, see also the Acknowledgements.

1. Anon. 15th century. In E. P. Hammond (ed.), *English Verse from Chaucer to Surrey*.

2–4. John Skelton. *Workes* (1568). (Scolar Press facsimile 1970). 2. lines 115–216; 3. lines 793–830; 4. lines 922–63.

6. Sir David Lyndsay. From Part I of *Ane Satyre of the Thrie Estaitis* in *Poetical Works* (Scottish Text Society, 1931), lines 2080–121.

7. Anon. From the 16th century Bannatyne MS., National Library, Edinburgh.

10–11. John Donne. 10. lines 1–70; 11. lines 43–110.

14. Joseph Hall. *Virgidemiae* (1598). (i) II.iii; (ii) III.i; (iii) IV.vi, 36–89.

15. William Rankins. *Seaven Satyres* (1598), 'Satyrus Peregrinans', lines 120–54.

16. Samuel Butler. *Hudibras* (i) The First Part, Canto I, lines 187–234; (ii) The Second Part, Canto I, lines 45–76; (iii) The Second Part, Canto I, lines 553–94; (iv) The Third Part, Canto I, lines 1263–1310.

17. John Cleveland. (i) lines 47–70; (ii) lines 101–26.

18. Henry Vaughan. lines 322–91.

19–20. Andrew Marvell. 19. lines 1–54; 20. (i) lines 1–12; (ii) lines 79–102; (iii) lines 885–906.

24, 26, 28–31. John Dryden. 24. (i) lines 16–38; 26. (i) lines 142–203; (ii) lines 529–68; 28. lines 406–509; 29. lines 1141–94; 30. lines 399–408; 31. (i) lines 1–86; (ii) lines 560–90.

32. Charles Sackville. F. H. Ellis (ed.), *Poems on Affairs of State*.

35. Anon. *Poems on Several Occasions by a Late Person of Honour* (1685).

38. John Wilmot, Earl of Rochester. lines 20–1.

42. Anon. Danielsson and Vieth (eds.), *The Gyldenstolpe Manuscript Miscellany of Poems by John Wilmot, Earl of Rochester* (1967). lines 1–20.

43. Alexander Radcliffe. *The Ramble* (1682).

44–45. John Oldham. *Works* (1684). 44. lines 175–90; 45. lines 1–128.

46. Anon. *The Post Boy* (12 December 1710).

47–49. Daniel Defoe. 47. (i) Part I; (ii) Part II, lines 1–50; (iii) Part II, 102–29; 48. (i) Part I, lines 84–115; (ii) Part I, 181–202; 49. lines 172–89.

50. Sir Samuel Garth. (i) Canto I, lines 107–33; (ii) Canto II, 93–150; (iii) Canto III, 11–40.

51. Thomas Brown. *Works* (1730).

57. Jonathan Swift. lines 33–58.

62. John Arbuthnot. *Gentleman's Magazine*, ii, 718 (1732); also in Pope's note to his *Epistle to Lord Bathurst* (1733).

63–64. John Winstanley. *Poems* (Dublin, 1742).

65–66. Edward Young. (i) Satire I, lines 51–76; (ii) Satire II, 57–94; (iii) Satire II, 211–82; (iv) Satire III, 237–42; (v) Satire V, 15–28; **66.** Epistle I, 291–310.

68. William Diaper. (i) lines 1–70; (ii) lines 122–70.

69–70. Anon. **69.** *The British Musical Miscellany*, i (1734); **70.** Dodsley (ed.), *A Collection of Poems* (1748).

72–82. Alexander Pope. **72.** lines 86–105; **73.** Canto III, lines 1–24; **74.** (i) lines 26–45; (ii) lines 408–35; (iii) lines 610–25; **75.** (i) lines 179–214; (ii) lines 231–48; (iii) lines 305–33; **76.** (i) lines 157–80; (ii) lines 215–48; **77.** lines 99–168; **78.** lines 1–22; **79.** lines 120–33; **80.** lines 17–44; **81.** (i) Dialogue I, lines 137–70; (ii) Dialogue II, lines 12–53; (iii) Dialogue II, lines 197–227; **82.** (i) Book I, lines 1–84; (ii) Book IV, 565–656.

83–85. Richard Savage. **83.** lines 1–20; **84.** lines 51–124; **85.** lines 45–92.

86–89. Soame Jenyns. **86.** lines 1–24; **87.** lines 1–106; **87.** lines 1–106; **88.** lines 11–52.

90–91. Samuel Johnson. **90.** lines 158–81; **91.** (i) lines 73–90; (ii) lines 135–60.

93. Edward Moore. *Poems, Fables and Plays* (1756).

94. William Whitehead. lines 85–130.

95–96. Oliver Goldsmith. **95.** lines 13–40; **96.** (i) lines 51–73; (ii) lines 251–302.

98. William Cowper. (i) lines 201–17; (ii) lines 364–403; (iii) lines 807–844.

99–104. Charles Churchill. **99.** (i) lines 179–216; (ii) lines 273–342; **100.** (i) lines 39–92; (ii) lines 185–224; **101.** Book II, lines 653–88; **102.** lines 195–206; **103.** lines 611–58; **104.** Book III, lines 667–810.

106. Robert Lloyd. lines 107–214.

108. John Wolcot. *The Works of Peter Pindar* (1812).

109. George Crabbe. Letter III, lines 1–165.

110. Anon. *The Rolliad*, no. 5 (1795).

114. Robert Burns, lines 49–66.

116. Richard Porson. J. S. Watson, *The Life of Richard Porson* (1861).

117. Robert Southey and Samuel Taylor Coleridge. Coleridge, *Complete Poetical Works* (1912).

138–143. George Gordon Noel, Lord Byron. **138.** (i) lines 540–59; (ii) lines 411–17; **139.** lines 568–631; **140.** lines 1–54; **141.** (i) stanzas i–xxiii; (ii) stanzas lxxxv–cvi; **143.** (i) stanzas i–xvii; (ii) Canto II, xcvii–c; (iii) Canto IX, stanzas i–x; (iv) Canto XI, stanzas vii–xi.

144–145. Percy Bysshe Shelley. **144.** (i) Part III, stanzas i–xxiii; (ii) Part VII, stanzas i–xxiv; **145.** stanzas i–xxi.

150–151. Winthrop Macworth Praed. **150.** stanzas 4–8; **151.** from the *Morning Chronicle*, 6 July 1825 in Allot (ed.) *Praed. Selected Poems* (1953).

152–153. William Makepeace Thackeray. *Ballads* (1855).

154. Charles Dickens. Kitton (ed.), *Poems and Verse of Charles Dickens* (1903).

155. James Russell Lowell. lines 1071–1120.

156–157. Arthur Hugh Clough. **156.** (i) Canto II, lines 247–67 (early draft variant); (ii) Canto II, letters I–IV; **157**. a variant of lines 130–97 from *Dipsychus*, printed in 1862 and 1863.

162. Sir W. S. Gilbert. *The Bab Ballads* (1898).

INDEX OF FIRST LINES

The references are to the numbers of the poems

447

INDEX OF FIRST LINES

INDEX OF FIRST LINES

INDEX OF FIRST LINES

INDEX OF FIRST LINES

451

INDEX OF FIRST LINES

INDEX OF AUTHORS

The references are to the numbers of the poems

INDEX OF AUTHORS